NORWALK

published for the
NORWALK HISTORICAL SOCIETY, INC.
by
PHOENIX PUBLISHING
Canaan, New Hampshire

*The Oyster Houses / photo
by George A. Lang*

NORWALK

being an historical account of that Connecticut town

by Deborah Wing Ray and Gloria P. Stewart

Endleaf illustration:
Landscape of Norwalk, painted by Charles Seely Gaylord in
1842 by commission of John P. Treadwell.
Collection of Lockwood House Museum.

Ray, Deborah Wing.
    Norwalk: being an historical account of that Connecticut
        town.
    Bibliography: p. 232
    Includes index.
    1. Norwalk, Conn. History. I. Stewart, Gloria P., joint
        author. II. Norwalk Historical Society. III. Title.
F104.N9R39   974.6'9   78-24441
ISBN 0-914016-56-3

First printing 1979
Second printing 1989

Printed in the United States of America
by Courier Printing Company
Binding by New Hampshire Bindery
Design by A. L. Morris

Dedicated
to the memory of
Sherwood H. Prothero
1912 / 1976

who initiated the writing of this history
while serving as
Vice President of the Norwalk Historical Society,
and who unselfishly served his community
as Executive Vice President
of the Norwalk Chamber of Commerce
from 1943 to 1976.

CONTENTS

Sponsors

This book was made possible in part by the generosity of the following:

Mr. & Mrs. Everett L. Baker
R.C. Bigelow, Inc.
Ralph C. Bloom
Mr. & Mrs. Andre Blumenthal
Douglas A. Bora Agency
Mr. & Mrs. Harry Boyd
James D. Bredice
Mr. & Mrs. Jay S. Buckley
Mr. & Mrs. Carroll Cavanagh
Mrs. Ruth Y. Court
Eric DeMarsh
Robert B. Devine
Dr. Bern Dibner
David Dibner
Fairfield County Savings Bank
Mr. & Mrs. Ferenz Fedor
Mrs. Elizabeth E. Freese
John Gaydosh
Mr. & Mrs. Nelson Taylor Hayes
Henry Richards Company, Inc.
Mr. & Mrs. Dudley D. Hoyt
Mrs. John Kellams
Keogh, Candee & Burkhart
Mrs. R.F. King
Mr. & Mrs. Andrew W. Kish
J.M. Layton & Company, Inc.
Capt. Frederick Lovejoy
Mr. & Mrs. Eric C. Malmquist
Mr. & Mrs. Harold S. Martin
Merchants Bank & Trust Company
Mr. & Mrs. Henry Meyers

Mr. & Mrs. Joel M. Morris
Nash Engineering Company
Norwalk Association of
Insurance Agents, Inc.
Norwalk Bicentennial Commission
Norwalk Board of Realtors, Inc.
Norwalk Company
Norwalk Savings Society
Norwalk Village Green Chapter,
DAR, Inc.
Everett H. Palmer
Mrs. Lawrence K. Paul
Pepperidge Farms, Inc.
Perkin-Elmer Corporation
Mr. & Mrs. Sherwood H. Prothero
Mr. & Mrs. Frank E. Raymond
Raymond Funeral Home
Mr. & Mrs. Lunsford Richardson
Rowayton Historical Society, Inc.
Rowlison Agency, Inc.
Mr. & Mrs. Dean G. Russell
Santaniello, Culhane & Allen
Sisterhood of Temple Shalom
Mr. & Mrs. Robert Slavitt
Mr. & Mrs. Douglas Smith
South Norwalk Savings Bank
Mr. & Mrs. John Steuber
Mrs. William F. Tammany
Dr. Edward J. Tracey, Jr.
John Vassos
Mr. & Mrs. Alfred I. Wirtenberg
Mr. & Mrs. John H. Woodward

PREFACE

The purported "histories" of Norwalk prior to the present volume were always a despair to me. They were obviously written by authors who — if they had any scholarly ability — made no effort to use it. Except for Edwin Hall's copies of the town records, the reader could never be sure if he was reading fact, tradition, fiction, or plain pipe dreams. I have been told that even Mr. Hall moved up dates in his genealogical records so that certain families would not be embarrassed to note a birth in their family tree which came too close to a marriage date. Although amateur genealogists continue to cite his volume, they are leaning on a thin reed.

When research for my biography of Robert Rogers led me to consult other town histories, I found that these histories of Norwalk were no exception. The typical town historian was an undiscriminating collector of stories which sometimes were published as "history." I presume they must have pleased a few elderly remnants of old families in various towns, but I cannot recall one which I felt to be reliable.

I thought about doing Norwalk's history myself. But I am wedded to America's eighteenth century. The period after 1800 is unknown to me. Of course, the events to this date are interesting, but present-day Norwalk cannot be explained by its colonial background. Without an intensive background study, which I was reluctant to undertake, I was not qualified to write a good history of Norwalk.

I suspected one would eventually appear. From a few examples which were sporadically produced, I feared the worst. However, my apprehension began to fade when the committee appointed by the Norwalk Historical Society early gave evidence that only a true scholar (or scholars, as it turned out) would be employed to compose a history worthy of its imprint. When the assignment was given to the present authors, I had only one lingering apprehension: How could Norwalk's story be compressed into one volume?

Well, they did it. Careful selection and expert wording have produced the full story within the covers of this single volume. When I read their manuscript, then, and only then, did I have any comprehension of the true history of Norwalk. I was stunned to realize how little I really knew, even of events which have occurred in my own lifetime. I am ashamed to admit that I made little or no effort to know more about my own family's modest contribution to the city's history. How I wish I could review some of the events in the book with my father and grandfather.

Therefore, I say to all Norwalkers — newcomers as well as those whose families go back to the first arrivals — here is a history of which you can be proud! Here is an outstanding account, engrossing, yet accurate as only able professional historians can produce. Best of all, here is a history from which present and future generations of Norwalk scholars will draw an inspiration to carry on the study of our city through the years to come.

John R. Cuneo
September 14, 1978

As the observance of America's Bicentennial turned the thoughts of its citizens toward the national past, so it led them to contemplate the history of their own towns. This volume, commissioned by the Norwalk Historical Society, has emerged from the revived interest in local history inspired by the Bicentennial. The authors have viewed their assignment as that of writing the biography of a city — its genesis, its early village years, its coming of age with nineteenth-century industrialization, and its maturity as a segment of Megalopolis.

Given the events of three centuries to describe within strict limitations upon space, it has been necessary to adopt a fixed beginning and ending. The authors have made no effort to investigate the pre-Norwalk lives of the planters of the town, for example, interesting though these might be, and we have rather arbitrarily set the cut-off point of our story at the end of Norwalk's Tercentenary decade. Even so, we have had to be highly selective, and if this were a film instead of a book many cherished scenes would be found lying on the cutting room floor. To offset this, a number of photographs have been chosen to augment, rather than merely amplify, the written material.

Researching this history has been as tantalizing as it has been satisfying. A singular lack of memoirs, diaries, and correspondence, the result not only of — to use Cervantes' phrase — the malignity of time, but the burning of the town in 1779, made research of the early period difficult and left unanswered questions about the character of colonial Norwalk. This has been compensated for by extensive reliance upon such records as the Norwalk Town Proceedings, the Public Records of Connecticut,

INTRODUCTION

and the Connecticut Archives. Records of the First Society, which would probably have provided even more information about local customs and mores than the Town Proceedings, are no longer in existence, having long since fallen prey to the parish house mice. Norwalk's lack of a historical figure of national prominence, except for Governor Thomas Fitch, precluded reliance upon the biographies and published correspondence that ease the historian's task. For the nineteenth and twentieth centuries a vast assortment of primary materials, including town and council records, church records, newspapers, letters, business ledgers and the manuscript census, made our work considerably easier. In fact, this abundance necessitated careful culling. Even for the later period, however, Norwalk's archives suffer a dearth of personal recollections and correspondence. Regretfully, too, descendants of the town's newer immigrants often tend to believe that their family stories or photographs are not "historical." We hope this book will change their views and lead to deeper studies of Norwalk's ethnic groups.

The authors are grateful to earlier Norwalk historians, each of whom contributed in a special way: Elsie Danenberg, whose pride in Norwalk was displayed on every page of her book; Edwin Hall, who preserved the town's ancient records; and Charles Selleck, whose massive volume clarified intricate genealogical relationships.

We appreciate the use of the facilities of several libraries. The Norwalk Community College Library provided a convenient room for our extensive microfilm research, and Raymond Cable of its staff made available his personal collection of early Connecticut works. The staffs of local libraries, George Krzyzak, in particular, were most cooperative, as was the staff at the Connecticut State Library. Local historical societies opened their archives. Mary Cohn and Harold Martin made special trips to the Seeley-Dibble-Pinkney House and the Town House to accommodate us. Through the kindness of Mrs. Roderick Williams we had access to records at St. Paul's-on-the-Green. Carol and Brad Taylor's collection was most helpful. Thomas Brigante shared his unique knowledge of the Norwalk Islands. City agencies and city employees consulted records, documents, and their personal memories to ferret out obscure facts. Those people listed in footnotes shared their special knowledge with us, as did the Reverend Zoltan Szabo, the Reverend John Ball, Janet Belward, Wallace Bell, Hazel Paxton Centner, Charles Gager, Mary McKinney, Captain Edison Morton, Carl Rowlison, Henry Streb, Andrew Wise, and several members of the League of Women Voters. Professor Mary Palmer read the first draft. It would be impossible to list the individuals who offered interesting tidbits of information or suggested the name of someone to interview. To all of them we are most grateful.

The Historical Society's book committee, Frank Raymond and John Cuneo, in particular, offered supportive encouragement over the past three years.

André Pardo permitted us to quote the poem with which this book closes.

Finally, it is hard to see how this volume could have been written without the archives of the Lockwood House Museum. This extensive collection of primary and secondary material about Norwalk, acquired almost single-handedly by Curator Ralph Bloom, makes these archives unique in Fairfield County. To Ralph, and to Inge Steer, the LHM Librarian, we owe our warmest thanks.

Deborah Wing Ray
Gloria P. Stewart
Norwalk, Connecticut / September, 1978

NORWALK

Two classes of footnotes are included in this volume. A superior numeral[1] refers to bibliographic annotations and sources which are listed by chapter beginning on page 226 of the appendices. An inferior italic numeral[1] refers to footnotes at the bottom of the referenced page and provides a further explanation of the text.

PART ONE

he valley, which lies along the

Norwalk river, and in which the

town is built, is beautiful. Few

FIRST TOWN

richer prospects of the same extent can be found

than that, which is presented from the neighbouring

eminences of this ground; the town . . . the

1651 / 1779

river . . . the farms . . . together with an unlimited

view of the Sound and the Long Island shore."

Timothy Dwight / 1822

1

OF HATCHETS,
HOES, AND JEWSE-HARPES

*Being
an Account of
the Plantation of Norwalke*

GENERATIONS of Norwalkers have proudly acknowledged the eminent colonial leader and lawmaker, Roger Ludlow, as the founder of their town. The truth is that Norwalk's founding father was a man considerably less eminent than Ludlow and one whose character was, at best, ambiguous. Yet this man, Daniel Patrick, was as important and useful in his own way as Ludlow was. During the Pequot War (1637-1638), Patrick came to Connecticut from Massachusetts, where he had been relieved of his high military command in that colony. Patrick may have lost his post because, despite the fact that he had a comely Dutch wife, he was a woman chaser, or because he had become, in the words of Massachusetts Governor John Winthrop, "proud and vicious." Whatever Patrick's personal failings, he was a tough, vigorous, capable soldier, and his timely arrival in Connecticut helped the English defeat the warring Pequots. It was during this war that Patrick, like Ludlow, first glimpsed the beautiful fertile area around the Norwalk River.

On April 20, 1640,[1] Patrick purchased some land to the west of the Norwalk River from the Indians of Norwake and Makentouh:

... the said Daniell Patricke hath bought of the sayed three indians, the ground called Sacunyte napucke, allso Meeanworth, thirdly Asumsowis, Fourthly all the land adjoyninge to the aforementioned, as farr up in the cuntry as an indian can goe in a day, from sun risinge to sun settinge; and two islands neere adjoining to the sayed carantenayueck, all bounded on the west side with noewanton on the east side to the middle of the River of Norwake ... for him and his forever; ...[1]

This deed gave Patrick all the land lying between the Norwalk River and what is now the Five Mile River. In return he agreed to give the Indians "of wampum tenn fathoms, hatchetts three, howes three, when shipps come; sixe glasses, twelfe tobackoe pipes, three knifes, tenn drills, tenn needles; this as full satisfaction for the aforementioned lande." A few months later the venturesome Patrick moved to the Mianus River area. In July he made a deal with Owenoke, son of the Siwanoy sachem, Ponus, to buy the area that is now Greenwich, and several years later took up residence there. He was killed during a quarrel with a Dutch soldier on the "Lord's Day," while God-fearing men and women were attending the Second Service. This event—an object lesson for lax Puritans—was recorded by Governor Winthrop. The moral was clear: had Patrick been inside the church, as he should have been, he would not have been killed.

In 1640 Roger Ludlow had purchased land on the Long Island Sound, a few miles east of the Saugatuck River, some miles eastward of the Nor-

---

[1] Confusion caused by simultaneous use of both the Julian and the Gregorian Calendars led to the assumption that, since Ludlow's purchase occurred in February and Patrick's in April, Ludlow was Norwalk's founder. Under the Julian Calendar, the new year commenced in late March. Ludlow's purchase date should read: February 26, 1640/1641, whereas Patrick's stands at April 20, 1640.

walk River, for the purpose of planting a town. He gave his new plantation the name Fairfield. The colonial government in Hartford, which had given Ludlow permission to start a plantation in a quite different area, Stratford, took Ludlow to task for his disobedience, but he presented a plausible explanation for going to western Connecticut—namely, his "apprehensions . . . that some others intended to take up the sayd place . . . which might be prejudicall to this Commonwealth."[2] The legislature accepted Ludlow's explanation, for it was indeed true that the Dutch in New York were expansionist-minded. Moreover the Colony of New

On February 26, 1640/1641, Ludlow, now residing in Fairfield, extended his land holdings westward by purchasing from Mahachemo and some lesser sachems in Norwalk "all the lands, meadow, pasturings, trees, whatsoever their is, and grounds betweene the two Rivers, the one called Norwalke, the other Soakatuck . . . from the sea a days walke into the country."[3] For this acquisition Ludlow agreed to give the Indians about the same mixture of wampum, tools, and trinkets that Patrick had given as well as "tenn jewse-harpes."

By 1650 the Fairfield farmers, especially the Bankside people whose land lay along the

The Purchase of NORWALK from MAHACKAMO~Chief of the NORWALK INDIANS~by ROGER LUDLOW~in 1640~

Mural by Harry Townsend in Council Chamber, City Hall.

Haven, then a completely separate entity from Connecticut, extended its authority over the town of Stamford, a dozen miles or so to the west of Fairfield, and could easily have claimed the Saugatuck and Norwalk River areas as well, if it planted a town there. In fact Daniel Patrick may have been acting as agent for New Haven when he purchased his Norwalk acreage. Ludlow's temerity in purchasing land between the Norwalk and Saugatuck Rivers gave the Hartford government a useful enclave, although authorities in the rival colony of New Haven were naturally annoyed at the time.

Saugatuck River, were prosperous and their farms exceedingly fruitful. No doubt this prosperity led to an interest in the land lying just to the west—the Norwalk properties purchased ten years earlier by Ludlow and Patrick.[2] A small group of men from the river towns of Hartford, Wethersfield, and

2 The earliest instance of Englishmen in the Norwalk area is recorded in the Land Records of the Town of Stratford, which state that in 1638 representatives of the colony met with Indian sachems to secure affirmation of English claims to the territory. Benjamin Trumbull declares that "a few scattered families" seem to have planted themselves in the town about the time of these purchases.

Windsor, led by Nathaniel Ely and Richard Olmstead, arranged to purchase Ludlow's tract lying between the Saugatuck and Norwalk Rivers. The agreement, made and signed on June 19, 1650, spelled out the terms of the purchase and the name selected by the new proprietors:[3]

Imprimis, the sayed NATHANIEL ELI and RICHARD OLMSTEAD, doe covenant and promise and agree, that they will set upon the plantinge of the sayed Norwalke, with all convenient speed; will mowe and stacke some hay upon the sayed Norwalke this winter, to the end that they may, in the spring next at the farthest, breake up some ground to plante the next season, following . . .

minister to them. Ludlow was willing to accept fifteen pounds, equivalent to the amount he declared he had paid for the land ten years earlier.

The Norwalk planters must have had some prior understanding about their project with the colonial officials for on June 26, only one week after the agreement with Ludlow had been signed, Hartford returned an answer to their request for permission to settle the newly-purchased lands. The colony's prompt action in this matter may have been related to fear of the Stamford Indians. In 1648 some of them had killed a white settler and another Indian war seemed likely. A plantation in Norwalk would

Mural detail.

Jew's harp. Collection of Lockwood House Museum.

The planters agreed to bring not less than thirty families to settle in Norwalk, none of whom could be "obnoxious to the publique good of the Commonwealth." They were also to invite an "orthodoxe and approved" clergyman   a Congregationalist—with all convenient speed, to

3 The other men on whose behalf Olmstead and Ely signed this deed were: Richard Webb, Nathaniel Richards, Matthew Marvin, Richard Seamer, Thomas Spencer, Thomas Hales, Nathaniel Ruskoe, Isaac Graves, Ralph Keeler, John Holloway, Edward Church, John Ruskoe, and "some others." Not all of them became residents of Norwalk nor were they all granted home-lots.

provide a buffer between the Stamford area and settlements farther east, Fairfield in particular. Indeed, this may have been one reason why Roger Ludlow was willing to sell his Norwalk acreage for a mere fifteen pounds.

Despite the threat from the Stamford Indians, the Hartford authorities gave a rather unenthusiastic approval to the Norwalk undertaking, remarking in their approbation that they "could not but, in the generall, approve of the endeavors of men for the further improvement of the wilderness" by settling new plantations in an orderly way. Colonial officials made no promise to help the new settlers in

INDIAN DEED TO ROGER LUDLOW
[East Side of Norwalk River]

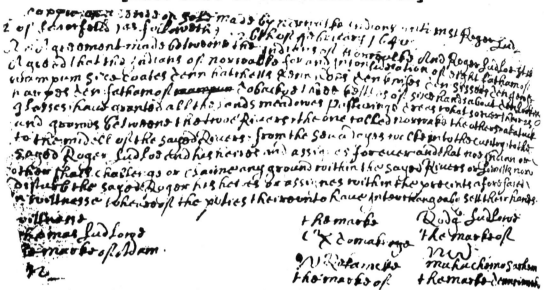

A copyie of a deed of sale made by Norwalke Indians, unto Master Roger Ludlowe, of Fairfield, as followeth, 26th February, 1640.

An agreement made between the Indians of Norwalke and Roger Ludlowe: it is agreed, that the Indians of Norwalke, for and in consideration of eight fathom of wampum, sixe coates, tenn hatchets, tenn hoes, tenn knifes, tenn sissors, tenn jewse-harpes, tenn fathom Tobackoe, three kettles of sixe hands about, tenn looking glasses, have granted all the lands, meadows, pasturinge, trees, whatsoever their is, and grounds betweene the twoe Rivers, the one called Norwalke, the other Soakatuck, to the middle of of sayed Rivers, from the sea a days walke into the country; to the sayed Roger Ludlowe, and his heirs and assignes for ever; and that noe Indian or other shall challenge or claim any ground with the sayed Rivers or limits, nor disturb the sayed Roger, his heirs or assignes, within the precincts aforesaid. In witness whereof the parties thereunto have interchangeably sett their hands.

Witnesse

Thos Ludlowe

the marke of

Adam

the marke
prosewamenos

the marke

Tomakergo

Tokaneke

ROGER LUDLOWE

the marke of

Mahachemo, Sachem
the marke of
(recorded in the Book of Deeds in the year
1672)

the event of Indian troubles. On the contrary, the approbation specified that those contracting to plant the town must take care to provide for their own defense and safety, so that "the country may not be exposed to unnecessary trouble and danger in these hazardous times."[4] The Norwalk proprietors had to comply with the requirements that they apportion their lands fairly, submit to the colony's jurisdiction in disputes, pay taxes, and obey "other wholesome orders" of the colony.

This approval cleared the way for settlement of the land east of the Norwalk River. The land west of

the river was still owned by Daniel Patrick's heirs. At this point a rather curious deed or transfer appears. On July 1, 1650, two Indians, describing themselves as the "surviving proprietors of the land lyinge on the other side of the Norwalke River" which had been "sold unto Captain Patricke of Greenwich," testified that Patrick had never fully paid for the acreage. He had failed to pay "twoe Indian coates and fowre fathom of wampum." These Indians were not the ones who had originally sold the land to Patrick. They may, of course, have been the only surviving proprietors. Whatever the true situation, these Indians deeded Patrick's land to Stephen Goodyear, one of New Haven's founders and a prominent merchant in that town. In return Goodyear gave the Indians the unpaid balance owed on the original sale.

The records are not clear at this point. Goodyear apparently transferred this land to the Norwalk proprietors shortly after obtaining it from the Indians. Perhaps Ely and Olmstead, *et al.* shared in paying the remaining balance owed to the Indians, or they may have bought the land from Goodyear. These transactions were probably necessitated by Patrick's relationship to the New Haven Colony. Whatever the situation in July, 1650, Goodyear never appears as a landowner in later Norwalk records. Moreover by 1654 the town of Norwalk was officially parceling out acreage from the Patrick property west of the Norwalk River to its own inhabitants, a clear indication that the town fathers considered this land theirs.

Another matter had to be settled before the proprietors could feel fully secure in their ownership of the area. This was to obtain title to certain shorelands and islands claimed by the Indian leader, Runckinheage, and Piamikin, Winnepucke, Pokessake, and Cockenoe-de-Longe Island and fellow sachems. On February 13, 1651/1652, these Indians confirmed transfer to the settlers of all their lands:[4]

... called and known by the name of Runckinheage [or] Rocaton ... Lying and bounded on the East upon ye land purchased of Captain Patriarke ... and the aforesaid Land bounded with the Brooke called as aforesaide Pampaskeshanke, from the aforesaide passage and path down along to the Sea ...[5]

This deed may be the first recorded instance of increasing land values in Norwalk's history for in 1651 the proprietors paid "thirty fathom of Wampum, Tenn Kettles, Fifteen Coates, Tenn payr of Stockings, Tenn knifes, Tenn Hookes, Twenty Pipes, Tenn Muckes [and] Tenn needles,"— considerably more in wampum and useful items than either Ludlow or Patrick had paid a decade earlier for substantially larger areas.

There remained a final step for the proprietors of the lands between the Saugatuck and Pampas-

keshanke Brook:[5] to obtain the colonial government's approval of Norwalk as a municipal corporation, entitling it to choose its own town officers, to distribute lands within its boundaries, and to send delegates to the legislature at Hartford. On September 11, 1651, Hartford gave this approval, declaring that "Norwauke shall bee a Towne."

By the time Norwalk was recognized as a town Connecticut had been a colony for a dozen years. Less than five years after the Puritans first settled in and around Boston a shortage of good farm land had developed in that area and original settlers as well as newcomers began to look toward the south and west, to what is now Connecticut. With the realization that a magnificent river flowed from western Massachusetts down through Connecticut into the protected waters of Long Island Sound, families began to drift in small groups into western Connecticut. It was not a difficult journey for they could follow the Great Trail of the Indians. One of the largest and most significant migrations, motivated both by land hunger and the desire for less rigid governmental and religious control, was the trek led by Thomas Hooker to Hartford in 1636. By 1637 the three river towns of Hartford, Wethersfield, and Windsor had been formed. Although far from Boston these people were still under the government of the Bay Colony.

About this time the coastal area of Connecticut was developed when John Winthrop, Jr., son of the Massachusetts governor, built a fort on Long Island Sound not far below Roger Williams' Providence plantation and made plans to establish a town there. Winthrop was acting as agent for a group of Puritan gentlemen in England who had obtained the land from the Earl of Warwick. Warwick in turn had received the land from the Council for New England to which King James I had given the entire New England area seventeen years earlier.[6] Winthrop proceeded to work out an arrangement with the western Connecticut towns to join in forming a simple type of government with his plantation, Say-

---

4 Names of some new settlers appear in this deed: Thomas and Joseph Fitch, Matthew Marven, Jr., Isacke More, and Nathaniel Haies, among them.

5 The exact location of Pampaskeshanke Brook, Norwalk's western boundary, mentioned in the Runckinheage deed, has been controversial. Since early settlers maintained that their land extended west of the Five Mile River and supported this claim in court, it is reasonable to assume that today's Goodwives River is Pampaskeshanke Brook.

6 Although some doubts exist as to the validity of this patent, it was apparently accepted as valid in early colonial times, and on its basis Connecticut was able to request existence separate from Massachusetts.

brook. Massachusetts gave consent to the new government which put young Winthrop at the head of a governing commission made up of two representatives from each town. About 850 persons now lived in Connecticut.

The new government came into existence none too soon for during the winter and spring of 1636-1637 the Pequot Indians attacked both at Saybrook and at Wethersfield, terrorizing the settlements, killing men and women, and kidnapping two Wethersfield girls. The western towns managed to raise an army of ninety men under the command of Captain John Mason. Soon Captain Daniel Patrick arrived from Massachusetts with forty additional soldiers. These two skillful and ruthless fighters, Patrick and Mason, managed to bring the war to a successful end, more than repaying the Indians for their depredations. By the summer of 1638 the Pequots were almost annihilated—their forts and villages demolished and their men, women, and children slaughtered.

Both the Indian war and the continued growth of the Connecticut towns indicated the need for a stronger and more efficient government than the existing commission. In 1638 Thomas Hooker, the most respected and influential clergyman in Connecticut, preached a thoughtful sermon on government, in which he declared that the people, by the will of God, had sovereign power not only to select their own officials but to place limits upon the powers of these officials. Thus Hooker was the spiritual and philosophical father of the famous document drawn up that year, the Fundamental Orders of Connecticut, which provided a system of government that placed ultimate authority in the hands of the freemen of the colony.

Most historians believe that, although Hooker's ideas were embodied in the Orders, the one man in the colony with sufficient legal training to put together this remarkable set of laws, or at the very least to put them into their final polished form, was Roger Ludlow. Ludlow, lately arrived in Massachusetts, had rapidly become one of the most renowned men in New England. He was one of the eight commissioners appointed to administer Connecticut's first government.

The Fundamental Orders created a simple but effective representative government, based upon principles stated in the preamble:

... well knowing where a people are gathered together the word of God requires that to mayntayne the peace and

union of such a people there should be an orderly and decent Government established according to God, to order and dispose of the affayres of the people at all seasons as occation shall require; [we] doe therefore associate and conjoine our selves to be as one Publike State or Commonwelth; ... [6]

Under the Orders each town could elect two deputies to serve as the town's representatives to the General Court or legislature. All admitted inhabitants of a town could vote for their representatives but only a freeman could serve as a deputy, magistrate, or governor.[7] Freemen were entitled to elect the governor and six magistrates. The magistrates and governor also acted as a court of law to hear cases brought by inhabitants of the colony.

The Orders began to function as a constitution in 1639 and lasted until 1662, when Charles II granted a charter to Connecticut. This charter legalized Connecticut's form of government in the eyes of the English king and Parliament, retaining the essential governmental structure of the Orders. It was a form that united Connecticut towns in a republican system unique for those times. This, then, was the government under which Norwalkers were to live for over a century and a half.

Although the men from the river towns who purchased Ludlow's property in 1650 had set down Norwalke as the name for their settlement on the deed of purchase, that seemingly straightforward spelling was mutilated by subsequent generations of penmen. The earliest known map showing Norwalk in some recognizable variation of its present name is the manuscript map of the Connecticut Coast Line in the Blathwayt *Atlas*. This map dated *circa* 1690 shows "Norwocke," a settlement situated between "Stanford" and "Fairfielde." Such spelling was not uncommon among English mapmakers. A 1660 manuscript, *A Brief Discription of New England and the Severall Townes therein together with the Present Government thereof*, described "Norwock" as a settlement in Connecticut Government some fourteen miles distant from "ffairfeild."

Since early scribes practiced imaginative spelling and were committing to paper approximations of sounds of a language alien to English ears, the use

---

[7] To be a freeman, a man had to be twenty-one years old and of "good conversation"—i.e., good conduct. He had to obtain approval of the General Court or a magistrate and fulfill a property requirement. In practice, freemen were generally Congregationalists.

of "Newark" as a variant spelling does not seem entirely strange. This designation for Norwalk appeared on a map in Cotton Mather's *Magnalia Christi Americana*, published in 1702, and was repeated in a 1717 Mariners' Chart of the coastline of New England from New York to Boston.[7]

At least three other maps have designations far less explicable. "A Mapp of New England," by John Seller, who bore the impressive title of Hydrographer to the King's Most Excellent Majesty Cum Privilegio, used the name Chechister in place of Norwalk. Seller transposed the letters to Chichester on a map of New England in his 1687 volume, *Present State of His Majesty's Isles and Territories*. Seller, who claimed that his charts and maps were "Gathered from the latest and best Discoveryes that have bin made by divers Able and Experienced Navigators of our English Nation,"[8] is known to have purloined plates from the Dutch, erased the Dutch titles, and substituted English titles over his own name.[9] The symbols on his 1675 Mapp of New England are exact copies of those on William Blau's *Nova Belgica et Anglia Nova* (1635). Seller's creative nomenclature seems to have been the result of his business acumen rather than of his scholarship.

Regularization of the spelling "Norwalk" dates to a 1720 map of Connecticut describing the ancient boundaries of the colony.[10] John Copp, Norwalk schoolmaster, doctor, and town clerk, is known to have been engaged by the colonial government as a surveyor during this time. He may have made the survey for this map, which would account for the familiar spelling.

A map cannot record the special physical features of the area that nurture a symbiotic relationship between man and nature. "The situation of this town is very agreeable, the soil fruitful yielding plenteously, the harbor safe, and the air exceedingly healthful."[11] So wrote the Reverend Moses Dickinson in 1731/1732. Almost a century later his assessment was corroborated by that inveterate traveler Timothy Dwight, who described Norwalk in this manner: "The valley, which lies along Norwalk river, and in which the town is built, is beautiful."[12]

Modern geographers classify Norwalk as having a typically New England physiography.[13] Millenia ago ice sheets moving southward across what is now Connecticut slowly pushed rocks, boulders and soil ahead of them. When these huge glaciers retreated, they left in their wake the topographical features of the present day.

The main glacial stream, the Norwalk River, carved a north-south swath through the region and deposited organic mud flats up to fifty feet thick along the edge of Long Island Sound. The mud flats created an environment conducive to the growth of plankton plants, which ultimately supplied sustenance for shell- and fin-fish.[14] Tidal salt marshes and sandy beaches rimmed the Sound at the lower reaches of the estuary. The first white settlers gathered ample quantities of oysters and clams and utilized the wealth of the salt marshes as a dependable source of fodder for their cattle.

As the waters of the river coursed to the Sound, they carved a narrow but deep channel, making the river navigable for a distance of nearly three miles upstream. This harbor was sheltered from the vagaries of storms, gales and tides by a chain of islands. Known now as the Norwalk Islands, they appear on seventeenth-century maps as the Ar-

Atlatl weight found on Ram (Shea) Island in 1962. Collection of Norwalk Historical Society..

chipelagoes, a name bestowed by Captain Adrian Block who sighted them on his 1614 explorations.[15] The islands, by current count·twenty-two in number, have a mystique of their own.[16] Each generation has viewed them in a different way: first, as farmland and pasturage; then, as outposts for harbor pilots; and in modern times as unique recreational resources and wildlife sanctuaries.[17]

As one moves toward the interior, a series of hills and ridges rise abruptly above the floodplain and marshes. The most picturesque is the uplift of stone known as "The Rocks." The back-country areas were eminently suited for raising grain, and in the southern reaches of the ridge extending between Norwalk and the Five Mile River the dark loam was immensely fertile. Early settlers knew this long before the geologists and had steadily pushed their agricultural endeavors northward.

NORWALK
*an historical
account*

10

Few minerals or precious metals have been found in Norwalk. Albite and garnet, two varieties of quartz found in the area, have not been mined. Investors in will-o'-the-wisp schemes of developing a silver mine, purported to exist in the northern reaches of the community, realized heartbreak rather than riches. This elusive vein has provided only the wealth of local color. In the late nineteenth century more prosaic silex, a variety of flint, was exported in significant quantities to manufacturing cities as part of Norwalk's coastal trade.[18]

Settlers found an ample water supply in the form of natural springs whose properties often determined their names: Cold Spring, Fruitful Spring and Hungry Spring. With the growth of population, wells supplemented and later replaced springs as the major source of water.

When early man stood on the heights of the ridges and looked southward he saw an unending carpet of virgin forest. The stands of basswood, buttonwood, hickory, pepperidge, sycamore, and whitewood are all but lost to our memory.[19] In their time they provided early inhabitants with a fuel supply, the raw materials for houses and tools, and supported a wide range of animal life. Deer, fox, and wolves populated their shadowy depths and, together with an abundance of turkeys, pigeons, and quail, supplemented the grain and fish diet of the area's inhabitants and provided them with such valuable products as pelts and quills.

It is entirely likely that bands of nomadic hunters of the Paleo period traversed the area in search of the wild animals that were the mainstay of their diet. Some early men inhabited at least three separate sites in the Norwalk area. Artifacts found at the Bitter Rock Shelter in the ledge high above Ward Street indicate that the site was occupied around 5000 B.P.[8], making it the oldest known human habitat in Norwalk.[20] Spruce Swamp, originally a fresh-water pond one-half mile north of Long Island Sound, was first occupied by Amerinds about 3000 B. P. Projectile points found here suggest that the earliest residents of this site were primarily hunters. Later occupants eventually added shellfish to their diet—first, clams, then when the waters became warmer, oysters. As the present Long Island Sound moved inland, Spruce Swamp became a salt-water pond, and the site was abandoned at some time between 1000 B.C. and 1500 A.D. In the layers of the midden, two unique objects—a decorated paintstone, which may have depicted an astronomical phenomenon or have been a plat of the original village, and the skull of an adult male, bearing healed scars that seem to indicate ante-mortem trephination—may provide important clues to the origins of these people.[21]

The third site, Sasqua Hill, some distance northeast of Spruce Swamp, was occupied for several

8 B.P. is translated "Before Present."

thousand years and may still have been used by the Indians residing in the area when white men arrived. Archaeologist Bernard Powell notes: "Aboriginal occupancy of the region was apparently in a state of decline by Contact Times, but Contact materials may be present at . . . Sasqua Hill . . ."[22]

The Indians living in the area in Contact Times, when Europeans came in contact with the Indians, were People of the Shell, coastal Munsees whose forefathers were the Lenape People of the Delaware Tribe. They were part of the Wappinger (Mattabessec) Confederacy, a subdivision of the Algonquian linguistic group which stretched from Canada to the Carolinas. The Wappinger Confederacy occupied lands reaching from the east bank of the Hudson River from Manhattan Island northward to Poughkeepsie and east to the lower Connecticut Valley.[9] On the east their lands were bounded by the warring tribes of Rhode Island and Massachusetts; on the west were the hostile tribes of the Iroquois Confederacy. With the advent of the white men who zealously planted settlements under their native flags, the Wappinger became pawns in English-Dutch power plays. These factors may explain their withdrawal to the north where they formed a band called the Ramapoo. The name, a combination of the Indian words meaning "en route," may signify that the Wappingers, who had a tenuous foothold in the territory, did not view themselves as permanent settlers.

The Wappinger Confederacy was divided into seventeen subdivisions called sachemships. The Five Mile River was the demarcation line between the Siwanoy sachemdom, which stretched northeastward from the Bronx, and the Tankiteke sachemdom extending eastward to Fairfield and inland to Danbury.[23] The chief governmental figure in each sachemdom was the sachem or sagamore, terms that were used interchangeably. Although the sachem's position was hereditary and handed down in the male line of a family, he derived his power from the support given to him by the lesser sachems in his jurisdiction. Lesser sachems governed small bands of Indians, thought to be related families, who inhabited particular properties within the sachemdom.

9 Recent research by N. A. Shoumatoff indicates that the Connecticut Indians, who were on the frontier's crest, pushed westward to Pennsylvania and Ohio. The main body moved on to Kansas, northeast Oklahoma, Wisconsin, and Ontario, Canada, where their descendants still live today.

Sixty-eight villages, many of them coastal settlements, dotted the landscape of the Wappinger Confederacy. Norwauke and Saugatuck were the major villages in the Norwalk area. According to local tradition the largest aggregation of Indians lived at Wilson Point in a village called Naramake after the sachem who resided there and from whose name Norwalk is said to have been derived.[24] In the early records there are entries alluding to the Indian fort on the east bank of the Norwalk River. Such forts are known to have been residences of chief sachems and it seems likely that this fort was actually the Indian village of Norwauke. Since the forts stood on the very lands which the English first settled, the Indian population at Wilson Point may have been swollen with Indians who had removed from the east bank of the river.

As few as two hundred and no more than three hundred Indians—men, women, and children included—occupied the coastal area and the adjacent islands.[10] At some time around 1667 the town clerk turned to the back of his record book and inscribed the names of twenty-seven Indians on a page already half-filled with official notations. Selleck, the nineteenth-century Norwalk historian, used this faded record to reconstruct a list of thirty-eight Indian names but for reasons unknown failed to include several Indians whose names are still legible on the original record, Mamachimens and Winepuk, among them.[25]

Not surprisingly the first name on the 1667 census is Mamachimens, head sachem and intrepid spokesman for the Norwalk Indians in their relations with the English. The settlers respected his authority and often called upon him to resolve questions involving Norwalk's boundaries. One of the earliest boundary disputes between Fairfield and Norwalk originated in Fairfield's claim, by right of purchase from the Sasqua Indians, to land in the vicinity of Muddy Creek, a brook flowing into the Saugatuck River. Tribal ownership of specific land was a recognized principle and Mamachimens insisted that the Sasqua Indians had sold land properly belonging to the Norwalk Indians. He was witness to the April, 1661, deed which settled the dispute in favor of the Norwalk Indians. Mamachimens was appointed by the townspeople to mark the boundaries of Norwalk twelve miles north in

10 Weed, *Norwalk After Two Hundred and Fifty Years* (Norwalk, 1902), 102, estimated there were three hundred Indians. Elsie Danenberg doubted there were more than two hundred. *The Romance of Norwalk* (New York, 1929), 28.

"The Norwalk Indians" by Tom Parker . . . 1964. Collection of Norwalk Historical Society.

1669 and in 1674 accompanied two townsmen in marking out the boundaries on the far side of Saugatuck River.[26]

The 1667 census of Norwalk Indians contains the name of at least one female: Towntom's Mother. She may have been included because of her stature in the Indian community, where property and power were sometimes transmitted in the maternal line. Interspersed between such venerables as Winnepuk and Cokkenew are the distinctly Christian names of Joseph, Jonas, and Alexander, who probably represent that generation of Indians born after the advent of the white settlers.

Contact between English settlers and Indians produced a clash between drastically different cultures and led many Englishmen to view Indians as "much addicted to idleness, especially the men, who are disposed to hunting, fishing, and the war, when there is cause."[27] As a result of the Pequot War, which had disrupted the flow of life in the colony, the colonial government enacted laws to regulate settler-Indian relationships. The Ludlow Code of 1650 incorporated earlier legislation and provided that when any group of Indians set down near an English plantation it had to identify the sachem, who was then held accountable for the behavior of the group. Englishmen brought a long-engrained tradition of respect for property to the New World and were often irked by the proclivity of the Indians for using land which the settlers had purchased but had not immediately put to use. The Ludlow Code specifically forbade Indians to trespass on the English plantations. Englishmen were enjoined from selling or trading gunpowder to the Indians; selling, bartering or giving them cider; or settling and joining them. Although the law protected Englishmen from the Indians it also protected the Indians from unscrupulous Englishmen by mandating that either the person or the town make restitution for wrongs done to Indians.[28] When Norwalk was accepted as a town by the General Court of the colony its inhabitants were automatically required to obey all colonial laws regarding Indians.

In pre-contact time the land had unstintingly given up its treasures to the Indians. Residual shell heaps testify to the importance of siwan (wampum) production by local Indians rather than to their voracious appetite for shellfish. Fishermen, hunters, and berry-pickers, these Indians were farmers, too. Unfettered by the laws defining property rights of which the English were so fond, the Indians planted their patches of maize, pumpkin, and squash where they chose. After 1651 their life-style was severely constrained, although Norwalk settlers initially maintained a policy of accommodation toward the Indians who lived within the town's boundaries. The townspeople set aside planting land for the Indians' use and, to guard against encroachments on such lands, forbade the settlers to plant "within the Indian Field." The settlers were bound to make restitution for any damage done by their hogs to Indian property. Indians as well as whites were entitled to bounties for killing wolves within town limits. Some Indians were employed by the town to burn off the islands and at least once the town paid an Indian, Jores, for the use of his canoe. Committees of townspeople adjudicated any serious differences arising between the Indians and the town.[29]

This live-and-let-live policy did not last long. As early as 1665 a town ordinance stated that "noe Indian sitt down within a Quarter of a mile of the Town," the first of a series of decisions that removed the Indians from the immediate environs to more remote and less desirable agricultural lands. The policy was born of the need for additional land rather than fear of these gentle Indians. In 1667 the town allocated three acres on the west side of the Norwalk River and three-score acres of pasture there to the Indians, moving them farther toward the periphery of the settlement. In the 1671 land division, English inhabitants who did not then have any estate for their children received a portion of land in the Indian Field. Even though the Indians were removed from the east side of the river the settlers continued to trade with them.

Only local Indians were tolerated. In 1702 Matthew Seamer and John Seamer were appointed to inform "all Strang[e] Indians for to depart from our towne to their owne place whereto they properly doe belong." Hereafter Norwalk's town records become strangely silent with reference to Indians. In the Colonial Census of 1756 no Indians were recorded as residents of either Norwalk or of Fairfield County.[30] A more assiduous enumerator counted five Indian females and four Indian males in Norwalk for the 1774 census. In the first Federal Census of 1790 their number was considered so negligible that no provision was made for enumerating Indians under a separate category. They "seem to have melted away unnoticed."[31]

2

OF FOUNDERS AND FIELDS

Being
an Account of
Life in Early Norwalke

CHANCE PLAYED the largest role in bringing together the little group that settled on the east side of the Norwalk River in 1651. Yet these people were not a random collection; they shared a number of characteristics. First and foremost they were all Congregationalist Puritans. Religion probably tied them more closely together than did their English heritage although all had come from England. Most of them had left England in the 1630s, had stayed in Massachusetts for a year or more, and then had moved to the river towns of western Connecticut.

The Norwalk settlers all had a similar ambition: to obtain better farmlands. Norwalk's founders had arrived in Massachusetts too late to obtain the best lands in the Bay Colony towns and they had not fared too well in the river towns of Connecticut. In those days a man's future depended upon his share of undivided lands held in common by the town in which he lived. Most of the Norwalk deed signers who came from Hartford ranked in the lower half of the valuation list of land owners there and could therefore expect to receive lesser portions of that town's remaining land. Matthew Marvin, considered well-to-do in Norwalk, ranked somewhere in the middle in Hartford. Norwalk's founders knew how hard it was to break new ground. They had moved twice before; some had moved three times but, considering their limited future in the river towns, it is small wonder they took advantage of the opportunity offered by Ludlow in 1650.

On the average these men were fairly young — in their middle-to-late thirties. Richard Olmstead, Matthew Marvin, and Richard Seymour had grown sons but most of the other children were well under

sixteen. The backbreaking tasks of clearing, plowing, and putting up fences would fall to the Norwalk men alone.

All the Norwalk proprietors could read and write but in a few instances the penmanship indicates that signing one's name must have been an ordeal. Within several families who entered the town in the 1650s and 1660s, fathers, sons, and brothers spelled their surnames differently. John Keeler wrote a good hand but Samuel Keeler scribbled "Keler" for his signature. Richard Seymour, who had matriculated at Exeter College, Oxford, in 1613, was one of the town's best-educated men. Unfortunately, Seymour—in his middle fifties when he arrived in Norwalk—died in 1656, the same year he was elected to the honorable post of townsman, comparable to that of selectman. His death was a blow for it deprived Norwalk of an educated leader who could have been influential on the town's behalf with Hartford's General Court. Another educated man of the original group, Richard Olmstead, was not only a selectman for two decades but was a deputy to the General Court for almost twenty sessions, served several terms as a King's Commissioner, was appointed to highly important boundary committees, and served as Norwalk's militia chief.

There may have been some Huguenots in the original Norwalk group, for many French Protestants had fled France for England during the religious wars. Richard Seymour, a signer of the Ludlow agreement, was apparently of French descent, the name having been St. Maure originally. The Seymours had been in England for years and the name was so anglicized that Connecticut scribes often spelled it "Seamer." Nathaniel and John Ruskow (later Rusco) may have been Huguenots, and the Boutons and Raymonds, other early settlers, might also have been French or of French descent. The best example of a French name is St. John, which appears in many early records as Sention or Sension, indicating that record-keepers heard the name pronounced in a French fashion.

Under the terms of their agreement with Ludlow the proprietors were required to settle at least thirty families on their new plantation "in a short time." During the first three years, however, it was not easy to attract settlers to the Norwalk River area because the war between England and the Netherlands gave rise to rumors that the Dutch and Indians were conspiring against English settlers. The greatest alarm was felt in the western towns of Fairfield and Stamford for they were not far from Dutch-controlled New York. Rather strangely, in view of the Indian scare, the General Court questioned why Norwalk was so slow to obtain thirty families and in 1653 the planters had to send Richard Olmstead to Hartford to explain matters. Fortunately Anglo-Dutch hostilities came to an end without a full-scale Indian war and Norwalk was able to continue the search for additional settlers.

In the meantime Roger Ludlow, angered at the failure of Connecticut to provide military support for his Fairfield plantation during the Indian threat, abruptly decided in 1654 to leave America and return to England.[1] Shortly before he left Connecticut Ludlow assigned his remaining rights in the "Plantation of Norwalke" to the inhabitants of the town. By this time the proprietors had probably been able to fulfill the obligation to bring thirty families for a 1655 list of "Estates of lands and accommodations" shows thirty-one property owners in Norwalk.[1]

Since several men on the 1655 land list were relatives of the original planters and there was also much intermarriage among the families of the little settlement, by the fourth generation almost all Norwalkers who were not rank newcomers were related to one another. Matthew Marvin's family alone supplied wives for several Norwalk men: Hannah married Richard Seymour's son Thomas; Abigall wed John Bouton who arrived in Norwalk about 1654; and Mary Marvin became the wife of Richard Bushnell who was voted admission in 1647.

[1] Ludlow may also have been disappointed because he had been successfully sued for slander in connection with a witch trial.

Not everyone who might wish to do so could become an "admitted inhabitant" of a Connecticut town—that is, to have full rights, privileges and, of course, duties. Everyone had to take an oath of fidelity to the colony and most towns had additional requirements, the major one being that admitted inhabitants must be Congregationalists. Norwalk had no such religious requirement although it is easy to tell from the signatures on church petitions that almost every Norwalk man was a member of the Congregational Church.

Norwalk did, of course, have to live up to the express prohibition in the Ludlow deed against people "obnoxious to the publique good." During the period of Indian troubles, though, the town fathers may well have turned a blind eye toward minor character faults. Certainly they ignored George Abbott's brush with the law back in Windsor in 1640. Abbott, an indentured servant although seemingly an educated man, was fined five pounds by the General Court for selling "pystoll and powder to the Indians."[2] Apparently the authorities didn't consider this a heinous crime for, beyond the heavy fine, Abbott was not punished but simply bound to his good behavior. Although Norwalk accepted him as an admitted inhabitant, Abbott's past may not have been forgotten. He lived for over thirty years in town but was only once elected to an office of significance.

As far as can be gleaned from early records only one person was rejected outright from living in Norwalk. In 1671/1672 in town meeting "it was by vote declared that the Town do not approve of John Crampton to be an Inhabitant in this Town either by buying or hiring of land." Crampton may have been a squatter who had somehow acquired a few acres. There is a 1665 reference in the Town Proceedings to "Cramp's Coal Pit," no doubt a peat bog, out on the Neck. What was wrong with him? Something fairly serious since he was forbidden even to rent land. But the unwanted Crampton must have stubbornly refused to leave, for three weeks after their first vote of disapproval the town meeting again took up the problem of Crampton, this time authorizing the selectmen to "prosecute John Crampton by law for the removing him out of the town."

A new Indian conflict, King Philip's War, provided the perfect opportunity for getting rid of the troublesome fellow. Each Connecticut town was asked to furnish troops to fight the Narragansetts in eastern Connecticut. If not enough men volunteered, it was the duty of the selectmen to decide who was to be sent off to fight. Usually the selectmen chose men who could most easily be spared but on occasion an unruly or shiftless man would be included. Norwalk provided twelve soldiers for King Philip's War. Among them was John Crampton.

Knowing from experience what they would need in the wilds of western Connecticut, the Norwalk settlers had brought with them tools, livestock, and food to sustain them during the first months in their new location. Diligence, determination, and dedication were the personal weapons each proprietor brought to conquer this wilderness. It was no easy matter to fell trees and hew the lumber needed to build houses, to burn off wooded areas and remove stumps, to prepare tillage land for spring planting, and to cut hay in the salt marshes for winter fodder—all in the few short months before winter settled over the land. No man among them could afford the luxury of indifference, despair, or half-hearted effort.

The first land prepared for tillage, known as the Planting Field, was located to the south and east of the home-lots in an area the settlers early came to call the Neck. Periodic expansion extended tillage lands into the Pine Hill, Saugatuck, and Fruitful Spring sections of the Neck. In any division or allotment of land for tillage purposes the settlers had to clear the acreage in its entirety before a crop could be planted. With fewer than eighty adult males in the community during most of the seventeenth century, a scarcity of labor deterred the plantation from tilling and planting all the arable land within the town's boundaries.

Indian corn, or maize, was the first major crop they planted. It was dependable, disease-resistant, and produced a high yield. Later the settlers planted winter wheat, rye, oats, and barley. Flour and meal were staples in every colonial home but to enhance the plain fare each settler maintained a garden in his home-lot where he raised peas, squash, turnips, and pumpkins. Fruit trees were tenderly nurtured and no home-lot was complete without an apple orchard to provide cider, the most common drink of the period. Women and children

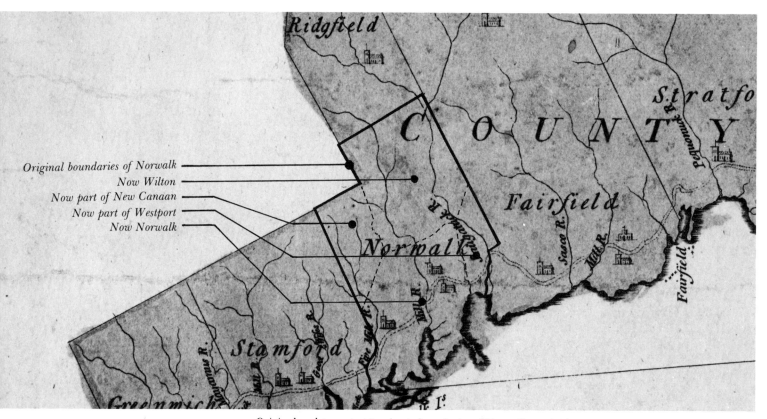

Original and present approximate boundaries of Norwalk overlaid on section of Moses Park's 1766 map.

scoured the hillsides for wild strawberries and huckleberries in summer and for nuts in autumn.

As additional lands were cleared flax and hemp were grown for local consumption. The women spun retted (softened) and beaten flax into linen thread and wove it into lengths of cloth that were fashioned into durable bed sheets and wearing apparel. Strands of processed flax and hemp were made into rope and cord, which were put to a multitude of uses. In 1699 the town paid James Hayes two shillings for two pounds of flax which were used to repair the cords of the town drum. In later years John and Ruth Hoyt maintained a manufactory where flax was processed into cart rope. By the 1700s flaxseed had become a lucrative export, shipped mainly to Ireland to replenish its supply since the Irish did not allow flax plants to grow to maturity. Through most of the eighteenth century Norwalk shared in this trade, shipping the flaxseed in locally-made casks to both Europe and the West Indies.[3]

In a subsistence economy whose very existence depended on grain crops reaching maturity, wandering pigs and cows created havoc when they roamed into a planting field and trampled the young grain. One of the earliest entries in the town records dealt with this problem:

... if there shall be found any swine in the _____ and planting field without youkes on, ... it shall [be] lawful for any inhabitant to kill any of such aforesaid swine ... [4]

The owner of the animal had to be immediately informed so that he could claim the carcass and butcher it, testimony as much to the scarcity of fresh pork as to the frugality of the settlers.

This ordinance gave way to a decision to erect a sturdy, thirty-foot square, post-and-rail pinnefold (pound) in which to impound roaming livestock, as required by the Code of 1650.[5] The pound was a prescription that did not cure the ailment and in an about-face the townspeople decided to pen up the crops instead of the animals. They voted to erect a fence around the Planting Field "sufficient to keep out all cattle and swine." Drawing on nature's generous supply, settlers piled stone upon stone to form the lower portion of the fence. On this base they erected a five-rail fence, allowing a space of only six to eight inches between the rails, which created a barrier about four feet high. Each man

was responsible for building and maintaining that section of fence which enclosed his portion of the common field. The "fence viewer" was an assiduous judge of the adequacy of the structure and could levy a fine of one shilling on those whose fences were found wanting. And wanting they were. In April, 1662, alone ten people were fined for such defects as holes, low places, and missing stakes!

Although the principle of private ownership was basic to Norwalk's agriculture it was distinctly tempered by communal activity. Decisions made in town meeting regulated the rhythm of daily life for all. Each proprietor held title to his lands but the crop he planted and the time and place he planted it were products of joint decision-making. When the townspeople decided "the Field called the Necke is to be laid in for a year for winter wheat," "the flock of sheep shall not goe into the Lower field two weeks after this date," "all Islands that have bin purchased by the towne shall be for the kepeing of calves onely and all other cretors ar by this order prohibited," they were creating an orderly and cohesive economic arrangement. They were also imposing a pattern of uniform behavior on all residents.

The beat of the drum became the measure of conformity. By the beat of the drum inhabitants were informed that the day was seasonable for burning about the common fences. Then all other activity ceased. After fences had been erected in the Planting Field the gates were opened at the end of September for a thirty-day period during which cattle were allowed to graze on the stubble. The drum announced that residents could drive their cattle to the fields and—relentlessly—its beat summoned them to drive out their cattle at the close of the period.

The settlers often established common services through shared resources or labor. Although these measures were intended to make work easier and more productive they inevitably curtailed individual competition. When the town decided to pay Nathaniel Richards £1 5s. for the use of his bull to service cows they not only guaranteed equal access to a scarce resource but they also ensured that Richards would not profit at their expense—as he might have, had he been free to negotiate individual transactions. Controls on charges accompanied the exclusive franchises given to the miller and the tavern keeper. When John Bartlett wanted to sell planks and timber for "shippework" he had to receive permission from the townsmen. Thus overt competition was severely limited and no man could profit at the expense of his neighbor. Through these self-imposed restraints Norwalk evolved into a small community of farmers with "steady habits," none very rich and few very poor.

In town meetings these hardworking men passed many hours trying to arrive at the most expedient method of caring for their herds. Annually in mid-May the milch herd was rounded up daily and pastured on the east side of the Norwalk River under the care of a cowherd. These cows, each bearing the distinctive mark recorded for its owner, were driven home nightly for milking and safekeeping in the owner's hovall (shed). During the summer months calves were isolated from other cattle and given to another cowherd, usually a young boy, who tended them in the pastures of the near islands expressly set aside for this purpose. At low tide the calves could be easily guided across the mud flats to the grassy island pastures.

On the first day of May dry cows were herded together and moved to the west side of the river where the dryherd keeper watched over them during the summer months. Every man shared responsibility for driving the cattle over the cart bridge spanning the Norwalk River and turning them over to the herdkeeper. Stephen Beckwith, for many years the herdsman, then drove the herd to the plain on the far side of Rooton Hill. As the herd increased in size and more grazing land was required, the area about and toward the Five Mile River was opened as pasturage.

Beckwith's job, his "whole Imployment," was a demanding one. He protected the herd from attack by wolves, killing at least five of these predators in 1667 alone. He tended the young bulls that "goe with the dry heard," supervised the pound on that side of the river, and for an additional two shillings a week kept an eye on the oxen pastured with the dry herd.

The early settlement functioned as a barter economy and little hard money actually changed hands. Beckwith, whose salary was twelve shillings a week, received "currant merchantable pay," or "country money" in lieu of coin. He was paid a half-pound of butter for every cow he tended and the remainder was paid in wheat, pease, and Indian corn. As the 1668 season drew near the townspeople—intending perhaps to rebuke him or to drive a sharper bargain—voted to "except" the butter from Beckwith's wages, threatening to hire

"some other sufficient man for the same wages" if Beckwith refused this offer. A man of Beckwith's experience was hard to find and the decision must have encountered opposition. In fact Beckwith was rehired with the half-pound-of-butter-for-every-cow provision restored to his pay but it was the last year he kept the herd. In 1669 Thomas Taylor was engaged to replace him. The town did not forget his many years of service and when Beckwith fell ill in 1699 James Jupp was paid to tend him.

Cows, oxen, sheep, swine, and ridgling boars were plentiful in the early settlement; the patrician of the animal family was the horse. Good riding horses were a luxury and owners often hired them out to transport a deputy to Hartford or to carry an emissary to Stamford in style and comfort.

The colonial government, which regulated many aspects of economic life, required each town to brand its horses. Owners placed a personal identification mark on their animals in addition to the O on the near shoulder, designated as Norwalk's brand.[6] The town's brander registered each mark in the brand book and entered all sales therein. The number of horses increased so rapidly that by 1679/1680 there were seven horse pounds in the community. People did not always conform to the law requiring branding and the sale of unmarked horses became a profitable enterprise. To curb such sales, reduce the number of strays, and bring money into the town treasury, an ordinance was passed allowing individuals who captured and sold unmarked horses to keep half the sale price, turning the balance over to the town. Such fees, fines, and other penalties became important adjuncts to regular taxes.

The early inhabitants of Norwalk were self-reliant but they were not individually self-sufficient. Fortunately the original settlers included several craftsmen among their number. When the town decided to build a frame house for the Reverend Mr. Hanford, the first minister, they utilized the skills of Ralph Keeler, a housewright, paying him in "wheate at the merchant's price" and the "rest in currant pay." So essential were the services performed by Richard Holmes, the blacksmith, that the town paid to have tools brought from Stratford for his use. When the town voted to provide inhabitants with home-lots and four acres for each child it rewarded the childless Holmes for his valuable service by including him in the grant. Joseph Fenn, a merchant from Milford, was given land behind the

The Home-lots, as shown on Edwin Hall's 1847 map of the principal parts of Norwalk.

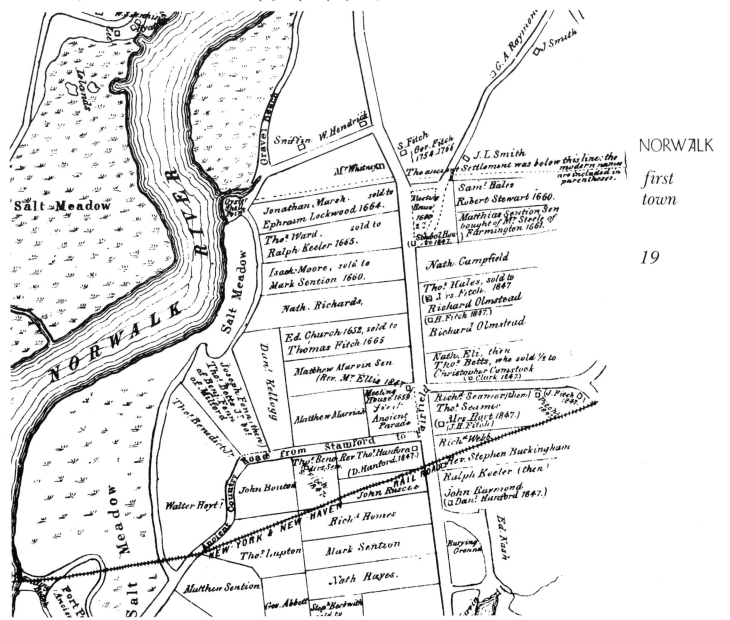

Burying Place, a central spot in town, for his house and shop.[2] He sold powder and shot, two of the great variety of items in his stock, to the townspeople. The list of resident craftsmen was further swelled by the addition of one James Beebe who was granted a home-lot on which to set up his trade.

Thomas Oviet of Milford was granted the right to establish "a house by the waterside . . . to put ashes in,"—the first potash and pearlash manufactory in

the community.[7] In a time-consuming process ashes were placed in large tubs with double bottoms and water was poured over the ashes. This was drawn off and the process repeated until the liquid was strong enough "for an egg to swim in it."[8] The liquid, lye, was then boiled in large pots until only black or gray ash was left. This product was potash, an important component of fertilizer and glass. If the ash was further refined by roasting in a kiln it became pearlash and was used for making soap, or as a leavening agent.

2 Hall's home-lot plan, however, shows Fenn located on the Ancient Country Road to Stamford.

This present wrightinge witnesseth that I Thomas
Ward of Norwalke doe by these present Bargaine sell
assigne and sett over unto Ralph Keeler of the same
my now dwellinge howse and howse bound orchard and
yardes and homelott ffences with all the accommodatio
ns of upland and meddowes within ffence or without
ffence with all the common ffences theire unto belonginge
with all the Divisions of lands allready laid out or
shall or may be laid out belonginge to the aforesaide
accommodations, as allso all the commonage privilidges
or Cimmunities belonginge or appertaininge to the sayed
accommodations all lyinge and beinge in the aforesaidde
Towne of Norwalke unto the aforesayd Ralph Keeler
and his heyers; An consideration and for the somd of
eightie poundes to be payed by the sayed Ralph Keele
r his heyers executors or administratores unto the
sayed Thomas Ward as by twoe Billes made and assig
ned by the saide Ralph Keeler unto the sayed Tho
mas Ward in manner and forme doe more fullye
expresse bearinge date this present hereof provided
the sayed Thomas Ward is to deliver up the possession
and enioiment of all the aforesayed howses orchard and
yardes and homelott ffences and upland and meddowes unto
the sayed Ralph Keeler in or upon the ithof maye n
xt ensuinge the date hereof; only the sayed Thomas Wa
rd doth reserue the workinge shopp the use thereof
for the abode of his wife if she shall haue occasion untill
the 29th of september next ensuinge the date hereof;
Allso the sayed Thomas Ward doth reserue to himselfe to
take away at his pleasure the Lockes upon the dwellinge
howse Doore and the younge nursery tres and 2 boardes
lyinge upon the Coller Beames; And unto the toward
faithfull performance hereof and every part hereof
I the sayed Thomas Ward doth by these binde my self
my heirs Administratores and assignes firmely by these
presents witnesse my hand this ithof september
Anno Domini 1665.

In the presence of   Thos   W
Tho ffitch sone   Ward
                                                      marke
being Ashford

The clustered home-lots provided a center for the craftsmen. The original ones were located on either side of Town Street (later East Avenue), which the proprietors had staked out upon a ridge that extended along the east side of the Norwalk River, beginning at the Sound end near a tidal pond and running inland just past the bend in the river. On its westerly side the ridge sloped gently down to wide, grassy salt meadows and marshes at the river's edge. The distance between ridge and salt marsh was such that four or five home-lots of about four acres each could be laid out between Town Street and the edge of the marsh.

The Deacon Thomas Benedict House on West Avenue . . . circa 1685.

The choicest lots were located at the heart of the new village where Town Street—still only a narrow dirt road—crossed the Stamford-Fairfield path. At this point the two roads united briefly in front of the meetinghouse lot. Owners of these lots could expect to make money through commercial ventures as the town grew. The best lot of all, on the Stamford path just across from the meetinghouse, was reserved for the minister. Proprietors who became acknowledged town leaders—Olmstead, Marvin, and Ely—and those men who arrived a few years later and quickly gained high posts—Thomas Benedict, Thomas Fitch, Matthew Campfield, and Christopher Comstock—all had homes close to the

meetinghouse lot and the intersection. Their names appear again and again in town records. Benedict is an interesting example.

Arriving in 1665, too late to participate in the original allotments, he nevertheless managed—probably by buying a portion of land from each of three adjacent property owners—to squeeze out a lot in a most advantageous location next door to the minister and across the street from Matthew Marvin, Jr. Benedict had been a man of some prominence on Long Island but after Britain wrested control of New York from the Dutch he found it more congenial to live in Connecticut among other Puritans than to live among Anglicans and he moved with his large family to Norwalk. The selectman system had just come into being the year he arrived, replacing the townsman system, and he was immediately chosen a selectman. He was also made town clerk, perhaps because of his firm, clear hand. At the same time he was elected to a much less prestigious post which he apparently willingly undertook—that of sweeping out the meetinghouse. He may have needed the twenty shillings the town paid for this work but it is more likely that as a good Puritan Thomas Benedict accepted this humble task for the glory of God.

Norwalk's first home-lots near the mouth of the river amounted to a miniscule portion of the common acreage within the town, some thirty-six thousand acres. Over the next eighty years this property was gradually parcelled out to both old and newly-admitted inhabitants. Strictly speaking Norwalk's proprietors, Ely, Olmstead, and the other deed-signers, were the only ones with the right to allocate this land. In practice all admitted inhabitants voted in town meeting on how and when to divide the acreage held in common.

In 1676/1677, for example, the town voted to give each man who had fought in King Philip's War a portion of land in the town. Those who had participated in "the direful swamp fight," in which the Narragansetts' major village was destroyed, received twelve acres each. Soldiers who had fought in lesser engagements were granted from four to eight acres apiece. Most of the men on this military list were sons of Norwalk families, but—quite surprisingly—John Crampton's name also appears. Crampton must have emerged from the expedition a hero for—not only was he allowed to return to Norwalk—he was granted more than eight acres of land.

Commonage was generally parceled out in two ways: in home-lots to newly-admitted inhabitants and from time to time in "divisions" of agreed-upon sections of still uncleared areas. Because of its effect upon the manner of Norwalk's growth it is worthwhile to describe land division in some detail.

A man's commonage rights were established when he was admitted and were seemingly dependent upon the contribution he made, sometimes in the form of services to the town. A right in commonage was somewhat like owning shares in a corporation where dividends were not paid in cash but in additional shares. Regardless of his property and commonage rights, however, each man had only one vote in town meeting. When an area was opened up for division the town's admitted inhabitants drew lots for their individual portions. Each

had to start with a fairly large initial share and live a long time, adding four or five acres here in one allotment, two or three acres there in another. By living into old age the town's first minister, Thomas Hanford, and another early leader, Thomas Fitch, Sr., managed to acquire estates of over three hundred acres each. In Fairfield by contrast John Staples lived about the same length of time and acquired almost fifteen hundred acres.[9]

The pace of land distribution quickened somewhat in the 1670s and 1680s. Various property owners began to ask for home-lots and shares in commonage for their grown children and in 1671/1672 every inhabitant who had not yet received a house lot for his children received one of at least four acres for each male child.

A second and more extensive allocation came in

*The Thomas Hyatt House on Willow Street, built in 1677, is
Norwalk's oldest residence.*

*The Platt-Raymond House on Silvermine Avenue
. . . circa 1680.*

division was carefully spelled out for the records. In the division of 1654 we read that the new allotments were to begin at the "hither plain where John Gregory moved last year, and to allot as far as the dead trees and . . . to come [to the] creek . . . " Thus with each new division every man added to his private holdings, some more, some less, in accordance with their original commonage rights.[3]

Unlike most other towns in the colony Norwalk was niggardly in its land dividends.[4] To acquire an

estate of any size through land division alone a man 1686 when Sir Edmund Andros, sent by James II to be governor of New England, challenged the validity of previous land titles. After ruling certain land grants in New York invalid, the dictatorial Andros now frightened Connecticut by declaring that lands granted to New England towns under the original patents were still the possession of the Crown. Hastily Connecticut's General Court issued new patents to the current proprietors of each town. After

---

3 Thomas Hanford's estate provides an excellent example of how the system of small land divisions worked. His allotments were scattered over the entire early town: Pine Hill, Saugatuck Plains, The Neck, Fruitful Spring, Coast Division, Planting Field, Other Side of the River, Indian Field, and various other areas.

4 Information about land allotments relies heavily on Erna Green, "The Public Land System of Norwalk, Connecticut, 1654-1704: A Structural Analysis of Economic and Political Relationships," an unpublished thesis, Department of History, University of Bridgeport, 1972.

Norwalk received its new patent it began to vote sizable dividends and continued to do so even when Andros was no longer a threat. In four short years some three thousand acres were allocated, about the same amount that had been divided during the first eighteen years of the town's history.[10]

Just why Norwalk remained stingy in land allotment for so long is hard to understand. At the time of settlement it was logical to open uncleared areas slowly and rely upon communal methods of planting and harvesting because of a manpower shortage. The conservative Norwalkers continued the policy of picayune land dividends for more than thirty years, however, and the system lay like the traditional "dead hand" on the town's economy. There was little trading in land for profit or speculation; most land transactions were simply exchanges for mutual benefit. Where the price of land rose in other Connecticut towns, Norwalk's land values remained low. Even newer towns surpassed it in land values. Since investors in land look for rising prices, Norwalk's system discouraged ambitious men from settling in the town and this in turn hampered Norwalk's growth throughout the seventeenth century.

3

OF MEETING-HOUSES
AND MINISTERS

*Being
an Account of
The Governance of the Town of Norwalke*

O FULFILL their promise to bring a clergyman to Norwalk the townspeople started to look for a minister willing to come to their frontier settlement. In New Haven they found a young schoolmaster, Thomas Hanford, who had been university-educated in England and had also studied theology under an eminent theologian in Massachusetts. He was not an ordained minister, however. The young man's New Haven pupils were poor scholars and he had become discouraged at the prospect of trying "to learn them to write [and] to bring them up to Latin as they are capable." With a new wife to support Hanford needed more than the twenty pounds he was earning. He welcomed Norwalk's invitation and arrived in the autumn of 1652.[1]

Members of the congregation must have taken the new minister and his wife into their own homes during the Hanfords' first year or two in the town. Not until December, 1653, do we find any mention in the Town Proceedings of a house for the minister. At that date the town assigned Ralph Keeler and Walter Hoyt the task of constructing a house for Mr. Hanford with instructions to finish the work by April. The frame house, sixteen feet wide and thirty-one feet long, was roofed over with shingles that Matthew Marvin, Jr., supplied. The minister's house was probably somewhat larger than those of the other inhabitants because it was designed to serve as home, temporary meetinghouse, and school. The detailed specifications indicate that Norwalkers gave great thought to the building.

Hanford's house is a typical example of the customary way of providing town buildings. Under the Congregational system the minister's residence, as well as the meetinghouse built a few years later, were considered town buildings. The meetinghouse served both as a house of worship and as the place where inhabitants met to discuss and vote on town business. Men such as Keeler and Hoyt with special skills were expected to contribute their craftsmanship to community undertakings. They were paid a modest but fair amount for their work, as was Marvin for the shingles. Other inhabitants made their contributions through a special tax. In large undertakings all men were expected to help unless they were old, ill, or had other time-consuming town duties.

Mr. Hanford quickly gained the respect of his congregation and over the years became ever more beloved by the people of Norwalk. The town settled upon the sum of sixty pounds annually as his salary, an amount that remained unchanged for almost his entire lifetime. Since sixty to seventy pounds was the average salary range for clergymen in New England in those days Norwalk did very well by its minister in view of its limited financial resources. In addition to his clerical duties Mr. Hanford served as the town's first schoolmaster, teaching Norwalk children in his own home. There is no record of how Mrs. Hanford[1] bore up under the

---

[1] After the death of his first wife shortly after their marriage, Hanford was married a second time in 1661 to Mary Miles Ince of New Haven, a widow with one son.

daily onslaught of pupils, well-disciplined little Puritans though they may have been, but the sixteen-by-thirty-one foot house must have been overflowing with children for the Hanfords had ten of their own.

Because a Congregational clergyman was hired by members of his church, and could be discharged by them, he could never completely forget that he was not only God's servant but the servant of the local congregation as well. Mr. Hanford's authority was, however, reinforced by a stern and powerful theology and by devoted lay leaders. The chief laymen, the deacons, kept track of church contributions, purchased sacramental wine, made sure that no one took the sacrament unless fully qualified to do so, and guarded the town's morals. Families of stability and substance provided deacons for the Norwalk Congregational Church generation after generation. Between 1665 and 1806 four generations of the Benedict family served in this prestigious post.

The tithingman also performed important duties. As the title indicates, he saw to it that every family paid its proper share of church expenses. During the week he checked to see that parents taught their children the catechism. On Sundays he awakened those who dozed during the sermon and kept strict watch over the children, who were apt to be fidgety during the long service.[2] Norwalk's children were not above reproach in this respect and in 1668 Thomas Lupton was chosen "to doe his best indevor to kepe them from playing and unsivill behavor" on the Lord's Day. A few years later Thomas Barnum was appointed to the same task for which he was specifically empowered:

... if he see any disorderly, for to keep a small stick to correct such with; oneley he is Desired to do it with clemency; and if any are incoridgable in such disorder, he is to present them either to their parents or masters; and if they do not reclaime them, then to present such to authority.[3]

It was humiliating to both child and family when Barnum seized an older boy by the arm and marched him off to sit with the younger children or paraded a little boy to the women's side of the church to sit with his mother. On the whole, though, Norwalk people were much more considerate of their children than were the people of Stratford who gave their tithingman instructions to "use such raps and blows as in his discretion meet."

It is not likely that Norwalk's meetinghouse was ever warm during the cold winter months even though the town did its best by voting that it should be "cated and dabed and made comfortable."[2] Between November and April New England churchgoers had to wear their heaviest clothing to worship. Even the minister might wear a skull cap or hood and keep woolen mittens on his hands while he delivered the sermon. Women wore bonnets called "punkin-hoods" which were filled with wadded wool and tied tightly about the face with a drawstring. Heated stones or bricks were brought to keep one's feet warm and later some people used footstoves filled with hot coals, although these created the danger of fire. But for the most part people just accepted the cold. Babies unfortunate enough to be born in winter were generally baptized with ice-cold water.

As backcountry land was settled noon-houses or "Sabbaday" houses were built to accommodate those who had to drive some distance and could not return home between morning and afternoon services. After the first service these "outlivers" would gather at the noon-house to eat food they had brought from home and to warm themselves at the fireplace. In 1713 the town gave John Taylor the right to erect such a "small house for his family convening on yᵉ Sabbath."[3]

Seating in a New England meetinghouse was determined by rank. This conformed to Puritan theology which, despite the Biblical injunction against pride, supported a class society on the theory that a man's success and prominence were surely some indication that he had found favor with God. It was not easy to serve on the committee that allocated pews. Men tried to avoid this assignment but they were usually unsuccessful in sidestepping either the task or the recriminations that followed. The practical Norwalkers tried to circumvent trouble by allocating pews in accordance with the taxes each man paid and even before the first meetinghouse was completed drew up a seating list based upon each man's estate. In recognition of their standing in the community, however, John Gregory, Thomas Fitch, and Thomas Betts, Sr., were

2 The settlers caulked the spaces between the rough-hewn boards to keep out drafts.

3 Most Sabbaday houses also had stalls for horses and in the affluent nineteenth century a member of the parish built a noon-house near the First Congregational Church just to keep the horses comfortable during meeting.

given the place of honor in "the round seat" until a controversy arose and this decision was revised: Mr. Fitch was given the "upper great round seat, as he is the King's Commissioner."

The custom of seating the town's chief citizen in the foremost pew symbolizes the close relationship between church and state in Connecticut. Just as, sitting in the round seat with the eyes of all upon him, Mr. Fitch could never allow himself the luxury of dozing during the sermon, so he and others like him were expected to set good examples in maintaining a godly and just government. This obligation was expressly stated in Connecticut law, was dinned into everyone's ears in the annual election sermon, and—it may be readily assumed—was self-imposed. As one New England historian has written: "The position in which God had placed them invested them with authority, and they were expected to give a good account of themselves."[4]

Norwalkers spent untold hours, individually and collectively, on town projects. Any matter involving the town had to be taken up at a town meeting which all adult male inhabitants were required to attend. At these sessions citizens elected officials, voted to admit new inhabitants, dealt with the local Indians, and made decisions on matters of public health and welfare. When the "fowre cotes"[4] paid to the Indian Mamachimens for marking the northern boundary of Norwalk turned out to be of inferior quality the meeting voted to sustain Mr. Fitch, who as selectman had promised Mamachimens "recompense for the badness" of the material. When Thomas Seymour refused to allow passers-by to drink from Hungry Spring on his property the town meeting "warned" him to permit "free passing of man and beasts to the sayd spring; he to remove any fence or incumbrance in the way."

Selectmen, usually five in number, were responsible for seeing that decisions were carried out. They were also called upon, as the Mamachimens episode indicates, to make day-to-day regulations as needed. As the town's highest officials they enforced Connecticut law as stated in the Code of 1650, the Ludlow Code, and in General Court statutes.[5] One of the selectmen's most important duties under the Code was to provide for local defense, ensuring that powder, bullets, and "good firelock muskets" were on hand at all times. Each

4 Lengths of material, not finished garments.

town had to equip and drill local militia or a "train band" from which no man was exempted unless already performing comparable military duty. The General Court early recognized Richard Olmstead's military capability and put him in charge of Norwalk's militia. These citizen soldiers drilled on the Common near the meetinghouse on training days. Sergeant Olmstead was so interested in this work that, for all his other obligations to town and colony, he continued the training activities and was rewarded with a special grant of sixty acres of land and the rank of captain.[5]

The town constable was another important official. He collected taxes, proclaimed new laws, and attended to a host of legal tasks. His law-enforcement duties included "Pursuits or Hue and Cryes" after felons and the apprehension of Sabbath-breakers and minor miscreants. The Code of 1650 provided harsh punishments for most crimes since lawbreakers were regarded as violators of the law of God as well as that of the state. Following the example of the Old Testament the death penalty was liberally imposed.[6] Those convicted of minor offenses might be sentenced to a term in prison, a whipping, the stocks, or payments of a fine.[7]

A variety of lesser officials were selected by vote at the annual town meeting in December. Posts seemingly low in prestige—chimney viewers, gate keepers, leather sealers, branders and surveyors—provided absolutely essential services. For this reason every man was expected to accept the position to which he was elected.

Even the man who beat the drum to warn town meetings and public gatherings or make other an-

5 The Code of 1650 included many useful regulations, such as a prohibition against the throwing of ballast into harbor channels, a provision for achieving honest and accurate weights and measures, and a requirement that anyone granted a home-lot must build on it within a year and keep his buildings in good repair.

6 To twelve crimes for which the General Court had previously imposed the death penalty—treason, murder, adultery, idolatry, witchcraft, rape, and the like—the Code added three more. Any youth over sixteen who cursed or struck his parents could be executed unless it could be shown that his parents had provoked the violence or had neglected to bring him up properly. A son over sixteen who refused to obey his father might also be punished with death, as could anyone who thrice committed burglary on the Sabbath.

7 There is no record of stocks or whipping post in Norwalk although these two instruments of correction must have existed in order to comply with the Code, which required anyone unable to pay a fine to be placed in the stocks.

nouncements played his part. This undemanding part-time job eventually fell to John Crampton who received forty shillings annually for beating the drum and sweeping the meetinghouse. If his miserably-scrawled signature is any indication, Crampton was barely literate and therefore well-suited to these simple duties.[6] The former outcast must have enjoyed a feeling of satisfaction and importance as he strode along the road beating his drum and passing on bits of exciting news. For well over a decade Crampton faithfully continued these tasks and just as faithfully the town's inhabitants elected him drummer and sweeper.

Under the Ludlow Code Connecticut settlements had to educate all children and apprentices so that they were able to read English and could understand capital law. Each town of fifty households had to provide a teacher and, after 1678, keep school in session at least three months of the year. The latter requirement may have been more than Mr. Hanford wished to undertake for in May, 1678, Norwalk voted to "hier a scole master to teach all the childring in the towne to lerne to rede and write." This atrocious spelling leaves no doubt that newly-hired Schoolmaster Cornish faced a formidable task!

Thereafter the town customarily hired a schoolmaster "if he can be obtained on Rationall termes," at a salary of thirty to forty pounds a year.[8] Since teachers were paid only "for each month of sayd work" and the school term was only the three months required by law, even though they may have taught for two terms per year, Cornish and his successors practiced considerable self-sacrifice.

Education was public but it was not free. Parents contributed one-half the schoolmaster's salary according to an intricate formula that encouraged parents to send children to school.[9] In addition to paying what was in effect tuition, parents supplied a half-cord of wood for every two children attending school. The town was obliged to pay the remainder of the schoolmaster's salary from a tax levied on the colonial list of estates and to provide a suitable classroom.

8 Preference was shown to local residents. Thomas Hanford, Jr., was hired in 1692 and John Copp became schoolmaster in 1700/1701.

9 This levied a tax equally on all children, except females, between ages five and twelve, whether or not they attended school, and on youths over twelve attending day school. Children attending night school paid one-third the tax levied on day-schoolers.

For many years this classroom was either in the meetinghouse or in a private residence "fitt . . . with conveniences for schooling," for the town did not build its first schoolhouse until 1699. This generously-proportioned twenty-by-eighteen-foot building soon proved to be inadequate. In 1707/ 1708 Over The River inhabitants constructed their own schoolhouse on Mill Plain and the schoolmaster divided his time between two institutions.[10] Either the Mill Plain school was overcrowded or, more likely, a flooding Norwalk River destroyed it for less than a decade later a new twenty-five-by-eighteen-foot structure was built on higher ground at Whitney's Corner.[11]

Residents of Dry Brook and Saugatuck, who lived a goodly distance from the town schools, successfully petitioned the town for a Dame School, one of three authorized in 1723. The Dame, a neighborhood woman, trained the children to count and to recite the alphabet in preparation for the rigors of formal learning. Actually a nursery school for children as young as two, during the summer months it allowed busy housewives to tend garden and lay away winter provisions with no small children underfoot.

Colonial lower schools were "essentially Congregational parochial schools."[7] The Congregational Society, almost indistinguishable from town government, managed educational affairs. Selectmen visited schools quarterly to scrutinize both the children's proficiency and the master's character and diligence. Masters had to manifest impeccable moral character and strong religious commitment so that they would not poison [children's] souls."[8]

In 1643 the General Court made local communities responsible for building and maintaining roads within their boundaries and for providing an intertown highway system. Sidestepping the intent of the law the towns often constructed little more than rough cart paths which had nothing to recommend them except that they were relatively free of underbrush, smaller trees, and boulders. Roads were built with little regard for proper drainage and their saucerlike construction turned them into

10 At first he spent two months in the original school and one month Over The River. Gradually he spent equal time in each school, a winter term in one and a summer term in the other.

11 It is more kindly to think that the number of children rather than competition dictated the larger dimensions. This structure must have had flooding problems too since the town allocated "refuse" boards from the new town house for use around the school's foundations.

reservoirs for heavy rain and melting snow. Travelers took life in hand when they used the narrow, rickety cart bridges that spanned the deeper rivers; they were forced to ford the shallow streams.

Colonial authorities continually rebuked local communities for their neglect of the country road or intertown highway. Norwalkers, more prone to talk than act, periodically discussed the need for a better bridge over the Norwalk River on the country road to Stamford. In May, 1680, the General Court ordered the town "to build a good and sufficient horse bridge." Two years elapsed before the townspeople agreed to survey the site, and an adequate structure was not erected until well into the eighteenth century.

Records left by travelers in the Norwalk area are a litany of hardship: "a most intolerable bad road;" "hazardous to the lives of travellers."[9] One tradesman claimed that his goods had been damaged in transit on a wretched stretch of road near Norwalk, "ye worst road,"—and that in the mid-eighteenth century! It was a humane gesture that colonial authorities required each community to establish an ordinary for travelers "for provision and lodgeing in some comfortable manner."

First selected by the townspeople, the keeper of the ordinary then had to be certified by two magis-

trates as "meet for that imployment." Once certified, the keeper adapted his home to the demands of his new enterprise. The needs of the beasts took precedence over the comfort of the traveler; whereas the law required the keeper to provide space sufficient for stabling two horses, it suggested only that a spare room be put aside for public use.

Ordinary keepers were the exclusive retail purveyors of wine and "hotte waters," the colonial term for liquor. Prices were set by law: cyder (hard cider) to be sold at not above four pence a quart and liquor at not above four pence a gill (quarter pint). Although the ordinary was meant to be a temporary home-away-from-home for travelers local inhabitants could visit there provided they tarried no longer than "halfe an hower att a time." Selectmen and constables kept a wary eye on those who frequented the ordinary, could warn them away, and fined persistent miscreants five shillings or one hour in the stocks. For his part in abetting such unseemly behavior the keeper of the ordinary paid a fine of twenty shillings.

A long succession of Norwalkers were elected to the job of ordinary keeper. The first was Walter Hoyt who started his business in 1659/1660 with a ten pound loan from the town. Patrons must have been few and the margin of profit slim for in addition to his duties in the ordinary Hoyt beat the drum on the Sabbath and swept the meetinghouse. Christopher Comstock, Matthias St. John, Matthew Seymour, and Andrew Messenger, all highly regarded inhabitants, succeeded Hoyt. Keeping a "publique house" was not generally considered woman's work but on occasion a competent widow like Mrs. Ruth Belden was licensed to continue the thriving business her husband had established. By the early 1700s travel had expanded sufficiently to warrant operation of two, then three, such establishments exclusive of a number of taverns catering primarily to local imbibers.

The grist mill was the most important business enterprise in the community. The earliest mill was operated by a Lieutenant Swain. In January, 1654/1655, a committee of freemen apprised him that he must leave the mill, a decision one supposes that stemmed from dissatisfaction with the desultory service this non-resident provided. The two years following were a time of great inconvenience. With no miller in residence the settlers had to convey their corn and wheat either to Fairfield or Stamford to be ground into "country flour," the coarse meal used by seventeenth-century farm people.

In 1657 an agreement was reached with one Jonathan Marsh to erect a mill either on the Norwalk River or the Mill Brook, as he saw fit. Sensing the urgent need for his services Marsh drove a hard bargain. He was promised the millstones, six acres of land, a piece of meadow and upland adjoining the mill, a monopoly for grinding grain in the community, ownership of the mill for himself and his heirs forever, and forty pounds in country pay to be paid both in produce and in three days' labor from each man. In return Marsh agreed to complete the mill in three months' time, to grind grain for local residents three days a week, and to take just the customary toll.[10]

The toll represented the miller's charge for his service, established by colonial law as one-twelfth part of each bushel of corn and one-sixteenth part of all other grains he ground. After grinding a customer's corn Marsh would scoop his toll dish, a "just" quart, into each bushel of flour and extract his share. To guard against an unscrupulous miller the toll dish was certified by the Sealer of Weights and Measures to be a true measure.[12]

12 The town also exacted one-sixteenth of each bushel as its toll.

Relationships between the town's inhabitants and Marsh were strained from the beginning. Marsh did not complete the mill within the specified three-month period. He seems to have had interests elsewhere or to have been neglectful of his job for in March, 1658/1659, the townspeople made an agreement with him that on the second, fourth, and sixth days of the week "he is to attend there that we may have free recourse to fetch and carry corn to the mill." A few years later when Marsh made strident demands for additional lands the town did not grant him the half-acre he wanted in the desirable Neck Planting Field but merely tendered an additional acre adjoining his mill lot.

Shortly after this, Marsh sold the mill, adjacent land, and scattered parcels of meadow and salt marsh to Nathaniel Richards for one two-year-old colt and two milch cows, appraised as equivalent to seventeen pounds. At the same time he sold his home-lot, house and contents, and his fruit trees to Ephraim Lockwood for one mare and one suckling colt. Marsh moved to a parcel of land in Stony Brook area on the outskirts of the settlement. There he erected a dam, an action suggesting that this consummate entrepreneur intended to build a mill to compete with the town-franchised operation at his old place of business.

Because of the town's constant need for a miller a local man, Nathaniel Richards, was given permission to operate Marsh's old mill "to the best of his ability and skill," but either Richards was unable to run the mill well or the mill no longer met local demands for only a year later the town removed it from his control. Finally in 1665 Henry Whitney of Jamaica, Long Island, who had followed the Benedicts to Norwalk, was voted an inhabitant and engaged to build a "good and sufficient corne mill" in a better location by the falls of the Norwalk River. This mill remained in Whitney hands for generations, passing first from Henry to his son John and in 1712/1713 to John's son-in-law Joseph Keeler.

In 1706/1707 Thomas Betts, Jr., and John Betts, Jr., were allowed to erect a corn or grist mill and also a fulling mill on the Mill Brook at the upper end of Dry Hill. In 1709 joined by Joseph Birchard, a newcomer, and John Gregory, Jr., they transferred their grain mill to the "crick" (pond) abutting Gregory's property. Although most mills of the time were situated on streams and derived power from the flow of water through undershot or overshot wheels this mill utilized tidal action. A hinged gate athwart a dam at the entrance to the pond opened to permit water to flow in on the incoming tide. As the tide receded the gate swung shut, storing enough water to turn the mill wheel for six to seven hours and providing a fail-safe method for storing water except in event of an extremely high tide. The process thus repeated with each change of tide provided an unfailing supply of water at Mill Pond, a prospect so attractive that Justus Brush of New York soon bought out the interests of the four partners. This mill was converted later to a lathe work operation and functioned well into the twentieth century.

Several decades passed before the inhabitants entertained the notion of building sawmills. These mills seem to have been franchised in tandem to serve both sides of the settlement. Matthew Marvin operated a sawmill on the west side of the river at the same time blacksmith Richard Holmes built one on the Five Mile River. In 1692/1693 when John Belden and Peter Clapham, some-time Norwalk resident, erected a mill on Stony Brook, John Reed, Sr., and his son were granted the right to open a sawmill "at the head of the salt" on the Five Mile River, with timber rights in the adjacent area. The Buttery Mill was built on the Silvermine River by Matthew Seymour in 1688 and became a famous landmark in the town with the distinction of being the oldest continuously operating sawmill in the nation.

The Reed grant was one of several in the Five Mile River area that brought a long-simmering controversy over the Norwalk-Stamford boundary line to crisis stage. Stamford proprietors claimed the land between Five Mile River and Pine Brook (Goodwives River) by reason of a 1643 gift made by the Indian, Piamikin. Norwalk settlers insisted the land was theirs under the Runckinheage purchase of 1651. This deed, signed by the same Piamikin and other local Indians, set the western boundary at Pampaskeshanke Brook which Norwalkers claimed was Pine Brook. Determined to exercise their right of ownership, in the summer of 1666 several Norwalk men deliberately cut hay on the west side of the Five Mile River, accompanied by Thomas Fitch who was to answer any challenge put by Stamford men. Attempts to arbitrate the issue locally failed miserably in spite of Norwalk's original intention to come to a "loving and neighborly" agreement. In 1673 the General Court intervened and established the Perambulation Line, determining:

That the five mile brook between Stamford and Norwalk, from the mouth thereof until it meets with the cross path that now is where the country road crosses the said River, shall be the bounds, and from there to run up into the country until the twelve miles be expired . . . [11]

Stamford did not concede the issue until 1715 when the Superior Court with Captain Joseph Platt of Norwalk presiding sustained Norwalk's right to grant land east of the Perambulation Line.

A similar controversy bedeviled relations between Fairfield and Norwalk. In 1649 at the behest of the Bankside farmers the General Court decreed that their property lay within Fairfield's jurisdiction provided that the land did not extend farther than two miles west of the bounds of Fairfield. When the line was drawn, however, it fell short of the Saugatuck River, leaving a slice of valuable farm land between Fairfield's legal boundary and Norwalk's eastern boundary as laid down by the Ludlow purchase. Local efforts to settle the matter always ended in a stalemate. The General Court intervened intermittently as an impartial mediator but even with the services of Governor Robert Treat it could not resolve the issue. Not until 1698 did the Court, with the approval of both contestants, vote that the Saugatuck River "shall be and remain forever . . . the dividing line between the said towns." [13]

These disputes pale into insignificance in light of a territorial question that threatened the very existence of Norwalk as a Connecticut town. In 1664 King Charles II granted his brother James, the Duke of York, a patent that threw all land west of the Connecticut River into New York colony, trimming Connecticut to an inconsequential strip of land and placing Norwalk under the jurisdiction of New York. Connecticut and New York commissioners soon redefined the boundary although the King never confirmed this decision and the matter remained unresolved for years. New York finally agreed to a boundary beginning at the Byram River and set on a line running north-northeast for some

---

13 A dispute erupted a century later when Norwalk and Fairfield became joint proprietors of that portion of a turnpike running between the two communities. When the question of fiscal responsibility for building a bridge over the Saugatuck developed, inflamed local residents again called upon the General Assembly to settle the disagreement. A commission set the dividing line at the mid-point of the river, and each town assumed the costs of constructing the portion on its side of the mid-point.

twenty miles. In return Connecticut agreed to cede a strip known as the Oblong or Equivalent Tract, roughly one and three-quarters miles wide from Norwalk to the Massachusetts line. New York's lack of good will, as well as a dispute over the exact point in Norwalk from which to run the line northward, delayed settlement until 1731 when the Oblong was finally ceded.[12] By this time a sizable number of the town's families had fanned out from the original settlement, taking up land in the Oblong, and its cession distressed both Norwalk and farmers in that area who became reluctant New Yorkers.

It would be pleasant to report that Norwalk's citizens took full advantage of the unique democratic rights to which Connecticut law entitled them. From the very beginning, however, so many men ignored town meetings that it was necessary to impose a sixpence fine for anyone who failed to attend after being properly warned. Soon the town found it necessary to double the fine and then impose an additional sixpence fine on anyone who arrived late habitually or slipped out early. Next they devised a system of calling roll at random times to catch anyone who had sneaked out. "The same meeting John Gregory came late, departed without leave," wrote a sharp-eyed town clerk. Even though the fine was increased to more than two shillings fewer and fewer men came to meetings. The sad fact that not many Norwalkers were interested in their town government was finally acknowledged toward the end of the 1600s when it was agreed that a mere twelve inhabitants together with a majority of the selectmen would suffice to transact business for the town.[14]

As anyone who has lived in a small town knows it takes a quarrel to bring people to town meetings. Norwalkers came out in full force during the great meetinghouse quarrel of 1679. After the townspeople had voted to build a new meetinghouse on the site of the old one it appeared that many people preferred a site farther north on a piece of common land known as Goodman Hoyt's Hill. The town divided into stubborn factions and, unable to agree, voted in December to leave the decision to a committee of out-of-towners. Accord-

14 This ordinance may have resulted from the desire of the Proprietors, descendants of the early families, to control town matters or it may reflect lack of interest because of this very control.

ingly they petitioned the General Court to send "three honest, indifferent judicious men" to view the two sites. Deputy Governor Treat and the two other men who, because of the bitterness, came to Norwalk with "trembling of heart," selected Hoyt's Hill with the proviso that should this be inconvenient for the ailing Mr. Hanford the town must provide him a house near the new site.

The losers promptly called a town meeting to "make voyd" the committee's recommendation. An entire day was spent in futile argument, not entirely unlike some modern committee meetings:

... the night being farr spent and after the day of that town meeting ... men being tired out with much tedious discours & agmt, many haveing not subscribed & som refusing; ... M_r Fitch sayd we had spent the day & done nothing ... [13]

Nevertheless opponents of Hoyt's Hill claimed victory. By this time the town had become a laughing-stock with its wrangling, and the General Court, standing behind its committee, sternly recommended that Norwalk's feud be "buried in perpetuall oblivion." This suggestion, alas, was not followed and the quarrel continued until the following May when the people of Norwalk again asked the General Court for help. In one final effort the Court turned to a Higher Power:

The Court ... doe heartily and affectionately recommend it to the good people of Norwalke ... to comitt the decision of this controversy to the wise dispose of the Most High, by a lott, which we hope may be that as will sattisfy and quiet the spirits of all the good people of that place ... [14]

The will of the Most High was clearly expressed when the lot was drawn: Goodman Hoyt's Hill.

The Reverend Hanford managed to remain on good terms with both sides during the acrimonious meetinghouse fight. Still the controversy was hard on the clergyman. One mid-summer day after the matter was finally settled, as he pondered Norwalk's troubles as well as his own, Thomas Hanford poured out his thoughts in a letter to a relative stranger, the eminent Increase Mather of Boston. Hanford was convinced that his quarrelsome parishioners had called down God's wrath upon the town. The previous summer "drought was our Judgm t," he told Mather, and now unseasonable rain was threatening the harvest. Only a few days earlier God had sent "a storm of lightning and thunder" that had struck dead nine working oxen. As for himself he was disheartened about his children's prospects. "God hath given me 10 children, 5 sons and 5 daughters," he wrote, "but as yet I see not how to bring up one of them to learning." The letter's final paragraph discloses Hanford's own loneliness dwelling in this frontier town among contentious parishioners:

Good S_r, pardon my boldness in troubling you with these rude lines, & let me intreat you (non semper saltem) not to leape over mee in your leisurable greetings by lines or otherwise in these parts; but let [me] bee accounted among the Numb_r, though (not of Reverend) yet of Brethren, & one who desires to bee

*Yours in the ffaith and ffelowship
of the gospell,*

Tho: Hanford[15]

During the rigorous first half-century of Norwalk's existence women surely must have contributed fully as much as men did to the community's wellbeing yet it is all but impossible to find references to the female sex in town records. A woman's birth, marriage, and death were recorded as required by Connecticut law but, except for widows whose names occasionally appear in estate listings, women's names are seldom found in the Town Proceedings. A search through other records produces only a fragmentary picture at best of women's role in the town. One learns from marriage records for example that it was not difficult for a young widow, especially one with full title to property, to find another husband. Indeed a large percentage of widows—even those without property—seem to have married a second time.

From records of the General Court or Assembly in Hartford one learns that women could and on rare occasions did bring suit for divorce. Although divorce was infrequent Connecticut was not illiberal on this subject and it actually may have been easier for a woman to obtain a divorce than for a man to do so.[15] At the end of the eighteenth century the wife of a Norwalk man and mother of thirteen children was granted a divorce on the grounds that he threatened her life during his frequent drinking

15 The Assembly took a lenient attitude toward women whose husbands deserted them or were lost at sea. After her husband had been absent for six years, or three years after he had been lost at sea, a woman could apply for divorce and remarry.

bouts. She received one-third of her husband's estate and guardianship of a minor child. Women sometimes brought lawsuits in their own names, usually in cases involving malfeasance of an executor.

Connecticut law permitted the widow of a man who died intestate to receive one-third of the household furnishings and to use one-third of his estate during her lifetime, or until she remarried. Husbands usually provided by will that their wives could continue to live in the homestead but title to real property generally went to the children, most often to the sons. Daughters usually shared in the household goods and could inherit real property, but sometimes this was willed to a son-in-law.

A revealing entry in the town records, giving each town-born boy a fifty-pound right of commonage, discloses the low status of Norwalk's women in land ownership. The grant originally included "all town born children" but the town clerk hastened to add for the record that "no female shall have benefits by this act, by their being born in y_e town."

Such limitations, combined with the lack of any formal voice whatsoever in town and church matters, left women legally dependent upon men. Yet the stability of society protected women and in daily life most men probably frequently consulted with and even deferred to their wives. Surely no woman could have been more cherished than Mary Benedict. When Deacon Thomas Benedict, "sound of mind but feeble in body," drew his will at the age of seventy-three he placed his wife Mary in full control of his estate during her lifetime. The will continues:

I also will and bequeath to my Grandchild Sammuell Bennedick [property and goods] provided he carry and behave himself dutefully and louvingly towards his Grandmother–so doing, I do also will and bequeath to y_e s_d Sammuell half of my sheep.
I do will and bequeath to Joanna Bennedick [property and goods], and what else of household her Grandmother shall bestow on her, provided she live with her and be tender of her while she shall Continue in this world.
Finally it is my will and I do hereby appoint my Son John and my Son Sam ll Bennedick to be joynt overseers of this my last will and testiment–willing these my loveing sons to be carefull of their Mothers comfortable living and to counsell her in y_e ordering of her affairs and disposall of goods . . .

Thos Bennedick, Sen_r[16]

4

PROSPERITY AND PERIL

*Being
an Account of
Norwalk's Growing Years*

HOMAS HANFORD died in 1693. He had been in declining health for some time, was gradually losing his eyesight, and was unable to carry out his customary duties. Although they could be contentious, Norwalkers could also be kind. When Hanford began to fail they urged him to "proceed in the work of the Ministry and therein to continue . . . until the Lord by his Providence shall dispose of him" and promised they would "endeavor to our ability for to give him due incouragement."[1]

It was no easy task to find a successor for their beloved minister but after more than a year's search they selected Stephen Buckingham, a recent graduate of Harvard College. The slender, scholarly-looking young man made such a good impression that the townspeople were willing to offer him a substantial eighty pounds annually after a two-year probationary period. Buckingham had excellent family connections. His wife Sarah, granddaughter of Thomas Hooker, is reputed to have been "the most accomplished lady that ever came to Norwalk" although she was but a girl of fifteen when the Buckinghams arrived.

The townspeople purchased a choice lot for the new minister's home-lot and gave Buckingham two other improved parcels and a large share in commonage. They set to work to construct a fine new house for him, a two-story structure with double chimneys and a "comely porch," considerably more elaborate than that provided for Hanford. To spruce up the meetinghouse for Buckingham's ordination in the autumn of 1697, to which prominent elders and messengers from other towns were invited, they added a spacious gallery.

Various bits of evidence contribute to a picture of a lively and prosperous Norwalk at this time. Although the 1690s saw the beginning of a long period of wars between France and England, for which Norwalk like other towns had to pay extra taxes, the town did not feel any need to pinch pennies. In 1699 it found funds to help John Crampton out of his financial troubles. Even with a substantial increase in pay, poor Crampton had fallen sadly in arrears in his mortgage payments and was also deeply in debt. Whatever the misfortune that had befallen him, some debilitating illness or the persistence of an old war wound, it stirred the sympathies of those strict Puritans for the townspeople agreed to advance part of Crampton's mortgage payments. In an untypical burst of generosity they also voted that in the event he died or was unable to beat the drum and sweep the meetinghouse "the said Crampton or his widow [are] to enjoy the house and lot so long as both or either of them shall live."[2]

Increasing affluence harmed the church throughout Connecticut. Church attendance declined and members flouted increasingly the warnings of their ministers. A colonywide inquiry in 1704 revealed disturbing tendencies: "neglect of attendance in the publick worship," intemperance, talebearing, and contempt of authority. To counteract the new independence a group of prominent ministers and lay leaders worked out a set of rules in 1709 known as the Saybrook Platform which created regional associations and consociations of clergy and laymen which could act as appellate committees in church disputes.

Norwalk's Congregational Church reflected the prevailing new attitudes. When the town added a splendid new belfry to the meetinghouse—further evidence of prosperity and growth—it was voted to top it with either a weathercock or pinnacle. In former times a pinnacle would have been deemed "Romish" and not countenanced by good Puritans; now architecture prevailed over religious implications. When a new meetinghouse was built (after another protracted quarrel) the town voted that it was to be used for church purposes only. Town meetings were to be held elsewhere, another indication of the more distant relationship between citizen and church.

proper conduct with the wife of a certain Mr. Lines. The town promptly cut off the minister's salary, appointed a committee of leading church members to investigate the charges, and arranged for young Thomas Fitch, Jr., a recent theology student at Yale and already a lay reader, to replace Buckingham temporarily in the pulpit. Again a quarrel rent the community, dragging on for two years with local meetings, consociation meetings, appeals to the Assembly, and even a day of prayer. Buckingham astutely countered the charge with an offer to appear before a consociation provided he could have

Rev. Stephen Buckingham from a portrait painted about 1700. Both portraits, collection of First Congregational Church on the Green.

His wife, Sarah Willet Hooker Buckingham, as painted during the same period.

The Reverend Mr. Buckingham added prestige to the town as he moved ahead in the Congregational establishment. He received a Master of Arts degree from Yale's predecessor, the Collegiate School, in 1702 and later was appointed a trustee for Yale. In 1711 the General Assembly invited him to preach the influential election day sermon at First Church in Hartford, a considerable honor for Norwalk and for Buckingham.

After thirty years of devoted service Stephen Buckingham found himself facing charges of im-

an opportunity to point out to its members "such public scandalls that any of ye members of this Church may lye under, in breaches of severall commands of the morall law, and other Scripture rules."[3] Not surprisingly the town rejected this proposal.

In 1727 the town invited the Reverend Moses Dickinson to be their pastor and the Fairfield (County) Association upheld his appointment, basing its decision upon the schism that had rent the Norwalk church. Thus the association did not meet the issue of Buckingham's alleged misconduct squarely. A group of church members, mostly outlivers from Five Mile River,[1] charged that "certain evill-minded persons," who wanted a minister they could engage at a lower salary and dominate, were "the Root of the Controversie."[4] The outlivers tried to hold their own church services with Buckingham as their minister but were locked out of the church by vigilantes from the majority group. The faithful Buckingham supporters then petitioned the Assembly for permission to form their own parish but their appeal was rejected.

Aside from its connection with the Buckingham quarrel the group's request was not unreasonable. For several decades families had been living so far away from the meetinghouse they were unable to attend church regularly in the winter. A snowstorm was no excuse in the minds of die-hard Puritans living in the center of town who were wont to remind the outlivers that they must have known about winter travel when they moved hence. By 1726 there were enough families in what is now Wilton to petition the Assembly for a separate church or society. Both the Assembly and Norwalk willingly granted the Wilton request and the parent church donated its old pulpit to the new "upper Society." In 1734 the Five Mile River group again petitioned for separation and after a row with the parent church lengthy enough to fill thirty pages in the colony's Ecclesiastical Affairs records their request was granted. The new society took the name "Middlesex"—now Darien. The Buckinghams continued to live in Norwalk for the remainder of their lives, in the house the town had provided. Records of the Middlesex Society show payments to Buckingham for preaching there.

Adopting the name of Prime Ancient Society, Norwalk's original parish divorced itself completely from the secular government, holding its own meetings and keeping its records separate from the civil records.

The Reverend Mr. Dickinson turned out to be another Hanford, serving the society for fifty-one years, "A man of good understanding, well informed by study, Chearful in temper, Prudent in Conduct . . ."[2]

[1] Samuel, Thomas, John, Daniel, Joshua, Ephraim, and Lemuel Raymond, probably all the younger adult males of that family, put their names to the petition, as did Thomas and Elnathan Hanford, James Pickett, John and Edmund Waring, James and John Olmstead, and a number of others.

[2] Inscription on his tombstone; Norwalk, Connecticut.

The quickened pace of economic life in eighteenth-century Norwalk may be attributed to an extraordinary change taking place in the region's agricultural system. In the 1600s a small population, a conservative policy of land division, and the limitations imposed by the cumbersome open-field system of farming had militated against any appreciable amount of surplus foodstuffs. Although "Wheat, Pease, Ry, Barley, Indian Corn, Porck, Beif, Woole, Hemp, Flax, Cyder, and Perry"[3] were shipped via the coastal trade to Boston and New York,[5] Norwalk's share of the total was very small indeed. When the populations of Boston, Providence, and New York began to burgeon in the early eighteenth century Norwalk farmers, totally unaccustomed to market pressure, now had to use tillage land to grow fodder crops to expand their production of cattle, beef oxen, hogs, and horses.

Norwalk became the hub of the area's agricultural enterprise as farmers from outlying areas as far away as Pound Ridge and Redding brought beef, pork, cheese, butter, and hides to Norwalk merchants, receiving in return sugar, molasses, tea, rum, cloth, books, spectacles, and household wares—to name only a few of the more popular items stocked by Norwalk merchants.

Using a barter system which developed out of the shortage of hard money, farmers exchanged produce known as "country pay" for articles they needed but did not make—a "kittle," for example, or small luxuries that added a touch of elegance to a farm wife's otherwise drab existence, a few yards of Persian cloth, perhaps. In a typical transaction Jonathan Grayham, a Salem farmer who also distilled considerable quantities of rum, shipped fifteen barrels of beef to Stephen Benedict, a Norwalk merchant whose customers came from as far afield as Danbury. Benedict sold the beef in New York, shipping it on the sloop *Anna* owned by Peter White, himself in debt to Benedict for rigging and overhaul charges. After Benedict deducted a service charge for repacking the meat and the cost of the salt used to preserve it he credited Grayham's account by thirty-six pounds against which Grayham made purchases in Benedict's store until the next autumn's slaughter. By carrying the beef to New York, White liquidated part of the debt he had incurred with Benedict for chandlering services and Benedict turned a neat profit—although not one shilling had changed hands!

[3] Perry was a pleasant-tasting liquor made from pears.

From such modest beginnings a prosperous trade developed. Enterprising merchants sought out markets beyond Boston and New York and found they could readily dispose of their goods in such faraway places as Charleston and the islands of the West Indies, which were destined to be Connecticut's major market. As sloops and schooners scudded into Norwalk harbor with greater frequency the old wharf at Fort Point began to buckle under the piles of merchandise waiting to be loaded for trips to Antigua and Barbados. Although inhabitants were encouraged to discharge their annual obligation of working on the highways by contributing their labor instead to the reconstruction of the wharf their efforts did not suffice. Norwalk's bolder merchants began to build private wharves, a calculated risk that paid off in expanded trade.

The development of sea-related occupations brought new faces to pre-Revolutionary War Norwalk. Whereas in the 1670s Captain Richard Raymond of Saybrook had been one of the few mariners plying the coastal trade from and to Norwalk, increasing numbers of masters, mates, and mariners arrived to man the vessels now homeported in Norwalk. Captain Josiah Thacher of Yarmouth, Massachusetts, who came to Norwalk in 1724 as a coastal mariner, in later years invested his savings in Whitney's grist mill and lived out his life a landlubber tending millstones. Eliakim Smith was another prudent man who owned his own schooner, unlike so many of his seafaring comrades who were wont to invest their earnings in silver buttons, sherry, and fine china tea sets.

The good life enjoyed ashore helped to counterbalance the wretched conditions at sea and lives imperiled by unseaworthy vessels as well as storms. On a voyage to Halifax, for example, Captain Thaddeus Raymond, master of the twenty-one ton sloop *Sarah*, was obliged to throw merchandise valued at £240 overboard during a severe storm "by reason of the sails of sd vessel being very old and much worn and unfit." He was also forced by these conditions to change his course to Barbados. He made the best of a bad situation by bringing a cargo of "Rhum" back to Norwalk, ending a disappointing voyage that became the issue of a suit and countersuit in the Fairfield County courts in 1759.[6]

An interesting example of the new commercial man who utilized agriculture and maritime pursuits to his own advantage is Nathan Mallory, born in Norwalk about 1725. Besides acquiring a consider-

able amount of land he engaged in shipping and also had a store at the head of navigation on the Norwalk River. In 1761 he joined with some other men to build a wharf at Oyster Shell Point on the east side of the river. Mallory left four sons, the best-known of whom, Lewis, born in 1763, built up his share of his father's estate and became one of the town's prominent and wealthy men in the following century.

Crown Great Chair attributed to Nathaniel Street ... circa 1700-1725/Collection of Mrs. Lillian Blankley Cogan.

Through no fault of their own Norwalk men who turned to shipping for their livelihood were restricted in opportunity during this remarkable maritime period.[7] In spite of its growth Norwalk remained in a secondary position because its harbor could accommodate only vessels of thirty to forty tons.[5] New Haven with first-rate wharves such as the famed Long Wharf and a harbor that could handle ships of up to three hundred tons became the major port of central and western Connecticut.

In 1709 New London gained a legal advantage to add to its natural one when England ordered all ships to be cleared through its customs house.[7] Shipmasters in western Connecticut were dismayed for it meant that ships plying between Norwalk and New York City had to sail to eastern Connecticut for the collector's signature. Although England eased up on this regulation a few years later Norwalk merchants suffered more than a temporary loss.

Fairfield provided additional competition. Settled a decade earlier than Norwalk, it quickly became the county's principal town. In 1666 Fairfield was made a shire town and the county seat, and by 1675 was one of the four leading market towns of the colony.

That Norwalk grew in spite of commercial rivalry is seen in the numbers of exceptional artisans who settled here in anticipation of a market for well-designed furnishings and accessories. Nathaniel Street was a dexterous cabinetmaker who had learned his trade in New Haven and set up a shop in Norwalk where he produced Crown and York chairs, elaborate new styles highly prized in Connecticut coastal towns.[8] Street had the misfortune of having his property flooded when Lieutenant Samuel Keeler built a dam across the Norwalk River but the town granted Street a more suitable parcel where he resumed his trade and eventually recovered his losses. His business was so flourishing that an inventory taken at the time of his death listed a stock of twenty-two chairs.

Norwalkers were eager to acquire articles made of silver—buckles, buttons, spoons, porringers, and tea sets—visible proof of their new affluence. At least three silversmiths practiced their craft in the town prior to the American Revolution. In 1737 Pierre Quintard, born in New York and appren-

ticed to Charles LeRoux, a leading silversmith of that city, settled in Old Well on the west bank of the Norwalk River. This man of many talents not only crafted silver but also kept a tavern and eventually became the owner of a ship.[9] Shortly after Quintard settled in Old Well, Peter White purchased more than twenty-six acres farther upstream on the same side of the river near the present West Avenue where he built his home and a shop for the manufacture of silver articles.

Jacob Jennings, a rival of Quintard and White, catered to such a prosperous clientele that when his shop was robbed during the night of April 6, 1762, the culprit made off with a silver cream pot, six large spoons, two or three dozen teaspoons, and many pairs of buttons, studs, and buckles, all valued at £100 lawful money. Through his brother, a Boston silversmith, Jennings advertised in the *Boston Gazette*, offering a twenty dollar reward to whoever apprehended the thief and committed him to any one of His Majesty's gaols.[10]

Heretofore Norwalkers had made their own clothing. Now Norwalk men could have their pantaloons tailor-made and their hats made to order. Samuel Cluckston, the first of a long procession of hatters, became a prosperous businessman and served several terms as town treasurer. Simple manufactories began to supply craftsmen with semi-finished materials. In 1709/1710 when the Betts brothers and their associate Birchard erected the fulling mill on Stony Brook their successful venture encouraged Jonathan Fairchild to build a similar establishment on the east branch of the Norwalk River. In a two-step process fuller's earth, a highly absorbent clay, was used to cleanse and scour fibers which were then thickened and compacted to a feltlike consistency. River water diverted into the manufactory through a sluice box carried off the dirt and grease removed during the process, an early example of polluting the river's sparkling waters with industrial waste.

Land in a convenient location was becoming expensive. In 1712/1713 Joseph Platt, Samuel Betts, and John Copp were given liberty to drain the "Boggs lying between the Rox and Camberry Plain path," a certain sign that the town's economy was changing. A century earlier no group of proprietors would have considered planting a settlement in an area devoid of boggy meadows since such lands provided fodder for their herds. When boggy meadow was drained, however, the land became

---

4 The Mallory family, one branch of which settled in Mystic, epitomized the difference between Norwalk and a superior port like that of New London. Although the Norwalk Mallorys did very well financially in local business circles, they never attained the stature of the New London branch of the family. See James P. Baughman, *The Mallorys of Mystic: Six Generations in American Maritime Enterprise* (Middletown, 1972).

5 Some sources state that Norwalk harbor was deep enough for sixty-ton vessels.

eminently suited to raising hemp and could command a high price. In 1741 Amos Monroe sold Cockenoe Island to merchant Ralph Isaacs for £300, a paltry sum when compared with the incredible £1,000 Monroe received for six acres of land in the Toilsome area north of the Rocks.₆

Norwalkers were demonstrating their new affluence in the construction of their houses as well as in furniture and silverware. The town's early houses, "one story and a half or two stories with back roofs running slanting and low," had been small, dark, and cramped, as were most early New England houses. Finished doors, hardware, and shelving were hard to come by, and those items were usually specifically mentioned in early deeds of sale. When Richard Raymond bought a house from Ralph Keeler in the 1660s Raymond was careful to see that

*Caudle Cup made by Peter Quintard.
Collection of First Congregational Church of Stamford.*

the deed included the "flores, doares, glasse windows, [and] shelfes." When Thomas Ward sold his house to Keeler a year or so later he reserved the right to remove the "locks upon the dwelling house doares" and even "twoe boards lying upon the collar beames."

By the eighteenth century, with finished lumber from the town's own sawmills and no lack of window glass, those items were no longer so expensive. Norwalkers could build larger houses and fit them out in greater style and comfort. The typical Norwalk style in window lights was nine-over-six, a well-balanced arrangement that created a double-hung window of respectable size. By the 1730s the

6 Even Selleck, who reports this transaction in *Norwalk,* fn 1, page 283, called this "a large price."

town must certainly have been more attractive than Madame Sarah Knight had found it when she had passed through Norwalk in 1704 and commented in her diary that its houses were "indifferent." Norwalk houses did not compare, of course, with those of Boston, Madame Knight's native town, or New Haven, whose wealthy settlers even thirty years earlier had "stately and costly houses."

By the third decade of the eighteenth century Norwalkers were living well beyond Five Mile River and several miles inland as well. Middlesex, Canaan, and Wilton parishes were still part of the town in civil matters and they were well-populated. To warn town meetings the proprietors had to post notices on many signposts—at the bridge over the Norwalk River, at Wilton, Canaan, on "Rhoton" Hill, and at the Saugatuck.

If a notable lack of educated men is any criterion Norwalk retained a somewhat parochial outlook even in the 1700s. No man from Norwalk is listed among Harvard's graduates during that eminent Puritan college's first century of existence, nor did any Norwalk man graduate from Yale during its first two decades. Since Yale, organized in 1701, was a creation of both the Assembly and the powerful Congregational Church, its graduates were more likely than other men to become part of the Connecticut "establishment," an amorphous political and social clique that became known as the Standing Order. Ties with that college were and still are politically useful. It is no coincidence that Thomas Fitch, Jr., the first Norwalk man to graduate from Yale (1721), became the first Norwalk man to become governor of the colony.

Norwalk was free from the epidemics that afflicted much of New England during the early eighteenth century. The "great sickness" of 1715 in Waterbury-Naugatuck, the smallpox epidemic in Boston in 1721 and 1730, and the "throat distemper" (diphtheria) rampant in all New England in 1737 seem to have bypassed Norwalk. By account of the Reverend Moses Dickinson the only general sickness in Norwalk between 1651 and 1732 was measles.¹¹

The town's early settlers had to be a hardy lot for they had only home remedies to cure their ailments. Poultices, powders and brews, compounded from assorted herbs, berries, bark and plants, were all part of the colonial housewife's pharmacopoeia.

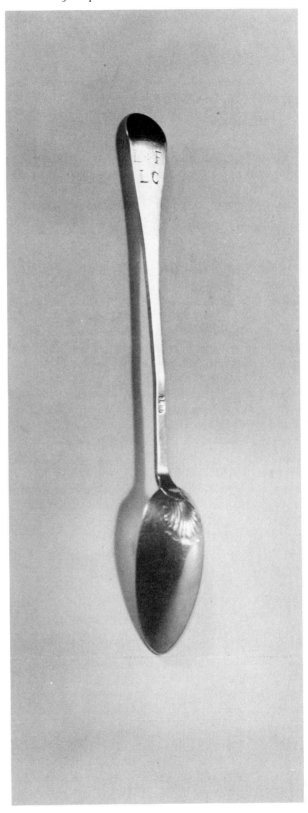

Teaspoon made by Jacob Jennings.
Collection of Ralph C. Bloom.

Many remedies had been learned from the Indians, such as the application of powdered white hellibore root over a coating of bear's grease to promote the healing of an open wound, or sumach boiled in beer to alleviate colds. Other remedies, elaborate medleys of ingredients, were time-consuming to prepare but had the virtue of relieving a variety of ailments. Consider the plight of the busy housewife who had first to collect the ingredients needed to concoct the following medicine, said to be "excellent for stuffing of the Lungs upon colds, shortness of wind, and the Ptisick."

. . . two gallons of Molasses Wart, Oak of Hierussalem, Cat Mint, Sowthistle, one of each handful, of Enula Cowpane root, one ounce, Liquorice, scrap'd brused and cut in peices; one ounce, Sassafras root cut in thin chips; one ounce annyseed and sweet fennel-seed, of each one spoonful brused; boil these in a close pot, upon a soft fire to the consumption of one gallon, then take it off, and strain it gently . . . put it up in glass bottles, and take thereof three or four spoonfuls at a time, letting it run down your throat as leasurely as possibly you can. [12]

During the eighteenth century home doctoring was slowly supplanted by licensed physicians who had generally received their training as apprentices to a practicing doctor. John Copp, sometime schoolmaster, surveyor, and town clerk, in 1705 also became Norwalk's first licensed physician. Although by mid-eighteenth century a few doctors were practicing in southern Fairfield County, Ezra Stiles included no one from Norwalk on his 1763 list of physicians. Less than a decade later Dr. Samuel Baker was practicing in Canaan Parish. The name of Dr. Thaddeus Betts appears often in Norwalk Town Proceedings during the Revolution.

Doctor-pharmacists compounded their own medications using an extensive inventory of drugs, compounds, phials, and corks that lined the shelves in Stephen Benedict's general store. Benedict also kept a stock of medical books and local physicians are known to have purchased such volumes as Brock's *Practice of Physick* and James' *Dispensatory*.[7] On occasion storekeeper Benedict supplied drugs directly to users. The Town of Norwalk was billed for opium supplied to a resident by order of one John Carter and Jesse Hoyt picked up an order of this painkiller for a Pound Ridge resident.

7 At one time Benedict had three copies of James' *Dispensatory* in stock, an indication of its popularity with householders as well as doctors.

It was not uncommon for the town to defray the costs of medical treatment. In 1759 Mrs. Andrew Achan, who for some time had been "in a Distracted posture of Mind," was sent to White Plains to be treated by a certain "Rev. Mr. Smith," a man of great repute for dealing with this kind of illness. The town magnanimously voted to pay him forty-five dollars if he cured Mrs. Achan; "otherwise nothing." When the dreaded smallpox appeared shortly before the French and Indian War those who contracted this highly-contagious disease were shunned by family and friends alike, and the town paid for the services of people willing to care for these victims. Moses Dickinson received eleven pounds as payment for providing care for Ebenezer Benedict's daughter and in a similar instance William Mott was granted six pounds out of the town treasury for tending John Lewis "when in the small pox."

At the end of the century Benjamin Trumbull reported that the life span of people in Connecticut was at least one-third and nearly one-half longer than in the world in general. It should be noted that he attributed this condition to "Temperance, chastity, a contented and quiet mind, and peaceful and righteous conduct, a cheerful confidence in GOD, and the reviving hope of His everlasting mercy."[13] He makes no mention of the medical practices of the time.

By Trumbull's day the religious movement known as the Great Awakening, when all of New England was transformed by the English evangelist George Whitefield, lay over half a century in the past. Whitefield traveled along the Connecticut coast in 1740, stopping at Norwalk among other towns and preaching there, wrote Trumbull, with his "usual popularity and success." This dynamic religious leader denigrated orthodox religion, urging sinful man simply to open his heart to God. Whitefield's ideas split the already troubled Congregational churches into the "New Lights" drawn to his theology and the "Old Lights," or strict Congregationlists. This schism was reflected politically with the New Lights predominating in eastern Connecticut, while western Connecticut remained orthodox.

Meanwhile other religions made headway in Congregational Connecticut. The most significant, the Church of England, grew through the work of its effective missionary organization, the Society for the Propagation of the Gospel. In western Connec-ticut the Reverend Henry Caner established Anglican headquarters at Fairfield and proselytized in the towns along the coast between Fairfield and Greenwich. After 1727 the Assembly permitted Anglicans to pay their church rates to the Church of England.[8] Norwalk then permitted Caner to collect from his local followers and a few years later granted the Anglicans acreage for a church and burying ground.

The Rev. Henry Caner, A.M., Minister of King's Chapel / Yale University Art Gallery, The John Hill Morgan Collection.

By 1757 Anglican strength justified a full-time clergyman in Norwalk and the Reverend Jeremiah Leaming became rector of the new St. Paul's parish. A devoted, hardworking man, Leaming was able to report in 1761 that in the preceding six months he

8 Baptists, Quakers, and other "sober dissenters," had already secured the right to attend their own churches and in 1729 were allowed to contribute only to their own churches. Heretofore everyone had to pay a tax to support the Congregational Church in his town.

had baptized "19 white and 6 black children and one negro adult, after proper instruction."[14] His little parish was prospering; the church was completed, and the parishioners had just purchased a six-hundred pound bell. The Congregational clergy was disturbed but Leaming tactfully carried on his duties "notwithstanding the great opposition we meet with from the dissenters" and was rewarded by seeing his religion tolerated. In 1770 he reported that "now there seems to be a friendly intercourse between [both religions] . . . they criticize their own clergy if they preach anything opposing Anglicanism."

The theological problems presented to clergymen in those days were often not subject to easy solution. Leaming once wrote to his superiors seeking advice on the following case: A newly-married sailor, taken prisoner at sea, was erroneously reported by the ship's captain as having died. Three years later his wife, believing herself a widow, remarried. Thirteen years passed before the wandering sailor presented himself at her door. Learning she had remarried and had children by her second husband, he took off and had not been heard from since. Now—three years later—Leaming posed the problem of the unwitting bigamists: "The man and woman who live here desire to be admitted to the Lord's Supper, and are very worthy people . . . " Alas—local records fail to show his church's response to the unfortunate couple's predicament.

One reason for Norwalk's continued prosperity throughout most of the first half of the eighteenth century was the series of wars between England and France. These were fought for economic reasons; in North America both nations wanted the lucrative fur trade and control of the Ohio Valley. It was this aspect involving Canada, New York, and the Ohio Valley that affected New England.

Norwalk, in little danger of attack by either French or Indians, nevertheless prepared for trouble by fortifying the meetinghouse and laying in extra powder and lead. Eventually a garrison was stationed on Sheffield Island. The town did not escape the exactions of war, however. It repeatedly supplied militia to supplement His Majesty's Regulars, especially annoying since these militia were not defending their own homes or even their own colony but were marched off to New York, Massachusetts, or some distant island in Canada to fight for terrain for which they cared nothing. Norwalk soldiers fought in the daring attack on

Louisbourg on Cape Breton Island, at Quebec, Crown Point, and Ticonderoga, among other campaigns. We find records like the following:

Out of Capt Ketchums Compeny ye first military Compeny in Norwalk Ten Good Effective men all of them Imprest . . . out of Capt. Clugstens Compeny ye second military Compeny in Norwalk Ten Good Effective men & all of Them Imprest . . . out of Capt. Marvens Compeny in Wilton Parrish Ten Good Effective men, one enlisted volunteer & nine of Them Imprest . . . [15]

The letter continues in the same vein as to Captain Carter's company from Canaan Parish and Captain Raymond's from Middlesex. Of forty-six "Good Effective men" only one was a volunteer. No wonder—they were being sent to "ye assistance of New York."

A scarcity of hard money—gold and silver—put an unwelcome restraint upon what might otherwise have been a booming wartime economy in Norwalk. New England always lacked hard money for its colonies bought more from England than they sold and the need for gold and silver was one reason the colonists traded secretly and illicitly with foreign nations like Spain and even France, the enemy. The scarcity of specie led Connecticut in 1709 to issue bills of credit, a form of promissory note, to pay soldiers and purchase supplies and in 1733, 1740, and 1747 the colony printed paper money. Counterfeiters had a field day. Even the customary punishment of cutting off part of a counterfeiter's right ear, branding a "C" on his forehead, or giving him twenty lashes on his bare back did not deter ingenious Nutmeggers from manufacturing their own bills of credit. Norwalk was outstanding among the colony's towns in that few of its citizens operated their own manufactories of paper money—at least only a couple were caught.[9] In 1718 John Raymond received a twenty-pound reward for informing the authorities about William Parker who was trying to pass two-shilling Rhode Island bills of his own devis-

9 Criminal cases in the colonial courts prior to the Revolution present a picture of an exceptionally law-abiding populace in Norwalk. In the first half of the 1700s one Norwalk man was charged with lying, another with selling goods by lottery, and a third was tried for fathering a Farmington girl's child. In a pitiful case arising in 1712 a man who would now be categorized as a chronic alcoholic was tried for uttering blasphemous words while intoxicated. Testimony indicated that he had managed to remain sober for several years but, having been given liquor for medicinal purposes, began to drink heavily and in this condition committed blasphemy.

ing.[16] Much later one Joseph Nichols, jailed as a counterfeiter, broke out, leaving behind two angry Norwalk officers, Samuel Olmstead and Thaddeus Mead, who had to petition the Assembly for reimbursement of the money they had spent to put him behind bars.

When the French and Indian War finally erupted in 1754 this great and final contest for control of North America dwarfed the previous wars. For Norwalk it brought dramatic involvement in military activities. Its outbreak also coincided with the elevation of Norwalk's Thomas Fitch, Jr., to the governorship of the colony.

When Fitch became governor proud Norwalkers asked him to select any place in the meetinghouse for himself and his family, offering to erect a suitably grand pew "at ye society's charge." But he refused to be treated in a special manner and after a year the townspeople were forced simply to "adorn the pew where the Governor now sits."

The Governor's signature

Fitch, Connecticut's fourteenth governor, was the great-grandson of the first Thomas Fitch to arrive in Norwalk. Young Fitch graduated from Yale in 1721 at the age of twenty-one. Although he studied theology at college he was also competent in the law and was considered a lawyer. Yale's president Timothy Dwight described Fitch as "probably the most learned lawyer who had ever been an inhabitant of the colony."[17] About the time he became Buckingham's temporary replacement Fitch was elected to the General Assembly. In 1734 he became a member of the Governor's Council. Among the many important committees on which he served was one to revise the Code of 1650 which had not been completely rewritten since Ludlow's day. When the other committeemen had to leave the work Fitch completed the job alone. The resulting compilation was so impressive that it was praised in England as well as in Connecticut as "the best code of plantation laws" ever published.[18]

One of Fitch's greatest talents lay in his ability to express himself clearly and exactly in letters and reports. He was also a master at making telling points in an offhand fashion, frequently accompanying them with an ambiguous remark slyly designed to abash or frustrate the recipient. When Fitch received word from New York's governor Sir Henry Moore that, as the new commander-in-chief of Connecticut's military forces, Moore intended to take a military tour through Connecticut, Fitch was quite capable of handling this interloper. He reminded Moore that some seventy years earlier another New York governor had attempted to exercise military rights in Connecticut and "how he Succeeded . . . and what Reception he met with it is needless for me to Mention." The result, Fitch informed Sir Henry, was that England formally acknowledged that Connecticut had full control over its own militia and "no New York governor has ever since attempted to test this arrangement." Fitch added graciously that he mentioned this, not to deprive himself of the pleasure of paying his compliments in person to Sir Henry but simply to acquaint him with the facts.[19]

Although Thomas Fitch could be so firm that one British official once called him "that Mulish Magistrate," his usual inclination was to resolve controversies in devious fashion through maneuvering in the background. Eventually such indirectness harmed him politically. Fitch did of course have firm principles to which he faithfully held. He was a devoted supporter of the Old Lights. His deepest loyalty was to his colony's Charter. As he observed other colonies being stripped of their rights by king or Parliament his ingenious legal mind was ever at work to preserve the Charter that gave his own colony its unique government.

Unfortunately Fitch antagonized a powerful group of speculators from eastern Connecticut who had formed the Susquehanna Company in 1752 to promote sale of land in western Pennsylvania to the land-hungry farmers of the eastern counties.[10] The General Assembly controlled by the New Light easterners enthusiastically supported the Susquehanna Company but both as deputy and as governor—Fitch refused to give formal approval to the scheme. Pennsylvania's objections coupled with Britain's disapproval precluded the Susquehanna promoters from making the quick profits they had anticipated. Rightly or wrongly the politicians of eastern Connecticut placed the blame on Fitch.

10 These speculators bought land from Indian tribes in Pennsylvania, claiming it belonged to Connecticut through the colony's original grant extending to the South Sea (the Pacific).

The year after the war began, the General Assembly voted to raise a troop of one thousand men to aid the British in their fight against France. As the war intensified the number was stepped up annually until at the height of hostilities in 1758 and 1759 as many as five thousand Connecticut men were under arms. Contrasted with the strong showing of volunteers from towns like Saybrook, Lyme, and Litchfield, Norwalkers dragged their feet; fewer than a dozen men enlisted in the first call-up. But what Norwalk lacked in numbers was more than made up in the fidelity of her volunteers. Thaddeus Mead is a superb example. Commissioned as a second lieutenant he took part in the Crown Point Expeditions of 1755 and 1756. When several area militia companies were called upon to come to the relief of Fort William Henry during the alarm of August, 1757, Mead was among the hundred horsemen who galloped northward from Norwalk to the foothills of the Adirondacks.[11] Advanced to first lieutenant Mead served in the Connecticut Provincials for eight months in 1758 and the following year rose to a captaincy and command of his own company.[20] In the summer campaign of 1760 in northern New York the seasoned officer led his company into the furious battle at Oswegatchie. The steady rain of French cannonballs and rifle volleys wounded and felled the veteran fighters. Among the dead was Captain Thaddeus Mead.[12]

The townspeople of Norwalk experienced firsthand the vexations of a war otherwise far removed from their interests. In November, 1757, inhabitants learned that Norwalk was to become winter quarters for three hundred and fifty British regulars for whom the town had to supply lodging. The following year, Norwalk, Stamford, Fairfield, and Stratford were commanded to supply "Quarters and Firing" for a large number of troops. Early in 1759 a flotilla sailed up the Sound from New York City, stopping at each shore town for soldiers to debark. Fifteen officers and two hundred and eighty-four men of the Forty-Eighth Regiment

under the command of Sir James Cockburn came ashore at Norwalk.

The town was ordered to build a guard house and a hospital, and to supply firewood for both buildings and bedding for the hospital. Although reimbursed for the costs of lodging soldiers, inhabitants detested quartering soldiers in private homes. Cockburn's orders acknowledged this: "It will be much for the advantage both of his Majesty's Service & the Country [they read] to have the Men Quartered in as Narrow Compass as Possible."[21] As might be expected, incidents occurred and Cockburn ran afoul of both town and colony when he defied the law by refusing to hand over to civil authorities some soldiers charged with misdemeanors. The selectmen took him to court on the matter and the Assembly gave them wholehearted support by voting to pay Norwalk's legal costs in the case. Inhabitants were happy to see the last of this regiment.

Early in the war Norwalk also had to accept a dozen French Acadians, who had been uprooted from their homes in Nova Scotia and scattered among Britain's colonies. Brought to each town by constables and lodged at the colony's expense with families willing to take French Catholics, these unfortunates were given little freedom although the Assembly did urge that families be kept together if possible. It is likely that some Acadians remained in Norwalk although no word about them appears in Town Proceedings, nor do new French names appear in subsequent town records.[13]

No account of Norwalk's part in the French and Indian War would be complete without reference to the Yankee Doodle story. Generations of Norwalkers have come to believe the charming tale that when a troop of citizen-soldiers, off to join with the British Regulars, rallied at the home of Thomas Fitch, the Governor's son, his sister Elizabeth, lamenting their unmartial attire, handed each man a feather to tuck into his hat. The motley crew is said to have arrived at Rensselaerville near Albany still rakishly sporting the feathers in their hats. Their outlandish appearance prompted Dr. Richard Shuckberg, a British army surgeon attached to several units of colonial troops, to compose a derogatory ditty. He set the verses to a simple but catchy

---

11 While they were stationed at Fort William Henry they had to give up their horses for lack of space and three Norwalk men, Peter Lockwood, Stephen St. John, and Nathan Mallory, drove the entire band back to Norwalk.

12 In 1761 Matthew Mead and Jeremiah Mead, administrators of Thaddeus Mead's estate, petitioned the General Assembly for permission to sell some of Mead's real estate holdings and use the proceeds to pay a £143 debt of the estate. Apparently Mead had been so often absent from Norwalk he had neglected to keep his accounts in order.

13 It is said that Witch Lane is so named because neighborhood children heard certain women living there speaking in a strange language. These could have been Acadians. The majority of the French-Canadians later returned to their homes in Nova Scotia.

melody long used by Englishmen for a nursery rhyme and a ballad deriding Cromwell's rule.[14]

Appealing though this account may be its authenticity is dubious. Thomas Fitch's name does not appear on the military rolls of the French and Indian War nor was the British Army commanded by General Edward Braddock anywhere in the vicinity of Rensselaerville during the summer of 1755.[15] History notwithstanding Norwalkers have adopted Yankee Doodle as theirs and have perpetuated the link between song and community with the Yankee Doodle Bridge, countless business establishments bearing the name, and the incorporation of the familiar air into Quinto Maganini's musical score, "Early Days in Norwalk Town."

[14] The origin of the simple melody is difficult to trace. Spain, France, Italy, and Holland all claim it.

[15] We are indebted to Lawrence Hochheimer for his careful research on this question.

5

THE BRITISH ARE COME

*Being
an Account of
the Break with the Mother Country*

THE DEFEAT of France in 1763 did not bring about the hoped-for tax relief. The very next year Parliament declared its intention to impose a stamp tax on the colonists on a variety of commercial transactions. Every governor had to take an oath to enforce the Act upon pain of a £1,000 fine. Governor Fitch detested the Act but his oath, his strong belief in obedience to lawful authority, and the fear that his colony might lose its Charter all kept him from opposing the act publicly once it was passed. Prior to its passage he prepared a memorial to Parliament arguing against a stamp tax and he appealed privately to Britain's secretary of state: "Suffer me my Lord to Intreat . . . that they may be excused from this new Duty which appears to them so grievous."[1] In spite of many such protests from America the Act was passed.

Events in 1765 moved too swiftly for Fitch to control them. In May he was able to muster only five votes, including his own and that of Norwalk's Joseph Platt,[1] against sending Connecticut delegates to a Stamp Act Congress in New York City. In September a threatening group of horsemen met the colony's new stamp tax collector, Jared Ingersoll, as he rode toward Hartford, and forced him to resign. On November 1, the day the act was to become effective, Fitch's effigy was buried in Hartford.

During those tempestuous days the people of Norwalk gave what help they could to the beleaguered Fitch. When the colony's merchants memorialized Hartford opposing enforcement of the act, not one Norwalk merchant signed the appeal. Shortly after the embarrassing effigy incident the town meeting went on record in wholehearted support of their governor:

Whereas there have been diverse routs and tumultuous and riotous assemblies of disorderly people in the land and some in this colony . . . the inhabitants of the town of Norwalk . . . do declare their utter abhorrence and detestation of all such . . . [and] will use their utmost endeavor in all proper and legal ways to prevent and suppress all such disorders . . . [2]

Now that there was no stamp tax collector Fitch was able to put his craftiness and legal skill into play to prevent actual enforcement of the act. When New York's governor informed him that there were bales of stamp paper for Connecticut in New York City warehouses Fitch explained that, since the Collector had resigned, there was no official legally authorized to receive stamp paper. The paper must therefore remain in New York. Next Fitch proceeded to inform London that although he would faithfully have carried out the act he could not do so because his colony had neither stamp paper nor collector. Nevertheless the anti-Stamp Act group and Fitch's old enemies were unwilling to give the Governor any credit and in the 1766 election they brought about his defeat. On May 12, accompanied by a sad and respectful group of well-wishers, Fitch rode home to Norwalk.[2]

---

[1] Platt was one of the most respected and popular men in Norwalk, being elected to fifty sessions of the Assembly between 1705 and 1770, according to Weed.

[2] Fitch tried again in 1770 but, in a narrow vote that showed how sectionalized Connecticut had become by this time, he was defeated by Jonathan Trumbull.

Fitch's drop in popularity unfortunately coincided with Norwalk's attempt to become the county seat. When the Fairfield courthouse was destroyed by fire Norwalk petitioned the General Assembly to be the county town. Danbury, Stamford, Ridgefield, and Redding all supported the plan, but Fitch's enemies in Hartford were not in the mood to be philanthropic toward his native town and Fairfield retained its favored status.

During the rest of the decade western Connecticut remained conservative while the eastern part grew more radical. Given their loyalty to Fitch and the conservatism of the entire area, Norwalkers were slow to be drawn into the storm that gathered strength during these years. The town prospered, ranking ninth in the colony's tax lists. The imposition in 1767 of the Townshend imposts on tea, lead, paint, paper, and glass—all much needed items—irked them but they were not inclined to join the eastern radicals.

Nor did Britain's tightening-up of customs collections following the French and Indian War bother Norwalkers particularly. Additional customs officers, broader powers of search and seizure, and clearance certificates even for the coastal trade were among the vexing new restrictions. Norwalk's imports and exports came under the Port of New Haven. It was not hard for Norwalk ships to evade payment of customs duties; they simply slipped past New Haven under cover of darkness or fog. As one harassed British official reported: "The Harbours, Rivers, and Creeks along this Coast are many and Commodious for smuggling."[3] As for the required certificates of clearance, another official complained:

A [new] Prevention officer resides at Stamford, Authorized to Enter and Clear Coasters, notwithstanding which all to ye Westward of fairfield go to New York without Clearances–10 Vessils makes trips to New York once a Week in ye Summer and once a Fortnight in ye Winter . . . Vessils from many parts of this District trade to the foreign West Indies–illicit trade carried on to a very great degree . . . [4]

The tightening of customs enforcement actually offered resourceful merchant shippers additional opportunities for profit through the sale of fictitious New Haven Customs House certificates of clearance. John Cannon—an audacious Norwalk merchant and twice a selectman—and his ac-complice and brother-in-law, John Pintard,[3] supplemented their regular commercial pursuits with the profitable sideline of forging clearance certificates. A New York informant claimed that Cannon and Pintard were the "persons that have procured most of these fictitious clearances, from the Customs House at Newhaven, for the merchants here (New York City)." In Cannon's own damaging words the two of them had "got several Vessels Clear'd . . . for Five shillings N. York Currency . . . we have Teen [ten] Pound for Our Trouble & Expenses."[5] The two men must have "Clear'd" more than forty ships to net a profit of ten pounds!

No action was taken against Cannon and Pintard for their shady operations. Cannon's fellow citizens continued to elect him to responsible posts. During the final years of the decade the townspeople continued much as before. Lawbreakers perhaps, but conservative ones, their town meetings were spent in discussions of roadbuilding, oyster beds, and annual elections of an expanding list of officials.

The year 1770 drew the town briefly into somewhat closer cooperation with other towns. When the Townshend duties, except for a tax on tea, were repealed some towns wanted to continue non-importation but others were already planning to import British goods. A proposed merchants' congress at Norwalk in June to devise an overall plan of action never came about. However in September Connecticut merchants met in New Haven. John Cannon, Colonel Thomas Fitch, son of the former governor, and Benjamin Isaacs[4] represented Norwalk at this gathering. Cannon's presence at this meeting is significant. The New Haven congress marks a point at which men like Cannon, evidently no longer satisfied with mere evasion of customs, began to cooperate with other merchants already in undisguised opposition to British trade policies.

Norwalk soon reverted to its parochialism, however, and officially, at least, took no steps in 1773 to form a local committee of correspondence although authorized to do so by the Assembly. Nor did it support Boston when that city was chastised for its

---

3 Pintard was the father of John Marden Pintard, a wealthy New York City merchant, prominent philanthropist, and founder of the New-York Historical Society.

4 Although still in his early thirties, Benjamin Isaacs, a merchant, had been a selectman, warden of St. Paul's Church, and was the founder of St. John's Masonic Lodge, which held its meetings at Isaacs' home on Wall Street. See *St. John's Lodge No. 6 F. & A.M., 1765-1976* (Norwalk, Conn. 1965).

December Tea Party by having its port closed. Norwalk's only cooperative venture in the spring of 1774 was to support a meeting of conservatives held at Middletown to put Fitch's name into nomination for the May gubernatorial election. This was Thomas Fitch's last political contest. He fell ill soon after the disappointing election and died in July.5

Over the summer months most of the towns of eastern Connecticut went on record in support of the Assembly's anti-British stand. Western Connecticut lagged behind. However, after the Continental Congress met in September, the western towns led by Stamford voted one by one to support the Congress. Norwalk delayed. After election of officials the annual town meeting in December was adjourned for a fortnight to decide what course to follow. When it reconvened the townspeople "tak-

hands, a strong Loyalist element was present in Norwalk.

When the meetinghouse bell rang in the new year 1775 few Norwalkers could have predicted the direful events that would follow—Lexington, Concord, the Battle of Bunker Hill, and by year's end King George's proclamation that the colonies were in rebellion and open to attack on land or sea. Although the disorders were still centered in Massachusetts, Norwalkers became increasingly sensitive to the vulnerability of their coastal port. A Committee of Inspection was appointed to see that suspected Loyalists turned in their arms. This committee took on the added task of investigating newcomers, requiring them to show certificates proving they were "friends to the liberties of these Colonies . . . " Five of the seven selectmen elected

The Benjamin Isaacs House on Wall Street.

ing into consideration the matters contained in the association come into by the Continental Congress," voted to appoint a non-importation committee.6 This lackluster resolution, in marked contrast to Stamford's sturdy resolve which had declared that town's determination to oppose "every design of a corrupt ministry to enslave America," has the appearance of a compromise proposal. Such it was for, although the patriots were now in the majority and the town's leadership would remain firmly in their

5 The Crown had offered Fitch a judicial post in India but he turned it down, saying he was too old to start a new life. He would have liked a pension if that were possible, he said, but if not: "I think I have learned to be content."

6 Several years later two members of the original committee, Gould Hoyt and Gershom Raymond, were declared Loyalists.

that December were Connecticut militia officers. Much of the credit for Norwalk's steady progress in preparing for war falls to Major Stephen St. John. His fellow citizens continued to elect this good patriot and conscientious officer first selectman or representative in the Assembly throughout the war years.

The town moved steadily toward rebellion and the Assembly did not have to send a committee to check into the Norwalkers' attitudes as it did in Ridgefield, Newtown, and even Stamford. Officially a moderate attitude prevailed toward Tories in 17757 but unofficially the Rebels, or Whigs as they called themselves, went about forcing everyone to sign in support of the new Continental Association. When some Whigs discovered, through intercepting his mail, that Asa Spalding, a lawyer living on Mill Hill, was corresponding with a man in England they chased him out of town. Informed that a mob had sworn to chop him up into "pound pieces," Spalding leaped upon his horse and fled, believing as he wrote later:

[it would be] neither true courage nor prudence for me to think of braving it out alone against a raving Mad Rabble, which, from what I knew, consisted of a hundred rough, infatuated, distracted desperadoes . . . I took my flight into the country, was pursued by 18 armed men for 20 miles, with guns, bayonets, powder, and balls.[6]

Reaching the safety of Pound Ridge he received word from his wife that unless he was prepared to join the rebels and sign the Association agreement he should not return to Norwalk for his life would be in danger.[8]

The Assembly had already passed legislation that forbade anyone taking up arms against Connecticut. When it met in October, 1776, after the Declaration of Independence, it absolved Connecticut inhabitants from all allegiance to the British Crown, declared the colony a free state, and permitted civil authorities to confine inimical persons in jail. There is more than a touch of hysteria in Norwalk's corresponding petition to the Assembly asserting that "Inhabitants that they call Tories or unfriendly persons" were combining to "contrive and Plot our Ruin and Distruction," and asking for permission to throw these people arbitrarily into jail and keep them there.[7] Yet Norwalk's agitation was not completely unwarranted: its proximity to British-controlled areas made it vulnerable and its many covert Loyalists were certainly not to be trusted.

No patriot in town could fail to be inspired by verses from the pen of the eloquent Peter St. John,[9] a local man who had been writing radical verses since 1765 when he composed "Taxation in America," in heated response to the Stamp Act. In 1779 St. John updated this to a 37-verse saber-rattling ballad that became a wartime favorite and has passed into the realm of classical American ballads. Indeed, no true patriot could fail to see his duty when he heard these resounding words:

We never will knock under,
*   O George! We do not fear*
The rattling of your thunder,
*   The lightning of your spear;*
Though rebels you declare us,
*   We're strangers to dismay;*
Therefore you cannot scare us
*   In North America.*[8]

St. John's personal misadventure was the inspiration for another of his many Revolutionary War poems for he himself was in the party of prisoners taken by the British in their 1781 raid on Middlesex Meetinghouse and was confined in the Provost Prison in New York City. In "Descent on Middlesex," St. John described the treatment he received:

An oaken plank, it was our bed,
An oaken pillow for the head,
And room as scanty as our meals,
For we lay crowded head and heels.
. . . .
The dread smallpox to some they gave,
Nor tried at all their lives to save,
But rather sought their desolation
As they denied 'em 'noculation.

The reader rejoiced with St. John when after eighteen days the surviving prisoners were released:

Four days before December's gone,
In seventeen hundred eighty-one,
I hail'd the place where months before
The Tories took me from the shore.[9]

Bruised in spirit but with his health unimpaired Peter St. John survived the ordeal and the war undaunted, his ballads an inspiration to fighting Americans.

---

7 Although required to turn in their arms, suspected Loyalists were apparently permitted to attend and vote in town meetings until December, when it was quite logically agreed that they should at least be denied the right to vote for the Committee of Inspection. NTP II, 157.

8 Unwilling to renounce his loyalty to the King, Spalding wisely avoided Norwalk.

9 Peter St. John was born in Norwalk in 1726, the youngest son of the prosperous cooper and landowner, Daniel St. John. After a stint at Yale, young St. John became a Norwalk schoolmaster. An inheritance from his father's estate provided the wherewithal that enabled him to live in New Jersey and New York for extended periods, to raise sixteen of his nineteen children to maturity, and, above all, to indulge his passion for writing verse. In 1793 the aging St. John composed his last renowned poem, "Historical or rather Conjectural Poem on the Death of Abel," an allegorical tale of the Revolutionary War. Orline Alexander, *The St. John Genealogy* (New York, 1907), 43-45.

By his EXCELLENCY

WILLIAM TRYON, Esquire,

Captain General, and Governor in Chief in and over the Province of *New-York*, and the Territories depending thereon in *America*, Chancellor and Vice Admiral of the same.

A PROCLAMATION.

WHEREAS I have received His Majesty's Royal Proclamation, given the Court at *St. James's*, the Twenty-third Day of *August* last, in the Words following:

BY THE KING,
A Proclamation,

For suppressing REBELLION and SEDITION.

GEORGE R.

WHEREAS many of our Subjects in divers Parts of our Colonies and Plantations in *North-America*, misled by dangerous and ill designing Men, and forgetting the Allegiance which they owe to the Power that has protected and sustained them, after various disorderly Acts committed in disturbance of the public Peace, to the Obstruction of lawful Commerce, and to the Oppression of our loyal Subjects carrying on the same, have at length proceeded to an open and avowed Rebellion, by arraying themselves in hostile Manner, to withstand the Execution of the Law, and traitorously preparing, ordering and levying War against us: And whereas there is Reason to apprehend that such Rebellion hath been much promoted and encouraged by the traitorous Correspondence, Counsels, and Comfort of divers wicked and desperate Persons within this Realm :---To the End therefore that none of our Subjects may neglect or violate their Duty through Ignorance thereof, or through any Doubt of the Protection which the Law will afford to their Loyalty and Zeal ; we have thought fit, by and with the Advice of our Privy Council, to issue this our Royal Proclamation, hereby declaring, that not only all our Officers Civil and Military, are obliged to exert their utmost Endeavours to suppress such Rebellion, and to bring the Traitors to Justice ; but that all our Subjects of this Realm and the Dominions thereunto belonging, are bound by Law to be aiding and assisting in the Suppression of such Rebellion, and to disclose and make known all traitorous Conspiracies and Attempts against us, our Crown and Dignity : And we do accordingly strictly charge and command all our Officers, as well Civil as Military, and all other our obedient and loyal Subjects, to use their utmost Endeavours to withstand and suppress such Rebellion, and to disclose and make known all Treasons and traitorous Conspiracies which they shall know to be against us, our Crown and Dignity ; and for that Purpose, that they transmit to one of our principal Secretaries of State, or other proper Officer, due and full Information of all Persons who shall be found carrying on Correspondence with, or in any Manner or Degree aiding or abetting the Persons now in open Arms and Rebellion against our Government within any of our Colonies and Plantations in *North-America*, in order to bring to condign Punishment the Authors, Perpetrators, and Abettors of such traitorous Designs.

Given at our Court at St. James's the Twenty-third Day of August, *One Thousand Seven Hundred and Seventy-five, in the Fifteenth Year of our Reign.*

In Obedience therefore to his Majesty's Commands to me given, I do hereby publish and make known his Majesty's most gracious Proclamation above recited ; earnestly exhorting and requiring all his Majesty's loyal and faithful Subjects within this Province, as they value their Allegiance due to the best of Sovereigns, their Dependance on and Protection from their Parent State, and the Blessings of a mild, free, and happy Constitution ; and as they would shun the fatal Calamities which are the inevitable Consequences of Sedition and Rebellion, to pay all due Obedience to the Laws of their Country, seriously to attend to his Majesty's said Proclamation, and govern themselves accordingly.

Given under my Hand and Seal at Arms, in the City of New-York, *the Fourteenth Day of* November, *One Thousand Seven Hundred and Seventy-five, in the Sixteenth Year of the Reign of our Sovereign Lord* GEORGE *the Third, by the Grace of God of* Great-Britain, France *and* Ireland, *King, Defender of the Faith, and so forth.*

By his Excellency's Command,
SAMUEL BAYARD, Jun. D. Secry.

WM. TRYON.

GOD SAVE THE KING.

In the spring of 1775 the General Assembly had sent out a call for troops. Local patriots responded by enlisting on the first call for a seven-month term in the Fifth Company of the Fifth Regiment, a unit recruited mainly in Fairfield County. Captain Matthew Mead, following in the footsteps of his father, Thaddeus Mead, commanded the small twenty-two man company ably assisted by Lieutenants Levi Taylor and William Seymour, Norwalk men who were veterans of the French and Indian War. As humble privates, jaunty drummers and fifers, proud standard-bearing ensigns, or harried officers responsible for turning the citizen-soldiers into a fighting unit, ninety-four Norwalk men enlisted in state military service during 1775.

A host of local inhabitants contributed their support and sometimes their lives to the war effort. Men could enlist in the Continental Army or in the more popular military units raised by the state. Some were men of position and repute; Lieutenant Colonel Thomas Fitch served as a member of the Committee of the Pay Table, that much-harried unit of Connecticut government responsible for dispersing funds for all war expenditures. Other volunteers were too young to have yet acquired name or fame; seventeen-year-old John Avery, only five feet five inches tall at the time of his enlistment in March, 1779, was a drummer boy in the Eighth Company, Third Connecticut Regiment for the duration of the war.[10]

For some, the war caused only minor hardship. Captain Eliphalet Lockwood, Commissary to the Fifth Regiment, Connecticut Line, who also raised a sixty-man company of Coast Guard stationed locally, remained in Norwalk during the entire war. At war's end he laid aside his military obligations, resumed his West Indian shipping business, and represented Norwalk in the state legislature. Others were less fortunate. When Theophilus Hanford journeyed to New York under a flag of truce to bring home his sick son, a soldier taken prisoner at Fort Washington and paroled after three months of inhumane and cruel treatment, that hapless man was himself captured and tried as a spy. Acquitted, he received news that his son had died. Hanford's ordeal was not yet over; when he attempted to return to Norwalk the British apprehended him and relieved him of his horse, saddle, and bridle.

Some Norwalk men would die heroes. Captain Seth Seymour, who had been captured early in the war and thrown into the infamous Old Sugar House

Prison in New York City, died there of camp fever in 1777. It is said that when General Washington, traveling through Norwalk, passed Seymour's former home on the Post Road he ordered reversed muskets and muffled drums. John Street, forty-eight years old at the time, enlisted in the Connecticut Line with his sons Davis, Nathaniel, and John. After he was killed in action during the Battle of White Plains in August, 1776, his companions in

Capt. Eliphalet Lockwood.

arms, picking their way through the enemy lines, carried his body home to Norwalk. The reputations of others would be tainted with charges of treason or desertion. Lieutenant William Seymour, who had enlisted at the first call-up and who later raised and commanded a company of matrosses (artillery men) to guard the Norwalk coastline, was court-martialled in August, 1780, by order of General Gold Silliman on charges of trading with the enemy and also deserting the garrison at Fairfield. Found guilty after proceedings held at Wentworth's tavern in Norwalk, he was cashiered.

Countless Norwalkers would suffer financial reverses through the war. As his part in the war effort Dann Finch chartered a vessel to transport state-owned war provisions. On one trip carrying salt from East Haddam to the Commissary at Stamford his ship was driven ashore on Long Island by a violent winter storm and it was immediately captured by the British. Finch escaped but was unable to pay the sixty-three pounds he owed for the charter and he was thereafter plagued by poverty. Only eight days after Lieutenant Jeremiah Beard Eells went on active duty in the Coast Guard he was captured and languished for almost two years in the filthy, disease-ridden Old Sugar House Prison where Seymour had died. By the time he received his back pay after his parole Continental currency had depreciated so much that the £183 due him had little value. All his efforts to rectify the matter were unsuccessful.

After the Continental Congress formed the Continental Army, or Regulars, in June, 1775, Connecticut had to furnish eight of the eighty-eight infantry regiments authorized. In turn the legislature assigned a quota to each town in the state. In the early years of the war Norwalk attempted to meet its quota by the traditional method of encouraging enlistment as a patriotic duty, suggesting that "virtuous sons of liberty cheerfully and readily engage in sd. service at this critical time; so that peace and rest may once more be restored to the United States of America."[11]

Initially a man could volunteer for a short-term enlistment but when this proved impractical for winning a war men were given only the choice of enlisting for three years or for the duration. Those Norwalk men who were reluctant to join for fear their families would suffer deprivation were assured that the town would supply provisions for them in the absence of the breadwinner. As the war dragged on and voluntary enlistments dropped off, Norwalk, like other towns in the state, attempted to meet its quota through the class system in which the town was divided into geographic sections according to wealth. Each class or section was responsible for providing, however they could, their portion of the town's quota of soldiers as well as their sustenance and clothing. For its part the state Assembly enticed recruits by offering a bounty of forty pounds

in addition to normal pay, "refreshments" (food ration), and family support. Even so Norwalk had difficulty meeting its assigned quotas; in 1780 the town fell eight short of the seventy-seven soldiers it was to supply that year. When the state applied pressure, by investigating discrepancies between the actual muster of recruits and the numbers reported, the town levied a tax of two pence per pound on the value of the estate of Norwalk citizens, using the money to pay soldiers. This procedure was used with fair success for the remaining years of the war.

Instead of serving in the Continental Army a man could enlist in one of the companies of state-levied troops used to guard sections of Connecticut susceptible to attack. Matross companies, commonly referred to as the Coast Guard, were assigned to protect the secluded coves and sheltered inlets of the coastline. Short-term six-month enlistments and the opportunity to care for family needs or conduct private business in off-duty hours and still discharge military obligations as a member of the locally-stationed Coast Guard were attractive features for Norwalkers. Captain Ozias Marvin, for example, was able to keep a public house of entertainment on the Post Road near Saugatuck bridge while commanding a company of Coast Guard.

State-levied troops were also detailed to areas of potential or actual conflict, particularly along the western frontier where British incursions were a constant threat. Occasionally they were called outside the state to reinforce Continental troops. In October, 1777, when British troops moved up the North River to join General "Gentleman Johnny" Burgoyne's forces in the north, thirty-six soldiers from various Norwalk-based Alarm List and militia companies were hastily dispatched to the Hudson River to prevent the union of the two British forces. "Without many clothes and some almost without shoes" because of their hasty departure, they were unable to replenish their attire when they reached Fishkill for they found an empty commissary and a barracks crowded with smallpox victims. Naturally they thought they could go home as soon as they heard that Burgoyne's army had been captured! But this spontaneous decision cost them dearly; upon their return to Norwalk the miserable wretches were charged with desertion. Insisting they had acted "from ignorance and not with open design," they were forced to wage a long battle to clear their names.

Seafaring men could utilize their special skills in the Connecticut Navy or in privateering. Some three hundred privateers supplemented the state's feeble navy. Captured enemy ships were brought into an authorized port where under the generous provisions of the law County Courts usually awarded one-half the proceeds of the sale of their cargo to the state and the other half as a prize to be divided among the owners of the privateers, the officers, and the crews. Norwalk was one of Connecticut's four authorized ports and had an official stationed here to enter and clear vessels and initiate proceedings for prize ships.

The first privateer commissioned in this state was the sloop *Gamecock,* carrying six guns and a fifty-man crew, commanded by Norwalk's Captain Lemuel Brooks.[12] Even the pluckiest fighter can lose in an uneven match; a few days into its first cruise this *Gamecock* was captured by the British frigate *Cerberus. Gamecock's* loss was more than made up during the long glorious cruises of the schooner *Ranger,* commissioned out of New York and commanded by William Smith Scudder, one of her seven Norwalk owners. Ranging up and down the Sound, harassing the enemy and seizing British merchandise, *Ranger's* crowning success was its triumphant entry into Norwalk harbor towing the British ship *Sally,* captured during combat at Cold Spring Harbor. The thrill of watching a captured vessel being hauled or even chased into the harbor and the hurly-burly enthusiasm of the privateers' crews brought a bustling excitement the Norwalk port had never experienced.

The narrow western end of the Sound, close to Long Island and British-occupied New York City, brought into existence a new type of small and sturdy raider, the whaleboat.[10] With captains and crews who knew every channel and shoal of the waters and serpentine shoreline of the Sound, whaleboats were used by both sides for night attacks on military installations, swift foraging raids, transmission of information, capture of hostages, and sometimes as privateers. Equipped with both sails and oars and armed usually with a swivel gun, the thirty- to thirty-five-foot whaleboats were capable of dealing surprisingly hard blows.[13] Jesse Brush of Norwalk commanded two whaleboats, *Refugee* and *Revenge,* and was able to capture the fifty-ton British sloop *Success* laden with lumber and provisions and bring it into Norwalk.

Unfortunately enemy whaleboaters could play at the same game, especially when they had among their number men from Fairfield County who knew the Connecticut shoreline as well as their rebel relatives did and who often volunteered to serve as pilots in the frequent forays for beef and other supplies purchased from Norwalk Tories or stolen from shorefront farms in Norwalk and Middlesex Parish. A local man, John Ketchum, a captain in the West Indian trade, had his estate confiscated as punishment for his help in piloting British expeditions across the Sound. With a twenty-four-man raiding party, another Norwalk Tory, Stephen Hoyt, stormed the house of Samuel Richards and "captured and took said Richards and 14 of the militia who were stationed there and two or three officers who were on their way home from the Sawpitts." This was one of the many exploits that gained Hoyt the reputation of "notorious renegade."[14]

One of the most spectacular escapades of the entire war was carried out by the Americans in November, 1778, when, under the very noses of British forces camped at Huntington, a flotilla of twenty whaleboats from Norwalk slipped past the enemy warships anchored in Huntington Bay and stealthily discharged its passengers. Making straight for The Cedars, a public inn kept by "'Mother Chid," whose proclivity for harboring Connecticut Tories was no secret on this side of the Sound, they managed to even the score. Sixteen Tories were taken prisoner and several killed before the raiders departed.[15]

Norwalk made significant contributions to Connecticut's well-deserved reputation as the Provisions State. The official ration for each Connecticut soldier was generous. It included daily rations of beef or pork, bread or flour, spruce beer (a fermented brew of molasses and essence of spruce), sugar, coffee, and vegetables. Weekly the ration included rice or corn meal, butter peas or beans, tobacco, candles and soap, as well as rum for men on fatigue duty. State-appointed commissaries ranged the state in search of provisions, often hampered by the forces of nature and the evil designs of war profiteers. Wheat crops ravaged by the Hessian fly, bold raids from across the Sound, and clandestine sales to black marketeers from New York and New

10 Nathan Hale is said to have sailed from Norwalk on his ill-fated mission in the sloop *Huntington,* a converted whaleboat.

Jersey all depleted available stock but the commissaries persisted. Even after the burning of Norwalk, Eliphalet Lockwood, provisioner for Connecticut troops, was able to supply those encamped at Redding with over 22,000 pounds of flour, 240 gallons of rum and 281 quarts of salt in a two-month period.[16]

Norwalk was a regular pick-up center for carters of the Continental Army who drove their teams of oxen between Norwalk, Stamford, Horseneck, the supply depot in Danbury, and Fishkill, carrying supplies to the troops. Seventeen-year-old Joseph Joslin was a carter who made frequent trips to Norwalk to haul oats and corn, picking up as much as two hundred bushels from one supplier alone, Nathan Adams, in less than a month's time.[11]

Norwalk was a beehive of manufacturing and mercantile activity. Since in addition to selling provisions for Connecticut troops each town was obligated to supply clothing for those of its inhabitants serving in the Continental Army, there was a constant demand for wearing apparel and cloth. During the dismal winter at Valley Forge Norwalkers, both men and women, worked to supply those woebegotten Continentals with shoes, stockings, woolen and linen shirts, overalls, flannel, linen and fulled cloth. Supply officers of Norwalk-based militia companies purchased flour, meat, and wear-

[11] Joslin had kind words for the hospitality extended by Adams and Matthew Marvin but, like so many passers-through, was most unhappy with lodging at a "Diabolical bad tavern" whose keeper they paid "Price Enough to ah burn him ah well."

Capt. Lockwood's provision report of June, 1779 / Collection of Lockwood House Museum.

ing apparel from local storekeepers. They were popular with the merchants since they sometimes paid their bills in "cash in Dollars." As rapidly as coopers could produce barrels, impatient merchants loaded them with provisions and contracted for even the smallest available space on vessels that delivered cargo to the supply depots along the coast. On one voyage alone the sloop *John* wallowed with the weight of ninety-nine barrels of flour shipped by Eliphalet Lockwood and another forty-four barrels sent by merchant John Cannon, all destined for Wadsworth's Brigade.[17]

One of the town's most successful wartime ventures was the saltpeter works, a refinery of potassium nitrate. This natural compound which is extracted from the soil was the oxidizing agent for black powder, the only kind of gunpowder used at the time. Bills of receipt show that as much as 413 pounds of this vital ingredient were carted from Norwalk to the powder mill at New Haven in a single load.

Norwalk's resources were strained by an influx of disabled soldiers "hospitalled" here after the disastrous battle of White Plains. The four to five hundred wounded men filled every vacant building and were even billeted in private homes.[12] The Committee of the Pay Table reimbursed both town and individual for the succor offered, as in the case of Thomas Madison who tended two men brought from North Cassel Church so critically wounded that they required the immediate ministrations of Dr. Baker. Often the battle-weary men needed little more than food and rest. Joseph Martin, a young army man detailed to nurse a small band of sick soldiers, marveled at their rapid convalescence, noting in his diary: "All they wanted was a cook and something for a cook to exercise his functions upon."[18] And a good cook they had; these particular men were quartered in the home of a prosperous Norwalk widower whose two Negro servants lavished their considerable skills on the patriot soldiers.

Young Martin believed that just about everyone in Norwalk was a Tory in those days. One elderly woman from whom the American troops purchased milk gave him a lecture on loyalty to good King George every time he went to her spring

12 State law required all towns to assist sick and infirm soldiers of the Continental forces, even those just passing through.

house. She was so fervent that some of the Americans were afraid to drink the milk lest it be poisoned. Even a slave in the house in which Martin was quartered scolded the young soldier for his disloyalty to the King.

Just how many Loyalists resided in Norwalk is impossible to say. A recent study shows that, excluding those from Canaan Parish, a little more than one hundred adult males and a half dozen women had their estates confiscated, were brought to trial for out-and-out Toryism, or later claimed reimbursement from Britain for losses because of their loyalty.[13] In 1781 town officials themselves estimated that at least a thousand persons had defected to Long Island.[19] Dozens of the town's young men had crossed over to enlist in Colonel Edmund Fanning's King's American Regiment, the Queen's Rangers, or the Prince of Wales' Loyal American Volunteers. That "notorious renegade" Stephen Hoyt raised an entire company for the Prince of Wales' Regiment. Infuriated Norwalkers turned his wife out of his house, converted it to a hospital for rebel troops, and confiscated the balance of Hoyt's sizable £2,000 estate.

Norwalk's Loyalists fit no single pattern although most of them can be placed in a few broad categories, of which Anglicanism is one. In Connecticut members of the Church of England were apt to be loyal to the mother country and St. Paul's parishioners were no exception. By no means were all the town's Anglicans Tories although a number of those whose estates were confiscated did belong to St. Paul's. Well-to-do farmers—and those in Norwalk were "reputed to be the most prosperous in the entire colony"—were also inclined to side with the mother country. To keep their flourishing farms they tried not to antagonize the patriots openly but they were not above secretly selling their fat cattle and swine to the British for high prices.

Kinship, friendship, respect, resentment, fear, even simple ignorance, had as much bearing on people's loyalties as political ideology. Five Mile

13 Lois Bayles, comp., "Norwalk Loyalists," unpublished list of Loyalists collected 1975. Archives Lockwood House Museum, Norwalk. This careful study, derived from Norwalk Land Records, Probate Court Records, confiscation proceedings, memorials of exiled Loyalists in Canada, and other sources, contains many clues to the status, wealth, and occupation of Loyalists. It is generally agreed that Fairfield County had the greatest number of Loyalists, with the best estimate based upon Stiles' report that in 1776 at least 25 percent of the people, or approximately 1,500 adult males, were Loyalists.

River men who had asked for a separate parish during the Buckingham dispute appear along with their sons on Loyalist rolls, indicating that the fires of the old quarrel may have continued to smolder for forty-odd years, stoked by the younger generation. In Deborah Quintard Fairweather's case kinship governed. Her family was well known for service to the patriot cause but her husband, Thomas Fairweather, helped Tories escape into British

Private of the 3rd Connecticut Line Regiment, 1778.

lines. Declared inimical, the middle-aged Fairweathers fled first to Long Island and later to New Brunswick.[20]

Both fear and ignorance were pleaded by a young Irishman, John McKee, from his jail cell in Litchfield in October, 1776. McKee kept an inn on the Saugatuck, a neighborhood that was home to an uncommon number of Tories, and confessed that

as a foreigner fearful of British vengeance he had allowed himself to be "unwarily seduced by sundry persons from Redding," who persuaded him to hide Loyalists in his house. Playing with Irish finesse upon Congregationalist heartstrings McKee bitterly regretted his actions, truly repented, and begged to be released so that he could once more support his "innocent, beloved, tender Wife and two helpless babes." The Assembly freed him but banished him to East Haddam where he remained under surveillance.

The stereotype of the well-to-do, conservative Tory might at first glance seem to apply to Asa Spalding who owned several valuable parcels of land. He was liberal enough, however, to have acted as attorney for the Wappinger tribe when no New York lawyer would take their case against Westchester County's powerful Philipse family, and he would become prominent in Connecticut's liberal party in the postwar years. Spalding was apparently motivated by genuine loyalty to his king, for he wrote:

... I do from my soul abhor the thought of rebelling against my Prince. But what to do I know not, to be absent from my family and business is cruel, 'tis hard ... This part of the world is filled with falsehood, and a lying spirit has gone forth in our land.[21]

Every passing week brought new problems to St. John and the other selectmen who, still responsible for day-to-day civil matters, also had to fill military quotas, impose extra taxes, and supply clothing and provisions for the armed services. They also collected donations for the "poor Inhabitants" of Boston, toward whom Norwalkers were taking a more sympathetic attitude than they had a year or so earlier. Barrack Master Eliakim Smith, already hard-pressed to find housing for all the state-levied companies stationed in the town, had to provide for as many as six hundred additional men when Continentals were temporarily bivouacked in Norwalk. At the governor's request the town studied the structure of the new United States government, the Articles of Confederation, and voted to approve them in general.[14] The town was thrown into a panic early in 1776 by a group of "nullifiers" in back-country Poplar Plains and Norfield (now Weston) who were advocating repudiation of all in-

14 These were adopted by the General Assembly in April, 1779.

debtedness and payment of interest. As fearful of the consequences to their pocketbooks as of having a lunatic label attached to their town, Norwalkers voted to do their utmost to suppress the scheme.

The value of Continental currency declined so rapidly that a town official who advanced his own money for military needs or made financial arrangements with the state for later reimbursement suffered a loss in purchasing power, even though receiving interest, unless he was promptly repaid. Ozias Marvin experienced such a loss when he agreed to accept 72 pounds Continental money to pay his matross company for guard duty and construction of gabions (earth-filled wicker baskets used as breastworks). Marvin frantically petitioned the Assembly and recovered some of his funds when it ordered that the balance due him be paid in highly desirable Connecticut Bills of Credit. Even the patriotic Colonel Stephen St. John and the men in his company were victims of shabby treatment. Although the men had enlisted with the understanding that they would be exempt from taxes, they were constantly harassed by tax collectors who exacted every possible penny to replenish the strained state treasury. Delegates from the towns in Fairfield County met several times to discuss this frightening inflation but the situation was too complex to be resolved locally or even on the state level. Michael Judah, a merchant trader who had settled in Norwalk about 1742 with the aid of a loan from Congregation Shearith Israel in New York City,[15] suffered severe financial reverses during the Revolution. Able to weather the dislocation of shipping and seizure of cargo, Judah incurred tremendous losses when, out of patriotism, he continued to hold wartime paper money until it became utterly worthless.

The town was not immune from wartime shortages. Salt was an absolute necessity for preserving the huge quantities of beef and pork required by the troops and for that reason it was often unavailable to civilians. A coastal town like Norwalk could offset this by producing some of its own salt through the slow process of evaporating water from the Sound in large metal pans manufactured at the cannon-casting plant in Salisbury. Demand always outstripped supply, however, and it frequently had to be rationed. Two local men received special per-

15 Judah became well-established in his new venture and married a local girl, Martha Raymond. Later their son David followed in his father's footsteps into business.

mission from the legislature to barter flour, corn, flaxseed, and pork in Massachusetts in exchange for salt. In another deal when a load of salt was obtained in Boston the townspeople cautiously dispatched three sturdy, responsible young men to ensure its safe arrival in Norwalk.

Under these conditions every effort was made to see that no useful goods left the state. Very early the Assembly had placed an embargo on the export of grains, flour, and pork, with authorities keeping close watch on movements of goods. Even importation of supplies was suspect for the chances were good that other produce had been bartered in exchange. After December, 1776, no inhabitant could leave any port in any craft without permission of the selectmen. In Norwalk they kept careful watch. Even in so personal and seemingly natural a matter as bringing a lawfully-wedded wife to Connecticut from her father's home on Long Island, Thomas Betts had to secure permission from the Assembly.

At the onset of the war Norwalkers, "apprehensive every moment of being attacked by our enemy and . . . in great danger of being plundered," were ill-prepared to defend themselves. Gradually, however, the town's fortifications improved. Two-hundredweight of gunpowder allocated by the Council of Safety was stored in a new magazine built on the hill near Mr. Leaming's house. Seventy-five townsmen were hired to keep watch along the shoreline and were soon supplemented by state-levied guard companies.

In the spring of 1777—and not one moment too soon—six cannon, two four-pounders and four three-pounders, secured from the furnace at Salisbury together with appropriate ball and grape shot, were mounted in salient positions. They must have been a reassuring sight for the townspeople who would soon see the enemy firsthand when British soldiers under Major General William Tryon marched to attack Danbury. Although Tryon had intended to land at Norwalk the six cannon forced a last-minute change of plans and he selected unprotected Compo Beach at the mouth of the Saugatuck instead.[22]

Even with the Stamford units that had ridden up to join them, local militia were too few in number to engage the two-to-three thousand British troops who disembarked in the early evening of April 26 at Compo Beach. During the long, chilly night, as they watched the Redcoats march past, the militiamen fortified themselves against the cold at Captain Marvin's tavern, consuming forty-five gallons of rum, sixty pounds of dried beef, and eight pounds of scarce white sugar. As he stated later in a petition for reimbursement, Marvin had gone in "hot pursuit" of the enemy and was unable to dole out provisions or collect payment for the militia's midnight meal.

When the British returned after sacking Danbury the Americans tried to make a stand at Saugatuck bridge but fell back in disorder, to the immense disgust of General Benedict Arnold who had hastened down from New Haven to take command. The Connecticut men almost succeeded in cutting off one British regiment on Compo Hill but the tired British soldiers made a charge with fixed bayonets, drove the militia back, and reached the flatboats that waited to carry them to their ships.[16]

For his part in the Danbury raid—joining the British at Compo Beach and, according to witnesses, looting in Danbury and chopping down the Liberty Pole in Ridgefield—Nehemiah Scribner was tried for high treason and given the death sentence, the only Norwalk Tory to receive so harsh a penalty. Scribner had made a successful getaway with the enemy following the raid but he made the mistake of returning to Norwalk for some clothes and was captured while trying to slip back to Long Island. At his trial Scribner denied he had looted but admitted that he had indeed been persuaded to follow the British. He appealed the sentence, pleading that he not be cut off "in the Bloome of Life," and the Assembly commuted the death penalty to an indefinite term in the hellhole Newgate Prison at Simsbury.

Following the attacks on Danbury and Ridgefield the British stepped up their raiding activity on Norwalk. The Council of Safety allocated one hundred rounds of shot and additional grape shot for Norwalk's field pieces and ordered the fullest company in the First Battalion transferred from New Haven to Norwalk, measures that did little to prevent the British from boldly stalking the area and firing on residents, terrorizing women and children. Norwalkers petitioned the state to purchase a six- or eight-gun armed sloop to protect western shores but the state, already forced to borrow money, did not accede to their request. Instead they provided funds for another matross company, replenished the supply of bullets and flints, and in October, 1778, when the First Battalion was transferred to the southwest coast, ordered another company from this battalion stationed in Norwalk. With these measures the townspeople had to be content.

[16] The raid did more psychological than actual damage to Norwalk, although its inhabitants later petitioned the Assembly for redress for "oxen, horses, provisions, cloathing [and] household goods," carried off by the Redcoats, and Eliakim Raymond and Lemuel Brooks asked reimbursement for ten hogsheads of rum cached by state order at Clap Raymond's house in Wilton and filched by Tryon's troops.

6

THE DEED MALIGN

Being
an Account of
the Burning of Norwalk[1]

PPREHENSIVE NORWALKERS found their fears realized during the anxious hours of July 10 and 11, 1779, when a British expeditionary force descended on the town and reduced it to smoldering ashes. Commanded by General Tryon the 2,600-man force had set sail from New York on July 3 with orders from Sir Henry Clinton to destroy the stores of foodstuffs, stockpiles of war goods, privateers and shipping at New Haven, Fairfield, Stratford, Milford, and "other parts of Connecticut," and to inflict "all injury consistent with humanity."[1] A coordinate force set out overland to take Horseneck and proceed eastward along the Connecticut coast.[2]

On July 5 Tryon's raiders landed at New Haven where with little opposition they destroyed provisions, ammunition, and vessels. The expedition made its way along the coast and struck at Fairfield on July 8 and 9. At the onset of his expedition Tryon had reproved Connecticut inhabitants for their "ungenerous and wanton insurrection"[2] and now found the perfect opportunity to vent his ill-will toward these "ungrateful" rebels. Antagonized

by the Fairfielders' stiff-backed resistance he ruthlessly ordered the torch set to private homes and public buildings alike.[3] Leaving the town in flames the convoy crossed to Huntington Harbor, ostensibly to take on supplies.[4] More likely the move was dictated by unfavorable winds that hampered westward progress along the Connecticut shore.

When news of Fairfield's burning reached Norwalk its inhabitants, who had been busy cutting and storing the July crop of hay, frantically gathered together clothing, household goods, and tools. All day Friday, July 9, they cached their possessions in makeshift hiding places in the hills surrounding the town. Those fortunate enough to own wagons or to hire the services of teamsters carted their belongings to Belden Hill or the farther reaches of Wilton Parish. Someone, perhaps Town Clerk Grumman, even remembered to secrete the town records in a safe place.

Family men evacuated wives and children to Silvermine and Wilton Parish where compassionate residents like Thomas Comstock opened their homes to shelter the refugees. In one instance twenty to thirty persons were crowded into a room only twelve feet square.

---

[1] The entire verse, cited in John C. Pease and John M. Niles, *A Gazetteer of the States of Connecticut and Rhode-Island* (Hartford, 1819), 176, reads:
Tryon achieved the deed malign,
Tryon, the name for every sin;
Hells [sic] blackest fiends the flame survey'd
And smil'd to see destruction spread;
While Satan, blushing deep, look'd on,
And infamy disown'd her son!

[2] If the clever tactical maneuver succeeded, not only would American supply lines be seriously disrupted but the British could move on West Point when Continental troops were siphoned off from the Highlands along the Hudson River to defend the Connecticut coast.

[3] This action is consistent with Tryon's earlier behavior. As lieutenant governor of North Carolina he had vigorously suppressed a rural uprising and as governor of New York had supported a large militia to crush dissidents. See Thomas Buckley, "Monument to a Royalist," *New York Times,* July 3, 1976, 10.

[4] Tryon cited the need for supplies as his motivation in his official report to Sir Henry Clinton but it is difficult to understand why it was necessary to deploy the total fleet of forty-eight transports and four escort ships on this mission.

Mrs. William (Mary Esther Belden) St. John.

"Mrs. St. J. and her husband and family, with what effects
they could carry, went up into the woods, at the East Rocks.
They had a bedstead which they set up; milked the cows
which they drove with them, drank the milk, and stayed there
that night. In the morning, the guns were firing; the smoke of
the burning house rose. Her husband said, 'The work is
begun; they are burning the town.'" From an interview with
Rev. Hall in November 1846 when Mrs. St. John was 94/
Collection of Lockwood House Museum.

Grumman's Hill.

Where would Tryon strike next? General Samuel
Parsons, hurriedly dispatched from the Highlands
above the Hudson River to Connecticut to coordinate its defense against Tryon, believed the British
general would move next against Norwalk. On the
night of July 9, Parsons, having just ridden some
sixty miles to view the destruction at New Haven
and Fairfield, tried urgently to muster an adequate
force to defend Norwalk. In the last moments before leaving his headquarters in Redding to assume
personal command in Norwalk he ordered various
state militia companies to join him there and requested General Washington to send one thousand
Continentals to bolster the local forces. He scraped
together an army of no more than one thousand
men.[5] The support he had counted on, such as a
company that left Milford on July 9 but inexplicably
turned back at Wilton, failed to materialize.[3] The
two brigades Washington dispatched from the
Highlands did not reach Ridgefield until two days
after Tryon had completed his mission.

On Saturday, July 10, Tryon's First Division
crossed the Sound and anchored about five miles
off Norwalk.[6] At nine o'clock in the evening, about
an hour after sunset, the British began to tumble
out of the small flatboats and bateaux which had
ferried them from the transports to the shallow
waters at "Cow" (Calf) Pasture. There they lay on
their arms awaiting the arrival from Long Island of
the King's American Regiment which finally joined
them at three o'clock the following morning.

On Sunday, July 11, at the point of day, that
instant when the skies begin to lighten with the
coming dawn, the columns of the First Division
made up of both Hessian and British soldiers began
their march up the east side of the Norwalk River.
Undeterred by scattered militia fire the well-

[5] The exact number is subject to dispute. Parsons himself,
who said in one account that he had no more than a
thousand, also estimated the number at between nine
hundred and eleven hundred in another account. Tryon
erroneously set the figure at two thousand, which may have
been a testimony to the valor of the Americans but was
more likely to have been the type of exaggeration British
officers were inclined to send back to London.

[6] The sequence that follows draws heavily from Charles
Hall's *Life and Letters of Samuel Holden Parsons* and from two
accounts written by General Tryon. The first, in his own
hand, was written aboard the *Camilla* in Huntington Bay at
seven o'clock in the evening of July 12, 1779, at the conclusion of the expedition. The second, dated New York July
20, 1779, is Tryon's official report to Sir Henry Clinton.
Both documents are catalogued in the Clinton Papers, The
William Clements Library, University of Michigan. A comparison of the two accounts shows interesting disparities of
fact and significant differences in tone.

Calf Pasture as seen from the Marvin-Taylor Farm in August of 1927.

organized British brigades pushed steadily on to-ward "Drummond's" (Grumman's) Hill. By 4:30 A.M. they had occupied the hill, the surrounding area, and the Norwalk Bridge, and had settled in to await arrival of the Second Division which was to march up the western bank of the river. With the coming of day frightened residents who had dared remain in town could see Grumman's Hill "all red" with British uniforms.

At about six o'clock that morning the main body of the American force, composed of eight or nine hundred troops under General Oliver Wolcott and Parsons' detachment of one hundred and fifty Con-tinentals, took up their positions on the heights beyond the Norwalk Common known as the "Rocks." From that vantage point, aided by two artillery pieces that sporadically lobbed cannon balls in the direction of the enemy, the outnum-bered Americans began to advance on the British. By nine o'clock their progress was checked but the Americans valiantly fought on until nearly eleven when the militia in their center gave way and beat a retreat.[7] The collapse of the American center coin-cides with the time the tardy British Second Division arrived at the bridge.

[7] Wolcott's horse troops retreated to Wilton Parish where the weary men found refuge from the rain and feed for their horses in the homes of such friendly residents as Clap Raymond and Benjamin Betts.

This division commanded by Brigadier General George Garth did not land at Old Well until seven o'clock Sunday morning.[8] About fifty spunky American militiamen fired down on the British col-umns from the heights above the Old Well where a cannonball found there years later, embedded in a rock, testifies to the invaders' sharp response. The handful of defenders in Old Well could not hope to stop the Redcoats' march up the western side of the harbor nor prevent them from setting fire to stores, barns, and homes as they moved up along the river. In spite of the incessant rain a stiff wind carried sparks to nearby buildings, multiplying the destruction.

When Garth's men reached Norwalk Bridge the day was lost for the Americans. Joining forces, Tryon's two divisions began to retrace the route to Calf Pasture in what Tryon described in his reports as an orderly retreat unmolested.[9] Parsons con-tended on the other hand that Wolcott's horse troops regrouped after their earlier retreat and

[8] Parsons reported that the landing began at 5 A.M.

[9] There is a shift in emphasis in Tryon's two accounts. In the official report (July 20, 1779), he used the word unas-saulted to describe the embarkation from Calf Pasture, rather than the retreat itself. The fleet was not able to set sail because of bad weather, and did not reach Huntington Bay until Monday afternoon. British and Hessian troops lay exposed to rain and wind on the crowded decks of the transports during the long wait.

Gould Hoyt House on Main Street.

Hezekiah Jarvis House on East Avenue.

John Belden House on West Avenue.

mounted so heavy an attack on the British that they "retreated with precipitation to their ships." Whatever the truth, Tryon's men did manage to set fire to the buildings they passed on the east side of the river, leaving behind "vast columns of smoak ascending from the conflagrated buildings" that were easily visible three miles away.[4]

Dwelling places, barns, shops, mills, and both churches were all ablaze.[10] Before they set sail the British also destroyed salt pans, magazines, five vessels, and two privateers under construction,[5] and carried off all the whaleboats they found. Only six houses stood untouched along the two routes. That some of these belonged to Tories so enraged Parsons that he confessed to Washington: "I hope our people will burn [them], as the burners are still here (Norwalk), and have committed no act by which the public can seize them."[6]

Well might Parsons have been embittered at the outcome of his confrontation with Tryon for the Americans under his command had failed utterly to prevent the British general from achieving his goal of destroying rebel war matériel. Since Parsons had arrived in Norwalk twelve to fifteen hours before the British landed and a full day before they began moving up from Calf Pasture, why did he delay positioning his troops on the "Rocks" until an hour and a half after Tryon's First Division had attained the heights of Grumman's Hill and seized the strategic Norwalk Bridge? And why did he select a site as far inland as the "Rocks" as the base from which to launch his counterattack when the center of the town lay well below this point? Positions on Grumman's Hill on the east bank and below the bridge on the west bank would seem to be better locations from which to protect the town.

The most likely explanation for selection of the "Rocks" is that the unhappy Parsons was stalling for time, hoping that his expected reinforcements would arrive; hence, he sought a spot where the various units could safely gather and coordinate their movements. The Americans fought bravely—Parsons had nothing but praise for officers and men. They also may have been hampered toward the end of the encounter by a shortage of

10 Parsons set the number at 130 dwellings, 87 barns, 22 stores, 17 ships, 4 mills, 1 church, and 1 meetinghouse. Weed, *Norwalk After Two Hundred and Fifty Years,* 141, uses the number 80 for dwellings. Nathaniel Bouton, *An Historical Discourse in Commemoration of the Two-Hundredth Anniversary of the Settlement of Norwalk, Ct. in 1651* (New York, 1851), 48, felt Parsons' count was inflated.

ammunition. Even so, judged on the basis of the number of British casualties, Parsons made a poor showing. More British troops were killed, wounded, and missing in each of the relatively undefended towns of New Haven and Fairfield than in Norwalk.[11] Still one cannot help feeling compassion for this desperately tired American general waiting for soldiers who never arrived.

As Tryon's troops began to re-embark, a number of Loyalists who had been willing to put up with vilification and abuse in order to remain in familiar home surroundings now decided to make the break.[12] One such householder, Jehiel Ketchum, told British authorities he had suffered "every species of vengeance that vindictive malice could invent." Some Norwalkers left because their houses had been burned along with those of the rebels. Elderly Jonathan Ketchum's house and contents were so completely destroyed that he, who had "never been under the necessity of supporting himself by labour," fell gravely ill and ignominiously had to beg financial assistance from British sources.

The circumstances of the Reverend Jeremiah Leaming's departure remain as ambiguous as his loyalty. Although this Anglican clergyman had lived in Norwalk for twenty-two years and had tried to live "in peace and unity" with the established church, he had also evidently been reluctant to alter the Book of Common Prayer to include an Independence Day Service and had shown his attachment to the mother country in other ways. He does not appear, however, to have been "as big a Tory as ever there could be on earth," a reputation derived from reminiscences of two elderly Norwalkers sixty years after the war.

11 Tryon's report, printed in a London newspaper and cited in a lengthy article in the *Connecticut Courant* of February 22, 1780, shows 28 British to have been killed, 95 wounded, and 32 reported as missing, in total, in all three raids, with figures broken down by town and regiment. Norwalk ranks lowest in all three categories (killed, wounded, missing), in spite of the professional military defense of the town. An early historian apparently reported the total figures above as referring to Norwalk alone, and later writers repeated them, leading to the erroneous conclusion that Norwalk had put up the best defense of the three towns.

12 Edward Arnold, a Tory who left with Tryon, was no doubt the man who had sold his remarkable collection of American Curiosities to Tryon, when he had earlier passed through Norwalk while still a governor. John Adams, who had seen the collection, was extremely annoyed when he learned that it had fallen into Tryon's hands and would probably leave the country. H.L. Butterfield, Marc Friedlander, Mary-Jo Kline, eds., *The Book of Abigail and John* (Boston, Mass., 1975), 256.

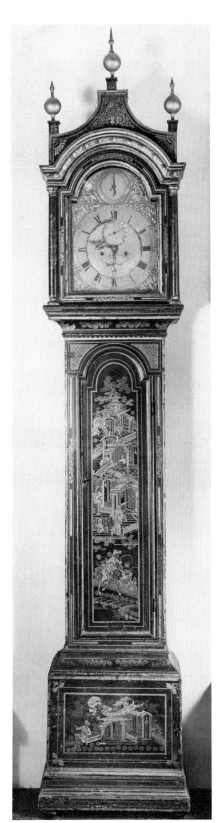

Survivors of the Tryon raid were this japanned Tall Clock made by George Prior of London and once owned by John Belden; and the three houses shown on the opposite page. Collection of Lockwood House Museum.

Leaming's departure with Tryon caused the townspeople to assume he had left voluntarily. As a result he was "dragged through mire and dirt," or so the Reverend Samuel Peters describes Leaming's treatment at the hands of the patriots.[13] One story has it that a group of Norwalkers coming upon his portrait retrieved somehow from the parish house nailed it head down to a sign post.[14] If one accepts Leaming's version of his departure, that he was captured during the raid by some Hessians and temporarily imprisoned, he did not leave town voluntarily but as a captive. That he left without making any provision whatsoever for the welfare of his personal slave lends some credence to the view that he left as a prisoner.[15] Leaming wrote later that his church was "laid to ashes, by which I lost everything I had, my furniture, my books, and all my papers, even my apparel, except what was on my back."[7]

Leaming's extensive property was confiscated and sold. He never returned to Norwalk but passed the remainder of his life in Stratford. Some years after the war in a petition for restitution he affirmed that he had always refused to take an oath of allegiance to Britain and had declined to accept the chaplaincy of a British regiment. The Assembly gave the now old and infirm clergyman a special grant of two hundred pounds.

As soon as Hartford realized the seriousness of Norwalk's plight the Assembly appointed a committee to investigate individual losses for tax abatement purposes and cut in half the town's quota of men for the Continental Army. In the fall Governor Trumbull appealed to other towns in the state for contributions for the sufferers in the three damaged shore towns but these donations were not distributed until the following January.

Fortunately houses on the outskirts and in the back country were still intact. Homeless families were able to move in with relatives or friends in Silvermine, Five Mile River, and Wilton. Aaron Cardoza opened his Wilton home to a band of Sephardic Jewish families who had already fled

once from the British when they left New York City to seek temporary haven in Norwalk. All from the same synagogue as Michael Judah, it was probably that connection that had brought them here. The most illustrious member of the colony was silversmith Myer Myers, one of the foremost artisans in America at the time.[16] Others of the well-to-do group were Myers' brother, Asher, also a silversmith; Joseph Simson and his sons, Solomon and Samson; Moses Isaacs, and Samson Mears,[17] two of whose daughters had married the Myers brothers.[8] Although these refugees had been able to evacuate all their women and children before Tryon's landing they had to leave furniture, tools, and stockpiled business inventories, the Myers brothers "being deprived of a very considerable part of their tools."

Somehow the inhabitants managed to weather the cruelly cold winter of 1779-1780. Later several burned-out families requested and received confiscated Tory property.[18] Rebuilding in the spring was delayed because the wartime embargo required obtaining permission from the Council of Safety for vessels to bring building supplies to Norwalk. Permission once received, the town sent its most skillful traders up the coast to Massachusetts and New Hampshire with instructions to use their talents to barter foodstuffs for boards, shingles, and glass.[19] Rebuilding was incredibly slow. Even so prominent a citizen as Stephen St. John was still living with his large family in a single room two miles from his farm and business a year after the raid. "I am Destitute of either House or barn," he wrote to Governor Trumbull.

13 Peters, an Anglican clergyman in Connecticut, was a noted Tory apologist.

14 This story lends credence to Loyalist charges that the rebels laid the torch to St. Paul's because of its large number of Tory parishioners. Tryon's official report unfortunately does not clarify the matter.

15 According to his supporters he remained in New York because of a hip injury sustained during his imprisonment.

16 Myers' knowledge of metallurgy was such that when the Connecticut General Assembly proposed to open a lead mine in Middletown, Myers was recommended as smelter and refiner above all other candidates in the New York region but there is no evidence that he became identified with the endeavor. In 1776 he had been elected president of the New York Silver Smiths' Society and received commissions from prominent New Yorkers, including British officials.

17 His efforts to conduct merchant shipping under wartime conditions in Norwalk were so frustrating that Mears had considered resettling on the Caribbean Island of St. Eustatius.

18 For example, the Assembly granted Abraham Benedict permission to take over a barn on the property of Tory Ebenezer Street whose estate was forfeited in October, 1779. In 1782 the Assembly also granted the First Society £500 from the sale of Loyalist property to defray the cost of rebuilding their church.

19 The need to insure fairness in collecting produce for export may have been the reason for appointing an exceptionally large thirty-four-man committee of "Inspectors of Provisions" in March, 1780.

Foraging raids which reached their peak during the winter and spring of 1780-1781 also hampered reconstruction. Encouraged by the town's disorganized condition, as well as by the continuous shortage of coast guards and ammunition, wanton pillagers now even had the effrontery to raid the very center of the village. One gang charged in at 4 A.M. on Thaddeus Betts and Eliphalet Lockwood and demanded that Lockwood hand over the payroll of the troops in the area. Lockwood managed to convince them he did not have the payroll and the marauders had to content themselves with ransacking the house and making away with "money, plate, arms, ammunition &c."[9]

Although some of the invaders were neither British nor Loyalist but simply profiteers and plunderers trading or stealing with equal vigor, the Tories and their sympathizers still showed surprising strength. The selectmen bombarded Governor Trumbull with pleas for additional guards. General Parsons, observing the situation from his headquarters at Redding, reported to George Washington that a secret spy ring existed in their very midst. In the spring of 1781, Washington, who himself suspected a Tory plot in Fairfield County, offered a skilled spy to Parsons to counter the suspected conspiracy. Anti-Tory feeling in Norwalk rose to a new high and a committee was appointed to check into all questionable individuals still residing in the town. They came up with a list of twenty-four inimical persons. Some of them who had been under suspicion for some time but for various reasons had been permitted to remain were now treated as out-and-out enemies and either fled or were imprisoned.

Norwalkers were not silent sufferers. On behalf of the town, St. John requested that 1781 losses be added to those from Tryon's raid and the Assembly spent untold hours reviewing petitions listing property losses.[20] Some Norwalkers were still requesting tax abatement in 1790! Still, lowered property taxes must have seemed small recompense indeed to someone like sixty-year-old Sarah Bouton. She had to move into a mean little ten-by-fifteen foot shop for which she had waited more than a year after she had lost her own home.

The state eventually reimbursed more than three hundred Norwalk residents for their losses.[21] Al-

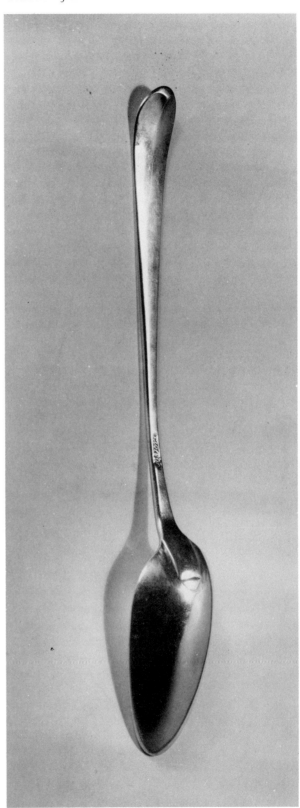

Dessert spoon made by Myer Myers ... circa 1780. Collection of Lockwood House Museum.

---

20 The Assembly also released Norwalk selectmen from a fine for failing to meet the town's quota of soldiers in 1781.

21 A full and accurate list was not completed until 1792.

though the largest claims represented the losses of stores, wharves, ships, and merchandise of John Cannon, Thomas Benedict, Eliphalet Lockwood, and Stephen St. John, a number of other residents had substantial claims. Women who had lost personal belongings and household goods appear here as petitioners, almost the only time women as individuals sought or received financial redress from the government. Altogether these claims amounted to about £29,000.[10] As further restitution the Assembly granted fire sufferers throughout the state the right to take up land in Connecticut's Western Reserve in the Ohio Territory where half a million acres known as the Fire Lands were set aside for their use.

It is not particularly difficult to envision the heartbreaking personal anguish that followed Tryon's raid when some families lost every

Sammis House on West Avenue, a temporary dwelling built in 1779 that remained for 117 years.

cherished possession but it is virtually impossible to appraise economic costs to the town as a whole. Sparse Town Proceedings indicate that almost four years after the burning Norwalk citizens apparently still felt that their standard of living was substantially lower than before the war. Even in 1789 George Washington noted on one of his passages through New England: "The Destructive evidences of British cruelty are yet visible both in Norwalk and Fairfield; as there are the chimneys of many burnt houses Standing in them yet."[11]

In October, 1781, only six months after the intensive raids that had reduced the townspeople almost to desperation General Washington accepted the formal surrender of Lord Cornwallis at Yorktown. The war was over at last. Ninety years later Cook St.

John, only ten years old when peace came, could still vividly recall the victory celebration. Asked if there was much of a demonstration the old man replied, "I guess you'd a thought so if you'd been there! I don't know that I ever saw such a universal turnout." He described how the jubilant crowd built a huge pyre around a mammoth log some twenty feet high, piling log upon log around it "as big around as this room," topping all with barrels of tar. "I tell you everything blazed."[12]

With victory came the problem of repentant Loyalists. The die-hard ones had long since moved to Long Island from whence some twelve thousand embarked for Nova Scotia, New Brunswick, or the Bahamas shortly after the signing of the Peace of Paris in 1783.[22] Now, however, many moderate Loyalists wished to be reconciled with relatives and former friends. The Assembly adopted a conciliatory policy toward those Tories who had not actually fought for Britain, allowing them to return home and take their places among their peers once more.

Norwalk's hatred of its own Tories burned as hotly as the tar in the victory bonfire. In no way was the town in accord with the Assembly's lenient policy. Early in 1783 ninety-four citizens sent a memorial to the "Free, Sovereign, and Independent State of Connecticut in America," urging that "those Tory Villains . . . who have been the Cause of so much Distress, Conflagration and bloodshed in our Country" and now came "cringing back" be forbidden to return. When the Tories "Saw their Countrymen breathing their last expiring Groans" they plundered their innocent neighbors. Now, said the memorialists, with "our murdered Brothers scarcely cold in their graves they want to return."[13] When a resolution that would have permitted Tories to return came up for a vote at town meeting it was naturally "Past in the Negative."

This vengeful mood did not last long. By the end of the year it was decided that the selectmen aided by a committee should have discretion to deal on an individual basis with those who had consorted with the enemy and now wanted to return home. Although this conciliatory measure was no doubt voted partly because families wanted to be reunited,

22 One small group composed primarily of people from Norwalk and Stamford, including Israel Hait [Hoyt], Widow Mary Raymond, Silas Raymond, James and Louis Picket[t], Widow Hester Burlock, whose husband had been shot to death on his own doorstep, John Marvin and three members of the disgraced Scribner family, became the nucleus of the town of Kingston.

Norwalk might also have been following the example of other Connecticut towns which passed similar resolutions with an eye to the dollar, recognizing the need for the capital and business acumen of well-to-do Loyalists in the postwar economy. Most of Norwalk's reconciled Loyalists seem to have been accepted, however, for other than financial reasons. Gould Hoyt, a typical example, was not a man of great wealth but esteemed enough to have been appointed to the 1774 nonimportation committee. The first year of the war found him exiled to Lebanon as a "convict tory." Allowed to return he became suspect again, especially when his house escaped Tryon. In 1781 he was listed inimical but his 1792 request for reimbursement for loss of property indicates that he was again in town and in the good graces of his fellows.

Besides passing muster at town level, those who wanted to have their confiscated estates restored had to appeal to the Assembly. Such appeals were not always granted. John Belden and Nathan Jarvis had made the fatal mistake of delaying taking their oaths of loyalty to the United States. Their farm directly opposite Lloyd's Neck was easy prey for nighttime visitors. This had led to the suspicion that they were trading with the enemy even though they lost all their farm buildings in Tryon's raid. At the height of anti-Tory feeling in 1781 they were placed on the inimical list. When they appealed for restoration of their remaining property all three selectmen as well as the justices of the peace supported their petition but the Assembly turned them down.[23]

Parcels of their estates were quite often sold to loyal Americans even before Loyalists' appeals reached the Assembly and few of them received their property intact. A sad case is that of Samuel Nash, Jr., who joined the British army when he was only sixteen. The Assembly granted his 1788 request for restoration of his property but only three acres and one-third share of a house and barn remained. Tories were also apt to find their property stripped of its timber for the patriots had found it convenient to cut firewood for troops quartered in the town from confiscated property.

The alleged disloyalty of certain individuals such as Captain Esaias Bouton appears to have been gradually forgiven and forgotten. Bouton, known to have had business dealings with General Tryon, also had extensive holdings in Wilson Cove, conve-

nient for the secret trading people suspected he engaged in with the enemy. After the war, Bouton, a pillar of St. Paul's, continued to live in seeming amity with his neighbors and the family became so respected that his grandson Nathaniel was invited to deliver the bicentennial address in 1851.[24]

Although patriots eventually took over the property of exiled Tories, Norwalk's records indicate that these lands did not end up solely in the hands of a few politically prominent men as in some other towns. Rather, Loyalist property was sold at public sale or occasionally given in lieu of money payment of a state debt. In this manner Captain Stephen

Sketch of the Congregational Church, rebuilt in 1788. Collection of First Congregational Church on the Green.

Betts received parts of the estates of Silas Raymond and Stephen Hoyt in lieu of back pay. It is true that Samuel Keeler 3d got the choice lot, storehouse, and wharf at the head of the harbor confiscated from the Rogers brothers, Samuel and Fitch. The latter, charged with commanding an armed vessel against the United States, had ranged the Sound in his sloop *Two Brothers*. Several members of the

23 Jarvis' name may have worked against him for the Anglican Jarvises were among Connecticut's most noted Loyalist families.

24 The selectmen had also been willing to exchange Bouton's teenage son Nathan who had fled to Long Island to avoid military service for an American in British hands, when Nathan was caught sneaking back for a visit with his parents.

Saint Paul's Church was rebuilt in 1786 on the foundation of its predecessor on East Ave.

Lockwood family leased or received quitclaim deeds to confiscated property but since this family was a large one these transactions do not imply impropriety. The Assembly took pains to be fair to families of exiled Loyalists and as a result not as much property changed hands as one might have expected, considering the large number of pro-British residents in the area.[25] Foresighted Loyalists had also transferred real estate holdings to reliable relatives prior to going over to the other side. Con-

25 The Assembly granted exiled Benjamin Jarvis' request for permission to collect some debts to buy a "desint pair of toom stones" for the grave of William Jarvis and to help educate the grandchildren of Widow Hannah Jarvis, still living in Connecticut. It gave Hannah Picket[t] Arnold the right to her father James Picket[t's] estate "as though no confiscation had taken place." RSC VII, 200, 363.

siderably more important in the development of Norwalk's postwar society and economy was the exodus of those prosperous Tory merchants and shippers such as Ketchum and the audacious Stephen Hoyt which left the commercial field open to new men.

In politics, however, like most towns in the land of steady habits, Norwalk continued to elect descendants of the early families to local offices. Following Stephen St. John's death shortly after the end of the war inhabitants gave the post of first selectman to Thomas Belden, a member of an old, well-to-do family. He was elected again and again. Its delegates went to the state Constitutional Convention in Hartford in January, 1788, with instructions to vote for the new Constitution of the United States, a generally conservative document.[26]

The years immediately following the war found the battered village mending slowly. Town finances were in dismal shape. Men who had advanced money to the town between 1776 and 1783, still not reimbursed five years after the signing of the peace treaty, now insisted upon repayment. In 1788 the town had to devote all tax revenues to these old obligations. Moreover taxes were hard to collect; some citizens had to be allowed to work them off by repairing town roads. To add to the distress in 1784 Hartford once again passed over Norwalk in handing out patronage, making Danbury a shire town over Norwalk's strong protestations. Local officials also pleaded with the Assembly for a Court of Probate but to no avail.[27]

In yet another respect the Tryon raid had taken a toll that would linger long after commercial activity had revived. Replacing essential dwellings, shops, and wharves took priority over rebuilding the town's schoolhouses which had been put to the torch and a generation of boys grew up with little or no formal schooling. Cabinetmaker Charles Grandison Street, the son of one of those boys, who himself had never had "aney Chance to have aney learning Much I was put to work when I had orto Ben in School," remarked upon this aspect of the "deed malign":

My Father had no schools when he was a Boy the Brittish Burned the town of Norwalk and Burned all the School houses and they had no money to build anny more he was ten years old then.[14]

26 The delegates were Major Hezekiah Rogers and Samuel G. Silliman.

27 In 1794, after years of appeal, Hartford condescended to let Norwalk have its own probate court.

PART TWO

SEAPORT VILLAGE

1779/1865

he valley, which lies along the

Norwalk river, and in which the

town is built, is beautiful. Few

richer prospects of the same extent can be found

than that, which is presented from the neighbouring

eminences of this ground; the town . . . the

river . . . the farms . . . together with an unlimited

view of the Sound and the Long Island shore."

Timothy Dwight / 1822

7

OF MERCHANTS AND MARINERS

Being
an Account of
Norwalk
During the Era of Yankee Ingenuity

INCHED AND IMPOVERISHED Norwalkers laboriously restored their battered village and gradually resumed the comfortable pace of the life they had enjoyed before the war. The laying out of new roads, improvement of old ones, and a surge of acreage transfers in the center of town are indications of a spurt of commercial growth. Once more stores and warehouses began to cluster around the bridge, so close together that businessmen feared what might happen if a single warehouse or shop caught fire, and a group of merchants purchased a fire engine and organized a company of twenty volunteers.

The town's commerce was the basis of this prosperity. The years after 1790 were golden ones for Norwalk's maritime-related business. As the coastal trade increased dramatically sloops and schooners threaded in and out of the harbor, their masters intent on catching the best winds for the outbound voyage or eagerly anticipating return to their homes on Pudding Lane.[1] Local wharves overflowed with heaps of cargo recently unloaded or waiting to be shipped to some distant port. Venturesome young men signed on as seamen for voyages to the West Indies or sealing expeditions to the faraway Falkland Islands.[2] In the custom of the sea, boys of thirteen or fourteen entered the coastal trade as raw hands or cooks and secretly yearned for the time they would be masters.

Men of the town found steady employment as ships' carpenters, spar makers, joiners, and caulkers in the port's flourishing shipyards. In one year alone, 1797, master shipbuilder Henry Johnson, Jr., supervised construction of three fine sloops, *Susan* and *Huntress,* commissioned by E. Lockwood and Sons, and *The Three Brothers,* which Eliakim Warren home-ported in Troy, New York. In addition to building the sturdy one-masted sloops so ideally suited to the coastal trade Nicholas Vincent, a master shipbuilder in both Norwalk and New York, launched many seaworthy schooners and handsome brigs down the Norwalk slips.[1] Possibly he faced the greatest challenge of his career when he built the U.S. frigate *Savannah* in his New York shipyard. Many Norwalk men helped to fit her out and the roster included familiar names like Selleck, Betts, Street, Finch and Odell.

To attract customers, packet owners began to schedule regular runs to the big coastal cities and even added new routes. By 1801 farmers and business men could ship produce to New York on the sloop *Griffin* which left Selleck's Hole every Tuesday.[2] *Griffin* was joined the following year by the

---

[1] Pudding Lane, the present Main Avenue, seemed to be "Seamen's Row." Many captains and masters lived in this area.

[2] Phyllis Kihn, "The Sea Journal of Captain Ebenezer Hooker, 1817-1818," *Connecticut Historical Society Bulletin,* Vol. 40, No. 1 (January, 1975), 8-18. At least two Norwalkers, Willet Hanford and Edward Bails, shipped on board the *Commodore Decatur* which, in company of *Ann,* left New York in 1817 for a sealing voyage to the Falkland Islands. Both ships were destroyed in the waters off St. Elena but many men managed to reach Buenos Aires, where they shipped on board *Pescadore* for a sealing expedition to Canton.

Juno which sailed from the slip at Thomas Lockwood's store on alternate Saturdays.[3] The sloops *Industry, Maria,* and *Alligator* made regular runs to Albany and Troy, New York.

Despite the groundswell in commerce, agriculture remained the way of life for most residents of Connecticut.[3] But high taxes and exorbitant land costs here, combined with availability of cheap, rich farmland elsewhere, drew many farmers to western New York and the Ohio Territory. When the Fire Lands were opened up many people pulled up stakes and headed west. Although a survey of the half-million acres in America's new West was not completed until 1807 several Norwalk men rode out earlier to view the area, returning with enthusiastic reports. In 1808 a drawing was held and a number of Norwalkers, using their own allotted shares or purchasing another's claim, set out to try their luck anew.[4]

Many Connecticut towns including Norwalk failed to grow during this period. The loss of farmers was so alarming that newspaper editors, both political parties, and even men of commerce united in a campaign to make farming more attractive and efficient. Agricultural societies were formed to foster pride among farmers and disseminate information to improve farming methods. Communities instituted lotteries to raise money for new roads and better bridges, realizing that better farm-to-market roads would aid both farmers and tradespeople.[5]

Farmers who improved their methods of production could live well and prosper. The Norwalk price for a barrel of prime pork was seventeen dollars and for a barrel of first-run cider almost two dollars, at a time when a man's napped hat of best quality retailed for about three dollars. Farmers who shipped their produce to New York could get as much as £3 4s. for a barrel of salted beef while a Norwalk tailor charged but £1 12s. for sewing up three pairs of pantaloons (men's trousers) and two vests. A Norwalk dairy farmer could clear about twelve dollars for nineteen churns of butter at a time when a female domestic earned a dollar a week for her labors. A clerk in a store was paid eight dollars a month; an industrious farm hand received thirteen dollars a month with board.[6]

Clearly farmers were not suffering unduly but they were dissatisfied, as were urban residents, with the rigid structure of the state government which placed control in the hands of a few well-to-do upper-class families. The Federalist Party was in the hands of these men. Such hegemony might not have been disagreeable in the old days of the Fundamental Orders when leaders felt a moral obligation to their fellow men, but New England had changed "from Puritan to Yankee" and the present elite all too easily set aside duty and restraint in favor of personal gain.

Many people felt that this situation had come about because of Connecticut's lack of a constitution. Connecticut had not adopted a constitution following the Declaration of Independence; the Assembly simply declared the 1662 Charter still in effect but without the customary allegiance to the Crown. The state did not have three separate branches of government. Instead, under the Charter, the Assembly controlled selection of governor, Council, and judiciary, permitting a tight little clique of Federalists to retain power.[7]

Even before 1800 Norwalk was becoming a center of anti-Federalist activity. Its farmers resented the taxing of farm land but not stocks or similar types of capital wealth. Its religious dissenters disliked the privileges of the Congregational Church. Anglicans, Baptists, and Methodists, all of whom had congregations in Norwalk,[8] could be expected to support anti-Federalist movements.

---

[3] In 1790 nine out of every ten male heads of households were involved in some form of agricultural pursuit during part of the year. By 1820, although jobs in commerce and manufacturing were siphoning off the farm population, there were still twice as many farmers as urban workers.

[4] Charles R. Sherman, father of Civil War General William Tecumseh Sherman, was one of those who moved with his family from Norwalk to the Fire Lands. As a child General Sherman must have heard many tales of the devastation left in Tryon's wake and it is very likely that the British general's destructive tactics provided the model for Sherman's notorious march through the South.

[5] Eli Morris and Company Lottery and Exchange Office located on the west side of the Norwalk bridge, which sold tickets and shares in all Connecticut lotteries, advertised in *Middlebrook's 1830 Almanac* that it had sold a ticket which had won a capital prize of $2,000.

[6] The prices for agricultural products and retail goods are taken from the account books of E. Lockwood and Sons. Archives, Lockwood House Museum, Norwalk.

[7] Qualifications for freemen, who elected the Assembly, were tightened over the years, and about 1800 a stand-up method of voting for the Council was adopted, which intimidated those voting for Council members.

[8] Jesse Lee, founder of the Methodist-Episcopal Church in America, is believed to have preached New England's first Methodist sermon under an apple tree by the roadside in

Anti-Federalists gradually coalesced into a political structure, the Republican or Democratic-Republican Party, whose short-term goals were to unseat Federalists in the Assembly and elect Republicans to national offices, and whose long-term goal was to obtain a constitution for the state. Local organizations calling themselves Republican (or Democratic) Societies were formed in several towns. In 1798 such a society was organized in Norwalk.[9] As its constitution boldly declared, the Norwalk Republican Society advocated a vigilant electorate, stating:

. . . to exercise the right of speech, and freedom of debate, recognized by the Constitution to perpetuate the equal rights of man, to perpetuate political knowledge, and to revive the republican spirit of '76, are the grand objects of this institution.[4]

Home of Judge Taylor Sherman on Main Street.

Democratic in character as well as in aim, the Society charged only 12½c for membership and held elections for officers annually.[5]

Some fragile, yellowed papers describing their occasional meetings between 1807 and 1811 reveal existence of a second organization, the Republican

Norwalk. In spite of a cool reception to Lee on that occasion, an informal group was soon organized and, led by Absalom Day, John Hoyt, Noah and Matthew Wilcox, Jesse Warren, and Ebenezer Crofut, raised money to build the first Methodist church building. Selleck, *Norwalk,* 417, 424. Ezra Stiles, *Itineraries,* 157, heard that Presbyterians numbered about one-third of the Congregationalists in 1751 in Norwalk, but Alexander Blaikie in *A History of Presbyterianism in New England* (Boston, 1881), 204-05, reports no church of that denomination in Norwalk even up to the 1850s.

9 This may have been formed in defiance of the proposed Alien and Sedition Acts as well as because of discontent with Connecticut politics.

Society of Flax Hill.[6] At its organizational meeting this group voted to "take in all that are friends of American Independence," to erect a liberty-pole, and to purchase a flag to celebrate Independence properly. "Thus was this young company so attached to their Beloved Country," wrote the Society scribe, "that they spared no cost nor pains to prepare for the celebration of Independence [which] they failed not [to] hail with the true spirit of Americans and with becoming zeal and return of the Memorable and famous 4th of July." When the liberty-pole blew down in the winter of 1811 the members voted to put up a new one, "determined not to let their zeal and love which they bare [sic] for their country fall and perish with [it]." Although liberty-poles were in fact popular symbols with political-action Republican societies, unless those simple preparations for Independence Day were a mere facade, the Flax Hill Society was more interested in patriotism than politics. What the records do reveal is that July 4th became enshrined in American hearts at a remarkably early date.

In May, 1800 Norwalk Republicans elected their first representative to the Assembly, William Maltby Betts, son of the respected Dr. Thaddeus Betts, and the following spring their Society was host to a statewide Republican caucus when the party nominated its first gubernatorial candidate.

Since Republicans were followers of Thomas Jefferson, an advocate and friend of France whose revolution and bloody Reign of Terror struck fear into many hearts, conservative Nutmeggers viewed Republicans with fear and suspicion and gave them a hard time when opportunity arose. Samuel Morse, publisher of a small Republican newspaper in Danbury, was forced to leave. "The Democratic printer in this town has blown out and moved to Norwalk," a local clergyman related in his diary in 1800. "The boys attended him out of town with bells, quills, etc."[7] For about a year, from a small shop near the Norwalk Bridge, Morse published his *Sun of Liberty* but after "opposition and difficulties" moved to New Haven.

Joseph Dennis, a Frenchman, next became publisher of the paper, soon named the *Independent Republican.* Although Dennis had to defend himself against the charge of being a foreigner he managed to last several years in the town and to obtain both advertisers and a fairly wide readership. Perhaps his success was due to his willingness to include local news which few papers of that day did. Dennis' difficulties seem to have stemmed more from business than politics. He once failed to publish because he ran out of paper and another time apologized for failing to put out a paper the previous week. His printer, "a stranger and friendless," had fallen ill and died, and Dennis not only had to handle funeral arrangements but was without a printer.*10*

No fanatical pamphleteer, Dennis was discreet in his Republicanism. Readers of the little newspaper were provided more than fair coverage of domestic and world affairs including news of Napoleon's activities and the wars in Europe. Occasionally he slipped in a few good words for his party, as when he reprinted an article defending President Jefferson against the charge of being an infidel. In the autumn of 1802 the Frenchman openly exulted in the election returns which showed that local voters had overwhelmingly chosen Republicans for both Assembly and Council. William Maltby Betts and Dr. Phineas Miller, "both inflexible republicans,"

This joke was mere wishful thinking for the Federalists were far from flat on their backs in Connecticut. They were in fact able to punish the town for its Republicanism by slicing off Canaan and Wilton parishes.*11* These were incorporated as separate towns over Norwalk's futile objections.

As Norwalk shipped ever larger quantities of local produce and manufactured goods to an ever-widening market, less and less could the community chart its own economic course. English designs on trade, European wars, and ultimately the assertion of America's economic independence all contributed to recurrent cycles of boom and gloom that Norwalk could not escape. The economic fate of its farmers, tradespeople, bankers, businessmen, and workmen were now tied irrevocably to national policy. After the United States adopted the Embargo Act in 1807 shipbuilding became a depressed industry. Conceived as a strategy that would force England and France to cease their harassment of

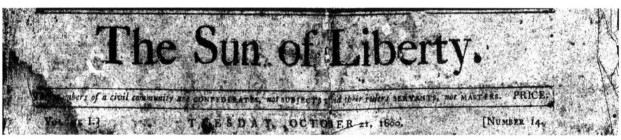

Masthead of Norwalk's first newspaper / Collection of John R. Cuneo.

were elected as the town's representatives to the Assembly.

Dennis didn't neglect his Federalist readers. Observing that they enjoyed jokes, he provided the following for their amusement:

First Federalist: *Do you not think that Federalism
                       is looking up?*

Second Federalist: *Yes, by _____,
                       for it is flat upon its back and can
                       look no other way.* [8]

10 Labor troubles may be inferred from the following advertisement appearing in the *Independent Republican* of December 26, 1802:

POST RIDER
Wanted immediately a Sober, honest & Steady man, who is not over fond of—High, Low, Jack and the Game, or too unsteady so as to learn a part of *Six* different Trades and not to stick at any. The papers are to be taken from this office, the route is advantageous, and can be rendered more so with [a] little care and punctuality.

American shipping during the Napoleonic Wars, the Embargo forbade any American ship to sail from a United States port to any foreign port. This act did unbelievable damage to New England's economy, ruining its many maritime-related businesses and doing great harm to farmers as well. The Non-Intercourse Act which came on the heels of the Embargo's repeal permitted trade with all countries except England and France and their colonies. This restored maritime trade to some extent. In Norwalk merchants Burritt and Cannon commissioned Vincent to build the brig *Benefactor* but this flurry of shipbuilding was short-lived. With declaration of war against England in 1812 empty cradles cast skeletal shadows across New England's deserted shipyards and in many sail lofts spiders spun their webs undisturbed.

During this entire period Norwalk's support of

11 These correspond roughly to the towns of New Canaan and Wilton today.

Presidents Jefferson and Madison put it distinctly out of step with Connecticut. Connecticut together with other New England shipping states lined up in vehement opposition to the war, refusing to cooperate in any way. The state's Federalists realized that they could not count on Norwalk in their antiwar tactics when Norwalk's town meeting passed the following grandiloquent resolution soon after war was declared:

Whereas Europe has long been engaged in a bloody & vindictive war... And whereas the right & interests of the United States have been totally disregarded in the savage exterminating war of the Belligerents particularly England, [which]... has kidnapped impressed & imprisoned known Citizens of the United States compelling them to fight her battles & shed her brothers blood. England has insulted our flag, outraged our territory & in peace shed the blood of our fellow citizens. England with piratical hardihood has seized condemned & pocketed millions of our property in ways practiced by none but by Arabs and Algerians. England has broken her public faith in scornfully disavowing the Act of her accredited Minister. England [postponed] and eluded negotiation with more than Carthaginian duplicity 'till her Syran [sic] Song of reconciliation & peace perfectly nauseating, we must defend our rights or bid them [an] eternal farewell. [9]

It is difficult to account for Norwalk's unqualified support of this war, since the traditional explanations do not suffice nor do available documents shed any light.[12] As to impressment of American seamen, a major source of antagonism toward Great Britain, samplings of files of appeals from sailors impressed between 1794 and 1815 reveal no Norwalk names. As for political patronage, loyalty to Jefferson does not seem to have been an open door to federal jobs for Norwalkers. True, President Jefferson had given Lewis Smith a commission in the U.S. Customs Service in 1805, but prime patronage went to Republicans from New Haven or eastern Connecticut. Moreover, Norwalk shippers suffered less financial hardship than merchants in

other coastal towns. Outdistanced in the West Indies trade by merchants from New Haven and New London, they had carefully built up their commercial connections with New York City and the thriving Hudson River valley towns. These modest routes proved to be a godsend, and even when British frigates patrolled the Sound during the war Norwalk's captains in their trim little sloops were able to slip along the coast to New York. Captain Daniel Merritt, in fact, became a local celebrity for his ability to elude a certain British commodore lurking offshore with his "Liverpool Packet."

One explanation for Norwalk's stance is its estrangement from the Federalist-controlled state government. Not only had Hartford never gone out of its way to grant the town any favors, but a few years earlier it had stripped Norwalk of its two rich backcountry parishes. Indeed, the town was held in such low esteem in Hartford that the *Connecticut Courant,* the state's major publication, completely ignored Norwalk's bold resolution.

Connecticut's governor refused to send militia out of state during the War of 1812 (the Assembly had declared the war unnecessary) but he did take steps to put these local forces into fair shape. One hundred and thirty-five Norwalk men served in the state militia during this war and nineteen enlisted in the regular army. Some men entered the U.S. Navy. Lewis Smith left the Customs Service where he had been placed in command of a Customs brig and entered the Navy in 1812, rising to the rank of captain before the war ended.

At war's end Norwalk may have been somewhat better off than larger towns for when Britain drastically cut prices of her export goods after 1815 American merchants could not hope to compete. Only merchants and shippers in the coastal trade were able to survive. Nevertheless the town's merchants worked doubly hard to broaden their routes and put new and better ships into service. By 1818 the *Mechanic,* whose three spacious cabins boasted forty-two berths, left Norwalk on Wednesdays and Saturdays for Peck Slip, New York, and in a spirited turnabout made the return trips on Mondays and Thursdays. At Rowayton's two wharves the *Stephen Raymond* and the *Julia*[13] took on farm produce for the New York market from the four warehouses in the village center.[10]

---

12 See Records of Impressed Seamen, Miscellaneous Correspondence regarding Impressed Seamen, Boxes 1, 2, 7, RG 59, Records of Jefferson Administration. National Archives, Washington, D.C. No clear picture of federal patronage can be obtained because a fire destroyed the U.S. Treasury Records in 1833. Certain correspondence from Connecticut Republicans to Jefferson indicates that Norwalk was not significant among the state's Republicans. See Records of Jefferson Administration, M418, RG 10-19-3, Roll 1, M418, RG 10-19-3, Roll 5. National Archives, Washington, D.C.

13 Alfred Seely had commissioned the *Julia* from a Nyack shipbuilder at a total cost of $2,823.09 (including rigging, compass, lead and line, stove for the cabin and a copy of the

The most remarkable mercantile establishment in early nineteenth century Norwalk was the family firm known as E. Lockwood and Sons. Eliphalet Lockwood and his two oldest sons, William and Buckingham St. John, were hard-working financial wizards who converted a single country store into a sophisticated mini-conglomerate. Merchants and bankers, accountants and landlords, these men counted among their many holdings the Danbury and Norwalk Turnpike, a fleet of ships that plied the coastal and West Indian trade routes, a sawmill, and one of the few rolling and slitting mills in America.

The heart of the original enterprise was the family store located near the west end of the Bridge. If you wished to buy Poland starch, spectacles, Gunpowder tea, pigtail tobacco, kirseymire, a riddle, Thompson's Eyewater, Palm sope (sic), callimanco or Geneva,*14* it was sure to be among the hundreds of household or specialty items on the shelves. Here weaver Thomas Carr bought indigo to color his yarn and carpenter Thomas Benedict acquired hammer, gimlet, and knife. Widow Sally Gregory stopped in for Scotch snuff and prosperous Dr. Jonathan Knight added a handsome bibelot to his home when he bought a japanned candlestick. The Reverend Matthias Burnett sent his Negro servants, Pomp and Dinah, to the store for a supply of his favorite Soushong tea with directions to select lengths of "callico and linning" for their new work clothes. Sall Syfax, a free Negress whose husband had his own carting business, bought white gloves as well as rum at the store. When the store stocked a small supply of silver-mounted buggy whips shortly before Christmas in 1805 they went like hot cakes to sporty local men who were willing to part with more than one pound for one of these elegant accessories.

The Lockwoods stocked their shelves with a great many locally-produced articles acquired when cus-

tomers reconciled their accounts. John Hyatt, a prodigious weaver, paid his bills in lengths of flannel, kirsey, and carpet, while Widow Lois Whitney knit woolen stockings and spun cotton cloth in exchange for her modest purchases.

Upon arrival of a Lockwood ship from the West Indies the store would display exotic tamarinds and oranges but customers were not apt to buy more than one or two at a time at a price of one shilling each. Not so with plaster (of) Paris—a twenty-ton shipment of this vital building material, sold in half-ton lots, was quickly expended, perhaps because it was also popular as a fertilizer.

When William who directed the Norwalk enterprises wished to replenish stock he requested his brother Buckingham, the firm's procurement, sales, and shipping agent in New York City, to make purchases and forward them to Norwalk. In October, 1808, for example, he advised Buckingham to buy twenty or twenty-four yards of scarlet cloth, noting that "it would sell as no one Else has any."[11] Orders to buy iron, a French grammar book, bottles of strong porter, or red and black feathers were interspersed occasionally with family concerns. A request to purchase "200 Good Bricks for an oven" was accompanied by the advice, "I think you had better come home . . . Especially if the yellow fever Rages as we have heard this day it does very much in New York."[12] But William also dispensed hardheaded business counsel. He recommended that Buckingham dispose of a shipment of corn and cautioned, "You may Sell for credit but be very Careful that the man you Sell to is good and Safe."[13]

In the days before formal banking institutions were chartered the Lockwoods acted as local bankers. You could, as David Selleck did, borrow twenty pounds cash "for a few days" at two pounds interest. Borrowers like Robert Cameron, a leather tanner, often paid off their loans in curried skins and tanned hides which the Lockwoods had no difficulty selling. E. Lockwood and Sons were also bookkeepers for the Norwalk First Society, regularly paying Ben Negro $2.33 every three months for ringing the church bell. They also supplied the wine used in church services. Acting in a similar capacity for the Norwalk School Society the firm collected tuition payments and after 1820 invested surplus school funds in shares of Bank of America and Globe Insurance and in United States Stock through their New York brokers.

A.F. McNeil, who regularly subscribed to New

Holy Bible), to replace the *Enterprise,* a vessel that drew too much water. Journal of Alfred Seely, Rowayton, Document No. 19, Sloops, Trade. Library Archives, Pinkney Collection. Rowayton Historical Society, Rowayton.

14 Tea rather than coffee was the favorite drink of the period and the store carried several varieties, including Louisberg, Soushong, and Gunpowder, a strong tea with a harsh metallic taste. Kirseymire and callimanco were only two of many varieties of cloth used at the time. Palm sope was a gentle bar soap made from palm oil; a riddle was a sieve. Pigtail tobacco was a rope of chewing tobacco. The most common alcoholic beverage was still rum, but Geneva or gin was gaining in popularity. In the early nineteenth century the cultured and affluent preferred sherry.

York and Wilmington, Delaware, newspapers, and Enoch Scribner, an avid reader of the *Spectator,* received their copies through the delivery service offered by the Lockwoods. Although post riders made regular stops in Norwalk businessmen found it quicker and safer to have their mail sent via the Lockwoods. Since the mail pouch was carried on one of the firm's ships on its regular run to New York the postage for a New York bound letter was only ten cents although postage to New Haven, a less frequent port of call, was fifty-six cents.

Between 1789 and 1820 Eliphalet, William, and Buckingham St. John Lockwood were owners or part-owners of at least twelve sloops and two schooners[14] which churned through the waters to Boston, New York, Charleston, and Savannah and up the Hudson River to Albany and Troy. The sleek *Huntress* carried tubs of butter, wheels of cheese, and barrels of preserved beef from Norwalk's rich hinterland to New York City and the sloop *Vermont* found a ready market for bushels of oats and rye and sacks of goose feathers in Boston. Captains Joshua Boulton and Stephen Jane were entrusted with the company ships plying the West Indian routes. These master seamen had full responsibility for disposing of Norwalk products in the Indies, loading quantities of rum and sugar, clearing customs and paying duties, and delivering the profitable cargo to the Lockwood wharf in Norwalk. Lockwood ships were occasionally chartered to local maritime men. In 1830 for example Captain Daniel James chartered the sloop *Eagle* for twenty dollars a month with any additional costs that he might incur, since "he is to Repair her and keep her in Repair at his own Expence & the Owners to be at no expence whatever,"—a good way for the Lockwoods to utilize their older ships and not a poor arrangement for a competent mariner.

The rolling and slitting mill located between the Norwalk River and the Danbury-Norwalk Turnpike near the present Glover Avenue was unique among all the Lockwood enterprises. Only a handful of such mills existed in the United States in the late eighteenth century.[15] The Lockwoods were probably able to buy in at a bargain price for the slitting mill had originally been the brainchild of two local men, Jacob Jennings and Nathaniel Den-

15 Benjamin French, *History of the Rise and Progress of the Iron Trade of the United States, from 1621 to 1857* (New York, 1858), 18, indicates that in 1810 there were thirty-four slitting mills in the entire United States.

man, who had grandiosely planned to combine manufacturing sheeted tin and linseed oil with iron slitting. They ran out of money in 1791.[16] Jennings managed to find another partner but the venture was still short of working capital and they had to sell shares in the enterprise. The Lockwoods almost bypassed this venture when William Lockwood turned down an offer of a share. Buckingham was chagrined that his ordinarily astute brother had overlooked an opportunity where "there will be no risqe [sic] equal to the profits that may arise" and informed William that a slitting mill could yield a clear profit of from five to six percent a ton the season 'round. Although concerned that William might tell him off "plump and plain" Buckingham recommended they buy as large a share as they could, "1/2 or 3/4 or 4/4." Buckingham prevailed and buy they did.

At a rolling mill the highest grade iron ore, imported crude from Sweden, Norway, or Russia and forged into malleable iron (often called "Bloom") at an American bloomery was brought to red heat over wood fires[17] and converted into sheets, plates, bars, hoops, and rods. Normally the rolled iron was then sent to a slitting mill often many miles distant where it was cut or stamped into nails, hoes, or leaf springs. The Lockwoods cleverly consolidated the two processes at one mill and were able to offer finished products at competitive prices. Esteemed New York firms such as Abel and Dunscomb, and Blackwell and McFarlan, often sent bundles of horse rods and plates to the Norwalk mill on Lockwood ships together with patterns and specifications for cutting them into the varieties of nails needed for shingles, clapboards, and lathing.[15]

This highly specialized operation was supervised by Lemuel Glover, a yeoman who owned property south of the mill. Glover received "half of what the mill has cleared" as salary, a handsome sum that amounted to as much as seven hundred dollars in a ten-month period.[18] Forgemen, many of whom lived within walking distance of the mill in the Winnipauk section of town, were paid a daily wage averaging five pounds a month although John Glover, Lemuel's father and a skilled ironworker in his own right, earned the respectable sum of a dollar a day. Single men received a salary and were boarded in the mill house at the Lockwood sawmill.

The Lockwoods' unerring ability to undertake successful ventures, coinciding as it did with seemingly boundless opportunities in a vigorously ex-

*Buckingham St. John Lockwood.
Collection of Lockwood House Museum.*

panding nation, led to handsome profits. Land in Vermont, Simapaug Turnpike stock and, after the incorporation of banks in Connecticut, shares in such area institutions as Fairfield County Bank, Stamford Bank, and Connecticut Bank were all part of the family portfolio. The New York brokerage

---

16 As a last resort they petitioned the Assembly for permission to hold a lottery to raise £600. They were refused. They made a well-reasoned appeal, pointing out in their petition that the project would "employ numbers of poor people who are daily emigrating from the State for want of work." Jennings and Denman were ahead of their time, for manufacturing sheeted tin, according to their petition, had never been attempted in the United States. Connecticut Archives, Series 2, Industry, 1747-1820, Manufactures, Mines and Mining, II, 142.

17 The wood needed for this process was cut on the Middlebrooks' property on the west bank of the river. Later coal brought to Norwalk on the Lockwood ships replaced wood.

18 A reconciliation in the Slitting Mill Account Book, 67, shows that between December 10, 1822, and October, 1823, the debit was $2,902.82 and the credit was $4,268.72. Glover got half the difference, $1,365.90, or approximately $700.

firm of Benjamin DeForest and Company, advising against highly speculative railroad stock, steered family investments into stock in conservative but fiscally-sound financial institutions in New York City. In company with those numerous businessmen who confidently invested in new American enterprises in the 1830s and 1840s, the Lockwoods helped to provide the capital that

had come to Norwalk by way of Nova Scotia and Quebec, where he had served as a journeyman tanner, he was licensed to practice "the Art, Trade and Mistery [sic] of Tanning Leather" by the Fairfield County Court in 1802.[16] Business flourished as he sold his product to a growing number of local shoe and boot makers. By 1815 the wooden building in which he tanned sole leather, made bootlegs, and

Norwalk potters . . . circa 1860 / Courtesy, Estate of Miss Mabel Thatcher.

America needed to become a significant commercial and industrial force.

Few businessmen in early nineteenth century Norwalk matched the mettle and stature of the Lockwoods but other industrious entrepreneurs supplied equally useful goods and services to local customers and jobs to local workmen. Robert Cameron is typical of this group. A Scotsman who

curried calfskins was licensed as a manufactory.

Algernon E. Beard on the other hand was a herald of a new type of American businessman. He is believed to have come to Norwalk from Massachusetts[17] and became a wholesale distributor of shoes which he purchased from independent local craftsmen. His agents made selling trips along the Atlantic seacoast from Boston to Richmond, Virginia, often selling as many as 646 pairs of shoes to one account in a three-month period.[18] This modest man, who took time to note in his diary that he "set a hen" and "went in [the] afternoon to help M. Hanford rais [sic] a barn," carved out a dominant place for himself in local economic circles. Unlike the Lockwoods who had broadened their financial scope, Beard reinvested his considerable profits in Norwalk undertakings.

One of the most important industries in Norwalk during the early nineteenth century was pottery-making with as many as five potteries at one time

mand as oystermen rushed to satisfy the seemingly insatiable appetite for that bivalve.

One of the earliest potteries was built on the Samuel Keeler property at the head of the harbor some time after 1781, when he acquired the property, and 1797, when he disposed of it to Joseph Meeker and Ephraim Curtis. Meeker and Curtis, potters who already owned an establishment at Rusco's Creek in Old Well, used the existing kiln on the Keeler property for "burning earthenware." Another early Old Well potter was Asa Hoyt who is known to have been in business as early as 1793. In

Mr. and Mrs. Asa E. Smith / Courtesy of Mrs. Robert Levers.

producing such familiar household articles as pie plates, milkpans, and pitchers, along with commercial ware.[19] Monkey jugs, ceramic water coolers that sold particularly well in the West Indies and were indispensable to the whalers of New Bedford, New London, and Sag Harbor, were fast-selling commercial ware items. Sag Harbor whalers briskly bought up one entire fifty-five ton lot of monkey jugs as soon as the shipment arrived from Norwalk. Oyster jars, commercial containers made in quarter, half, and one-gallon sizes, were in great de-

1796 Hoyt sold the potter house to Absalom Day who had come to work for Hoyt some three years earlier. Hoyt relocated about one and one-half miles south of Old Well along Village Creek, an ideal location for unloading potter's clay. He suffered such reverses during the War of 1812 that he never recovered his losses and a few years later offered the property for sale.

Absalom Day, an itinerant Methodist minister, founder of Norwalk's first Methodist church, farmer, and master potter, preferred to work with

his native New Jersey clays and to fire his ware with resinous Virginia pinewood. He not only peddled his ware along the coast, presumably preaching as he moved from town to town, but also distributed his pottery through local merchants. In 1831 Day deeded his land and business to his two sons but it was not long before one son quitclaimed his interest. Noah Day, Absalom's favorite son, continued the business and for a while went into partnership with his cousin Asa E. Smith who in 1825 had established his own pottery on the property formerly owned by Meeker and Curtis.

They managed to maintain a respectable wholesale and retail business despite competition from the Quintard Pottery, a manufacturer of domestic ware and door knobs run by the partnership of James Quintard and Henry Chichester, and the Gregory Pottery on Half Mile Isle where John Gregory produced earthen and stoneware. Smith and Day were incompatible in other respects, however, and the partnership abruptly dissolved after Smith was arrested in New York City, held responsible for his partner's personal debts under the law of the time.

Smith continued to manufacture pottery, taking

Residences of Asa E. and Asa Smith from an 1858 wall map / Collection of the Norwalk Historical Society

The partnership of the two cousins Smith and Day[19] brought together two master craftsmen who produced work so superior that they won an award at the American Institute Annual Fair in 1844.

19 Asa Smith served his apprenticeship under Absalom Day. Gregory and Quintard probably learned their trade from Day as well. Not all apprentices were willing students, however. On at least one occasion Day advertised a 1c reward for information about Jason Merrills, a runaway apprentice. Watkins, *Early New England Potters and Their Wares*, 200, points out that Merrills must have been apprehended since he was identified in a group picture of Norwalk potters taken years later.

his oldest son Theodore into the firm and placing him in charge of the New York City warehouse at Peck Slip, one of the city's busiest wharves. Later when Asa's two younger sons, "Young" Asa and Howard, joined the firm its name was changed to A.E. Smith and Sons. This commercial operation— the largest in the region—employed as many as fifty men to manufacture yellow ware and Rockingham ware as well as the stoneware and brown earthenware that were so popular in the southern and western markets. Smith pottery was distinguished by charming slip decorations of crude designs, triple wavy lines or phrases like "Mary's Dish," "Mince-meat Pie," and "Oysters and Clams," which some potter, perhaps one named Chichester marked in Spencerian-style handwriting.[20]

Norwalk's fifth pottery was a button manufactory. L.D. Wheeler in partnership with Dr. Asa Hill, a successful Norwalk dentist, specialized in brown clay or mottled glaze buttons made either in the flat four-hole style or fitted out with metal shanks. The potters were a closely-knit fraternity and it is not surprising that Enoch Wood, a Bennington potter who came to work for Wheeler, married his daughter and bought half interest in the business and operated it in partnership with his brother-in-law.[21]

Redware plate believed to have been made in Norwalk to commemorate General Lafayette's visit in 1825 / Courtesy, Estate of Miss Mabel Thatcher.

Until fire destroyed his plant Wood used mixed clays to produce "mineral" knobs that were unique among New England potters.[22]

In 1808 during Jefferson's embargo Republicanism had been halted but only temporarily. Continually pushing for a constitutional convention the various anti-Federalist or Republican groups gathered strength and under the umbrella of the Toleration Party won a majority in the Assembly in the May 1818 election. The stage was set for a state constitutional convention.

Towns had already begun to pass resolutions instructing their delegates to work in the Assembly for a new constitution. Norwalk was somewhat behind other towns in passing such a resolution but in mid-March the town, "deeming it highly important that the power and authority of the Government . . . should be distinctly difined [sic]," instructed its representatives to support a constitution[23] which was adopted by the voters of the state in October. A new era had begun for Connecticut's citizens.

[20] With introduction of glass bottles and jars and metal housewares, the Smith pottery gradually became insolvent. In 1888 it sold out to a group of local merchants who were eager to keep the potters employed. Renamed Norwalk Pottery Company and managed by "Young" Asa Smith it continued in business for a number of years.

[21] Enoch Wood, a descendant of the renowned Wood family of potters in Staffordshire, England, was a skilled mould-maker. He had been named after his great-granduncle Enoch Wood who is sometimes called "The Father of English Pottery." See John Spargo, *The Potters and Potteries of Bennington* (Southampton, New York, 1926), 234-235.

[22] Both buttons and knobs, today rare collector's items, may be viewed at the Connecticut State Library.

[23] At the constitutional convention John Eversley and Moses Gregory represented the town.

8

BY LAND AND BY SEA

*Being
an Account of
Norwalk During the Era
of Turnpikes and Steamboats*

HE JOURNAL of a young Scotsman fleeing one of New York City's recurrent yellow fever epidemics in August, 1822, provides a rare description of Norwalk at that date. The young man's preconceived notions may have contributed to a somewhat unflattering view of the town, for he had been warned about Connecticut Yankees who were sharpers and swindlers, and "capable of [the] most mean and contemptible shifts and tricks, for the sake of accumulating money." As his sloop docked in Norwalk he thought that now "every face looked sharper and every eye rolled more obliquely," and he saw the town as an "unpleasant, crooked and confined-looking place." Nevertheless he must have heard about Norwalk's salubrious reputation for he felt himself free of fear of contagion and set off through the countryside, passing through balmy buckwheat fields and abundant apple and peach orchards. He thought the fields only tolerably well-cultivated but attributed this to a deficiency in the soil rather than to careless husbandry.

As night drew near he sought lodging but was directed from one house to another. No one "appeared kind" probably because Norwalkers too feared yellow fever. At last a tanner consented to put him up for the night. All evening the old fellow talked endlessly of his skill, his superb manufactory, and the high prices he could command for his leather products, while out of the corner of his eye the yawning visitor observed the tanner's plump young wife as she "winked and blinked" with a young male boarder. The following morning the

traveler decided to have a look at the tanning establishment. He found:

. . . one lime hole and four old bark pits, surrounded with rubbish and grass, and a hut with some bark in it, which a black boy was chopping small with a knife, for the tannery. I could not help smiling as the Prince of Tanners . . . in his ox hide habiliments . . . was bustling about in his antediluvian "factory."[1]

Had the Scot taken a more careful look at the town he could easily have found a number of more modern and efficient manufactories than the miserable tannery but it is true that, at the time, most Norwalk establishments still operated on a small scale. At this date, some twenty years prior to general use of coal for energy, Norwalk lacked the one essential for industrial development: reliable water power. The Norwalk River was a far cry from the powerful Connecticut River which, along one stretch, dropped sixty feet within a single mile. There were of course small waterfalls and places where the stream could be dammed. The terrain rose so gently, however, that in winter when the river was frozen over, children were able to skate from a dam near today's Belden Avenue and Forest Street upriver for almost a mile on its flat surface. Furthermore in a dry summer the Norwalk River, fed by only a few small brooks, fell too low to be useful. The town, therefore, did not attract the great new textile factories that were beginning to make fortunes for their owners and dingy mill towns out of peaceful New England villages. Those

New Arrangement...Commencing on Monday, August 4th, 1845.

FOR

RIDGEFIELD,
WILTON & NORWALK.

Fare through $1,00

The Old Line of Stages will leave Ridgebury every

MONDAY, THURSDAY & SATURDAY

AT HALF-PAST TWO O'CLK. A.M.,

And RIDGEFIELD at FOUR o'clock, passing through WILTON and arriving in NORWALK in time for Passengers to take the Steamboat for New-York.

Returning, leave Norwalk on the same days, on the arrival of the boat from New-York.

AUGUST, 1845.

D. HUNT, Proprietor.

factories needed reliable water power for their spindles and looms.

A comparison of Norwalk with nearby towns indicates that it was developing in similar fashion to its neighbors.

COMMERCE AND INDUSTRY
SOUTHWEST FAIRFIELD COUNTY SHORE TOWNS[2]

Type of Business	Fairfield	Stamford	Greenwich	Stratford*	Norwalk
Grain Mills	9	29	9	3	5
Woolen Factories			1		1
Slitting and Rolling Mills					1
Cotton Factories	1		2		2**
Fulling Mills	2	2	2		3
Tanneries	5	2	4	2	2
Carding Machines			4	2	2	4
Tinware Factories					1
Paper Mills				1	
Mercantile Stores	25	14	9	23	16

*Includes Bridgeport
**One large factory

Visitors traveling by stagecoach along the Boston Post Road could obtain a much better view of the town than the Scotsman was able to do. Under ideal travel conditions a Boston-bound coach leaving New York City in the morning could reach Norwalk by nightfall. After an early morning departure from the Bowery, the horse-drawn, spring-mounted open box wagon would lurch northward along the rutted city streets and lumber through the pleasant Westchester countryside toward the Connecticut border. At the Byram River passengers had to transfer to the "state Waggon" owned by William Maltbie Betts of Norwalk who held the franchise for transporting passengers on the Post Road between the western boundary of the state and Stratford Ferry. As the vehicle swayed and bumped over the wretched road, driver and passengers were in constant danger of being pitched from the four backless wooden benches that provided seating. A canvas stretched over the top of the wagon, with leather and woolen side flaps that could be rolled down in inclement weather, offered little protection from sun, rain, wind, or snow. Such was the plight of the traveler who chose to journey by land in the late eighteenth century when the stage coach was in its infancy.

In New England during the half-century following, stage coach became the most common type of travel, a development that owed much of its im-

petus to establishment of a federal postal system.[1] Norwalk was designated one of the nine U.S. Post Offices in Connecticut, all located on the New York-Boston highway, the familiar Boston Post Road, which was part of the Great Atlantic Road that connected Wiscasset, Maine, and Savannah, Georgia. Federal contracts to carry mail along the post roads were powerful incentives for new stage coach companies. To expedite delivery Congress ordered the states to repair bridges and post roads, a directive Connecticut's General Assembly promptly passed on to the selectmen of towns along these routes, together with its own enactment forbidding any gate or fence to be erected or remain standing across the Public Post Road.

After 1827 as the Concord coach began to replace open box wagons the assurance of a more comfortable ride induced greater numbers of Americans to indulge in the already well-established custom of long visits with relatives who had moved to distant parts. Stage coaching expanded to meet the demands of this already-mobile population.

As the stage made its way across western Connecticut passengers could mark their progress by the red sandstone milestones that towns erected on post roads and other heavily traveled routes by order of the General Assembly.[3] Spying marker 49 the well-seasoned traveler knew he was fast approaching Norwalk. Just beyond the marker the stage crossed over the Five Mile River on a wooden bridge built in 1805 after the town had appropriated a small portion of that district's highway tax and provided the wood for its construction. Once across the river, at the intersection with the road to Roton Point, the traveler could spot Stephen Raymond's store, conveniently located for residents of Five Mile River. Soon the stage began a precipitous descent to the center of Norwalk. Past Captain Raymond's and the Hoyt property where the town's first flax manufactory had stood, the stage bounced down the hill to the intersection of the Post Road and the main road to Old Well.

At this intersection a sharp-eyed passenger peering off toward Old Well might catch a glimpse of Quintard's Inn. Required by law to have a "compleat sign" bearing the name of the landlord, James Quintard is reputed to have added this message:

1 Although post riders had carried mail from New York City to Boston as early as 1673, the new American government attached paramount importance to a unified postal system.

"Norwalk Bridge in 1856" by G.R. Cowles.

Since man to man is so unjust,
You cannot tell what man to trust,
I've trusted many to my sorrow,
So pay today and trust tomorrow.[4]

As the stage trundled into Norwalk's main thoroughfare on the west side of the Norwalk River it passed Wentworth's, a popular Norwalk tavern—located as so many inns and taverns along the Post Road—at a milestone marker. At marker 51 the coach stopped at Reed's, a house of entertainment that was also a stop for mail coaches.[2] While the mail pouches were being transferred and fresh horses hitched to the coach, weary passengers could rest, dine, or fortify themselves for the trip ahead with hot negus, buttered flip, or a tumbler of cherry cordial.[3]

Crossing the Great Bridge over the Norwalk River at the head of the harbor was enough to make even the most courageous traveler catch his breath. This narrow, rickety wooden structure dangling high above the river was not improved in any substantial fashion until the 1850s. Ordered by the state to repair bridges on the Post Road, Norwalk decided to build a durable stone bridge and to raise the necessary funds by lottery. But when a study of the cost of a stone bridge showed that the five hundred pounds they hoped to raise would be insufficient the lottery was canceled. The new bridge, about thirty feet long and rising fifty feet above the water, was once again built of wood.[4]

The Great Bridge was literally and figuratively the hub of Norwalk proper. Near the bridge the Post Road curved into a sweeping S in order to make the crossing at a more narrow point of the river. East of the river the road expanded into Lockwood Square, known in the nineteenth century as St. John Place. In the vicinity of the Great Bridge several hostelries competed for the favor of travelers. As coach travel became more customary, old-fashioned taverns and inns expanded in size, service, and comfort, and were called hotels. By the

2 A house of entertainment was generally an inn or public house that did not provide lodging.

3 Negus was a popular drink of the time, made of wine, water, sugar, nutmeg, and lemon. Flip was a hot drink made of beer, spirits, and sugar, to which a dollop of butter was added.

4 Although need for a sturdy span over the Norwalk River at Wall Street had been discussed at countless town meetings during the colonial era, an adequate bridge had never been erected. The bridge, such as it was, was destroyed in Tryon's raid and its replacement built immediately after the war was washed out twice by floods.

1840s Norwalk had two very adequate hotels. West of the bridge on today's River Street stood the Norwalk Hotel. East of the bridge Hezekiah Whitlock's old tavern, built in 1775 and for some reason spared by Tryon, had added rooms in every direction and taken the name Connecticut Hotel.[5] The three-story Greek columns that adorned both buildings gave distinction to the commercial area.

After the stage driver had guided the team carefully across the bridge he urged the horses up State Street (Mill Hill) past the centrally-located signpost where public notices of land and goods taken for nonpayment of taxes were posted. Passengers not preoccupied with regaining their composure after the perilous river crossing could admire the churches around the green. A new St. Paul's built in the 1840s with an ornate roof and lancet windows was a charming illustration of the ability of local carpenters to express Gothic details in wood. Opposite St. Paul's stood the First Congregational Church₅ and on the east side of the green stood the Greek Revival edifice of the Baptists. Although surrounded by the homes of many of Norwalk's elite the green was poorly cared for. Grazing cows were evidence that town officials still regarded it as suitable for its original purpose, a pasture. Not until 1855 did the town give a committee authority to enclose the green to keep cattle out, to grade the sidewalks, and to plant trees—all at the committee members' own expense.

At the far end of the common the stage turned right and made its way past the extensive Lockwood and Platt properties. At milestone 54 the wagon passed the old Marvin's Inn which George Washington had noted was "not a good house . . . [although] the people of it were disposed to do all they could to accommodate me."[6] Passing the two roads to Wilton and milestone 55 the stage lumbered on toward the Saugatuck River and Norwalk's eastern boundary.

From colonial times the town had only fulfilled halfheartedly its obligations for road construction and maintenance. Unless a particular road was commercially important the town sloughed off its obligations. As trade with Ridgefield increased the two towns jointly agreed to construct a highway but a similar project with Wilton was not undertaken until its residents brought action against Norwalk in Fairfield County Court. Even under pressure from

₅ This church burned and the congregationalists built the next church on Park Avenue in 1849.

all quarters Norwalk never seemed to work out a plan for providing decent in-town roads and inter-town highways. Under one early nineteenth century policy the town was divided into eight districts, each district maintaining its own roads out of its portion of highway taxes. This did little to comfort the traveler in sparsely-settled districts. In similar fashion when residents complained about highways leading to other towns Norwalk often tried to squirm out of its responsibility. After Samuel Sherwood, Esquire, won a suit in County Court for a bridge and better maintenance on the road to New Canaan the town quibbled over the court's decree, claiming that Middlesex should share in the cost since its inhabitants also used this road. Again, little was done. Dusty or mud-mired roads remained the rule.

NORWALK HOTEL.
D. Stephenson.

Besieged by strident demands for better roads and bridges, the towns gave their support to the turnpike movement, a post-Revolutionary War phenomenon that flourished throughout New England for four decades. One of Connecticut's earliest turnpikes was operated by the Norwalk and Danbury Turnpike Company incorporated by the legislature as a joint stock company in 1795. The company was granted the sole right to repair, maintain, and collect tolls on the "Great Road" that ran from Belden's Bridge in Norwalk through Redding to the SemiPog Brook in Danbury. Capitalized at $2,833 with Eliphalet Lockwood and Timothy Taylor, a Danbury man, as major stockholders the Norwalk and Danbury Turnpike Company rebuilt the eighteen-mile road at a cost of $129 per mile.[7]

All persons using this turnpike except neighborhood farmers and those en route to funerals and Society or town meetings had to pay a toll ranging from twenty-five cents for a four-wheeled carriage down to one cent for each sheep or hog.

Turnpike companies were granted franchises for as long as it took to realize the original investment with twelve percent annual interest. Men of means scrambled to invest in enterprises with such high dividends. In 1829 the Newtown and Norwalk Company began to operate a turnpike extending from the Great Bridge in Norwalk to the foot of Main Street in Newtown. Even the venerable Bos-

mere eight percent. Costly repairs, inhospitable terrain, recalcitrant toll collectors, and canny "shunpikers" presented insurmountable problems to the turnpike companies. Many lost money. Eventually the roads reverted to the towns through which they ran. Norwalk assumed its portion of the D&N Turnpike from the Great Bridge to the Wilton line, voting in 1848 to assume costs of repair not to exceed fifty dollars per year. In 1851 the Newtown road, still known today as the Newtown Turnpike, passed into the hands of the towns through which it ran.

An attempt to set up a turnpike through South

The Green.

ton Post Road was not immune from the clutches of turnpike speculators. However, a committee appointed by the Assembly in 1795 to determine feasibility of making it a privately franchised operation recommended that the road remain an open public highway with cost of maintenance to be borne by the towns.

While turnpike fever raged speculators who dreamed of returns as high as twenty-four percent clamored for franchises. But the golden promise did not materialize; the average yield for the Norwalk and Danbury for the years 1795-1802 was a

Norwalk gives insight into the divisive brand of small-town politics that was just beginning to plague Norwalk and would eventually lead to a split between the uptown and downtown communities. When Samuel Gibbs applied for permission to set out a turnpike on a "lower route" from Fairfield to Stamford through Old Well, Norwalk town authorities found all kinds of reasons to oppose the plan. Opponents declared that it would obstruct navigation of the lower Norwalk harbor, injure commercial and agricultural interests, divert travel from a populated area to an unsettled part of town, and be out of the way of the seat of business and correspondence. The petition was emphatically denied and a project that would have added substantially to the whole town's economy was aborted by the uptown interests.

Bypassed, ignored—or worse, scurrilously belittled—by pompous uptown residents, South Norwalk flourished nonetheless. In the 1830s the former Old Well[6] boasted three potteries, a half dozen hat factories, a carriage manufactory, and many modest enterprises including a smithy and a stone-cutting shop.[8]

South Norwalk owed its rapid economic growth

St. Paul's Episcopal Church.

at this time to its superior location along the deeper portion of the Norwalk River. Small wharves and warehouses dotted the shoreline and ships of all sizes from tiny sharpies to bulky steamboats clogged the waters of the lower harbor. The hub of this bustling port was Quintard's Wharf at the foot of Marshall Street. Commercial buildings clustered on both sides of upper Marshall Street and spilled over into nearby Ann Street with its jumble of small

6 The names Old Well and South Norwalk were used interchangeably although by 1840 South Norwalk seems to have been the more common designation.

shops and private dwellings. Before too many years had passed South Norwalk had become the principal port surpassing Norwalk Borough which could accommodate only "vessels of light drought."[9]

Steamboats had begun to ply the waters of the Sound in 1815 but Connecticut companies were effectively barred from engaging in this new commerce for a number of years. Two wily New York businessmen, Robert Fulton and Robert Livingston, enjoyed a monopoly that prevented Connecticut craft from steaming into New York State waters. Only after Chief Justice John Marshall handed down a stunning decision in the case of *Gibbons* vs. *Ogden* was the way opened for Connecticut steamboat companies to trade legally with New York City.

Practical South Norwalk investors took advantage of this decision to build Steam-Boat Landing on Water Street just a stone's throw north of Washington Street. To satisfy residents of outlying areas who wished to travel to New York City by steamboat the Danbury Stage extended its route to Steam-Boat Landing and offered a combination ticket. Waiting passengers could tarry at Ward Chichester's Steam-Boat Hotel, conveniently located within a few rods of the landing.[10]

One of the earliest local entries into the steamboat race was the Norwalk and New York Steam Boat Association, incorporated in 1824 as a common carrier of goods and passengers between Norwalk and the West River, New York City.[11] The company operated the *John Marshall,* a fully-equipped sidewheeler with multiple decks, fittingly named for the man who had made possible Connecticut's access to New York waters. This company was plagued by losses of cargo in transit and by such low cash reserves that in 1827 Sheriff Charles Isaacs attached two long boats and one stove from the ship itself to satisfy a plaintiff's claim for muskrat skins lost in transit between New York City and one of Norwalk's hat factories.

More serious than conventional losses of cargo was the competition that developed between rival companies. By 1825 sixteen to twenty steamboats puffed in and out of Norwalk, docking at Steam-Boat Landing or at the uptown landing near the Great Bridge. Waiting passengers and curious townspeople often congregated on the porches of the Mansion House to indulge in the popular pastime of cheering for a neatly executed docking at

NORWALK

*an historical
account*

90

the uptown wharf.₇ From this vantage point sight-seers could watch the night boat, the *Citizen,* depart for New York City, giving fair competition to the *Fairfield* which left at 6 A.M. and the *Nimrod* which sailed at 1 P.M.

Safety, low prices and speed were essential if a steamboat company hoped to remain competitive. When business dropped off after a rash of boiler explosions some companies refitted their ships with copper boilers and advertised them as the safest on the Sound. Others competed by slashing prices. A one-way passage between Norwalk and New York City fell from twenty-five cents to twelve-and-a-half cents. Occasionally rival competition took owners to the law courts. Commodore Cornelius Vanderbilt, whose boats docked at Old Well, not only engaged in ruthless price competition but enraged local men of the waters by his "impudent way of crowding into and holding the regular boats' dock against the

---

7 Known as the Mansion House in 1830 it is shown as the
Stevens Hotel on Hall's 1847 map. Selleck, *Norwalk,* refers
to it as the Arnold House at a later period.

protest of its [sic] owners." The court found for the local owners and nightly Sheriff Isaacs went down to Old Well to serve a writ of arrest on the Commodore, who conveniently never came to Norwalk.

Every effort was made to change the design of the clumsy sidewheelers to increase their speed. In steamboating's finest hour a streamlined iron steamboat like the *Pegasus,* 225 feet long and with an astounding capacity for 1,830 passengers, could make the trip from Pier 4, North River, New York City, to the landing at Wilson's Point, Norwalk, in two hours and thirty-eight minutes with only thirty pounds of steam in her boilers.

Travel by steamboat introduced an element of danger considerably beyond that encountered by sailing vessels. For one thing steamboats were less maneuverable than the latter and therefore more easily ran aground. Such a mishap was minor in comparison to the great disaster that befell passengers on the *Lexington.* Bound for Stonington, Connecticut, on January 14, 1849, and carrying 144 passengers, twenty-five crew and large quantities of baled cotton, the *Lexington* caught fire in the Sound, midpoint between Eaton's Neck, Long Island, and Sheffield Island. The family of Gershom Burr Smith, living on Sheffield Island, watched the burning ship in horror but was unable to help because in the bitter -18° weather Smith's ice-locked boats could not be dislodged from their moorings. There were only fourteen survivors, those who had had the wit to jump on the floating bales of cotton and tenaciously cling to the floating lifelines until they drifted ashore or were picked up by passing sloops.[12]

In contrast to this overwhelming disaster the sinking of the New York-Norwalk steamer *Harlem* while docked in South Norwalk borders on the absurd. Carelessly moored, the ship sank to the harbor floor when water flooded her ash chute on the rising tide. Unable to aid herself, the *Harlem* was pumped out

Southern view of Norwalk Town House.

and raised with help from the nearby steamship *City of Norwalk* and was able to steam off to New York at noon the same day. But the incident left bad feelings for the *Harlem's* request to the local fire company for help in pumping out the water had been denied. The firemen's *Phoenix* steamer had been polished and readied for a parade and fire officials were reluctant to get it dirty![13]

The almost do-nothing attitude of town officials toward maintaining roads, bridges, and public buildings was nowhere better illustrated than in the shameful condition of the Town House on Mill Hill. Rebuilt after the war, it had been allowed to become so dilapidated that in 1835 some anonymous "regulators" took it upon themselves to tear it down one dark night, leaving the debris in a prominent spot

by the roadside. The town then erected a handsome red brick Town House but again allowed it to fall into such disrepair that visitors often wondered at its disgraceful appearance.[8]

Ever since the early part of the century, however, individual householders had been trying to beautify the town. New Haven had set the pace in city beautification in southwestern Connecticut by embarking upon a tree-planting program in the 1790s. Norwalk, more parsimonious or simply more shortsighted, undertook no such program and allowed individual property owners to set out trees on the "publick highway against their own land," only if they themselves carefully maintained the plantings. Many elms and maples were set out and as the years passed they grew to lofty heights, shading and enhancing roadways throughout the town.

After 1820 Americans became intrigued with several new vogues in architecture. Fashionable Norwalkers followed these trends and built Gothic cottages whose roofs and verandahs were or-

8 *Ballou's Pictorial* (November 24, 1855). The actual perpetrators of the Town House destruction are still shrouded in mystery. It is believed that a certain "Ensign Andrews" was the major culprit.

The Lawrence M. Stevens residence, Norwalk's most notable Gothic Revival house.

namented with lacy scrolls of fantastic design; bell-towered Italianate villas; and houses with colonnaded porticos resembling Greek temples.[9]

The grandest of the Greek Revival houses was "Rockcliffe," the house Algernon Beard built on a rocky eminence along Flax Hill in 1842, raising the central part of the structure in the old-fashioned way with the help of neighbors. Four massive Ionic columns extending two full stories dominated the facade with a pediment extending another story. Visitors reached "Rockcliffe" by way of an impressive circular driveway or by a stiff climb up a series of steps chiseled from heavy granite blocks. For over a century Beard's Greek temple stood guard above South Norwalk.[10]

William Kellogg James, an importer who "through close and laborious application and sharp practice of economy" was in the process of amassing a fortune, built a Greek Revival mansion on Wall Street in 1840. Even more splendid in its furnishings and the details of its interior than Algernon Beard's temple, the spacious James mansion contained exquisite Chinese antiques, rare Wedgwood bowls and vases, eighteenth century Spode, magnificent silverware, and handsome Duncan Phyfe furniture. It well merited New York's Metropolitan Museum as the final resting place of its *objets d'art.*[11]

Although this period has been called the Age of Affluence, as indeed it was for a dozen or so families, most Norwalkers did not share the affluent life. What they did share were the benefits of many new inventions and gadgets that made life more comfortable and chores less time-consuming. The wood-burning kitchen stove, a great advance over the fireplace, was now in common use. A housewife's work was further lightened by gas cook stoves which, as advertised in the local paper, could heat a "Smoothing Iron, Cook a Steak, Stew Oysters, and Boil . . . Coffee in FIVE MINUTES."

In a sense this period provided the best of two worlds: while enjoying the benefits of the new technology people in small towns still retained their farm heritage. Most families kept at least one cow, a few chickens, even some pigs and sheep as well as the horse needed for transportation. When William and Julia (Seeley) Tristram set up housekeeping in Five Mile River in 1853 their very first household

9 Almost none of Norwalk's austere but gracious Federal houses remain undespoiled in the center of town although a few may be seen around France Street and some line the river side of East Avenue north of the Connecticut Turnpike. A particularly handsome Greek Revival house built in 1846 by William K. Lewis still stands on Lewis Street.

10 The Beard house was mysteriously destroyed by fire in 1963.

11 After the death of James' widow in 1910 the listing of the contents of the house bequeathed to the Metropolitan Museum filled nineteen typewritten pages. Among the items were samples and bolts of costly eighteenth and nineteenth-century fabrics. Some James furniture went to other recipients, including the New-York Historical Society and indirectly to Lockwood House Museum. See Will of Maria Philips Selleck James, 1911, LHM Archives.

The Seeley-Dibble-Pinkney House in Rowayton . . . circa 1870 / Collection of the Rowayton Historical Society

expenditures included $55 for a horse, $26 for a wagon, and $50 for a cow.[14] The young Tristrams were able to live a very comfortable life on only $583 the first year of housekeeping.

Since families could supply some of their own food even Norwalkers of moderate means were able to eat very well. Besides a variety of meats they had scallops and oysters in abundance and fish and clams for the taking. Many households maintained kitchen gardens and orchards. By the 1820s Connecticut nurseries could supply asparagus, watermelon, "cantelope," lettuce, cucumbers, several kinds of lima beans, and "sweet sugar corn."[15] Local nurserymen offered several types of fruit trees, the most common being peaches, pears, and apples. Many people grew several varieties of grapes.

An 1841 cookbook used by a Five Mile River housewife reveals that some families enjoyed rather sophisticated dishes. Its wide selection of recipes includes instructions for a most elegant aspic and also recipes for rich Tory Wafers, humble Whig muffins and for Portable Soup. This last was made with highly-seasoned beef or veal broth reduced to a thick paste, allowed to dry in the sun, and then cut into small cubes. "Whenever you wish to make a soup," the author stated, "nothing more is necessary than to put a quart of water to one of the cakes and heat it very hot."[16]

Bombarded by advertisements in the local paper Norwalkers acquired a myriad of gadgets now available to them in specialty shops and stores. Hardware stores began to compete with blacksmiths and tinsmiths; furniture stores supplanted cabinetmakers. A number of merchants catered exclusively to the ladies, offering yard goods, hats, gloves, jewelry, and other adornments. Thrifty Julia Tristram seldom purchased exotic personal articles for herself but had she wished to do so she could have found *eau de toilette*, Persian Rose and Chinese Musk Soap, curling fluid, cold cream, and Grecian Dye in profusion in Mr. Stevens' Drug Store. D'Artois' ice cream shop in South Norwalk carried nine flavors of ice cream and eleven different ices.

Itinerant portrait painters found Norwalk well worth a stop. Ezra Bisbee, a Brooklyn artist, did portraits of the William B. Lockwood family among others during his stay in town. On one visit Jesse Talbot, a leading landscapist and portraitist, painted several prominent Norwalkers, among them Dr. William Cooper Mead, rector of St. Paul's, and summer visitor LeGrand Lockwood, an investment banker. In 1842 John P. Treadwell, a New York City businessman who maintained a home on North Avenue, commissioned Charles Seely Gaylord of Gaylord's Bridge, Connecticut, to do a painting of Norwalk. The artist was delighted with the assignment, his first commission for a landscape, and he painted a charming view of the town, seen from a vantage point at a bend in the Norwalk River about a quarter of a mile east of the bridge.[17]

Excursion steamer "Americus"... circa 1870.

Connecticut people were slow to accept theatrical entertainment but Norwalkers managed to devise their own cultural activities. Many homes contained pianofortes at which women and girls played the popular melodies of Stephen Foster. A Lyceum Society organized in the early 1830s for "mental improvement" met at the Town House where members heard lectures on topics of the day or debated controversial issues. Some of the debates must have lasted well into the night for they involved such questions as: "Has the discovery of America, by the Europeans, resulted in more good than evil?" and "Is a man justifiable, who inveigles into a clandestine marriage, a minor?" Norwalk's book store kept up with current topics, stocking among its volumes *Dr. Gall's System of Phrenology* and the latest works of the Connecticut poetess, Mrs. Lydia Sigurney, and its circulating library contained volumes ranging from *Lectures on Politeness* and *Domestic Manners of Americans* to *Westward, Ho* and *Kenilworth.*

Every year in a combination of reverence and rampage the entire town gloriously celebrated the Fourth of July. The format was always about the same: a fourteen-gun salute at sunrise followed by the ringing of all the church bells. Midmorning, a procession of old soldiers, leading citizens, guests, militia, and a band marched to the Town House where prayers, a reading of the Declaration of Independence, and one or two lengthy orations were interspersed with "Hail, Columbia" and other appropriate musical selections. Fourth of July orators customarily thanked God for making America the greatest nation in the world but they also warned that the people must keep it so. "It is not enough that our political men be great, they should be good, also," the Reverend William Hayes reminded the townspeople in one typical speech. Families poured out of the Town House to enjoy games, gossip, and hearty picnic fare in the afternoon. In the evening prominent citizens attended a formal dinner that included toasts and musical entertainment. After dark, the fireworks—one expense on which the town didn't stint!—Roman Candles, Chinese Bowers, Peruvian Crosses, Firewheels, Golden Palm Trees, Italian Streamers, Rockets, Stars, and Serpents filled the nighttime sky with golden showers and thunderous explosions.[12]

But life also held many bleak, heartbreaking

Symbol of opulence... Mrs. William K. James' fan, imported from France by Tiffany & Co. about 1870. Collection of Lockwood House Museum.

The Algernon E. Beard residence, built in 1842, was Norwalk's grandest Greek Revival house.

moments. Throughout the nineteenth century the mortality rate was high. Medical practices of the day, a vast improvement over those of colonial times, left much to be desired. Sufferers turned to patent medicines (some issues of the *Gazette* are filled with ads for cure-all elixirs) or took up fads like hydropathy, which employed the internal and external use of water to treat a variety of diseases, or the Graham system which advocated a grain diet.

Norwalk had no shortage of doctors or dentists although people sometimes traveled to Bridgeport for dental care. The inventive Dr. Asa Hill devised a "plastic filling" for teeth, used by dentists throughout the nation. Hill never revealed his secret formula but the filling material may have contained some potter's clay for Hill was part-owner of the button factory. The advertisements of a Dr. Easton, "Surgeon and Mechanical Dentist," whose office was on Wall Street, reveal as much about the state of the dental art as about his skill:

> *Oh Dear Dentist how I thank you*
> *For the ease you gave my jaw;*
> *When from the socket you extracted*
> *Four double teeth without a flaw.*[18]

12 The editor noted gratefully on one occasion that although "the streets were crowded throughout the day and till a late hour of the night with a merry throng who were all hilarity and mirth [yet] there was no fighting, no brawling. No accident occurred to mar the festivity of the joyous occasion." *Norwalk Gazette,* July 11, 1838.

Children were as frequently victims of impure water or milk and incorrect medical diagnoses or treatment as they were of dread childhood diseases. The pitiful tombstone of the Remson children, George Henry, six weeks old, who died in September, 1858, and his two-year-old sister, Katie Amelia, who died only five days later, probably tells the story of one of the routine "summer ailments" wont to strike during August and September.

Nor were young adults strangers to fatal diseases. Julia Seeley Tristram's account book details page by page her husband's rapid decline only a decade after their marriage. In 1860 William may have become too ill to work for they had to borrow money even though they had drastically reduced expenses. Then came the doctors' bills—only "$.25" for the first one, but finally $12.50 for a single bill from a consulting specialist. There were payments too for paragoric and laudanum, and as William Tristram lay dying frequent purchases of whiskey, brandy, and "anodynes." On October 10, 1862, Julia duly recorded purchase of one hat ($4.50), one collar ($.90), one pair of gloves ($.60), and one coffin ($20.80).[13]

Understandably people became preoccupied with death, and funerals became elaborate and expensive. Although it had been customary in New

13 Julia Tristram continued her careful records in ever more shaky handwriting until September, 1863. She died in 1864.

England to inscribe some brief fitting phrase upon a grave marker, now lengthy poems dwelling upon the circumstances of death or a family's grief were carved into the stones. The tombstone of seven-year-old Eliza Page next to the grave of her brother Samuel, who died at the age of two, is inscribed:

A widowed mother's lovely child
Last of my earthly ties,
I place her here in certain hope
To meet her in the Skies.[19]

Americans also became more interested in the problems of the ill, indigent, and aged. Ever since the days of John Crampton the town had provided for its less fortunate members. Connecticut towns generally tried to discourage persons incapable of supporting themselves from becoming residents but each community had at least a handful of orphans, widows unable to support themselves, and aged, infirm, or indigent adults. Norwalk was no exception.

During much of the nineteenth century selectmen "bound out" orphaned children to "good families." Under the family's tutelage boys learned a useful trade and girls performed domestic chores until they reached maturity or were released by reason of marriage. Widows and indigent or aged adults able to care for themselves lived in humble dwellings provided by the town and made do as best they could with a small stipend from town funds. Less mobile unfortunates were boarded with residents; Jason Smith was paid for the support of Widow Keziah Hoyt, a town pauper. The town was never lavish in dispensing money, however, and when the poverty-stricken sisters Louisa and Polly Crawford sought funds for badly-needed repairs to their tumbledown hovel the town denied their petition. The selectmen were assiduous in ferreting out funds from other sources[14] and when Hannah Darrow, originally an inhabitant of New Canaan, became infirm and unable to support herself the town typically demanded the cost of her support from New Canaan.

Early in the nineteenth century these somewhat casual arrangements were augmented by a new institution, a house for the poor. In an unusual spirit

14 For at least thirty-five years after the Revolutionary War the selectmen worked to obtain pensions from the federal government for disabled veterans, even resolving to take matters to the Secretary of War if they received no satisfaction at a lower level.

of harmony the neighboring communities of Fairfield, Weston, and Wilton joined with Norwalk to purchase land somewhere between Saugatuck Bridge and Beer's Trip Hammer (forge) and build a poor house. Each town agreed to pay one thousand dollars initially and thereafter to contribute an annual sum based on the number of poor it sent to the home. When the other towns neglected to pay their share of the costs Norwalk to its credit bought them out and maintained the poor house for its sole use.

A new attitude toward the woebegotten elements of society swept the nation in the 1830s: those who could must work. In line with this trend Norwalk purchased a sizable piece of property for an Alms House or Work Farm. Here residents who were able tended the vegetable crops that were the

The Down Town District School House on East Avenue.

mainstay of their diet. The property served many functions; there was also a House of Correction used until the new lock-up (jail) was built at the foot of Mill Hill. In 1852 another story was added to the old part of the Alms House and a pest house constructed for those with contagious diseases. Meant to serve the unfortunate from birth to death the facility included a home for children and a burying place for town paupers.

After the turn of the century the Norwalk School Society, a separate entity from town government, became accountable for public school education. Under state law a School Society Committee composed of three elected members and one represen-

COMING FROM SCHOOL

The bearer Miss Julia Lockwood receives this as a token of the praise merits for her faithfulness and good behavior in school: from her teacher Timothy Taylor

tative from each school district within the Society's purview was delegated power to delineate boundaries of school districts, erect school buildings, and tax residents for educational costs. Although the Old Society District with over four hundred children was the largest, new districts were carved out with regularity as population shifted from the center of town. Middle District, Pudding Lane, Flax Hill, and Over River were created in the 1820s; mergers and realignments of old districts and the organization of new districts brought the total to twelve by 1840.[15]

In addition to teaching the three Rs, schools were by law responsible for moral and religious instruction. The task of assessing the district school's success in achieving these goals fell to nine Overseers on the Visiting and Examining Committee. Overseers made annual visits to district schools, examined students and teachers alike, and submitted recommendations to the Society. Since there was always a healthy sprinkling of ministers on the Visiting and Examining Committee—in 1837 alone four of them were men of the cloth—one must

assume Norwalk children learned their prayers as assiduously as their sums.[16]

Schools received some state support from interest on the School Fund established by the Assembly with proceeds from sale of the western Fire Lands. The tidy sum of $350 that Norwalk received from the Fund's April, 1821, division alone went a long way toward the cost of educating its 808 school children.[17]

In 1837 Connecticut towns received what in effect was the first federal subsidy to education when the federal government distributed the Surplus Fund of the United States. Although the money was to be used to promote education each town was free to determine exactly how it wished to spend its share. Norwalk deposited its allocation and loaned it out in sums not exceeding three hundred dollars, turning over the interest earned to the School Society. But the town was not above transferring a small

15 The twelve districts were South Middle, Down Town, Old Well, Flax Hill, Over River, Pudding Lane, Northwestern, Northeastern, North Middle, South Five Mile River, Middle Five Mile River and North Five Mile River, each with its own school. *School Society Book,* 1840. Lockwood House Museum Archives.

16 Even in the last decades of the nineteenth century, school children practiced the highly-touted phonetic system of speech by reciting The Lord's PrEr and The Gos/pel A-CORD/ ING Tu St. Mark, two exercises in Knudsen's *A Primer for Use in Schools and Families for teaching Correct and Distinct Articulation in Reading and Speaking,* one of many text books published by the South Norwalk firm of Golden Brothers.

17 The money was apportioned among the several districts. Old Society got $192.77 of the $350; it enrolled 445 of the 808 children.

The Children's Retreat as drawn by B.C. Palmer.

Drawn from Nature by B.C. Palmer. Published for Friends of Lockwood House, Inc., 1973 by Silvermine Production, Norwalk, Conn. Lith. of Jones & Newman N.Y.

portion to the town treasury "for the use and benefit of said town."[18]

Advocates of "better education" in the 1830s and 1840s lamented the shameful inadequacies of Connecticut's common school system: poorly trained teachers, deteriorating buildings, and a paucity of schools above the primary level. Concerned citizens organized branches of the statewide Association for the Improvement of Common Schools and shared their convictions at conventions in Hartford. Statewide agitation eventually led to reform and in 1856 School Societies were abolished and the towns themselves assumed control over education.

Of the shortcomings identified in Norwalk none loomed larger than the charge that the town was "entirely destitute of a first rate school of higher order than the primary school." Parents with the wherewithal to pay tuition enrolled their children above the age of ten in one of the private or select schools that prepared them for higher studies or instructed them in the niceties of gracious living.

Middle-class parents could enroll their children at the Norwalk English and Classical Academy; the South Norwalk Academy which boarded pupils with private families for two dollars a week; or at

Miss Mahettable H. Selleck's Select School where students studied in a specially-furnished classroom set up "in the second story of the South Wing" of her father's house. Miss Susan Betts ran a coeducational boarding school, the Children's Retreat, on France Street in an idyllic country setting with broad areas perfect for rolling hoops and skipping rope that must have enchanted more than one little New York City boarder.

The 1830s and 1840s found Americans taking religion as seriously as education. Strict laws in every state required citizens to keep the Sabbath with Sunday School and Bible societies and the Society for the Promotion of Good Morals flourishing. Protestantism nevertheless became rent with competition and disputes. The drawing power of the Unitarian Church which had discarded the harsh Calvinist belief in predestination hit the Congregationalists very hard. The Episcopalians were also attracting many members; by 1850 St. Paul's-on-the-Green had a membership of five hundred.[20] Dr. Edwin Hall who had taken the pulpit of First Congregational in 1833 felt called upon to engage in pulpit debate with the Episcopalians from time to time and also devoted several sermons to an attack upon the Baptist custom of adult immersion.[19]

18 By December, 1844, the town deposit fund amounted to $7,877.09. Total interest was $500.88. Of this amount $371 was allocated to the School Society and $100 to the town treasury.

19 A Mormon church, the Church of Jesus Christ of Latter-Day Saints, was organized in Norwalk in 1841 by missionary Charles Wesley Wandell. Joseph Bouton and Albert Greg-

Like all threatened institutions orthodox Congregational churches resorted at times to "zeal not according to wisdom" to keep their members. The First Congregational's Prudential Committee was its instrument for maintaining orthodoxy in Norwalk. The mission of the laymen on the Prudential Committee was to investigate reports of immoral or heretical beliefs or conduct, to reform offenders, or as a last resort excommunicate them. Misconduct ranged from prolonged absence from the Lord's Table to adultery and Universalism. A few examples will suffice. At one annual meeting of the church the Committee reported that Widow S. had been guilty of gross profanity. Despite her rebuttal that one of the leading members of the Prudential Committee was guilty of the same sin she was excommunicated. When Mr. L. made a public confession of adultery in 1833 the church voted this unsatisfactory and excommunicated him. Habitual intemperance frequently led to expulsion from the church. One can only surmise what unspeakable guilty secrets were ferreted out by the Committee in 1842; the pages for that year have been torn from the record book.[20]

After 1835 a second Congregational church in Old Well gave Congregationalists living across the river the option of attending services in their own neighborhood.[21] Sharing in South Norwalk's rising fortunes this church thrived from the very beginning.

Roman Catholic families who lived in Norwalk in the 1830s and 1840s were able to worship formally only when a traveling priest from Bridgeport rode into town and said Mass in a private home.[22] When the number of Roman Catholics increased to more than seventy a lay committee petitioned the Bishop of Hartford for a resident priest. Impressed by the group's sincerity and their carefully worked-out plans the Bishop assigned the Reverend John G.

Rev. Edwin Hall, D.D.

Brady to be their pastor. Father Brady and his parishioners purchased a plot on Chapel Street and built a modest thirty-six-by-forty-foot building that was dedicated in 1851.

---

ory, whose cottage on Gregory's Point was used for Mormon meetings, became ordained Elders. The unusual theology of this group excited the disapproving interest of Norwalkers. There were rumors that Brigham Young himself had baptized converts on Ram Island. Largely because so many of its members moved to Utah the Norwalk Mormons had to unite with those of Westport. John J. Wolfinger, "A Test of Faith: Jane Elizabeth James and the Origins of the Utah Black Community," "Journal History of 1845." Archives, Church of Jesus Christ of Latter-Day Saints, Salt Lake City.

20 From time to time the congregation voted not to continue this committee's activities. About 1875 its character and duties changed. It became involved with such things as obtaining new church personnel.

21 The move may have been motivated by disapproval of the Prudential Committee's tactics but the founders of the new church averred that it was solely to accommodate the many families now living across the river. Letter, Request to Separate, Jan. 24, 1835, Daniel N. Nash, James Quintard, John Bouton, George Benedict, Committee, to Congregational Society of Norwalk. File Box, Second Congregational Church. LHM Archives.
There was also a Methodist Church in South Norwalk by the 1850s.

22 Lynn Wilson, *History of Fairfield County,* Vol. I, 493, states that Mass was said not only in the private homes of Michael Cooney, Lawrence Martin, John Connors and John Kelly, but also in George Belden's tin store.

Support from Protestant clergymen like Dr. Mead of St. Paul's and donations from local non-Catholics reflected the good will in the community at the time. When Paul Bresnan and Terence Reynolds, two members of the lay committee, paid a visit to Dr. Mead to solicit funds Mead asked Bresnan, "Paul, how is it that you came to me first, why not go to the Congregational minister, Dr. Hall?" Bresnan replied, "Well, Doctor, we know you to be an offshoot from the parent stalk."This answer left the Episcopal clergyman with one response; he took the subscription list and wrote his name at the top.[21]

Rev. William Cooper Mead, D.D.

In this period of population growth and industrialization, urban dwellers now living closer to their neighbors became more aware of social problems. Norwalkers like their other fellow Americans applied their energies to a variety of reform movements. Temperance led all other reforms in popularity. Virtually all local clergymen were active in this drive although the Congregational clergy led the way. The earliest Temperance Society meetings were held at the Congregational Church and the Reverend Roswell Swan, its pastor, gained statewide acclaim as early as 1807 for opposing use of spirituous liquors. In one sermon Mr. Hall reminded his listeners that when the first barrel of rum was brought to Norwalk the town fathers had returned it to the ship's master, declaring, "A whole barrel of rum would corrupt and ruin the community." Hall was considerably more sympathetic than punitive but warned problem-drinkers that their only hope of escape was "immediately, totally, and forever" to abandon the use of strong drink. South Norwalk's more militant Second Congregationalists unanimously adopted a single resolution at their organizational meeting: that the making, the trafficking in, or the use of spirituous liquors was sinful.

Laymen were if anything ahead of the clergy in this movement. The editors of the *Norwalk Gazette* threw their influence on the side of temperance, seeing to it that among the many doleful stories from far and near that appeared in their weekly paper two or three described lives blighted by heavy drinking. Typical of the *Gazette's* methods are a short story, "The Drunkard's Grave," and a poem, "I've Thrown the Bowl Aside," both of which appeared on the front page of a single issue. The last verse of the poem contained encouragement for the reformed drinker:

> *My path henceforth is plain,*
> *In honesty to live—*
> *To shun Intemperance and its train,*
> *By industry to thrive.*

In 1843, the same year a J.A. Allen opened his Temperance Hotel in South Norwalk, the Sons and Daughters of Temperance was formed in Norwalk. Members promised to take spirits for medicinal purposes only and to lead moral lives. South Norwalk's Rising Star Division of the Sons of Temperance which appeared a few years later waxed and waned but lasted for seventy-odd years. Happily, more of its members were expelled for nonpayment of dues than for "breaking the pledge."[22]

During the reform decades the United States enjoyed great economic progress despite overexpansion and unwise speculation in certain areas of the economy, and in spite of panics and depressions and a growing shortage of hard money. The mansions of Norwalk's entrepreneurs gave visible proof that there was money to be made. Although domestic servants and the laboring men and women hard at work in the town's new factories received only small nibbles of the economic pie, even their share was growing. A visitor to Norwalk in 1855 found a town quite different from the "crooked and confined-looking place" observed by the young Scot in 1822. Viewed from any one of the surrounding hills, remarked the later visitor, Norwalk appeared "beautiful in the extreme"—

Rows of neat white cottages [he added], with their green blinds, neat and beautiful dooryards and gardens in the rear, lose themselves in the more plain and substantial farmhouses, surrounded by orchards, fields, and meadows, filled with cattle, grain and fruit, and showing evidence of that thrift and application which are proverbial with the Yankee farmer.[23]

NORWALK

seaport village

101

9

FURS, FELTS, AND FACTORIES

Being
an Account of
Industrialization in a Nineteenth-Century Town

HOSE "rows of neat white cottages" comprised a large share of the 774 dwellings the census taker counted in Norwalk in 1850. Although a wealthy handful could afford to build Greek Revival temples and Italianate villas most residents were wage earners with modest incomes. They worked as tanners, turners, and tobacconists; as coopers, carmen, and clerks; as bakers, blacksmiths, and basket makers; and as saddlers, sailors, and ships' carpenters. The five most commonplace occupations in Norwalk were hatter, boatman, shoemaker, farmer and laborer.[1] Although few people were desperately poor (only four paupers lived in the Alms House in 1850) self-employed fishermen earned so little that they generally had to work at other jobs to make ends meet.[i]

Norwalk was little more than a village. In 1830 its population stood at 3,702, an increase of 1,000 over the two previous decades. A net gain of only 157 by 1840 is probably attributable to the loss of a small portion of Middlesex to Darien in 1820[2] and the loss of Saugatuck which became the independent township of Westport in 1835. The Panic of 1837, whose effects lasted for several years, also limited the town's growth. The 1850s saw the first dramatic population increase as a host of immigrants poured

in; the figures jumped from around 4,600 in 1850 to some 7,600 in 1860, a gain of 64.5 percent.[3]

In spite of its limited water power, by 1840 up-and-coming Norwalk had established itself as one of the state's leading manufacturing centers. Its output of $434,500 in 1839 placed it fifth in the state in value of manufactured goods. Its factories attracted skilled workers, often migrants from northern European countries. Lounsbury's wool manufactory hired German-born dyers and woolsorters; English-born potters worked at Smith's Pottery while their Scottish cousins found jobs as hatters and shoemakers.

A few Irish had settled in Norwalk in the 1830s and after a decade of hard labor had become men of property. Michael Cooney, one of the first Irishmen to bring his family here, in 1850 owned real estate valued at $1,800, as much as the town's carriagemakers and coasters could claim. The trickle of the 1830s turned into a flood of Irish immigrants in the 1840s and 1850s. Although a few such newcomers found employment as saddlers and shoemakers, almost all Irish-born males on the 1850 Norwalk census enumeration were common laborers employed either on railroad construction and maintenance crews or on the larger farms in the area. Young single, Irish-born women who came in comparable numbers readily found jobs as live-in servants for Norwalk's middle-class families. Many of them found husbands as well. Although Irish-born females living in Norwalk married Irish-born males more frequently than Norwalk-born, non-Irish men, love sometimes triumphed over prejudice.[2]

---

[i] The situation of the simple worker was undoubtedly preferable to the few whose livelihood is clouded in mystery. Since the census enumerator routinely used the entry "uncertain" in cases where he could not determine a man's occupation, one can only guess at the personal animosity or righteous indignation that compelled the 1850 census taker to describe one resident's occupation by the simple word "questionable."

Ownership of real property, a symbol of stability and permanence,[2] was confined to the middle and upper classes. In Norwalk in 1850 property valuation fell into three distinct categories. A considerable group of men owned real estate valued from a thousand to two thousand dollars. Among them were the "coasters," men like Captain William Ferris and Captain William Allen who, sailing the waters from Nova Scotia to Georgia, were the lifeline between Norwalk's manufacturers and their markets. Carriagemakers and shipbuilders, who had migrated to Norwalk from New York and Maine, set up workshops on property valued at the same level. Even "pedlars" became property owners. Although many were young men who traveled the length of New England and central New York State hawking their wares, persistence and the "hard sell" must have paid off since mature "pedlars" had the means to purchase property at this level.

Those men who owned real estate valued at between three thousand and five thousand dollars were for the most part self-employed and native-born. Their occupations ranged from mason to jeweler and farmer to lawyer. Among the few salaried workers in this classification were some elderly potters, apparently men with such special skills that they had commanded a lifetime of high wages and were able to spend their golden years "comfortably fixed."

The most substantial group owned real estate valued at ten thousand dollars and upwards. In this class were Edward Bissell, a twenty-eight-year-old accountant; David Stevenson, innkeeper of the Norwalk Hotel; and Deputy Sheriff Charles Isaacs who, in accepted middle-class custom, took in Dr. Asa Hill as a boarder. Among the merchants[4] of stature were George Betts whose extended household consisted of a wife, eight other relatives, and four servants, all living under one roof; and Lawrence Stevens, a merchant and farmer with di-

versified holdings. Among manufacturers in this group John Lounsbury, owner of the largest woolen factory, was outstanding and must have served as a role model for ambitious young men who came to Norwalk to open small, cottage-type manufactories. Typical of these aspiring manufacturers was Asa Hagerman from New York City who set up his small woolen manufactory in a building that served as both workshop and home for himself and two young employees. Farming was still important and men like Uriah Seymour and Jonathan Camp represented the most successful practitioners of this occupation.

Land speculation and real estate holdings were popular methods of adding to a man's income from business or profession. Ownership of three, four, or even five houses was not unusual. Charles White, owner of a great many shares of corporate stock and so rich that he possessed six coaches, still retained title to three dwellings. Men of lesser eminence also favored real estate. Even Giles Seymour, a carpenter, held title to two dwellings assessed at nine thousand dollars.

Men who had inherited land in a growing area were able to live nicely by selling it off piece by piece. Charles Raymond, whose comfortable farmhouse stood on the corner of Wilson and Highland Avenues, owned almost all of Five Mile River between Wilson Avenue and Roton Point. He no longer had to farm for a living as his ancestors had done but over the years was able to dispose of plots in this desirable shorefront area.

The value of a person's real estate holdings was not the sole determinant of social position. Clergymen were highly esteemed citizens whose prestige and influence bore little relationship to their economic circumstances. Connecticut-born Dr. William Cooper Mead, rector of St. Paul's, was at age fifty-one an independently wealthy man with real estate holdings of forty thousand dollars. His Congregational counterpart, the admired Dr. Edwin Hall, owned real estate worth a mere $2,500. Both men were indeed affluent compared to the minister of the Union Church in Five Mile River

2 See Lester Card, "Norwalk Records (Marriages), Supplementing Hall's Annals of Norwalk Bringing The Records to 1875." Typewritten manuscript, LHM Archives. In an analysis of fifteen marriages involving Irish-born females residing in Norwalk between 1851 and 1865, eight married Irish-born males and four married Norwalk-born, non-Irish males.

3 Clyde Griffen, "Workers Divided," in Stephen Thernstrom and Richard Bennett, eds., *Nineteenth Century Cities* (New Haven, 1969), 59, noted that "persistence [remaining in a community] has a stronger association with ownership of real estate than with any other variable available in quantifiable sources."

4 Nathan Trock, twenty-six years old, listed his occupation as merchant, too, but owned no property. His distinction derived from the fact that he was born in Poland and was the only person of Slavic birth residing in Norwalk at the time of the 1850 census. Since the designation "merchant" was a broad one, used for those engaged in importing and exporting, for wholesalers and for retailers, we cannot distinguish the precise nature of their businesses.

The Benedict Hat Co. factory was built about 1790.

where the people were "too few in number and too poor to support more than one church." His congregation, mostly oystermen and clammers, paid him the equivalent of four hundred dollars annual salary in shellfish at the current market price. Although they agreed to sell the minister's portion first, huge piles of clam and oyster shells at either side of the parsonage doorstep were sorry testimony that shellfish were the mainstay of the family's diet.[4]

During the nineteenth century hat manufacturing became Norwalk's most prominent industry providing at its peak jobs for well over two thousand men and women. Hatting was an old industry in the town dating back before the American Revolution. Hatting establishments had to be small prior to Independence because the Hat Act of 1732 limited the number of a hatter's apprentices to two. The man's hat of those days was the popular tricorn, made of felt from beaver fur. Tricorns of good quality were expensive; beaver pelts commanded considerable in the way of bartered goods at Indian trading posts. The reason for this aside from the beaver's superior pelt was that the animal had to be

trapped, not shot.[5] An Indian might ask one shirt or two pounds of gunpowder or a silk handkerchief for a single beaver pelt.[5] The inventory of Governor Fitch's estate gives some idea of the value of a beaver hat for although appraisers generally gave used wearing apparel a low estimate the governor's best tricorn was given a value equal to a pair of silver tea tongs.

About 1810 American men began to adopt the styles popularized some years earlier by the French revolutionists. Just as trousers replaced knee breeches so brimmed hats replaced the tricorn. Ownership of a brimmed beaver hat became a mark of wealth and when a gentleman had his portrait painted he often posed with his "beaver" in hand. As fashion dictated that the crowns of hats should grow ever higher so did prices rise for the felt was made of pelts obtained from ever more-distant forests.[6]

---

5 If shot on or near a pond, a beaver would simply sink irretrievably to the bottom.

6 Oliver Wendell Holmes described not only high fashion but disappearing wildlife when he handed out this tongue-in-cheek advice:
> Have a good hat, the secret of your looks
> Lies with the beaver in the Canadian brooks.

One of Norwalk's earliest nineteenth-century hatters was Isaac Jennings who disposed of his excess output to the Lockwoods, trading hats for food and other necessities. Within a decade other small establishments, often partnerships, were engaged in hatting. In 1836 South Norwalk alone had six or seven such firms. By 1839 Algernon Beard had added hats to the other items his agents were peddling up and down the coast. Buying from several fabricators, of which Charles St. John was the foremost, Beard also dealt heavily in furs and managed to make money at both ends of a transaction. Entries in his cash record book indicate that he sold pelts to St. John and received hats in exchange for groceries purchased by St. John.

Norwalk was ideally located for development of this type of light manufacturing. Not only could the town's growing number of hatters reach a wide market through local entrepreneurs like Beard and the Lockwoods but they could readily send to nearby New York City for imported ribbon trim, buckles, fancy fabrics, and accessories to finish off the hats. From the city also came an unfailing supply of workers. The process of hat-making required a number of distinct steps and it was not long before certain fabricators specialized in a single portion of the process, improving and enhancing the quality of the final product. Between 1820 and 1850 a number of new inventions hastened manufacture of the felt or improved its quality. In 1822 a Danbury man invented a manually-operated wheel that allowed thirty-six hats to be dyed at one time, markedly speeding up this previously slow and tedious stage. Control over key patents may have been one reason Danbury quickly surpassed Norwalk as a hatting town when Norwalk had every advantage of transportation.

When the European silk hat appeared in the United States during the 1830s Norwalk hatters learned how hazardous it could be to depend for one's living upon the public's whims and fancies. Competition from the silk hat compounded the financial troubles generated by the depression of 1837. Workers were laid off in droves and the fabricators themselves struggled to keep their heads above water.[7] By 1840 men of fashion and means had turned exclusively to the silk top hat. The price

7 Algernon Beard was forced to "give up" Charles St. John's past-due note for the sum of $6,995.00 as a bad debt during this recession.

of a beaver pelt plunged from six dollars to one dollar. When members of the New York Stock Exchange adopted silk hats and swallowtail coats as their daily business clothing the day of the beaver hat and Norwalk fur-felt hatters appeared to be at an end.

Fortunately for its laboring men Norwalk's other manufactories began making felt from sheep's wool. Lounsbury and Bissell, later known as Winnipauk Mills, whose factory was located at the site of the old fulling mill on the Norwalk River, made wool felt for many uses.[6] In 1836 on the strength of a patent he was granted for a unique process for felting wool, George G. Bishop formed the Union

The original Crofut, Knapp & Co. factory.

Manufacturing Company which made felt carpet among other things.

A fluke of history revitalized the fur-felt hat business. In 1851 the Hungarian patriot and reformer, Louis Kossuth, arrived in America to plead the cause of the oppressed Hungarians. As he traveled around the country Kossuth wore a dashing costume that included a wide-brimmed soft top hat of black felt with a plume and buckle. Men all over the nation hastened to adopt the Hungarian's romantic attire. The Kossuth fad was the beginning of a great new era for the fur-felt hat business. Although silk hats retained their popularity as dress hats for men, felt hats were steadily worn by both men and women for almost a century.

In 1858 James H. Knapp, an experienced hatmaker, took advantage of the new popularity of fur-felt hats and invited Andrew J. Crofut, a hatter whose specialty complemented Knapp's own expertise, to join him. They adopted the name Crofut and Knapp although James Knapp was always the dominant partner. From the very first the company prospered, probably because the partners were not afraid to be innovative. In 1860 Crofut and Knapp made the first derby hat manufactured in the United States. C&K continued in the forefront as inventions and new techniques changed the process of hatting and as new fashions influenced American buying habits. John B. Stetson for whom the famous Stetson hat was named learned his trade at C&K. Although other hat manufacturers and a number of small hat shops did business in Norwalk C&K was by far the largest.[7] When a man said that he worked at the hat company everyone knew he meant Crofut and Knapp.

The steps required to make a fur-felt hat remained essentially the same from the earliest days of hatmaking. The back skins of rabbit, muskrat, otter, and coney were frequently used but the thick, rich, soft pelt of the beaver surpassed all others. After washing the fur of the aquatic animals in a strong whale-oil soap mixture the next step was to pluck out the long coarse protective hairs from each pelt. These were pulled out one by one with tweezers and discarded. Then in a process known as carroting the skins were dipped into a bath of nitrate of mercury, a hazardous task for the workman. After this the fur was shaved from the skin and the better fibers separated from the poor ones. Carroting released many tiny barbs on each fur fiber and set the stage for the next major step which was to mat the thousands of fibers into a cone-shaped hood by means of a vibrating process. In early times this was done by beating the fibers with a bowlike instrument of catgut but later a forming machine using the same principle came into use. This process demanded highly-skilled and experienced operators for each piece of matted, tangled felt had to be of uniform thickness throughout, without a single tear or weak point.

Next the material was hardened by the process of sizing (shrinking) by being dipped into boiling water. An operator could handle only a few hats at a time and had to keep a large bucket of cold water handy in which to dip his hands before plunging the felt into the boiling water.[8] The treatment was repeated until the felt had shrunk to about half its original size. This too was a ticklish step for it was

[8] Even in the 1920s some shops still did sizing by hand.

The Lounsbury & Bissell Co. Winnipauk Mills about 1860.

important not to set a crease in the material during sizing. Dyeing the hardened felt was equally delicate for the dyer had to achieve an absolutely even color. Dyeing completed the "wet" steps of the process.

In the first of the "dry" steps each piece of felt was formed into a hat through blocking or shaping. Derbies were then dipped into a mixture of shellac and alcohol to stiffen and waterproof them. Turning of the brim was important, especially in the derby, as was pouncing or sandpapering the felt to remove any possible remaining long hairs. After the ribbon trim and inner facing were stitched on, the hat was complete.

James Henry Knapp.

Hatting was by no means the only large industry in Norwalk although it was the one responsible for the most activity. An enterprise that was to assume a dominant place in the town, the Norwalk Lock Company, was organized in 1856 by a group whose major shareholders included Algernon Beard, Ebenezer Hill, and Henry H. Elwell. Hill was made president of the new corporation and Elwell, who owned a process for plating cast-iron keys, was appointed superintendent and given a place on the board of directors.[8] Using coal for energy, in contrast to the wool and felt factories that had had to locate on the river to obtain power, Norwalk Lock was able to build its plant in South Norwalk, conve-

nient to the Boston and New Haven tracks.

The depression of 1857 struck within a year after the lock company's operations got underway but with careful management and some good luck Ebenezer Hill managed to guide the firm through that crisis. The good luck came from an order for an ingenious new household gadget, the Yankee Apple Paring Machine, an order so large that thirty tons of iron were required to fill it. The company also obtained substantial orders for institutional locks such as one from the state of Michigan to equip all of that state's prisons, hospitals, and alms houses. Soon Norwalk Lock was turning out more than twenty-five hundred locks and latches and twelve hundred pairs of doorknobs daily besides

The elegant Dobbs derby.
Collection of Lockwood House Museum.

special orders. In 1859 the company netted an astounding 30 percent profit.

The manufacture of locks and keys lent itself nicely to the assembly line method. From the casting of individual parts in the foundry to polishing and fitting of the finished products, the process was broken into efficient segments. The skilled workmen needed at almost every stage had often learned their trades in England or Germany.

The company brooked no nonsense from its workers. Men in the brass foundry, where the black lead crucibles sometimes cracked under the intense heat required to melt the ores, had to provide their own crucibles. The management found that this regulation "work[ed] most advantageous." Workers in other departments were paid only for the pounds of perfect work turned in. It was noted that this, too, was of "incalculable benefit to the stockholders in the prevention of waste and loss of time." The owners further justified it on the basis that it "served as a great stimulus for exertion, and [engendered] the laudable spirit of emulation . . ."

The Morrison & Hoyt Shirt Company, a sizable concern of more than three hundred employees, was as modern in its operations as the lock company and considerably more advanced in personnel practices. Morrison & Hoyt offered workers stimulating cultural advantages including a well-stocked library for which Mr. Hoyt himself carefully selected books

Ebenezer Hill.

of high moral and educational value. With generous wages that ranged between one and two dollars per day, shirt factory girls were able to live in comfortable boarding houses and spend money freely in local emporiums.9 These benefits, ob-

9 The *Gazette,* May 10, 1859, viewed these young women as a decided benefit to local merchants because of their spending habits. The Census of 1860 shows several boarding houses with women residents, Connecticut-born and the majority between the ages of eighteen and twenty-two, who listed their occupation as "shirt factory." By 1870, according to the Census, the shirt factory was attracting women from nearby states, even Canada. They continued to live in boarding houses.

served the *Gazette,* attracted "the better class of young ladies."

The town's lone bank, the Fairfield County Bank,10 could not meet growing demands for working capital from expanding local industries. In 1849 the Norwalk Savings Society was organized and in 1857 Eben Hill formed the Bank of Norwalk. Not long afterward the Mechanics Savings Society of South Norwalk opened its doors, changing its name within a few years to the South Norwalk Savings Bank. Banks were only one of a variety of service enterprises necessary to the operation of factories and other businesses. There were at least two printing establishments in town, some new office buildings, a paper box factory, lumber yards, a brick works, and the ubiquitous livery stables. There were also several small fire insurance companies and an assortment of lawyers.

The traditional railroad conductor's cry of "All aboard! All aboard who are going aboard!" did not ring out in Norwalk until shortline railroads had become commonplace in most of New England. With heavy investments in steamboats and harbor facilities and satisfied with the existing steamboat and stage service, Norwalkers systematically resisted all proposals for railroads throughout the 1830s and 1840s. Danbury businessmen, eager to construct a north-south shortline connecting that city with the tidewater, got little encouragement from their Norwalk counterparts.9

When optimistic spokesmen for the Housatonic Railroad Company explored the feasibility of an east-west line connecting Bridgeport with Saw Pitts (Port Chester), Norwalkers swiftly rallied in opposition.11 Even after the New York and New Haven Railroad received a charter to construct a line between New Haven and the Bronx local businessmen failed to see its potential for increasing trade. Alexander Twining, the august Yale engineering professor, had no sooner completed a survey of the route for the N.Y. & N.H. than agitated Norwalkers took exception to his plan for a drawbridge spanning the Norwalk River. Ostensibly concerned about the effect on river traffic they insisted the

10 The Fairfield County Bank is now the Merchants Bank and Trust Company.

11 Prior to completion of a direct Boston-New York City rail line, New York-bound passengers usually traveled by rail to Providence, and completed the trip by steamer, via Long Island Sound.

General Assembly authorize a draw in the bridge at least sixty feet wide.

In spite of obstructionist tactics that led to design modifications and heavier construction costs the New York and New Haven Railroad began full service in December, 1848, from Mill River Junction in New Haven to Forty-Second Street in New York City, passing through South Norwalk.[10] Low fares, comfort, and the novelty of trains captured public interest and they became the stylish and practical mode of travel. Toward the end of the century New York-bound Norwalkers had a choice of twenty-seven trains daily. Ten trains leaving South Norwalk between 5:16 and 9:36 A.M. and a one-way fare as low as eight cents made commuting to New York an attractive feature of living in Norwalk.

Although commuters could take solace in figures showing that Connecticut rail lines had better safety records than those in other parts of the nation[11] the townspeople witnessed their share of catastrophes. Norwalk's most disastrous rail accident occurred in midmorning on May 3, 1853, when the Boston Express reached Norwalk eight minutes late. Speeding through South Norwalk at twenty miles an hour to make up lost time the engineer rounded the curve leading to the bridge and hurtled on, unaware that the draw was open. The engine and five passenger cars plunged into the void killing forty-five persons and seriously injuring twenty-five others.[12] Townspeople rushed to the aid of the victims and sympathetic residents opened their homes

12 Harlow, *Steelways of New England,* 181, points out that the *American Railroad Journal* criticized the New York and New Haven for cutting costs when constructing the line, and charged that the sharp curve at the Norwalk River Bridge was responsible for the 1853 accident. Edward Tucker, the engineer on the ill-fated train, survived the catastrophe, but apparently never overcame his feeling of guilt. He later committed suicide. *Norwalk Gazette,* Sept. 14, 1858.

New York & New Haven Railroad train crosses the trestle at South Norwalk.

to them, ministered to the injured, and diligently contacted survivors' relatives. Local telegraphers furiously hammered out descriptions of those victims who could not be readily identified because their papers had been lost in the river's waters.[13]

This tragedy prompted the state legislature immediately to pass a law requiring all trains to come to a full stop before crossing a drawbridge or the tracks of another railroad. Train riders could henceforth travel with greater ease of mind.

The New Haven-New York City connection rekindled interest in construction of a shortline between Danbury and Norwalk. Norwalkers who had responded to Danbury's earlier overtures "with coldness and distrust" reconsidered after Danbury raised nearly seventy-five thousand dollars toward construction and began probing alternate routes. A group of distinguished businessmen which included farmer-banker Jonathan Camp, pottery manufacturer Asa Smith, and lumberman-merchant-banker Eben Hill, joined with Danbury financiers to construct the twenty-three mile line. The real hero of the project, however, was S. Edwin

Olmstead, a local wholesale and retail grocer who held the contract to feed all men and horses employed in laying the trackage. When the contractors, Beard, Church and Company, of Derby, Connecticut, abandoned the work because they had miscalculated costs, Olmstead stepped in and directed completion of the track.[14]

Travelers deserted stage coaches for the clattering little cars that bowled along the tracks. The Danbury and Norwalk which had modestly scheduled two southbound and two return trips a day when the line began service in 1852 plowed its profits into additional rolling stock and increased the number of daily runs.[12] Incredulous viewers marveled at the puffing, wood-burning locomotives that hauled as many as thirty-eight passenger and freight cars, a load that probably necessitated the quaint custom of halting on the upgrade trip near a spring in Georgetown. Here passengers could debark and quaff a cool draught of water, scrambling aboard when conductor W. H. Banks called out, "All who are going will get on board, for when we start, we start sudden."[13]

During the height of the Civil War control of the

---

13 In the case of Dr. Butler Wilmarth, a renowned practitioner of hydropathy and president of the American Hygienic and Hydropathic Association, identification was made only after a worried associate came to Norwalk and viewed the remains.

14 Olmstead, who had built a grist mill on James Street to grind the grain needed to fulfill his contract, was probably protecting his investment.

Danbury and Norwalk passed to LeGrand Lockwood. Under his guidance and with his uncle Edwin as president the line began to expand. Two branch lines, fingers reaching into the surrounding countryside, fed into the main tracks. The line's most innovative venture was extension of its tracks from South Norwalk to Wilson Point where the company built an enormous steamboat pier that extended two hundred feet out over the water. Even though construction had proceeded slowly, an engineering misjudgment necessitated raising the roadbed across the head of the cove to grade so that "an engine driver can now run a train at high water to the Point without a harbor pilot." When the line began service in 1882 there was immediate proof that steamboats and railroads were compatible. New York City and Brooklyn ice companies contracted for as much as thirty thousand tons of ice a year. Ice blocks whacked out of ponds close to the tracks in Wilton and Redding were hauled by trains making a downgrade run to Wilson Point and loaded into steamboat holds for delivery to the metropolitan area.

Cutthroat competition and a nationwide movement to consolidate shortlines, both characteristics of late nineteenth-century railroading, had a direct impact on the Danbury and Norwalk. In 1886 the Housatonic Railroad leased the D & N for ninety-nine years and in turn the Housatonic and its lessees were absorbed into the New York and New England line. This did not sufficiently strengthen the N.Y. & N.E. for the fierce combat it had to wage against the New York, New Haven and Hartford. In a brilliant but costly maneuver designed to corner Boston-New York rail traffic the N.Y. & N.E. devised a unique combination of rail and ferry service under the name Long Island and Eastern States Line. Specially designed locomotives capable of mile-a-minute speeds pulled gaslit, mahogany-paneled cars furnished with elegantly upholstered plush seats toward Wilson Point. In this widely-acclaimed "wedding of Boston and Brooklyn" a twin-screw iron train ferry carried both passenger and freight cars across Long Island Sound and deposited them onto the Long Island Railroad tracks at Oyster Bay for the remaining trip to Brooklyn and Long Island City.[14] But the line never matched performance to its grandeur. Delayed traffic on the long stretches of single track, storms that buffeted the ferry as it crossed the Sound, and frequent accidents marred service. Wags shortly renamed the Long Island and Eastern States Line the "Long Interval and Empty Seats Line."[15]

Local businessmen always had an eye for investment opportunities on a smaller scale and were excited by the profits to be made in intra-city transportation schemes. When David Swords established the Omnibus Line in the 1840s local residents with a preference for a particular store or seeking a sharp bargain could trade in either Norwalk Borough or South Norwalk with relative ease. Five times daily the horse-drawn wagon left from Peck's Store in South Norwalk for John Weed's Store uptown, carrying passengers to the lower district on alternate hours. The first trip in the morning and the last in the afternoon were timed to accommodate Norwalk Academy students who paid reduced fares.

In 1862 the Omnibus Line fell victim to an improved intra-city transit system when the Norwalk Horse Railway Company, formed by LeGrand Lockwood, introduced its handsome red cars with upholstered crimson plush seats. During the first year of operation the Red Line, as it was known, ran cars from uptown Norwalk to the South Norwalk railroad station using the Danbury and Norwalk tracks. One can only imagine the horrified reaction as passengers on the horsedrawn cars careened toward a spur to avoid collision with an on-coming D & N train. This hazardous arrangement quickly gave way to a single track laid on West Avenue. The improvement was not without its disadvantages for as the horses pulled the cars along the stationary tracks on the unpaved street they kicked up such clouds of dust that "if you have on black clothes you will look like a miller."

To provide similar service for the east side of town a group of South Norwalk businessmen organized the Gregory Point Horse Railroad Company shortly after the Civil War. The enterprise had

15 Foreclosure proceedings against the subsidiary that operated the train ferry took place in 1893 and the spur line from South Norwalk to Wilson Point was abandoned eventually. The final chapter of the D & N is hidden in the history of the New York, New Haven and Hartford line. When the N.Y. & N.E. line was forced into bankruptcy in 1893 the majority of its stock was purchased by the New York, New Haven and Hartford Railroad Company. The Danbury and Norwalk, so long a feature of Norwalk's economic life, was absorbed by that line in the course of consolidation.

It is interesting to note that in 1977 there was a revival of interest in the spur when the Berkshire Railroad Company filed an application for permission to conduct freight and passenger operations from Wilson Point to the Massachusetts border on the Danbury line of Conrail.

NORWALK
seaport
village

111

no difficulty in securing a charter of incorporation nor in disposing of a thousand shares of stock at twenty-five dollars each. But when the original cost calculations proved to be unrealistically low, stockholders saw their promised dividends evaporating and inveighed against the directors. The company found it impossible to meet its obligations and collapsed.[16] The east side of the river did not acquire trolley service until late in the century when the Norwalk Tramway Company, known as the White Line, constructed horse-drawn railway trackage along East Avenue from Van Zant Street to the foot of Mill Hill. At the Wall Street terminus both Red and White Lines shared common trackage, turntables, and switches, a circumstance that led to animosity between the two companies[17] but Norwalk benefited from the ensuing competition. The needed East Avenue line was so successful that the White Line was encouraged to build connections between East Norwalk and South Norwalk via the bridge at Washington Street and between East Avenue and Gregory Point. It then extended service to Roton Point and built a line along Main Street that terminated in Broad River.

Thrifty Norwalkers, at least those in no great

16 The outcome is revealed in a brief pathetic attachment to its contract with the construction firm: "In consideration for the sum of $25, Sidney Miller forever releases and absolves said company from all and singular the covenant agreements and promises."

17 The story goes that when an out-of-towner got off the train in South Norwalk and asked a Red Line employee where the White Line trolley stopped the loyal Red Line worker would swear he had never heard of the White Line.

rush, took advantage of the five cent fare for the ride between uptown Norwalk and South Norwalk via the White Line's East Avenue-transfer-Bridge route. In a desperate move to recapture lost business the Red Line electrified its West Avenue route and advertised a faster, cleaner ride. It also snared the franchise for the last two lines to the fringes of the expanding community, building one route along Newtown Avenue and another to Winnipauk. In a magnificent counterstroke, that clinched the victory, the White Line built the Westport-Norwalk trolley line and extended service from Roton Point to Stamford, thereby making it possible to journey from Bridgeport to Stamford by interurban cars that could carry up to one hundred and fifty passengers and were also used to transport short-haul freight.[18]

During the pre-Civil War years two parties, the Whigs and the Democrats, dominated Connecticut politics.[19] In Norwalk the Whigs quickly became the

18 By the end of the century both Red and White Lines electrified their lines. The Board of Water Commissioners of South Norwalk became concerned that electric current from the rails was traveling to the city's water pipes and that resulting electrolytic action would irreparably damage the pipes. A study by the Board of Electrical Commissioners laid the matter to rest when they found the voltage to be so minimal that damage was unlikely.

19 The Federalists had disappeared after their defeat on the state constitution, and the next dozen years saw several different parties maneuvering for power. The Democratic-Republicans broke up into factions and eventually their dominant group adopted the title of Democrats. The anti-Democrats coalesced into the Whig Party.

Wilson Point Steamboat Pier about 1890.

Waiting for Dobbin at Commerce and Wall Streets about 1890.

majority party. It is interesting that Norwalkers lined up under a political banner with men who would have been comfortable in the old Federalist Party. This pro-Whig stance so congenial to the Yankee-businessman power structure undoubtedly reflected the town's prosperity and middle-class orientation. A group of Democrats nevertheless provided lively competition with enough anti-Whig sentiment in town for a few years during the 1830s to permit publication of the *Democratic Star.* Norwalk's Democrats usually had to read the Stamford *Democratic Sentinel* to obtain fair reportage of their party's activities and to learn about any misdeeds of the Whigs for the *Norwalk Gazette* was a loyal Whig paper.20 The two parties squabbled over the spoils

of office on both state and local levels while real issues such as abolitionism and the growing prohibition movement drew their advocates into small, single-minded parties.

Between 1830 and 1860 three Norwalk men distinguished themselves in state and national politics: Thaddeus Betts, Clark Bissell, and Orris S. Ferry. Of the three, only Betts was actually born in Norwalk; the other two settled in the town in later life. Although the three moved up the political ladder in somewhat different ways they had two things in common; all were lawyers and all had attended Yale, a connection as useful21 as it had been in Fitch's day.

Thaddeus Betts, twice lieutenant governor22 of

20 The *Norwalk Gazette* was a weekly newspaper begun in 1818 by Roswell S. Nichols and Philo Price using, it is said, the Ben Franklin Press left behind by Joseph Dennis. It was sold in 1848 to James N. Hoyt and A. Homer Byington. Byington sold his interest to Hoyt in 1849 but repurchased the whole paper in 1851, taking as partner Henry W. Hyatt. After Hyatt's retirement Joseph B. and George N. Ells joined under the firm name of A. H. Byington & Company. The *Gazette* was a respected newspaper in the state. In 1890 it became a daily but was unable to compete with the Norwalk *Hour,* and went out of business ten years later. Osborne, *History of Connecticut,* II, 148-150.

21 In spite of the town's increasing wealth Norwalk failed to keep pace in higher education. Only twenty-five Norwalk youths graduated from college between 1721 and 1849, whereas eighteen men from Wilton went to college between 1761 and 1849 and eighteen from New Canaan graduated between 1791 and 1837.

22 The Whigs nominated Betts in spite of some discreditable actions on his part. He had assaulted an opposing lawyer in a courtroom and had also been sued for striking a neighbor's child, if the *Stamford Sentinel* of Feb. 16 and March 23, 1835, are to be believed.

the state, was the first United States senator to come from Norwalk. His father, William Maltby Betts, had represented the town's Democratic-Republicans in the state legislature. That the son, Thaddeus, was a Whig reflected Norwalk's political conservatism in the 1830s.

Clark Bissell, Connecticut's governor between 1847 and 1849, was a poor farm boy who taught himself Greek and Latin to prepare for college. He entered Yale wearing a homespun suit his mother had made and worked his way through college by teaching in New Haven schools. He was graduated with honors and after studying law in a local

Captain Joseph Hubbell.

lawyer's office set up practice in Norwalk in 1809. Bissell was elected to the state's supreme court in 1829 but because his judge's salary was too low to support a growing family he returned to private practice. About the time he decided to run for governor on the Whig ticket he was offered a professorship at Yale Law School. He won the election but took office at a time when the two major parties had to face up to the problem of slavery. The Whigs were torn apart on this and other issues. The unfortunate Bissell was unable to hold them together and in the following election was rejected by his party.

Another Whig was elected governor and Bissell returned to teaching at Yale.[23]

Orris S. Ferry, Norwalk's second United States senator, had considerably more impact upon governmental policy than either Betts or Bissell. As a boy Ferry was expected to follow in the footsteps of his father, a hat manufacturer, but he disliked this occupation so intensely that his father released him from an apprenticeship and gave him an education. Ferry entered the practice of law in 1846 and at almost the same time became involved in politics. In 1859 he was elected to Congress for a term and after the Civil War was elected to the United States Senate where he had a distinguished career.

On the local level government was in the hands of well-to-do businessmen who made up the first Court of Burgesses when the Borough of Norwalk was chartered in 1836. The Borough had been formed in response to the needs of the district around the bridge. It comprised a large area on both sides of the river, residential as well as commercial, and was roughly similar to—but smaller than—Norwalk's present First District. Its government consisted of a warden and six burgesses, elected annually, who possessed the same general powers as selectmen. The Borough remained part of the Town of Norwalk and its inhabitants continued to vote for selectmen at the general town election. Its laws could not conflict with those of the town.

The Borough's charter and by-laws reflected the concerns of those who lived and worked in this densely-populated part of Norwalk—a need to keep streets open to traffic, to maintain and improve the uptown harbor, and to keep the residential area quiet and attractive.[24] Above all, residents worried about the danger of fire and at least half the by-laws were concerned with fire prevention. Bonfires in this compact area were forbidden; chimneys had to be kept in good condition; haylofts and

23 Clark Bissell's connection with Lounsbury and Bissell, as noted in Osborne, *History of Connecticut,* IV, 279, is difficult to trace. This felt company was formed in 1845, only a year or two before Bissell began to teach law and run for the governorship. He may have been a silent partner, lending his name only. Neither his obituary in the *Gazette* of Sept. 22, 1857, nor the *National Cyclopaedia of American Biography* mentions any connection with Lounsbury and Bissell.

24 Residents were forbidden to fire guns except to kill some "mischievous animal which cannot otherwise be destroyed." Anyone making a noise or causing a disturbance in the "night season" was liable to being locked up until the following day.

warehouses were subject to inspection. A small army of fire wardens, fire inspectors, and chimney inspectors investigated fire hazards as assidously as the old time fence viewers had ferreted out broken rails. Two large volunteer fire companies, each with its own apparatus, were organized under the tight supervision of a fire engineer.[15]

Names of the central district's businessmen appear regularly in Borough records. Algernon Beard for example served for years as chairman and member of the board of relief, a committee concerned not with the welfare of the poor, as one might suppose, but with tax appeals. Most of these officials were public-spirited men who worked for progress in the Borough. Since what was good for business in those days was also regarded by most citizens as good for the town, there was apt to be little disagreement on the general direction Norwalk should take. Captain Joseph Hubbell typifies the stranglehold some businessmen with narrow interests had on the town between 1836 and 1860. The self-made Hubbell had risen from grocery clerk to secretary-treasurer of the Norwalk Savings Society, *de facto* head of the bank, by 1856. Popular Captain Hubbell sat on the Court of Burgesses time and again—indeed, he was the first warden. He also served consecutive terms as the Town of Norwalk's first selectman as well as a member of the Court of Burgesses.[25]

Although the Town House stood neglected and Norwalk Bridge was hazardous, in spite of constant complaints by citizens, the burgesses spent hour upon hour reshaping the center of town, realigning streets, and widening thoroughfares, primarily for the benefit of the commercial interests. Woe to the store owner or citizen who inadvertently placed an awning or a hitching post in the public street where it might interfere with traffic. Only after a horrendous flood in 1854 toppled the Union Manufacturing Company's plant, damaged Asa Smith's pottery and Lounsbury and Bissell's factory, and swept Captain Joseph Hubbell's mill into the river did Borough officials agree to build a solid stone bridge at Wall Street.[26]

[25] A farm boy, Hubbell went to work at the age of fifteen as a grocery clerk in Bridgeport. In four years' time he had somehow managed to learn enough about navigating the waters of the Sound to become captain of a ship plying between Bridgeport and New York City. At the age of twenty-eight he opened a store and mill in Norwalk. He was one of the organizers of the Norwalk Savings Society and served as Warden of St. Paul's-on-the-Green.

If there was one area of disagreement between citizens and burgesses it concerned spending money for public services. Always tight with a dollar the burgesses delayed spending money and when they finally did they often opted for makeshift solutions instead of doing the job properly. Every so often Borough voters tossed out the incumbents but for the most part, in a kind of round-robin arrangement, the same little clique controlled the central district's top offices. Just at the time the nationwide depression hit in 1857 citizens of both town and borough were beginning to question why more was not being accomplished and why the little

Governor Clark Bissell.

that was done cost so much.

The brief recession checked Norwalk's economy only temporarily. "Taking in perhaps a little sail, yet pushing forward with close reefed canvas—and not a single instance of shipwreck." Thus describing this business squall Byington of the *Gazette* expressed gratitude in October, 1858, that not a single family in town had been in want during the previous winter. He proudly pointed to many signs of

[26] This long-overdue structure was completed at the end of that year.

business recovery: the Union Manufacturing Company was completing a tremendous warehouse; Winnipauk Mills had just built a comfortable cottage as an on-site residence for its foreman; a new brick foundry was under way; the old Quintard Pottery was switching to coal-burning furnaces to manufacture ceramic doorknobs. In South Norwalk one whole business block of brick was under construction and all of it already rented!

Barely a month after these confident words appeared the entire business district around the bridge was consumed by fire—the greatest disaster since Tryon's men had made their malevolent march through town. Suddenly it became apparent that borough officials had been almost criminally delinquent in fire protection. While the fire companies tried futilely to raise the steam in the engines the fire raged through the wooden buildings. In desperation the town appealed to neighboring communities for aid but help arrived too late. Fully one quarter of the business area fell in flames: the Danbury and Norwalk depot, the Isaacs block of office buildings, a lumberyard, grocery stores, saddle and harness shops, warehouses, a host of small stores, and Terrell and Down's cabinet shop where the fire had started in a defective chimney. William Kellogg James' mansion was barely saved; he lost his office and a storehouse. The new Bank of Norwalk was rescued only by pulling it with chains from its foundations and hauling it out of reach of the flames. Many small shopkeepers who had stocked their shelves for the coming Christmas season were crushed for they were underinsured or not insured at all.

Norwalk's calamity, declared the *Stamford Advocate,* arose from "the niggardly policy of the citizens of that place." The *Danbury Times* reported that the Norwalk Fire Department had been completely unprepared. The *Gazette* reprinted these harsh judgments without comment.

The only mitigating feature of the devastating event was the destruction of the "Liberian Hotel," a house of ill-repute operated by a Mrs. Phineas in a building owned by Samuel Lynes.[27] Few tears would be shed, prophesied Byington, over this loss. It was in fact "a much needed moral and physical purgation."

Norwalk's businessmen promptly set to work to

rebuild the burned-out district. Officials now insisted upon strict compliance with an 1853 ordinance prohibiting construction of wooden buildings within the "fire limits" of the central area.[28] The *Gazette* put up a three-story, iron-front brick building large enough to house its own editorial and printing departments, the telegraph office, the U.S. Post Office, and "the entire legal fraternity of Norwalk." The D & N depot and other structures were rebuilt in a modern manner. Wall Street was widened to fifty feet. When the imposing Methodist Church at the intersection of Wall Street and West Avenue was erected it crowned the handsome new architecture that rose out of the ashes of the great fire. This gracious edifice bestowed the assurance

The Norwalk Methodist Church.

that all was well with Norwalk, with Connecticut and with the United States of America.[29]

But the burgesses had not learned their lesson. Agreeing to order one new fire engine and buying a

---

27 This Samuel Lynes was a "gentleman" and not the well-known Dr. Samuel Lynes who for years was warden of the borough.

28 In spite of a serious fire in 1855, which had started in Captain Hubbell's warehouse and destroyed nearby wooden buildings, officials had ignored this ordinance. At that time the *Gazette* took burgesses to task for their laxity, making the point that Asa Smith's brick buildings had withstood the flames.

29 This double-towered structure completed in 1860 had some Gothic traits and a few Italianate features, added to a combined Federal and Greek Revival design, and probably represented the compromises of a large building committee.

lot for an engine house only after "ordered by vote of [the citizens of] the Borough," they refused to replace Engine No. 2 which continually needed repairs. In 1860 angry citizens forced the call of a special meeting to authorize purchase of a new engine. The Borough clerk's laconic minutes give a tantalizing glimpse of this confrontation. Someone on the burgess' side "moved that the petition for a new fire engine be not granted. Motion lost. Motion to adjourn. Lost. Voted that Fifteen Hundred Dollars . . . be appropriated for purchase of New Engine. Adjourned."[16] Even so the burgesses ignored the mandate until voters called another special meeting and instructed them to carry out their wishes.

The same stingy recalcitrance prevailed in the matter of installing street lamps. Many people including businessmen wanted street lighting and had formed an *ad hoc* committee to obtain a gas supply. When forty-nine residents petitioned for street lamps the burgesses stalled by merely appointing a committee to see "how many lamp posts and lanterns can be put up without expense to the Borough." A disgruntled citizenry pushed through a motion to have the lamps erected at public expense and then took its case to the ballot box. After the next election only one or two familiar faces appeared in the Court of Burgesses. Hubbell's was among the missing.

As selectman Captain Hubbell also ran into stormy waters. At the annual town meeting in December, 1858, his Alms House practices were called into question and he was directed henceforth to purchase supplies wholesale. Voters also demanded that selectmen balance the ledgers, keep a strict record of the funded debt, keep track of outstanding bills, and account for moneys spent by the surveyors.[30] But Captain Hubbell rode out the storm and a year or so later even managed to obtain the not insignificant post of town auditor.

In the Borough of Norwalk, however, the newly-elected reform burgesses hastened to disassociate themselves from the old clique and were only too happy to carry out the wishes of their supporters. When the new lamp posts arrived for distribution in the Wall Street area they pointedly placed one in front of the Fairfield County Bank, one in front of the Bank of Norwalk, but none in front of Joseph Hubbell's bank.

30 For at least two years town voters had complained about financial practices of the selectmen. Taxes had risen by 27% between 1857 and 1858, although this may have been partly due to the recession. In December, 1857, citizens took the first step in curbing the clique; they decided to select the Registrar of Voters by ballot. Heretofore the only elected officials had been the selectmen, constables, and School Visitors.
Although Hubbell had severed his connections with his grocery business, his son still operated the store, and it is possible that Alms House supplies were being purchased from Joseph, Jr.

10

SAVING THE REPUBLIC

Being
an Account of
Norwalk During the Civil War

ITIZENS in the North had long been concerned about the continued existence of the slave system. No simple issue, this involved moral and constitutional law, political and psychological attitudes, and North-South business relationships. Connecticut's textile manufacturers had strong ties with Southern businessmen from whom they bought cotton and to whom they sold finished goods. Steamers plying Long Island Sound between Connecticut ports and New York City relied upon textiles to fill their holds.

It was still legally possible to own slaves in Connecticut after 1800 but there were only a few and in 1848 a law wiped out the last vestiges of the evil institution, culminating a century's effort to erase human servitude in the state.

The earliest written record extant pertaining to slaves in Norwalk is a deed of sale recorded on March 9, 1748/1749, for the transfer to Moses St. John of Dick, a black man, by his five co-owners.[1] In another legal document, a will probated in 1751, John Copp set aside the princely sum of 400 pounds from his estate for the care of his two highly esteemed slaves after his death.

When the economic scales began to tip in favor of trade and commerce in the eighteenth century Norwalk's merchants became prosperous enough to own slaves, most of whom were employed as domestic servants.[2] The number of slaves in the community steadily increased from 94 counted in the first census of 1756 to 136 in 1774. Some of the community's prosperity rubbed off on the slaves themselves. The estate of Cesar, the Negro man of Abijah Comstock, was a replica in miniature of his master's. Like his master, Cesar drew up a will nam-

ing members of the Comstock family as recipients of his library of twenty books, numerous animal traps, beaver hat, silver spoons, knee buckles, and sleeve buttons. To Dwer and Belinda, his fellow slaves, he left his chest, caps, and handkerchiefs.[3]

The War for Independence was a time of momentous change for Connecticut's slave population as spirited white men who chafed at their own bondage to England became aware of the condition of bondage called slavery. Reflecting a growing concern for freedom the colonial legislature prohibited importation into, or the sale of any slave within, the colony.[1] Although free blacks and slaves alike served in the militia without incident during the early months of the Revolutionary War, colonial leaders had second thoughts about arming slaves and abandoned the use of blacks in the military. In 1777, however, facing a critical shortage of white enlistments, the legislature allowed any able-bodied person regardless of hue or status to substitute for any two white men. Masters were encouraged to grant freedom to slaves who enlisted for three years. Under this policy almost every Connecticut town supplied one or two blacks for the Continental forces. When Richard Camp of Norwalk "for and in Consideration of the sum of Thirty pounds Currency of the States of America recd" declared his slave, Frank, free,[4] Frank had probably "received his freedom with his flintlock."[2]

---

1 Benjamin Quarles, *The Negro in the American Revolution* (Chapel Hill, 1961), 40, points out that the action may have stemmed from the overstocked condition of the American slave market.

2 This expression for the exchange of slavery for freedom by fighting in the war is from Quarles, *ibid.*, 68.

Other slaves took a different route to freedom. After Tory-minded Jeremiah Leaming departed from Norwalk, leaving his slave behind, Pomp memorialized the General Assembly and was granted his freedom. Pomp Leaming as slave and as freeman was a man of substance for he sustained property losses exceeding fourteen pounds during Tryon's raid. Nor was he the only property owner in the black community. Syfax Negro, emancipated by John Ingersoll in 1777, received an abatement of over twenty pounds for property burned or destroyed in that same raid. Not so fortunate, however, were Job Bartram's "two valuable and likely negro men," who escaped to Long Island and sought protection of the British. Bartram crossed the Sound, repossessed and sold them.

A series of enactments gradually gave freedom to Connecticut slaves. No Negro or mulatto born in the state after March, 1784, could be held in servitude after age twenty-five. A later law lowered the age to twenty-one. After 1792 slaves could not be transported out of the state for sale in another state and when Stephen Betts 2d of Norwalk sold four Negroes out of state, Isaac Hillard, a zealous abolitionist from Redding, brought charges against him.

The effect of the gradual emancipation on Norwalk's black population is readily seen in the census figures. In the first federal census of 1790, which treated Norwalk and Stamford as one unit, sixty-seven families held a total of 117 slaves. Among Norwalk residents, Thomas Fitch, the Reverend Matthias Burnett, John Cannon, Jr., and Gould Hoyt had two slaves apiece while Matthew Marvin, Ozias Marvin, and Stephen Betts each had one.[5] In the 1810 enumeration only twelve slaves were listed in Norwalk. These belonged to various members of the Hoyt, Gregory, Lockwood, Nash, St. John, and Raymond families.[6] The more striking figure is the 113 listed under the column "other free persons."[3] These include black heads of households, like Eben Ingersoll, Ben Hanford, and Primus Quash. A list compiled from the Norwalk Land Records shows that between the end of the war and 1816 at least thirteen Negroes were granted freedom.[7]

Free blacks worked as servants and general laborers. The Lockwoods, for example, employed Enoch Negro for thirteen dollars monthly wages and kept a strict accounting of the days "you was

unwell [and] staid home," "went to Doctr Betts praising," and "you took to yourself [to] plant your garden." However, it was still possible to read advertisements like the following:

FOR SALE
A likely stout WENCH, of about twenty-four years of age; she is perfectly acquainted with all kind [sic] of housework; and suitable either for a tavern or a private family. The reason of her sale is owing to being dissatisfied with her owners. For further particulars inquire at this office.[8]

By 1830 Norwalk's free black population had reached 132 and by mid-century 150. They worked

Onesimus Brown.

as hatters, barbers, servants in private homes, maids in hotels, and as waitresses and shuckers in "oyster saloons." Only one black, ninety-year-old Jane Buckley, resided in the Alms House as a pauper. Eighty-seven-year-old Onesimus Brown who proudly listed himself in the 1850 census as the "voluntary slave" of Miss Phoebe Comstock was an anachronism in the mid-nineteenth century.[4] The

---

[3] "All other free persons, except Indians not taxed," was the designation for listing free blacks.

[4] Onesimus was sold to the Comstock family in 1773. When Miss Phoebe's aunts, Sarah and Phoebe, died, ownership passed to Miss Phoebe. On-e, as he was familiarly known throughout the town, died in 1857.

NORW∆LK
*an historical
account*

120

increase in size of the black community is reflected in the number of marriages recorded in Norwalk Records where the clerk was careful to specify the couple as "colored," although he neglected to record the ages of the partners.[9]

Black residents who had been holding church services in hotels and houses hoped for a church of their own. The selectmen failed to act on their petition for a lot on which to build a church but Henry Brush, spokesman for the black community, persisted. A second petition, this time asking for land on Town House Hill, spurred the town to find "a piece of common land [that] can be spared for their accommodation." The African Methodist congregation was too poor to build a church, however, and for decades continued to use the Town House as a place of worship, free of charge.[5] When in 1858 the African Methodists held a donation party for their pastor, the *Gazette*'s editor urged his readers to contribute generously in recognition of the minister's untiring efforts to bring about "a moral and religious elevation of the African race." To the modern reader his words sound patronizing but then they showed a vast attitudinal distance from the 1790 colonial law that prescribed whipping "not exceed-

ing forty stripes" for slaves who uttered defamatory words.

Although it is evident from the above that by mid-century Norwalk's blacks were making some economic and social advancement it had not always been that way. Norwalkers were slow to accept the anti-slavery viewpoint. By 1839 forty-five chapters of the American Anti-Slavery Society had been organized in Connecticut but none existed in Norwalk or for that matter anywhere in Fairfield County.[10] In 1838 at a time when nearby communities were engaging in anti-abolitionist riots the *Norwalk Gazette*, ordinarily sympathetic to the anti-slavery movement, briefly retreated from that position. The newspaper did editorialize while reporting on riots in New Jersey and Pennsylvania, admonishing its readers not to engage in mob action.[6]

Many individual Norwalkers opposed slavery, however, and held abolitionist meetings in private homes or in churches where representatives of the

---

[5] When in 1886 the First Congregational Church gave its Lecture Room to the Bethel AME and it was moved from Lewis Street down Mill Hill to a site on Knight Street the tiny congregation had its own home at last.

[6] Strother, *Underground Railroad in Connecticut,* 35, and Charlotte Case Fairley, "A History of New Canaan, 1801-1901," in *Readings in New Canaan History* (New Canaan, 1945), 223, cite *Charter Oak,* May, 1838 (Strother cites it for May, 1839) as their source for statements that Norwalk was the site of severe anti-abolitionist riots at that time. This seems to be a misreading of the *Charter Oak,* for that abolitionist newspaper describes these troubles as occurring in Danbury and "Reading," not in Norwalk. In May, 1839, according to *Charter Oak,* Norwalk was host city to an anti-slavery gathering.

American Anti-Slavery Society spoke. The Norwalk branch of the American Colonization Society held its meetings in the Second Congregational Church and occasionally collected money for such things as education in Africa.

Just how controversial the slavery issue was is evident from the Reverend James Knox's farewell sermon to the Second Congregational Church: "Choose not a man [so] intent upon the . . . abolition of slavery [that he] will deem it a duty to bring the subject into the pulpit," he warned regarding his successor. Nor should they accept a man with just the opposite view. Given the agitated state of the public mind, either one would bring discord and division into the church.[11]

Norwalk is reputed to have been one of the stops on the northward land route of the Underground Railroad. Several trunk lines emanated from New York City, a central point in the escape route. One of these passed through Greenwich, Darien, Norwalk, and Wilton.[12] A few houses still standing have secret chambers or passageways that could have been used to hide runaways but no documentation exists that firmly pinpoints one particular house or even one area. Tradition has it that a house at 69 East Avenue was Norwalk's stop on the Railroad. Located on both the main highway from New York and the road leading to Wilton, in the twentieth century this house still contained a small round windowless dungeon, with a ceiling opening that might at one time have led to a staircase or hidden passageway.[7]

Except for that brief period in the late 1830s the *Gazette* never hesitated to speak out against slavery and even suggested several times that free Negroes should be granted the right to vote. When A. Homer Byington became editor and publisher in 1848 the *Gazette* moved even more solidly into the anti-slavery camp. Twenty-two-year-old Byington was a kindly young man frequently taking time to insert small announcements—free advertisements, actually—into his paper to help some man down on his luck who was trying to become a house painter, or a frail maiden lady who was attempting to eke out a living as a seamstress. His own circumstances may have contributed to his generosity toward these unfortunates; he had hoped to attend Yale but, forced to earn his own living, had become an apprentice in the newspaper office.[8]

Byington used his editorial power freely to attack slavery. He roundly condemned continued sale of slaves in Washington, D.C., demanding: "When shall this free republic be relieved of such infamous exhibitions?" He decried an incident in Philadelphia where a "Gentleman of color" was asked to ride on the outside platform of a trolley while a "disgusting white loafer" was allowed to ride inside.

Toward the middle of the century many voters were attracted to the American Party, a new party that advocated "governing of America by Americans." Popularly known as Know-Nothings, its members felt threatened by the thousands of immigrants, especially the Irish, pouring into the United States. Because this party also opposed slav-

Orris S. Ferry.

ery it found favor with both dissident Whigs and anti-slavery Democrats. The American Party was briefly popular in Norwalk, as elsewhere in Connecticut. During the few years of rampant nativism the little Catholic church on Chapel Street became the target of violent anti-Catholic feeling. When their attempt to burn it to the ground failed, nativists sawed off the gilded wooden cross atop the structure. Even the kind-hearted Byington regarded the Irish with indifference although he opposed the

---

7 This house stood on the present site of J.M. Layton & Co.

8 Byington's father had received one of the first patents for felting wool and brought his family to Norwalk when he went into business with G.G. Bishop. This partnership broke up and the Byington family moved to Rochester, New York, where Byington, Sr. died.

Know-Nothings. Norwalk's Irish residents were never mentioned by name in the *Gazette*. "We hear that three Irishmen were sunstruck in Westport on Saturday, one of whom has since died," Byington reported laconically in one issue. The editor could write without a trace of pity: "An Irishwoman was found dead near 'Finchville'—cause, general bad usage and worse rum."9

Discontented Whigs and Democrats soon found a new political home in the Republican Party which took hold in Connecticut in the late 1850s. The American Party also declined as a result of the drawing power of the Republicans with their free-soil, anti-slavery orientation. In 1859 during the "Ferry and Freedom" campaign that sent Norwalk's Orris Ferry to Congress, Byington headed the town's new Republican organization. He himself was elected to the state assembly.

Ferry's slim margin of victory in this election—only 654 to 446 in his own community and less in other towns in the Fourth Congressional District—presaged a questionable future for the Republicans of the area and for the United States itself. During the next campaign in 1861, which occurred during the unsettled period between the secession of South Carolina and the firing on Fort Sumter, Ferry's speeches and votes in Congress demonstrated his loyalty to the Union. "We must not compromise," he stated privately to some newspaper men in Washington. "We have got three things to do: first, to do right; second, to overthrow forever the power of slavery; third, to save the Republic."13 However, in the 1861 election, held just before the outbreak of war, Ferry lost to his Democratic opponent, receiving an even scantier plurality in Norwalk than he had received two years earlier.10 Indeed Norwalk was almost the only town in western Connecticut that went Republican.

"There is no course left but for the government to vindicate its dignity by an exhibition of its strength," Ferry insisted to his former colleagues in the House of Representatives after all efforts to reconcile the differences between North and South had collapsed and the surrender of Fort Sumter had been announced.

9 By the 1860s, however, the Irish were regarded as individuals, and the *Gazette* often referred to them by name and in a friendly fashion.

10 The vote was 740 to 605 in Norwalk. The Democrats, although not actually in favor of slavery, hoped to avoid war and appease the South.

With columns edged in heavy black the *Gazette* reported the somber details of the loss of Sumter and President Lincoln's Proclamation of War. It was indeed a time for mourning. Governor William A. Buckingham immediately called for volunteers to help the beleaguered government "vindicate its dignity." Under the prodding of Eben Hill, Union supporters promptly gathered in Lynes' Hall to show their loyalty and passed a resolution giving the President their full support. Nearly every one of the town's businessmen was there, as well as most of the clergy. As the band struck up "The Star-Spangled Banner," every man in the hall leaped to his feet and spontaneously joined in the chorus.

Within days five thousand dollars had been raised to aid the families of volunteers and the amount was speedily augmented. These contributions provided ten dollars at the time of a man's enlistment and five dollars monthly during his term of service.14 Officers of Eben Hill's Bank of Norwalk offered Governor Buckingham thirty thousand dollars to help the state procure weapons and supplies for its volunteer regiments. A special town meeting was also called at which voters authorized funds to equip and supply local volunteers. Not only well-to-do, older men supported this war; employees of the Norwalk Lock Company contributed their nickels and dimes to buy a large new American flag which soon waved over the factory.

During this shortlived burst of patriotic fervor Norwalk men enlisted for three months' service in various companies within the five Connecticut volunteer regiments raised during the spring and summer of 1861. Of companies within the five regiments, one, Company A, Third Regiment, drew its entire complement of sixty and its officers solely from Norwalk residents. This regiment was immediately dispatched to Washington, D.C., to relieve the Cassius M. Clay Guard, a valiant band of "wide-awakes" that had been guarding the city around the clock against Rebel attack. Two Norwalkers were already in the Guard—Orris Ferry11 and newspaperman Byington who had gone to Washington immediately after the war started. Company A's gentle introduction to warfare was but a brief interlude for before the Third's term of enlistment ran out its men took part in the bloody battles of Manassas and Bull Run.

11 Ferry joined the Fifth Connecticut Regiment as a colonel and was later promoted to the rank of brigadier-general.

The defeats handed to Union forces in the summer of 1861 were convincing evidence that the war would not be speedily concluded. News about local boys was uncommonly distressful. In June Lieutenant Thomas Horton, Company D, Seventh Regiment, was struck down by heavy grapeshot in an engagement at James Island. Less than a month later Corporal Oliver Brady was a casualty of the Battle of Cedar Mountain where the Connecticut Fifth Regiment was "broken in pieces."

Governor Buckingham called for volunteers to fill four additional regiments and the Sixth through

Le Grand Lockwood.

Ninth Regiments were organized. Once more Norwalk volunteers were randomly assigned to several companies in three regiments although Company H, Eighth Regiment, was almost entirely a Norwalk company. Many of its men had followed the example of its commander, Captain Douglas Fowler, and reenlisted at the end of their three-months' term.

The Ninth, the Irish Regiment, had a complement of eleven companies, nothing short of a miracle when one considers the shabby treatment meted out to this ethnic group in those days. Although

prejudice and discrimination had left the Irish as a whole opposed to the war many Irish families in Norwalk were staunch Unionists. When every Norwalk church except the one on Chapel Street showed the colors some people worried about Irish patriotism. Questioned about this, Father Mulligan, pastor of St. Mary's, explained: "Our church is not a church of North or South. We minister to all ... but you will find my flock truly loyal to the Union." No greater example of devotion to country exists than that of Patrick McQuillan who doughtily maintained: "I've sent me boys, and if the ould man is needed to save me adopted country, I'm ready to go, too." Irish boys from Norwalk joined all regiments but were prone to enlist in Rhode Island, New York State, even Ohio volunteer units instead of in Connecticut's Irish Regiment. In fact only one Irishman from Norwalk, John O. Mahoney, served in Connecticut's Ninth.

There was a discernible slowing-up of enlistments during the winter of 1861-1862. Bounty payments of $150 were no real incentive to men from Connecticut's industrial communities who could find steady work in war industries either at home or in nearby towns. In Norwalk Lounsbury and Bissell had begun to make gun wadding and the Norwalk Lock Company was turning out hardware for guns and ships. Foodstuffs too were in great demand—even onions which William Marvin raised on his farm near Calf Pasture and sold to the federal government for the whopping price of forty-two cents a barrel.

The call for manpower continued. It was with considerable difficulty that the Tenth through Thirteenth Regiments were filled. In this callup Norwalk again had no single company but counted thirty-eight local men in Company E, Twelfth Regiment, with Captain Stephen Byxbee of Norwalk commanding. Local enlistees as usual were sprinkled throughout the companies of the four regiments, often with no close friend or comrade in the same company. Nineteen-year-old Charles Knapp, for example, was enrolled in Company D, Thirteenth Regiment, when it was mustered in on February 20, 1862. When the regiment left New Haven on March 17, en route to New Orleans to join General Benjamin Butler's forces, young Knapp was not among those who boarded ship. Listed initially as a deserter poor Knapp was actually a victim of smallpox, virulent in the New Haven camp that winter.*12* Army authorities had callously resorted to this method of keeping news of the epidemic from the public. The young soldier's tombstone proclaims the courage he never had a chance to test:

> *Sleep Soldier still in honored rest*
> *Your truth and valor wearing:*
> *The bravest are the tenderest*
> *The loveing are the dareing.*

Once again the state called for volunteers. Fairfield County responded by manning the Seventeenth Regiment. Norwalk supplied sufficient troops to fill Company A commanded by Douglas Fowler and Company F under Captain Enoch Wood.*13* The pride of Norwalk was Company F, the Lockwood Guards, which was raised in three days after LeGrand Lockwood offered one thousand dollars bounty to its volunteers. As the Seventeenth passed through South Norwalk en route from mustering in at Seaside Park, Bridgeport, a premature discharge from a cannon shattered the arm of one soldier who died shortly after the limb was amputated. This inauspicious beginning was the first in a chain of ill-fated events that befell this uncommonly courageous regiment during its three years of active duty, although life seemed uneventful enough when the troops first reached Baltimore and were assigned to defend that city. In a monotonous round of activity the troops rose at daybreak, drilled five hours a day, busied themselves digging wells and building an abatis around the fort, and fell in at 9:15 P.M. taps. During a respite from military duties in the evening hours the men organized a Union Temperance Association of the Seventeenth Regiment and enrolled sixty-five colleagues with little effort.

Norwalkers contributed to the war in a number of ways. Captain William Allen whose two sons were fighting with the Union Army commanded the steamer *Huzzar*, transporting troops and war materiel. Gilbert Secor was an officer on the *Thos. Collyer* which plied the Potomac River carrying

members of the Sanitary Commission to Bermuda Hundred and bringing back Rebel prisoners of war to Washington on its return trip. At home people gave generously to such causes as the Fund for Chaplains' Tents or Thanksgiving dinners for soldiers in the field. South Norwalk's Ladies Patriotic Society met regularly at Ely's Hall to stitch shirts, drawers, and socks, and to knit mittens which they packed off to the Norwalk men of the Seventeenth together with dried apples, mustard, and Bibles. Homer Byington expedited delivery of these packages to the front by sorting them out from among the heaps of backlogged materials in Washington's storehouses. As a newspaperman covering battles and marches he searched out Norwalk soldiers for friendly visits and raised morale at home as well as in the field for he was careful to send back the most encouraging and complimentary stories about individual soldiers. Still other Norwalk residents patriotically bought "Five-Twenties," the registered U.S. 6 percent bonds offered for sale by Fisk and Hatch, New York bankers, who advertised these bonds in the *Gazette*. The Reverend Augustus Field Beard alone purchased one thousand dollars worth at one time.*14* LeGrand Lockwood maintained a proprietary interest in "his" Guards, paying for necessities such as eighty blouses packed off to the front to keep the men warm and comfortable during the winter of 1863.

Although they received less publicity than those in the Army a number of Norwalkers served in the United States Navy during the war. Rear Admiral Francis Hoyt Gregory, known as "a brainy officer," held the highest rank of all Norwalk men in the Navy during these years. Gregory, who had made the Navy his career, was considered for command of the Atlantic coast fleet but was passed over because he was "very old, [with] face and hair like tissue paper." His expertise, however, made him invaluable in superintending the building of Union war vessels in non-government shipyards, the post to which this fine old officer was assigned during the war.*15*

---

12 In the *Adjutant-General's Record of Service* published in 1869, Knapp was listed as a deserter. In *The Record of Service of Connecticut Men in the Army and Navy of the United States During The War of the Rebellion* (Hartford, 1889), Knapp's record was corrected.

13 Wood survived the war but came home to find his pottery had been destroyed by fire. He resettled in Perth Amboy, New Jersey, where he became superintendent of the Hall Pottery.

14 See A.F. Beard's Personal Account Book. LHM Archives. According to a family letter from his sister, Augustus Beard may have had some influence in persuading President Lincoln to dismiss General George B. McClellan from his command of the Army. Ltr., Eliza Beard to Edward Beard, Nov. 14, 1862. File Box, Beard Family Letters, LHM Archives.

15 During Gregory's long career in the Navy he fought in the

A few months after hostilities began, a Norwalk photographer, E. T. Whitney, attached himself to the Army of the Potomac as one of several assistants to the now-famous Civil War photographer Mathew Brady. Although he himself seldom ventured into the actual battlefields, Brady always claimed credit for all pictures taken by the men in his employ and it is therefore impossible to single out Whitney's contributions to Civil War photography. He was almost certainly the only cameraman with General George B. McClellan's troops for some weeks in the spring of 1862. This came about after general headquarters had temporarily forbidden photographers at the front, but a guard ignorant of the orders permitted Whitney to approach McClellan's headquarters. The general gave the Norwalk man a special pass and permitted him to stay. Pictures of the Army of the Potomac between early March and possibly on into April can probably be attributed solely to Whitney. When the troops went into winter quarters Whitney became superintendent of Brady's Washington Gallery from whence Byington reported: "Our photographer friend Whitney is still at Brady's perpetuating the life and death scenes of the war." Although gaining a reputation Whitney gave up this position after a few months, perhaps because of difficulties in working with the temperamental Brady, and returned to Norwalk where he set up a studio in the *Gazette* building.[15]

Bad news from the front continued almost unabated during the first two years of the war. By 1863 some people were saying that the fighting should be brought to a halt even if this meant allowing the South to go its own way. To Unionists this was treasonous talk. Nevertheless such talk grew and the spring elections found the Peace Democrats taking control of that party in Connecticut, forcing the nomination of the outspoken Thomas Seymour for governor. Republicans ran the incumbent, Buckingham.

In western Connecticut Norwalk stood almost alone as a Republican town in a county even more Democratic than when the voters had stripped Orris Ferry of his Congressional seat in 1861. Emboldened by the turn of events at the state level, Peace Democrats flaunted shiny copper pennies in an attempt to turn the opprobrious term "Copperhead" by which they were known into a proud title. Norwalk's Copperheads became more defiant as their numbers increased. Even children were drawn into the wrangling. One little fellow at Over the River School was expelled when he refused to obey his teacher's command to remove the copper penny his father had insisted he wear as a badge.

The Whitney family in 1861.

The petty incident became a local *cause célèbre* and the *Gazette* fulminated: "Pity the child whose father is so brutalized and bestial as to compel his little boy to wear one of these open insignia of treason."

During the election campaign the newspaper ran several emotional appeals from the men in the Connecticut Volunteers to counteract the Peace movement's growing popularity. The soldiers of the Seventeenth Regiment declared that should the Peace Party triumph in Connecticut the state would be "stained by one of the foulest blots of all history." Signed by two dozen officers, with Lieutenant Edgar Hoyt of Company B, Captain Enoch Wood

War of 1812 on Lake Ontario, was captured and spent eighteen months as a prisoner in England. In the exciting 1820s, in command of the twelve-gun schooner *Grampus*, part of a squadron suppressing pirates in the Caribbean, the swashbuckling Gregory let a Puerto Rican pirate ship "come down close before opening fire and reduced her to sinking in three minutes." Promoted through the ranks to captain, Gregory next commanded a forty-four-gun frigate in the Mexican War and later was placed in charge of the African Squadron. Fletcher Pratt, *The Navy, A History* (Garden City, N.Y., 1941), 221, 313, 342.

of Company F, and the popular Captain Douglas Fowler of Company A leading the list, this appeal must have carried considerable weight. Even so the election was nip-and-tuck for the pro-Union Republicans.

"Our Flag is Still Here," cried the *Gazette* after the election. "Connecticut is Saved!" In western Connecticut the Union flag was still flying but just barely. All the towns around Norwalk went Democratic; Buckingham won in Norwalk by only 168 votes and in the state by a small majority. Westport and Greenwich were solidly Democratic and Stamford evenly split. Fortunately for the Republicans the election took place before the disheartening news of Chancellorsville reached the North.

The Seventeenth had joined General Joseph Hooker's Eleventh Corps in the Union's drive toward Richmond. During the tedious march south, slogging through interminable mud—"Old King Mud" as William Godfrey of the Lockwood Guards called it—put a damper on the spirits of all but the most hardy. "Old Warrier" Godfrey also expressed a fear that "the boys will not stay . . . mutch longer . . . should have paid us three months ago but not a damed cent yet—and some of the men has not been paid in eight." Godfrey frankly admitted he would prefer to be home drinking cider to "fighting for the Almighty Nigger."[16]

Hooker was stopped short at Chancellorsville when Generals "Stonewall" Jackson and Robert E. Lee outmaneuvered the indecisive Union general. Connecticut troops bore the brunt of the fighting in this engagement. Indeed one of the first forays in the battle was an attack by Jackson's men on Lieutenant Albert Wilcoxen's Norwalk troops while they were on picket duty. As the battle raged on, Union artillery succeeded in checking the Southern advance, temporarily relieving weary infantrymen. The Norwalk troops were so exhausted they flopped to the ground and fell asleep amidst the roar of the battle. "While the ponderous diapason of the artillery rolled along the vibrating air, and the solid earth trembled with the oft-repeated concussion, I fell asleep," wrote Wilcoxen, "and, with the serenity inspired by a good position and heavy artillery, rested pleasantly till Sunday morning." The battle continued all next day and night with heavy losses on both sides and when it ended the Confederates had won.

News of local boys killed, wounded, or taken prisoner at Chancellorsville filled almost an entire page in the *Gazette*. Among the dead was Corporal Thomas Brown whose wedding Company A had attended the morning they left town. Brown died in the hospital "just as he finished singing a patriotic song." Sergeant Rufus Buttery's letter to his wife narrates the fate of Company A, commanded to hold its position in a small garden:

As the rebels came out of the woods [he wrote] they had to come over a level clear lot, and as that traitor flag came out of the woods, a thrill ran through my veins, and I waited for the bearer of it to get near enough for my shot to reach him, about that time we had the order to fire. I drew as close a sight on him as I knew how, and that rebel fell with many others.

A. Homer Byington.

After fighting some time, I looked around to see how things were going on, and to my surprise, there were only three or four of us in the garden. I had heard no order to fall back, all I heard was one of the men said "We will have to fall back," and I told him that we could hold our ground.[17]

Buttery was taken prisoner and marched off to the barbarous Libby Prison in Richmond. After four days without food the weakened prisoner was taken to City Point, a Union area, to be exchanged for a captured Southern soldier.

The Seventeenth moved on to Gettysburg. On July 1, 1863, with the indomitable Douglas Fowler, now a lieutenant colonel, leading the left wing, the regiment took part in the first assault of this fratricidal encounter. Fowler, so ill at Chancellorsville that he had directed his troops from an ambulance pallet, was killed in this charge. The *Gazette's* columns were again draped in black when news of his death reached Norwalk, for the brave young officer had had admiring friends throughout the town. Although news of the Union victory in Pennsylvania cheered all, lamented the editor, Fowler's death showed how costly it was. He was "the bravest of the brave—every inch a soldier." The gallant Fowler's death in battle was later commemorated in a song, "Comrades, I am Dying," published in 1865:

> *Comrades, comrades, I am dying!*
> *See the crimson fountain flow,*
> *Sick and wounded I am lying,*
> *On the field among the foe.*
>
> *But the angels hover round me,*
> *They will guard me while I sleep . . .*
> *Comrades, onward to the battle.*
> *Do not for the soldier weep.*[18]

Even as Norwalkers mourned this valiant soldier hero they delighted in the exploits of Homer Byington, a civilian hero at Gettysburg. Byington had become a war reporter for the *New York Tribune* and arrived at Gettysburg to find the telegraph lines cut. In short order he had the lines repaired, ferreted out an operator who had hidden his telegraph machine under a bed, and pressed both man and machine into service. For two days Byington monopolized the line, sending off detailed dispatches of the action while rival reporters fumed and sent theirs by courier. Byington's accurate and informative reports, which had to be sent via the War Department before release to the newspaper, impressed the Department and even caught the attention of the harried President.

The costly battles of Chancellorsville and Gettysburg had thinned the Union ranks. The short-term voluntary enlistments utilized at the onset of the war did not meet the demands of sustained campaigns. When President Lincoln stepped up the call for men and also lengthened the period of service to three years, Connecticut communities found it more difficult to meet their assigned quotas. To lure volunteers Norwalk gradually had to raise its original fifty dollar bounty to three hundred dollars by 1863 but—with a three year term—even such munificence failed to attract enlistees. In March, 1863, Lincoln finally had to institute conscription.

Under conscription regulations all males twenty to forty years old were liable for service but a man could circumvent the draft by providing a substitute, obtaining a medical or religious commutation, or purchasing an exemption. This system especially strained the poorer elements of society but allowed an affluent man like George St. John, "a gentleman of leisure," to purchase a substitute for one hundred dollars to replace him in the draft of September, 1863. Too often draftees were unconcerned about the physical or psychological condition of their replacements as long as they were alive and breathing. St. John took care to procure a substitute who "was apparently sober and understood what he was doing."[19]

St. John's behavior was typical of Connecticut

Cap made by Comstock Bros. of Norwalk for Buckingham Post No. 12 of the G.A.R.

draftees in 1863. Of the 11,539 men drafted, 2,248 hired substitutes and 8,000 others purchased exemptions or obtained religious or medical commutations. "White liver," a hitherto unheard-of disease, reached epidemic proportions and threatened to extinguish Connecticut's male population of draftable age. When news of the threatened draft call reached the ears of "Old Warrior" William Godfrey he warned his friend "Gyp": "Tell Hary to look oute for his Oxen for I think they will draft everything that is not over Thirty-Five . . . Hogs Sheeps Chicken and so fourth."

Violent draft riots broke out in New York City and raised fears of similar reactions in Connecticut.

As a precautionary measure Governor Bucking-ham detailed rifles and ammunition to large towns along the major railroad lines. He entrusted sixty guns to Thomas Guyer, a Norwalk doorknob man-ufacturer and commander of the militia. The riots never occurred but draftees did their best to avoid the new law by somehow scrounging the money needed to buy their way out. The records show that individual Norwalk residents paid out almost eight thousand dollars for bounties to substitutes and volunteers, and an additional nine hundred for commutations. The town itself spent $73,967.91 for commutations, bounties, and support of soldiers' families.[20] On the other hand Norwalk's volunteer soldiers offset its reluctant conscriptees. The town supplied altogether almost seven hundred fighting men for the Union forces.

After Gettysburg the decimated Seventeenth Regiment was moved to a different kind of combat. Following a respite at Folly Island it moved on to St. Augustine, Florida. Here Henry Allen, one of "coaster" Captain William Allen's sons who had

served in the New York Volunteers prior to joining the Seventeenth Connecticut, was promoted to major. Albert Wilcoxen who had received two promotions since Chancellorsville became lieuten-ant colonel as Fowler's successor.

While in Florida the regiment was given the dangerous assignment of foraging for foodstuffs. Often traveling seventy-five miles or more into Rebel territory, its small raiding parties sometimes brought back a thousand head of cattle in a single strike. On one daring foray to seize some baled cotton, the raiders, hampered by their slow-moving wagons, were attacked by Dixon's Cavalry and more than thirty men were taken prisoner. Wilcoxen was severely wounded and was captured after his horse was shot from under him. He was removed to a Rebel hospital in Tallahassee where he died in March. His death so close to the war's end was particularly ironic for Wilcoxen was a peaceable man who, in spite of his soldierly demeanor and uncommon bravery, had been studying theology before his enlistment. His family learned of his death at the very time the welcome news of Lee's surrender was received.

It seemed as if joy and mourning were to be forever commingled. Hard upon the news of the Union's great triumph came the horrifying report, just two days before Easter, that the President of the United States had been struck down by an assassin's bullet. Norwalk people, looking forward to the first really joyous Easter service in four years, found themselves listening to somber sermons delivered from black-covered pulpits. Every yard of black cloth in town was sold out the following day as their owners draped houses and shops in mourning. On Wednesday the grieving town turned out for a funeral procession and memorial services for the fallen President.

All through the day muffled church bells tolled. A procession marched with slow tread down West Avenue, across Washington Street Bridge, and up East Avenue to the Green. The Phoenix Fire Engine, displaying a large black-bordered picture of President Lincoln, moved slowly along the route with the hook-and-ladder which carried a banner with the words: "We Mourn Our Loss." The highlight of the procession was a funeral car on which rested a draped catafalque covered by an American flag. This vehicle was drawn by twelve black horses, each led "by a colored man wearing deep mourning badges, for the memory of him who was their God-appointed Moses to lead their race out of bondage."

The Fourth of July passed quietly that year. The traditional old-fashioned noisy celebration seemed out of place, not alone because of the President's death but because the Seventeenth Regiment had not yet been ordered home. Until the men of the Seventeenth were back the war was not over. The Fifth, Sixth, and Seventh Regiments, each of which had a few Norwalk men, had promptly returned to Connecticut. But the Seventeenth, about to leave for Hilton Head for the return journey, was abruptly rerouted to Jacksonville for two months to reconstruct the Tallahassee railroad and its men were not mustered out until mid-July. Then when the regiment finally landed in New Haven citizens of that city, led by Governor Buckingham himself, insisted upon heaping honors and praise upon its brave soldiers. Companies A and F did not arrive home until the first of August. Lieutenant Colonel Henry Allen, who had been only a lieutenant in Company A when he had joined it in 1862, now led the veterans home as the ranking officer.

With prominent citizens vying to serve on the Committee of Arrangements and every fire band, every fife and drum corps, every civic society, and all church organizations coming forward to help, Norwalk organized a day of celebration beyond any the town had ever seen. Again everyone turned out for a procession ending at the Green, but this time it was an exuberant one. Judge Thomas Butler's[16] heartfelt speech of thanks and welcome was warmly and fittingly answered by General Orris Ferry. Then the "boys in blue" and their ladies partook of a sumptuous collation prepared by the women of the town and later were honored at a splendid reception.

Joyous and festive as the day was, no one seeing the Seventeenth's tattered battle flag could forget that some men had not come home. "Beneath the soil of almost every battlefield of the war," Ferry reminded the throng at the Green, "lie buried some of the dead of Norwalk." Fowler lay in an unmarked grave at Gettysburg; Wilcoxen in a Rebel cemetery in distant Florida. Was there any recompense for the loss of so many heroic men? Ferry believed there was. "The triumphal arch of the Republic spanning the continent," he assured his fellow townsmen, "is their monument."

16 Butler was prominent in Norwalk, not only as a judge but because of his interest in agriculture and meteorology.

PART THREE

INDUSTRIAL

COMMUNITY

1865/1913

11

WORKINGMEN AND GENTLEMEN

*Being
an Account of
Norwalk's Victorian Days*

HE WAR'S end found the town poorer "in numbers and riches." Norwalk factories had failed to receive the volume of lucrative war contracts handed out to companies in some Connecticut towns. No counterpart to the Remington Arms Company developed in Norwalk. On the other hand the town did not suffer from the forced blooming experienced by little villages in eastern Connecticut which turned out quantities of guns and gunpowder and then were left to wither after 1865.

South Norwalk was now very definitely the industrial although perhaps not the social center of town, and it was fitting therefore that one of the first banks to be chartered in Connecticut under the 1863 Banking Act was established in that section. Algernon Beard was a founder of this, the First National Bank of South Norwalk, and served as its first president.

One large new enterprise appeared at the end of the war, the Norwalk Iron Works Company, which began to manufacture mining equipment, steel pumps, and—later—air and gas compressors. This was a sister firm of the Norwalk Lock Company with Ebenezer Hill and Algernon Beard among its principal stockholders and directors. Other "regulars" who acquired a share in this—as in each new undertaking—were George G. Bishop of the Union Manufacturing Company and Henry Hoyt of Morrison & Hoyt, together with a few newcomers such as former New York businessman Dudley P. Ely. The Iron Works made steady although not outstanding progress and by the end of the century, with 375 workmen in its foundry and factory on Water Street, it was one of the town's larger employers.

In 1868 a new Stamford company, Yale and Towne, which manufactured a small, flat latchkey, threatened to put Norwalk Lock out of business. The mechanism of the new lock and key was a unique advance over the traditional long-necked key which required a thick, heavy door for its lock and bolt and was susceptible to an even moderately talented lockpicker. Yale and Towne successfully protected their patents from would-be imitators and soon Yale Lock was a household word throughout the world. Norwalk Lock continued to manufacture the old-fashioned long-necked key but it had to concentrate on other products in the highly competitive builders' hardware field and to emphasize design and finish rather than locks.

All in all the years immediately after the war saw Norwalk's economy neither outstandingly good nor depressingly bad. The town's greatest asset was its growing reputation as one of the most attractive residential cities in the state. The lovely harbor with its many scenic islands was almost unmatched along the eastern seaboard. Hills rising close to the shore afforded breathtaking views of the waterfront as witness this advertisement for a sixteen-room house for sale in South Norwalk, on one acre of land, well stocked with shade and fruit trees and only five minutes from the New York and New Haven depot:

The Prospect from the premises is unsurpassed for beauty and extent, embracing a view of the town, Norwalk Harbor, and islands, and thirty miles of Long Island Sound and shore.[1]

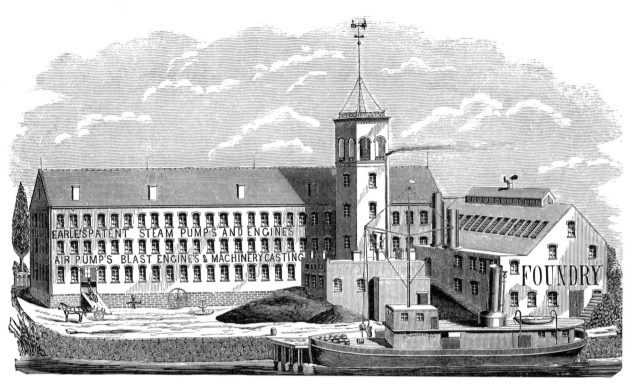

Prospect Hill, half a mile farther inland, rose still higher and the fortunate families who could afford to live in this fashionable neighborhood situated their houses so that the wide, curved verandas looked out over river, harbor, and the blue waters of the Sound. Land prices skyrocketed for a few years after the war and property changed hands so rapidly that newspapers dubbed the situation "real estate fever." A growing number of prosperous New York City businessmen, well-to-do retired men, and "gentlemen" brought their families to the charming seaside community.

One "Yorker" whose presence left a lasting mark was the well-known publisher, George Palmer Putnam, who purchased a house in Five Mile River in 1862 and brought his family there every summer. Putnam overwhelmed the unsophisticated Five Mile River people with his constant efforts to improve their lot. He brought celebrities like Horace Greeley to speak at the little Union Church, made generous contributions to repair the edifice, established a children's library in the Sunday School, and started a public library in the village. Putnam expected that all these benefactions would promote "a large sense of corporate village feeling and of fellowship."[2] The local people failed to appreciate his efforts on their behalf.

Undiscouraged, Putnam applied to the government for a U.S. Post Office for Five Mile River. To meet the Postal Department's minimum mail requirements the indefatigable publisher brought mail from his New York City office and posted it from the village. The Postal Department thought the existing name, South Five Mile River Landing, too lengthy for postmark cancellation, so Putnam researched old records and proposed the name "Rowayton." This was promptly accepted at a town

Patented steam pump manufactured by Norwalk Iron Works.

meeting and although resentful villagers fought to have the old name restored Rowayton it remained. The publisher plunged ahead with his good works, next persuading the New Haven Railroad to provide a station stop at Rowayton. Old-time natives insisted the stop be called Five Mile River—and it was.

Only after Putnam's death in 1873 did his old neighbors realize what he had done for their little community. Resolutions acknowledging his public service were passed at town meetings and a commercial sloop that docked at a Five Mile River wharf was rechristened the *George Palmer Putnam.*

Of the many rich newcomers none excited the interest of local people as much as millionaire

tural examples of America's Gilded Age. The finest Italian marbles, exotic ebony and rosewood, specially designed Aubusson carpets—nothing but the best was used to construct and furnish Lockwood's house. "Elm Park," completed in 1868, was four years in the building and cost nearly two million dollars. One hundred gardeners labored to landscape the grounds which contained greenhouses, an arboretum, a splendid orchard, grape arbors, a small lake, and a carriage house with room for seventeen carriages.

By no means as acceptable or popular as Lockwood but as willing to spend money were four henchmen of New York City's William Marcy

The "Elm Park" rotunda with Albert Bierstadt's "Domes of Yosemite."

Le Grand Lockwood's "Elm Park" was under construction from 1864 to 1868.

LeGrand Lockwood as he set about to build the most extravagant and elegant mansion ever to rise in Norwalk. Not in actual fact a newcomer, Norwalk-born Lockwood had moved to New York City as a youth, had accumulated a fortune in the stock market through his own efforts, and was adding to his millions every year.[1] Still in his early forties this portly financier wanted to show the hometown folks what a local boy could achieve. His forty-room mansion, designed in French neo-Renaissance style, stands today as one of the most beautiful architec-

("Boss") Tweed. These "Lords of the Ring," John H. Keyser, Elbert A. Woodward, James Ingersoll, and Andrew Garvey, purchased adjoining shore-front estates at the mouth of the Norwalk River leading out to Bouton's Island (later Keyser Island and now Manresa Island).[2] They may have been trying to emulate "Boss" Tweed who summered in Greenwich and were probably attracted to the Norwalk shore area because they were poker-

[1] Lockwood was married to Ann Louise Benedict, a descendant of the early Benedicts. The couple had six children.

[2] Elbert A. Woodward should not be confused with Asa Woodward, a rising young attorney of that period, a former town moderator and member of the state legislature.

Mayor Ely's residence . . . circa 1870 . . . stood on the present site of the main post office building on Washington Street.

Andrew Garvey's estate, now Shorefront Park.

playing cronies of Lewis O. Wilson, owner of Wilson Point. Each man had made a fortune padding his bills for goods and services to the City of New York. Garvey, "Prince of the Plasterers," had charged five hundred thousand dollars for one job and within months received a million for repairing the work he had just completed.[3] In their summer homes on the shore the Lords lived the lives of country gentlemen, beautifying the grounds of the estates with specimens of exotic fruit trees and flowers. Although the unsavory sources of their wealth were known to everyone the Lords seem to have been fairly well liked. The trusting councilmen of South Norwalk appointed Woodward a street commissioner and he also sat on the board of the First National Bank of South Norwalk. Both he and Keyser gained local reputations for philanthropy which served them well when their patron was thrown in jail a few years later.[3]

The doubling of Norwalk's population in the two decades after 1860, a modest gain compared with that of similar cities in the state, created overcrowding in the older sections and put stresses on the governmental structure. The cry during the last half of the century was for more city services—schools, electricity, a water system, clean paved streets, sewers, trash disposal. "Dear Editor," wrote one disgruntled Borough resident:

I live on Main Street . . . It is filthy . . . The Borough officers ought to enter their solemn protest, if nothing more, against any one merchant throwing more than six rats per day onto the street . . . If I had time I would speak of the number of barrels, boxes, tubs, baskets . . . now lying on the sidewalks in front of some of our drygoods and grocery stores.
UNFORTUNATE CITIZEN, with eyes and nose and no rubber boots.[4]

South Norwalk's business district was in even worse shape with "garbage, swill, and refuse" tossed daily into its streets. The danger of polluting nearby wells led to demands for a public water system but South Norwalkers could do little about this until 1871 when the state legislature granted that area a charter making it the City of South Norwalk. This charter permitted South Norwalk to control its own

affairs much as the Borough of Norwalk did, with only a modicum of control by the town. With Dudley P. Ely, the City's first mayor, presiding over an elected council of twelve members,[5] South Norwalk could move ahead to provide its own amenities, unhampered by lethargy or opposition from other areas of Norwalk.

The Borough of Norwalk was the first section to obtain a water system when in 1871 water from Grupe's Reservoir in New Canaan was pumped to the central district.[4] South Norwalk asked to have this system extended to supply its residents but the

Mayor Dudley P. Ely.

Borough was unwilling to promise to share water with South Norwalk in times of extended drought. The latter municipality had to develop its own water supply and in 1875 obtained water from reservoirs in Wilton. Toward the end of the century South Norwalk's system was extended to East Norwalk and Rowayton.

---

[3] After Tweed's downfall all the men fled, to Europe and elsewhere, but none was imprisoned as Tweed was. Keyser and Woodward returned to Norwalk where the latter went into several business ventures, including real estate.

[4] This supply was augmented by several additional reservoirs. The system marked the beginning of the First Water District.

Workers at the Volk Hat Company.

South Norwalk also developed a city-operated electrical plant supplying current for street lamps in the business district. Except for Saturday nights when the city fathers deemed it wise to keep the streets well lighted, the lamps were lit only when there was no moonlight and even then were turned off at midnight. Electricity was soon extended to mercantile establishments and finally to private homes.

This modern form of illumination gained South Norwalk nation-wide fame. The municipality was fortunate to have an unusually capable man, Albert A. Winchester, design the plant in 1892. He was invited to remain as its general superintendent. Visitors from all over the country came to observe and study the South Norwalk electrical plant. Winchester was invited to be a member of the eminent National Civic Association's Commission on Public Ownership and Operation, frequently lectured on electrical technology, and was a United States delegate to an international convention of electrical engineers in London.[6]

The modest but pleasant prosperity Norwalkers enjoyed after the war was eroded by the depression that began in 1873. If anyone in Norwalk doubted that a serious economic crisis had struck the nation

he had only to drive along West Avenue where LeGrand Lockwood's mansion, emptied of its luxurious furnishings and works of art, its shutters closed, awaited a buyer. Lockwood was dead, his business in ruins, and his widow evicted for non-payment of the mortgage.[5] Norwalk managed to weather these depression years rather more successfully than might have been expected but people did feel the pinch. Every newspaper edition carried three or four notices of tax sales. Tax receipts fell off so sharply that in 1876 the Borough had to reduce wages of its policemen from $2.00 to $1.75 per day. Householders were plagued by tramps, sometimes twenty in a single day, forlorn, out-of-work wanderers who would chop kindling or do other chores for a free meal and overnight shelter

[5] Lockwood was dealt a heavy financial blow through no fault of his own during the Black Friday gold manipulation of Jay Gould and Jim Fisk, and he had to mortgage "Elm Park" to pay his business debts. He died unexpectedly in 1872 before he was able to recoup his losses and put his firm into sound condition. His sons were unable to keep the firm afloat when the depression hit. Through ownership of a railroad that had taken the mortgage on "Elm Park," Commodore Vanderbilt held the mortgage and when Mrs. Lockwood was unable to make the final payment of $80,000 he foreclosed. Prior to this time she had had to dispose of most of the furnishings.

in barn or carriagehouse. These "turnpike sailors" were apt to steal as well as beg and the selectmen warned citizens not to encourage them but to direct them to the lock-up which was expanded in 1877 to handle the influx of tramps. Here a man was given a supper of hearty soup and overnight lodging, for which he was expected to break rocks the following morning before he was sent on his way.

All the town's old, conservative companies managed to survive this, the longest depression up to that time in the United States. In 1877, however, Norwalk Mills, formed a dozen years earlier to manufacture overcoat woolens, went under and the two hundred employees at its Winnipauk mill were thrown out of work temporarily until it was reorganized by the Hill interests and resumed business.

Of the several fire insurance firms in town the Fairfield County Fire Insurance Company was one of only four in Connecticut able to pay its losses in full on the great Chicago fire in 1871. Ironically Elbert Woodward was this company's president. Tweed's old henchman must have acquired considerable financial expertise for his company also survived the depression.[7]

A few brave enterprisers mostly in the fur felt and hatting fields dared to embark on new ventures. One of the largest, the Volk Hat Company formed in 1875, gained a reputation for making headgear for uniformed services and received orders from such diverse customers as the New York City Police Department and Pinkerton's detectives. The following year the Central National Bank opened its doors for business in South Norwalk. It ran afoul immediately of the national banking law by making excessive loans to two local shirt manufacturers, an indication that firms other than Norwalk Mills were in financial distress. By the beginning of 1878, however, Central National was not only able to pay dividends but to continue them regularly, a certain sign that its borrowers were meeting their obligations.[8]

The Lockwood mansion, standing empty for three years, was a stark reminder that the depression continued. Rumors that it was to be purchased by the ex-Emperor Napoleon III, by a Catholic bishop, or even by the Pope himself were duly reported in the papers but always turned out to be unfounded. Finally in 1876 Charles D. Mathews, a retired businessman from New York City, purchased the grand house as a summer residence for his family for a mere $90,000, the unpaid balance of the mortgage plus interest. Norwalk merchants re-

garded the event as a godsend for the Mathews' standard of living was almost equal to that of the Lockwoods. Seven full-time servants, a cook, a butler, a nurse, two seamstresses, a chambermaid, and a coachman cared for the daily needs of the family, with the aid of a half-dozen day workers. A sizable outside staff took care of the grounds. This single household provided more employment for Norwalkers than a moderate-sized business.

During the depression oystering continued to be a mainstay of the local economy. Fortunately Americans and Europeans had acquired such a taste for the delicacy that Norwalk's oystermen had little difficulty disposing of their catch. English gourmets had a special affinity for the small, tasty East River bivalve found in Long Island Sound between New Haven and New York City.[6] Though there is no extant record of her response to Norwalk oysterman William Merrill's gift, even Queen Victoria received a barrel of choice local oysters "sandpapered and polished so that they could be handled with kid gloves." A wistful commentary in a letter from Oliver Seeley of Afton, Iowa, to his sister, Hannah Dibble of Rowayton, gives us an inkling of the widespread distribution of Norwalk oysters:

We had a No. 1 feast. The oysters were some of them damaged in thier [sic] transit though some of them were good and very forcibly reminded us of old times by the seaside and we have preserved some of the shells for memorys [sic] sake.[9]

The Norwalk coastal area was an ideal environment for the two-shelled mollusk. The estuary of the Norwalk River furnished essential nourishment and its tidal flow provided a clean habitat. The saline content and water temperature of the Sound were highly congenial to oyster propagation.[10] Heaps of shells on pre-Contact Indian sites attest to the fact that river and Sound have long combined to provide a bounteous food supply to inhabitants along their shores. Early settlers eagerly consumed the readily available natural growthers, as un-

6 The smallest oysters were liked best by the English and received the trade name "London Stock." In one season alone, between Oct. 9, 1880, and May 14, 1881, the total number of barrels of oysters shipped from New York to Europe was 70,768, of which 68,140 were destined for Liverpool. See Ernest Ingersoll, *A Report on the Oyster-Industry of the United States,* (Washington, 1881), 131-134.

planted oysters are known, to supplement their monotonous meat and grain diet.

The supply of oysters has never been limitless. Natural predators such as fish, jellyfish, and crustaceans consume the helpless free-swimming spawn and spat.[7] Lucky survivors attach themselves to hard, clean surfaces, lying on the floor of bay and river, growing to maturity in four to five years. Here the sedentary bivalve is the target of drills, boring snails, winkles and mussels. Their greatest enemy is the starfish, which can consume as many as seven oysters in a single day.

Finding that the most severe predator was man himself, as early as 1721 Norwalk authorities limited the privilege of raking or gathering oysters within its waters to residents only. Unscrupulous inhabitants circumvented the intent of the ordinance by selling the day's catch to outsiders who anchored their vessels near the oyster grounds. The town was so concerned that it voted to pay the expenses of any resident willing to bring suit against miscreants but efforts to curb the lawbreaking were ineffectual.

When colonial law invested the towns with authority to protect oysters and clams within their territorial jurisdiction, Norwalk took advantage of the law to establish annually a mid-April to September closed season on gathering shellfish. To ensure a future supply the town made it mandatory for oystermen to "leave old shells and stones where the same was taken, whereunto any young oysters may be fixt and growing." Since the oyster was believed to be endowed with medicinal properties, Norwalk's selectmen could grant special permission to gather one bushel of oysters or round clams out of season if "any person . . . stands in such need . . . that it may endanger his or her health by being prevented of them." The dispensation was extended to "longing" women; apparently, pregnant women hankered for oysters as much as for pickles!

In the early 1800s oystering became a business venture. The technique of oyster planting proved

---

7 John Kochiss, *Oystering From New York to Boston* (Middletown, 1974), 5-8. An invaluable source for the history of oystering, this book devotes one section to the physical features that are conducive to oyster propagation and to the growth and development of the oyster. Spawn are the free-swimming fertilized eggs. When the larvae reach a length of about 1/75th of an inch, they are known as set or spat. At this stage they seek out a hard surface on which to attach themselves and begin the process of growing to maturity.

to be the answer to the public's insatiable appetite for this shellfish. In 1840 Nathan Roberts and several cohorts applied for permission to "mark, stake out and inclose" an underwater lot near Tavern Island. Smaller oysters were taken from the natural beds in the shallow river waters, replanted in the staked-out lot, and harvested at maturity. Captain Henry Bell of Bell Island converted the idea into a more sophisticated form of submarine agriculture known as oyster cultivation. In this process, still used today, oyster larvae in the free swimming stages were "caught" on shallow water beds specially prepared with one to two thousand bushels of clean shell per acre. When the "set" was two to three months old the spat were removed to deeper waters to mature.

Opening oysters in 1902.

This businesslike approach to oystering created much ill will. The public felt so deprived of access to oysters that a town committee had to be appointed to balance the needs of the planting interests with the rights of the public. Fierce competition between oystermen also led to illegal enclosure of planting grounds without the town's permission. Although by law no one could receive more than two acres of underwater land, a miniscule amount for large enterprises, aggressive businessmen managed to enlarge their holdings by acquiring land from relatives and friends willing to quitclaim their allotments.

The pressure to control shoreline waters was relieved after 1865 when oystermen discovered that oysters could be propagated in off-shore waters at depths of twenty to twenty-five feet, but operations in deeper water now brought state control. The State Shellfish Commission became the agent for disposing of these valuable properties and it was some time before equitable allocations of oyster beds were worked out.[11]

Technological improvements drastically altered nineteenth-century oystering methods. Hand rakes and tongs had been the traditional tools of oystermen sailing over the natural beds in their fragile-looking but eminently satisfactory small craft called sharpies. In the 1860s the dredge came into widespread use. This simple mechanism, a rake with a large bag attached, the whole pulled by a chain along the watery floor, increased the day's haul appreciably. Sharpies and skiffs were replaced by the oyster sloop, a vessel specifically designed to accommodate the large daily catch.

Norwalk's Captain Peter Decker further revolutionized the business when he devised a small, steam-driven drum and installed the mechanism on two family-owned oyster sloops. The device, powered by a small steam plant that burned three to four bushels of coal a day, replaced the backbreaking labor of hauling in the heavy dredge by hand. In 1874 the ingenious Decker installed a large steam engine on his sloop *Early Bird* and thereby made sails obsolete. Competitors and legislators so opposed Decker's innovation that the steamers were allowed to work only two days a week lest their mighty hauls completely deplete the oyster supply. The fear was unfounded and by the 1880s steam-driven oyster boats ruled the waves.

The change from sail to steam created a surge in Norwalk's shipbuilding industry. Large oyster planters hastened to follow Decker's suit by converting their sail fleets to steam. William Isaac Stevens, owner of Rowayton's largest oyster company, was one of the first to commission a steam-propelled oysterboat which he named *Mable C. Stevens*.[8] Master carpenters Richards and Weed in one short six-year period between 1882 and 1887 built eleven steam-powered oyster dredge boats in their South Norwalk yard. One of the most renowned oyster steamers, *William H. Lockwood*, was sixty-three feet long with four dredges. The craft operated in all seasons, took up five hundred bushels of oysters a

day, and had a storage capacity of one thousand bushels.

About 1900 steam gave way to gasoline engines and then the diesel replaced gasoline. A noteworthy twentieth-century technological modification derived from the fertile mind of the well-known Norwalk oysterman, Captain Frederick Lovejoy. Lovejoy designed the boom dredge rig, fashioned somewhat like a derrick with a scoop that plunged down through the waters, dislodged quantities of oysters from the floor, and disgorged them on the vessel's deck.

The oyster industry reached its peak in the years between 1885 and 1910. The fiercely independent small oystermen who harvested natural growthers in the public beds within the waters of the harbor

NORWALK
*industrial
community*

Captain Decker's oyster sloop "Early Bird."

were driven out by the competition. Their successors, primarily planters and shippers, bought the annual catch of 100 to 1,500 bushels from the few remaining free-lancers at one dollar a bushel. In Rowayton alone there were thirty-five planters and oyster firms of significant size, including Oliver Cook, Craw and L'Hommedieu, Aaron and George Stevens, and the Lowndes brothers.[12] The Rowayton-based fleet of twenty-eight sail and steam-powered vessels bore such unpretentious names as *Lida May, Lizzie, Ruby, Emma* and *Josephine*, but the acknowledged queen of the fleet was the glamorous *Nena L. Rowland*.[13] Even in a very poor year like 1879 the Rowayton fleet gathered nearly fifty thousand bushels of oysters, most of which

---

8 This Stevens is not to be confused with Aaron and George Stevens, also Rowayton oystermen.

Oysterman Alfred Harris shucking for market in 1969.

were shipped to New York City. Fifty large planters and shippers operated out of South Norwalk, among them the well-established Hoyt Brothers, Graham Bell, Oliver Weed, C. Remsen, Raymond Saunders, and Peter Decker, plus wholesalers Reed and Housman. Annual production reached sixty-five thousand bushels in the 1878-1879 season, the haul of two steamboats, a dozen sloops, and about thirty sharpies.

As they made their way to the oyster houses fronting Water and Raymond Streets the adroit oystermen had to dodge river traffic and skirt nearly two dozen "arks," the floating oyster houses fashioned out of old canal boats and scows. At the oyster houses the mollusks were culled or separated from the shells and stones that had been dredged up with them. They were then graded into sizes, starting with the largest, or extras, down through box and culls to the smallest, or cullenteens. They were care-

fully packed into wooden barrels or bags and freighted to New York City in shipments of as many as 670 barrels at one time.[9] From there, some were transshipped for sale across the continent or across the Atlantic.

This was the era of oyster bars, oyster saloons, and restaurants featuring chilled oysters on the half shell. Few consumers wanted the tedious and sometimes bloody task of opening oysters and local oyster houses hired shuckers for this distasteful duty.[10] Working in the arks that floated in the harbor or were moored along the waterfront and extended partially over the water, shuckers adeptly opened five hundred to seven hundred bivalves an hour,

[9] A barrel contained two to three bushels or between 500 and 750 oysters, depending on size.

[10] At its peak, the Radel Oyster Company employed 200 shuckers.

Hauling in the dredge.

separating the tender morsels from their casings. The shucked oysters were then packed in half-barrel wooden casks, surrounded by ice, and within twenty-four hours were on the tables of New York connoisseurs.[11]

As the century progressed oystering and hatting continued to be central to the town's economic life. Cigarmaking, an industrial latecomer, blossomed in Norwalk as in many towns in the state when it was discovered that Connecticut tobacco blended well with Cuban leaf. About a dozen tobacco and cigar firms existed in the town. Most were small with merely a handful of employees in each, as was typical in this business.[12]

Working women found employment in Hutchinson, Pierce & Co., whose Star Shirt Factory had supplanted Morrison & Hoyt, and in the R&G Corset Company's factory. Connecticut was one of the largest producers of ladies' corsets and it is strange that Norwalk, so close to the New York City market, did not attract more such factories. R&G Corsets owned by Messrs. Roth and Goldschmidt employed about a thousand workers in 1901, almost all of them women. Since the heavy, boned-and-laced corset was an essential part of women's clothing, R&G was easily able to sell the 650 dozen garments it turned out daily.[13] Each corset contained fourteen curved or gored pieces of heavy cloth and the women at the sewing machines had to be skillful indeed to sew these together in a smooth hourglass shape and to stitch firmly padded pockets for the steel stays so they would not poke the wearer. Clean, light surroundings were needed to keep the corsets immaculate and aside from having to listen to the constant din of the eyeletting machines R&G employees enjoyed steady, year-round work with good pay in pleasant working conditions.

Dozens of small enterprises in shops along the side streets struggled to make a living. These firms,

11 After several epidemics of intestinal disorders were attributed to oysters, the Department of Agriculture banned use of wooden casks. The packers began to use metal containers which would not absorb the melting ice water.

12 For awhile it appeared that with four or five shoe factories in Norwalk and South Norwalk the town might become an important center for this industry, but it died out. The F.H. Ruscoe Shoe Company employed about one hundred workers in 1887 while Lounsbury, Mathewson & Co. employed about twice as many.

13 It is likely that the size and output of this company, noted in Weed, *Norwalk After Two Hundred and Fifty Years,* p. 364, are somewhat exaggerated.

generally employing fewer than twelve workers, put together laundry machinery, automatic paper fasteners, stoves and heaters, office furniture, toys and games. They mixed and bottled flavorings, wood alcohol, horse remedies, and elixirs like Dr. Dick's Medicine and Loxa Tonic. They extracted fish oil and processed fertilizer from menhaden catches. They manufactured baking powder and packaged starch for stiffening ladies' shirtwaists. Supplying for the most part a market with a limited radius, these little companies came and went. Some of the smaller ones must have led a hand-to-mouth existence. One wonders, for example, about Julius W. Miller who manufactured "all kinds of Hatters' Tools and Machines," and employed seven men with a monthly output valued at only five hundred dollars.

The nature of many of these small concerns indicates that Norwalk possessed a wealth of workmen skilled in woodworking, carpentry, and metalwork. Wagons, carriages, hearses, wheelchairs, and baby carriages were among the finely-crafted items built by Norwalk artisans. Carriages, ordered now mostly for in-town travel, since the railroad and trolley supplied intercity transportation, were custom-built works of art. The lightweight brougham which could be drawn by one horse and the Victorian

phaeton which became fashionable in the 1870s were the most popular. To make either required expertise in several crafts. The body, of walnut or other fine wood ornamented with brass moldings and decorative touches, had to be meticulously mounted on springs connected to the axles. It then had to be fitted out with upholstery, side glass windows, and lamps. Wheels had to be light but sturdy enough to thwart the bumps and potholes of unpaved streets.

Carriagemakers had all too brief a day. Their business was stimulated by the new wealth of the Victorians but they suffered in the depression of the 1890s and the advent of the motor car finished them off. Luther V. Wright, a carriagemaker with a large establishment on Madison Street, South Norwalk, tried to meet the changing times. Originally a blacksmith, by century's end he was describing himself as a "Manufacturer of Wagons, Carriages, and Automobiles." Alas for the proficient and versatile Mr. Wright, South Norwalk was not destined to become another Detroit.

In the aftermath of the depression of the 1870s even the vaguest rumor of a new manufactory coming to Norwalk was worthy of mention in the newspaper. Advocating inducements and concessions to potential investors, the editor of the *Hour* stated the case clearly: "The more manufacturers, the more people; the more people, the more money; the more money, we all know what that means."

What, in fact, did this mean for Norwalk's large pool of industrial workers? Labor's spokesmen had already called attention to the growing economic gap between "the class that labors and the class that lives by others' labors,"[14] a theme the *Hartford Courant* reiterated when it noted that there were too many millionaires and too many paupers. The average per capita income was three hundred dollars, and only very skilled workers received the top daily wage of four dollars.[15] Since Fairfield County businesses customarily paid their employees only twice a month, workers found it difficult to stretch

R & G Corset Company advertisement of 1900.

their wages and frequently were forced to patronize credit stores where they paid higher prices.[14] Few factory workers had the wherewithal to buy steak, roast beef, or lamb chops, all twenty cents a pound at the butcher shop of Jacob Schaub, who catered to Norwalk's "quality trade."

In the post-Civil War era American manufacturing changed dramatically. Complex machines and team production reduced skilled craftsmen to machine tenders and destroyed their pride in the finished product. When Crofut and Knapp in-

14 A report by Labor Commissioner Arthur Hadley showed that it cost about 16 percent more to purchase an average year's food in a credit store in Norwalk than in a cash store.

stalled hat curling machines, each of which shaped two hat brims per minute, the artistry of hand curlers, the most highly-skilled operatives in the hatting business, became overnight a superfluous accomplishment. Sensing that their plight stemmed from competition between man and machine, American laborers resisted the new devices.

Connecticut factories were dismal places. Handsome exteriors masked cheerless interiors. The law required all factories using machines to be well-lighted, adequately ventilated, and "as clean as the nature of the business will permit" but failed to regulate night work, meal periods, and drinking water. Everywhere, habitual spitting exacerbated health problems. Cuspidors were seldom supplied and although some factory managers prohibited the ugly practice of expectorating workmen ignored the rule. A particular hazard of cigarmakers was "tobacco heart,"[15] but workers continued the time-honored practice of biting off excess tobacco at the end of a cigar and smoothing the head in their mouths, long after machines made the nasty habit unnecessary.

Low wages, unrelieved drudgery, and persistent fear of unemployment were the lot of skilled and unskilled workers alike but it was from the ranks of skilled labor that Norwalk's first trade union drew its members. In 1854 disgruntled hatters had organized the South Norwalk Local of the National Trade Association of Hat Finishers of the United States, a strong national union promoting the "bread and butter" issues of hours, wages, and working conditions.[16] Later when cigarmaking became a flourishing local industry Local No. 26 of the Cigar Makers' International Union energetically forwarded the interests of its membership. Resolute in its strike threats, in 1880 this militant body successfully forced Old Well Cigar Company to increase wages. Local No. 26 also cleverly mounted an advertising campaign urging those interested in "fair wages for a fair day's work," as well as a good smoke, to buy only cigars manufactured under the union label. Neither Old Well Cigar Company nor Hoyt & Olmstead, another South Norwalk firm, quibbled with the demand for, in this rare instance, what was good for labor was good for management.

Norwalk's first prolonged labor dispute erupted in the hatting industry in the fall of 1884. There was little evidence beforehand that labor-management

15 Tobacco heart was a form of nicotine poisoning that occurred from swallowing scraps of tobacco.

relations would deteriorate into a six-month strike, since hatters had long endured seasonal employment and wage reductions without resorting to strike action. Certainly the *Sentinel's* glowing report that Crofut and Knapp employees had presented an elegant clock to A.J. Crofut on the occasion of his fiftieth birthday gave no hint of the violence that would erupt.

That autumn, in the Hatting Notes section of the *Sentinel,* readers were informed that "the trade is dull," "we have no orders ahead," and "manufacturers [are] running close to the wind." When the "temporary" slump showed every sign of being permanent, the four major Norwalk hat manufacturers announced reductions in wages ranging from 12 percent for sizers to about 43 percent for trimmers.[16] The Committee of Makers, Finishers and Trimmers, spokesmen for the workmen, countered with the charge that the employers had unilaterally foisted the wage slash on the workers with no comparable reduction in the price of hats. In their eyes this clearly demonstrated the owners' intention to destroy the union. Refusing to accept a reduction that would leave them "little better than paupers," the incensed hatters struck.

Determined not to knuckle under, the Norwalk "big four"—C&K, Alden Solmans Company, Coffin, Hurlbutt and Company, and Adams Brothers—responded as one: severe competition forced them to establish uniform wages for the same work in all factories. They inveighed against the hatters' underhanded tactic of demanding a 25 percent wage increase on threat of a strike when orders were backlogged during busy seasons, and condemned union resistance to labor-saving devices as well as union efforts to limit apprenticeships. Both sides implacable, the shops remained idle.

The first strikebreakers, hatters from New Jersey, arrived in late November to begin work at Crofut and Knapp's No. 2 plant. Rumors flew that entire crews would arrive shortly from Boston. Those "foul" hatters who were not induced to depart upon their arrival found it safest to live in the plant, for they were set upon and beaten if they ventured on the streets. Union sympathizers intimidated, assaulted, and spat upon boarding-house keepers who furnished room and board to "certain" hatters.[17]

The Norwalk business community showed little sympathy for the strikers. The heads of the largest local factories, reaffirming their esteem for this "Christian gentleman," took special pains to refute the slanderous charge that A.J. Crofut had attempted to induce them to reduce their own mechanics' wages. Officers of Norwalk banks and the publisher of the *Sentinel* stood foursquare behind the employers and condemned the strike as "unAmerican" and "repulsive." Thus cloaked in moral righteousness, the hat manufacturers refused to meet with officers of the struck union's national association who came to Norwalk with an offer to arbitrate. The owners even visited Bridgeport with a view to relocating where they could maintain an open shop. With a mere 140 men at work in all the struck plants, "all that business at present warrants," employers actually had no need to concede to the union.

On the night of January 16, 1885, a charge of dynamite, carefully positioned on a window sill of C&K's No. 2 plant, detonated, spewing glass and debris, punching gaping holes in walls and ceilings, and tossing sleeping scabs from their cots. No one was injured. The employers publicly blamed the malicious act on the striking hatters; the hatters labeled it an owners' plot perpetrated to further discredit the union. Between the time of the explosion on Friday night and six o'clock Saturday morning, the *South Norwalk Sentinel* wrote, set in type, and printed an extra. Their efficient reportorial skills gave rise to the charge that they had been in collusion with the employers and knew about the incident before it actually happened. Despite substantial rewards offered by the union, the owners, and the South Norwalk City Council the culprit remained unidentified. Although receiving far less attention, a fire of suspicious origin in early February gutted the Cooperative Hat Company, a worker-managed factory recently established by the hard-pressed strikers in a vacant plant on Main Street. Fire consumed the entire building and its contents and spread to a hat box factory next door.

As the strike dragged on through the winter and

---

16 The owners claimed they were reducing prices no more than 10 percent, a miniscule amount, since, they claimed, they normally paid high wages. See Employers' Statement, *South Norwalk Sentinel,* Dec. 25, 1884.

17 Feelings developed along ethnic lines. When Hans Burchardt, who was charged with assault and battery upon one Charles Weege, appeared before Judge Ely, Burchardt condemned Weege as "the only German" to provide room and board for scabs.

early spring,[18] some disheartened hatters moved away and found jobs in independent plants in Danbury and other hatting centers. The breakthrough finally came in April. When C&K and Alden Solmans Company agreed to recognize the union the strike ended. However, Adams Brothers and John Green of Danbury, who had bought out Coffin, Hurlbutt and Company, retained open shops. Hat manufacture did not rally as a consequence of the strike settlement. Buried among such engrossing stories as the one describing the sudden illness that overtook forty-three girls attending the Methodist Church social, the *Sentinel* continued to record: "The trade is dull."[19]

An important repercussion of the hatters' strike, however, was the uncommonly rapid growth of membership in the Knights of Labor, a national association that promoted solidarity of labor by enrolling both skilled and unskilled workers. Connecticut workmen had shown little interest in the Knights in the 1870s and by 1883 there were fewer than a thousand members statewide.[17] Early in 1883 a vanguard of Norwalk workingmen founded three local Knights of Labor assemblies in South Norwalk, Winnipauk, and Norwalk. A generous contribution to the striking hatters by the national executive board of the Knights undoubtedly helped some lukewarm workingmen make up their minds

to join. Between July, 1884, and July, 1885, there was a massive surge in membership with 1,140 initiates in the South Norwalk local alone. The following year the Norwalk locals and their brothers in Georgetown and Stamford joined together in a governing unit known as District 113, South Norwalk.[18] But the rapid growth of the Knights locally was matched by an equally swift decline. When the National Board denied the District Assembly's request for a loan to sustain striking members, many workers let their membership lapse. Furthermore labor troubles like the Chicago Haymarket riot hurt the labor movement as a whole. In 1888 District Assembly 113 ceased to exist. Yet for one shining moment worker unity had achieved a stunning victory; in the South Norwalk municipal election of 1886 the labor ticket won.[19]

In some small unorganized shops ruthless employers intimidated workers as a means of guaranteeing labor tranquility. When Hungarian immigrants employed at R.G. Millard's West Norwalk fur shop struck for higher wages Millard summarily dismissed every employee except the foreman and hired another complete crew of Hungarians. *The Evening Hour* uncharitably reported the event under the headline: "Prompt Way to End a Strike."

18 The *Sentinel* editor on January 15, 1885, took exception to the "fairness" of Norwalk hatters working in independent shops in Danbury when Danbury men who came here were intercepted by a "persuading committee" and coerced into not accepting employment.

19 The illness must have been food poisoning. The blame was placed on ice cream which Mrs. Tuttle, at whose home the social was held, had made in a tin freezer with a galvanized bottom.

12

CHANGING PLACES, CHANGING FACES

*Being
an Account of
Norwalk's Newcomers and how They Lived*

FLOOD OF IRISH immigrants in the 1850s had already transformed the character of this conventional New England town. Now during the first two decades after the Civil War a spate of German-speaking people with names like Lichtblau, Gunther, Weisheit, and Kreger, settled in South Norwalk. In the same interval there was a smaller immigration of Swedes and Norwegians, Englishmen and Scots, together with a soupçon of French Canadians and Central Europeans.[1]

In a veritable parade of nationalities, a Cuban cigarmaker, a Spanish farm laborer, a French domestic servant, and Canadian telegraphers all sought their fortunes in Norwalk. A family of enterprising Polish barbers, the Pakulski brothers, opened a public bath that was immediately patronized by many South Norwalkers whose living quarters were devoid of bathtubs and at separate ends of town Ying Lee and Sam Wing each operated a Chinese laundry.

Most of the German-speaking immigrants came to Norwalk equipped with desirable industrial skills acquired in their native states of Prussia, Saxony, and Silesia.[2] Although a few worked at menial jobs as common laborers and teamsters the majority found employment as machinists, iron molders, cigarmakers, and hatters.[1] Frequently all the males in a family worked in the same factory. When Herr Frederich Bacchus, for example, set off in the morning for his job at the Norwalk Lock Company his two sons sixteen and twenty years old accompanied him. John Pellenstein's three children did not have so far to go; they simply moved into the workroom cigar manufacturer Pellenstein had set up in his home.

The Germans had a propensity for setting up their own small businesses. German-born proprietors presided over the bars of South Norwalk saloons dispensing gemütlichkeit along with ale and lager from Julius Hermann's Oriental Bottling Works on Water Street. Along Washington Street and Washington Street Bridge spicy smells emanating from the shops of sausage and bologna makers vied with the tantalizing aromas from Lichtblau's Bakery where father, son, and two employees produced batches of dark bread and delectable kuchen. On Railroad Place George Schaub operated the Germania Hotel, a haven for newcomers until they found permanent quarters in one of the many German-run boarding houses in South Norwalk.

A strong sense of community existed among German-speaking residents. Since the greatest number were of Prussian origin and therefore Lutheran it was quite natural that they organized the German Evangelical St. Peter's Congregation

---

[1] Norwalk had 7,582 residents in 1860 and 13,960 in 1880.

[2] In the census enumerations, the German-born used the designation of their native states (Prussia, etc.) rather than the term Germany. This is understandable, since German unification was not completed until 1871 and parochialism prevailed.

which met for Sunday worship in the Old Presbyterian Chapel on North Main Street, South Norwalk.[3] The congregation provided free German lessons for members' children every Saturday morning. J.W. Ellendorf of the local German community owned and edited the *Fairfield Anzeiger,* a countywide weekly German-language newspaper that kept these newcomers abreast of the news about their countrymen.[4]

Two clubs, Arion Hall at 135 Washington Street and Germania Hall at 162 Washington Street Bridge, abounded in opportunities for convivial gatherings. Smaller social and cultural societies, including the Freundshafts Bund; the Daughters of Herman, Louise Lodge; and the men's counterpart, the Order of Herman, Humboldt Lodge, met in the Germania Hall. As early as 1868 some thirty German residents joined together in the Norwalk Sanger Club "Frohsinn," the first of a group of singing societies that became a popular form of recreation.[5] In the 1870s and 1880s the Arion Hall sponsored the Arion Singing Society; the Germania Sangerbund met at the Germania Hall. Friendly competition developed between the groups and a third rival, the Hermannsohne Liederkranz, which met weekly in the *Gazette* building.

Reputed to be industrious, frugal, and law-abiding, the Germans suffered little of the contempt and abuse Norwalkers had showered on the Irish. Local newspapers seemed to relish reporting cases of intoxication and assault arrests of the Irish but had few stories of this ilk to print about the Germans. Such tolerance may be attributed to several factors, not the least of which was that the

3 Some confusion arises from the fact that the German Evangelical Synod of North America, of which the German Evangelical St. Peter's Congregation was a member, maintained an office in the Old Congregational Church on North Main Street, South Norwalk. See *Norwalk City Directory* for 1892, 1895, and 1900, for the distinction. Sunday service at the Old Presbyterian Chapel was held at 10:30 A.M. Rev. Neelo Yansen had his office at the Old Congregational Church.

4 From 1885 to 1893 he also published the *Mechanics' Journal,* a weekly touted as "Champion of Labor."

5 *Statuten Fur Norwalk Sanger Club "Frohsinn,"* a document in the possession of the Norwalk Quartette Club, which traces its origins to the by-laws of this organization. There is some question about whether the group existed after 1869; it is possible that the Arion Singing Society and Germania Sangerbund developed out of the original group, for some of the names are connected with both groups. See *Program, Centennial Anniversary Concert,* Norwalk Quartette Club, November 16, 1975.

Germans were no financial burden to the city. Few sought public assistance or were paupers since the German community made its own provisions for caring for its members. The Universal Working Men's Sick and Death Benefit Fund, which despite its grandiose name was organized by and for Germans, contributed to the costs of the two worst financial disasters a workingman's family faced. Second and most important, because the Germans were Protestant, they were free from the stigma of Papism and did not suffer the whiplash that native Americans unleashed on Catholic immigrants. A third factor was the kinship tie that developed with

Christian Swartz.

the native-born Norwalkers through marriage. The first wave of German immigrants to Norwalk were mainly single males and since there were few *mädchen* in the area many of these young bachelors married American girls.[6] Christian Swartz who married Adora Flynn, a Ridgefield girl, became a leading cigar manufacturer and outstanding South Norwalk businessman, politician, and philanthropist. Bridging the two cultures, Swartz was the

6 In a sample of twelve marriages involving German-born males in the years 1863-1875, eight married American-born females.

acknowledged spokesman for the German community.

A few German Jews also settled in Norwalk around this time. Generally of Prussian, middle-class origin, they had a proclivity for establishing small retail mercantile enterprises. Seemingly drawn by the economic potential of this growing community, many came here after a stint in the tumultuous world of New York City. One such newcomer, Israel Davis, opened a clothing store in South Norwalk after the Panic of 1873 wiped out his wholesale clothing business in New York City.[2] Silversmith Adolph Orlich worked in New York for at least five years before he set up a jewelry store in Norwalk. Orlich's skill brought the community's richest families into his shop but if the prices he charged the Beard family are typical he didn't grow rich. He cleaned Miss Hattie's ornate French clock for two dollars and a half, took a dent out of a thimble for fifteen cents, and replaced the hook on an ivory buttonhook for a mere half-dollar.

These Jewish retailers nevertheless made a comfortable living for themselves and their families in the attractive community that was more like the small Prussian cities they had known than was hurly-burly New York. Louis Stadelmann's furniture store supported his family and that of his brother-in-law who clerked in the store. Davis' clothing establishment flourished and in later years was run by two sons as Joseph Davis Clothiers. Orlich's two daughters became teachers.

Blood-curdling pogroms in eastern Europe brought yet another tide of Jews to America's shores. A remarkable number of these Polish-born and Russian-born newcomers with little formal education and few resources except the will to work hard were absorbed into the middle class within a short time.[3] Two examples illustrate the spectacular success that some of Norwalk's eastern European Jewish people achieved. Lithuanian-born Joseph Abrahams began with a modest grocery store on the corner of Ferris Avenue and the Boston Post Road. Reinvesting the profits, he opened a second store and then another, until there were thirteen in all throughout Norwalk. The string of stores known as the Modern Grocery Company was a precursor of modern-day supermarket chains. In fact Abrahams' enterprise later merged with First National Stores.[4]

The amazing career of Samuel Roodner was in the best Horatio Alger tradition. The strapping young student who fled from Russia to avoid conscription stoked furnaces in Newark, New Jersey, before he settled in Norwalk. His first job here, clerking for five dollars a month in a Fort Point grocery store, was equally inauspicious. But Roodner calculated that if a man could earn five dollars a month he could borrow fifty. This conviction paid off; Roodner soon opened his own grocery business on Cedar Street. As the years passed this capable businessman established a wholesale grain, hay, and feed company; purchased scattered

Samuel Roodner.

parcels of business property; and financed, wholly or in part, construction of many new mercantile buildings on the main thoroughfares of Norwalk and South Norwalk.

Samuel Roodner lived by the maxim that a man should "walk with kings and with peasants and be equally comfortable with both."[5] At ease serving on the hospital building committee with several millionaires Roodner rarely let a day pass without visiting the facility to chat with patients from all walks of life and lend a helping hand. In one typical gesture of generosity he sped in his chauffeur-driven car to a burning farmhouse, ordered the dazed farm family into his automobile, brought them to his comfortable Flax Hill home, and gave them temporary lodging. He was as egalitarian in the last days of his life as in the first. When his former laundress and chauffeur came to visit, the ailing Roodner accorded them the same gracious hospitality he had just extended to a prominent United States senator who had departed minutes earlier.

Religion played an important part in the lives of the eastern European Orthodox Jewish community. For many years the small band held services in makeshift quarters in Hoyt's Theater and rented hotel rooms in South Norwalk. Plans for building a synagogue were repeatedly shelved because the most influential and wealthiest member of the congregation always maintained that the time was not right. "When the time is right," he said again and again, "I'll be the first to make a contribution." To many it seemed the time might never be right. Then one day during Yom Kippur service the long-sought miracle happened. The agitated lay leader stepped up to the platform and informed the worshippers assembled at the Clifford Hotel: "I have just learned that while we are holding our service on the second floor of this hotel, there is a house of ill-fame on the third floor. The time is right."[6] In 1906 the long-awaited Beth Israel Synagogue, a brown shingled structure with onion domes reminiscent of Eastern Orthodox architecture, opened its doors to the peripatetic band.

Of the Scandinavian immigrants to Norwalk, Swedes comprised the largest single group. Erich Ericson from Dalarna Province was among the earliest arrivals.[7] After he had found steady employment as a teamster he brought his family here and moved into a house in East Norwalk next door to Henry Carlson, a carman. Shortly the area encompassed by Fort Point Street, Van Zant Street, and Third, Fourth, and Cove Avenues was a Swedish enclave where one could count as many as thirty-five Andersons alone. Although a few moved on to Minnesota or returned to Sweden, by 1889 the community was large enough to organize the Swedish Bethlehem Covenant congregation and build a church on Van Zant Street. By 1892 the pastor of the Swedish Congregational Church, yet another denomination, had a congregation large enough to support weekday prayer meeting and

Sunday services in addition to Sunday School. At the Society Scandia, Swedish newcomers enjoyed fellowship and at the same time kept alive native traditions and customs.

Across the river in the Springwood section of South Norwalk a profusion of flower gardens and fruit trees in the front yards of the houses along Bouton Street, Ely Avenue, and Lexington Avenue bespoke the presence of a Hungarian colony. Vivid blooms contrasting with whitewashed fences, stoops, and walls, created a familiar touch of the homeland. As a stream of wives, relatives, and neighbors from Abauj-Torna County[7] joined the handful of men who had come to Norwalk in the mid-1880s Hungarian families soon outnumbered the German, Irish, and black families in Springwood's "Whistleville."[8] Within walking dis-

Beth Israel Synagogue, built in 1906.

tance of their homes Hungarians could trade at butcher shops and tailoring establishments or tarry at tea gardens and saloons, all run by compatriots.[9] Many a child raced up Nagy's Hill on Ely Avenue to the Hungarian-owned grocery store for a measure of paprika or poppyseeds.

A few Hungarian farmers who had settled in West Norwalk regularly delivered farm produce and dairy products, ladling out rich whole milk from large metal cans or selling freshly-dug potatoes.[8] From horse-drawn buggies their wives

7 The greatest number came from the villages of Vilmany, Hejcze, Goncz-Ruska, and Fony.

8 The Vargo farm on Richards Avenue (now St. John's Cemetery) and the Shimko farm on North Taylor Avenue were examples.

Scene from "The Gypsy," an operetta presented by the Hungarian Choir Group in 1918.

peddled bowls of clotted sour cream and mounds of creamy cottage cheese. On their routes they were apt to pass Dr. Wolfe or Dr. Burnell making a house call in the company of Stephen Tomas who served as interpreter for the doctors. At the foot of Cliff Street school children dawdled in front of Deacon Taylor's house listening to stories of his Civil War escapades. They would reluctantly scatter to make way for the heavily-laden buggy but no sooner had it passed than the goggle-eyed youngsters would crowd around the diminutive ex-slave again, coaxing from him yet another tale.

The farm horses always quickened pace as they passed the fur factory on Franklin Street for the foul odors and clouds of fur clippings that swirled about the building choked man and beast alike. The horses, familiar with the route, knew just where to stop so the farmer could deliver fresh country eggs at one house, a plump hen at another. The faithful animals could be depended upon to bring the wagon safely home even when a convivial farmer had lingered too long at a Whistleville saloon.

The man who dominated Lexington Avenue was the Reverend Gabriel Dokus, a personage of aristocratic mien whose stiffly-waxed mustache never once quivered as he paced to and fro in front of his tiny white church. He greeted children cordially on their way to school but occasionally whipped a walking stick out from under his cape to administer a sharp rap on the head of an unmannerly boy who had forgotten to tip his hat. Known to many residents from their school days in Hungary, school teacher Dokus was summoned to Norwalk by his former students to organize a Hungarian Reformed congregation.[10] For thirty-eight years the Reverend Dokus ministered to his people, first at the white wooden church on Lexington Avenue and later at the red brick church perched high on a rocky bluff across the street. In addition to his regular pastoral duties this man of boundless energy conducted a Hungarian school during summer vacations where children learned to read and write the language of their parents and sang folk songs of the old country. Dokus helped to found new churches from New Jersey to Nova Scotia, yet with all this he managed to find time to visit each communicant's home once a month, as much perhaps to savor the potato pancakes made specially for his visits as to collect church dues.

Yankees and second-generation Irish looked down on the "furriners" who lived in Whistleville within earshot of the warning blasts of trains as they rounded a sharp bend in the tracks and crawled toward the South Norwalk station. But for the

Rev. Gabriel Dokus.

Hungarians, living near the tracks had its compensation. As the train crept along, youngsters gathered to taunt the crew, who reciprocated by pelting the children with lumps or an occasional shovel of coal. Each youngster scurried to gather the scattered pieces and bring them home to supplement the family's fuel supply.

"We were never hungry; mama made big pots of soup," recollected the children of one family whose male breadwinner, like so many of the Hungarian newcomers, found employment only as an unskilled factory worker. Other new arrivals worked

in the fields at Hoyt's Nursery[9] or as yardmen and gardeners on estates in Tokeneke and Rowayton. Still others were steamboat hands or earned five dollars a week shoveling coal for the railroad from the holds of ships docked at Wilson Point. The luckier men were hired as iron molders at the Norwalk Lock Company or as cutters at Lounsbury, Mathewson & Co. on Haviland Street. The J.J. Asch Company, Royal G. Millard, and Martin Bates, Jr. & Company, three firms specializing in processing hatters' fur, hired entire crews of Hungarians. Eventually nearly one thousand Hungarians were employed in hatting, sought after by employers who valued their hard work and conscientious effort.[11] Only a few of these workers—those whose Anglicized names disguised their origins or who had learned to beat and shape fur at an uncle's side as children in Hungary—moved up to well-paying jobs. Even in the get-rich-quick 1920s some Hungarians in hatting were still earning only fifteen cents an hour.[10] Hungarians had no access to other skilled trades for by 1900 the Irish had a stranglehold on the skilled crafts. No matter how industrious or competent, a Hungarian was locked out from apprenticeship, union membership, and referrals for jobs in the construction trades.

With little hope of economic advancement and ignored by the town in general, Springwood people might have despaired; they did not. They worked hard, prayed hard, and laughed a great deal for life in Whistleville had its joyous moments. A singing group would rehearse for months to produce a light opera or drama and stage the production on New Year's Eve at Novak's Hall, the only neighborhood building large enough to accommodate the crowds. When Hungarian-speaking touring troupes made one-night stands Whistleville's Magyar population flocked to the Music Hall on South Main Street and marveled at the palatial furnishings, which reminded them of European opera houses. Lonely young men often walked miles from Hoyt's Nursery to Whistleville, to spend an afternoon in a tea garden, saloon, or the Hungarian Reading Room at Ely Avenue. Here they read poetry, discussed literary

9 There was little hope of advancement; the bosses were always Irish.

10 Hungarian employees at the Lock Company brought home eleven to fifteen dollars in wages every two weeks. On the other hand, one highly-skilled fur beater earned thirty-five dollars a week during the Depression.

classics, and rehearsed plays and comedies that were staged at Kish's Hall.

Picnics in the grove on upper Lexington, dances in various halls, and Sunday-afternoon English classes for children were all church-sponsored events, for the social life of the community centered around its churches. Norwalk had ignored the spiritual needs of the Springwood population until 1889 when a little Hungarian girl was killed crossing the grade-level tracks. The tragedy inspired the South Norwalk Congregational Church to organize a Hungarian Mission and secure a Hungarian-speaking Bible Reader. Members of the congregation pledged a monthly contribution to help support the Hungarian Mission; the Beard family papers show that Edward Beard faithfully contributed four dollars every month to this mission. It eventually evolved into the Hungarian Congregational Church whose parishioners met for many years at the Springwood Union Chapel on Ely Avenue. Some of those who felt uncomfortable in the Congregational fold withdrew and organized the Hungarian Reformed Church at which time Gabriel Dokus was invited to be pastor. After the turn of the century there was also a Hungarian Baptist Church with services conducted by a lay reader from Bridgeport. Hungarian Catholics met in the basement of St. Joseph's Church until a new parish built St. Ladislaus Church on Cliff Street.

Community spirit was at its finest in times of adversity. During the severe depression of the 1890s Hungarian farmers dumped wagonloads of potatoes in Whistleville streets for the taking since few of their compatriots could afford to pay the store price of ten cents a bushel. A death in the community brought out the uniformed Hungarian Band whose thirty-five members took time off from work to march behind the horse-drawn hearse and play solemn dirges as the cortege made its way to Riverside Cemetery. Members of the choir who sang at the committal hopped the trolley to guarantee their presence at the gravesite before the procession arrived. If the deceased had belonged to the Hunyadi, Rakoczy, or Verhovai Sick and Benevolent Society an assessment on each surviving member tided over the widow and children. For above all else it was concern for its members that helped the Hungarian community combat bigotry, contempt, and the difficulties of adjusting to a new environment.

The winding dirt roads adjacent to Lexington and Ely Avenues became home to yet another wave of immigrants, the Italians. Like the Hungarians, many of the earliest Italians to come to Norwalk were lone men who worked long hours as common laborers and lived frugally until they had saved enough money to send for their wives and children. At the urging of those who had already settled here, dozens of relatives and former neighbors left Minturno, Miletto, and the small Calabrian towns to emigrate to Norwalk. The prosperous appearance of a native son like Mr. Ganario, the popular Norwalk peanut vendor who returned to visit his old homeland, spurred others to resettle, for he signified the wealth that could be made in America. These reunited families together with relatives and friends were attracted to Wood, Laura, Olean, and Chestnut Streets, where cheap rental housing cost four to six dollars a month.

On the feast days of St. Ann, St. Vincent, and St. Mary Morgia, Ely and Lexington Avenues hummed with activity as Italian families from all parts of town joined in glorious celebrations. Often the milling crowds were so thick that families from outlying areas had to tether their horses and wagons several blocks away on Lowe Street and make their way on foot to the festivities on Ely Avenue. Here Italian bands made up of sprightly old neighborhood musicians shared the spotlight with entertainers from New York City. Whirling couples danced the tarantella while the more sedate sampled regional delicacies offered at decorated booths. Crowds always congregated about the greased pole that sported two provolone cheeses and a ten dollar bill securely attached to the tip. Many a young man ruined his best and sometimes only suit in a vain attempt to shinny up the slick pole and capture the elusive prize. The glow from the strings of colored lights adorning the booths at nightfall was eclipsed by the flamboyant fireworks display that signaled the close of the gala.

Columbus Day was no less important. The 1909 celebration, the first observance of this special Italian holiday, set a precedent for years to come. Staging the elaborate parade that began in front of the Italian Court of Foresters Hall on Railroad Avenue and proceeded through South Norwalk was a joint effort involving all of the Italian societies in town. Heading the line of march were the Grand Marshals on horseback and a platoon of white-gloved police carrying American and Italian flags. Next a corps of carriages rolled along carrying municipal leaders and prominent businessmen. Then wonder of wonders, the floats, the resplendant floats! The Luigi Zappetta Society's float of the Santa Maria was "manned" by ladies dressed in bright blue sailor uniforms who drew cheers of approval from the solid mass of onlookers at the corner of Washington and South Main Streets. Even this dazzling sight was surpassed by the Sons of Columbus entry: fifty boys, aged eight to fifteen, all clad in white, escorting a miniature ship drawn

hods of cement for bricklayers, often walking as far as Darien to earn a dollar a day. With luck a man might become part of a work gang whose padrone spoke English well enough to contract for a job repairing railroad trackage or shoveling ballast. Gangs of stone masons who had mastered the art in Italy were also under tutelage of a padrone who not only found them jobs but frequently provided housing.[11] Others were barbers or shoemakers or ran fruit and confectionery stores. Success could come rapidly. John Fanzilli who advertised his mason-builder business in the 1895 *Norwalk Directory* had

Italian immigrant to Norwalk, Giacomo Cuneo.

First-generation American son, Lawyer John F. Cuneo.

by a goat. The day's heady events culminated in a Knights of Columbus banquet at the Clifford Hotel where revelers dined on a sumptuous meal and danced away the evening.[12]

Such occasions were a respite from what was all too often a harsh and impoverished daily existence. Many of the immigrants, rural people with little education and no industrial experience, worked all their lives as pick-and-shovel laborers. They prepared streets for paving, dug ditches, and carried

been Giovanni Fanzilli, a mason, just three years earlier. Most Italians, however, were doomed to a life of common labor and seasonal work. More than one girl who grew up seeing her father idle during the winter months vowed to marry a man with a steady job!

11 In 1895, at least sixteen men, all listed as common laborers, lived at 27 Chapel Street. Nine stone masons resided in a house at Pine Street near the railroad. Neither dwelling was listed as a boarding house or hotel in the *Norwalk Directory*.

Their old-country ways helped the Italians surmount their poverty. Each family had a garden plot and raised rabbits, geese, and chickens in the back yard. Families who lived off Perry Avenue or had farms on North Taylor Avenue raised goats, pigs, and often one or more cows. Every housewife canned garden vegetables and dried tomato paste in the sun. A thrifty woman preserved perishables like eggplant and peppers in stoneware jars and stored cabbage and onions deep in the root cellars. Italian farm women peddled much-loved specialties such as goat cheese and pigeons, door-to-door. Few families could afford "store bought" foods. As a special treat a mother might buy three oranges which she carefully divided among ten children.

Ingenuity often had to save the day. More than one young girl made her First Communion at St. Joseph's Church wearing a cut-down dress and a veil made from a window curtain gathered onto a band of ribbon. A length of rope often served as a belt for trousers for a young man seeking his first job. Since everyone in the neighborhood was equally poor there was little cause for embarrassment, except perhaps to the children of one family who had to go to school wearing rope-soled shoes which a desperate but resourceful father had fashioned to replace the worn-out soles.

Whistleville children explored the vast expanses of woods off Ely Avenue, a perfect place to play cowboys and Indians or roast potatoes over a campfire. Children of Italian families in Winnipauk cherished their rare trolley rides downtown to gaze at the enchanting toys displayed in store windows. A dollar-and-a-half doll became the stuff dreams were made of, too costly ever to possess! The most memorable expeditions were the full-day family outings to Roton Point, the day spent playing in the sand, watching the boats from New York dock, and making frequent forays to the lunch-basket which always seemed bountifully stocked. Farm children from West Norwalk had no time for such pleasures. Their days were filled with a never-ending round of chores. Rising at sun-up, they chopped wood, hoed

vegetable patches, gathered huckleberries and raspberries, picked grapes for the winter wine supply, and filled the seemingly bottomless concrete tub that was used to wash clothes.

In Italian families there was always a father to account to—a stern, uncompromising father who counted the children seated around the kitchen table at eight o'clock and locked the door for the night. Economic necessity dictated that sons and daughters alike leave school the day they turned fourteen and find jobs in South Norwalk's factories. A father or older brother customarily escorted a young woman to and from work for—as in the old country—unmarried young women were not allowed to walk along the streets unaccompanied. Fathers decreed that their daughters wear their hair long, even well into the era of bobbed hair, although occasionally a man succumbed to the persuasive argument that long tresses were hazardous near belted factory machines. Fathers collected unopened pay envelopes from all members of the family. A daughter who had worked all week trimming, pinning, and boxing children's clothes on a piecework basis at two cents a dozen might be allowed to keep twenty cents of her pay to buy a pair of stockings.

Courtship was carried on at home under the watchful eyes of parents. The visitor spent the evening singing or playing cards with his fiancee. Rarely did the engaged couple go to the ten-cent movie at the Springwood Theater or to the Rialto on Washington Street. A young woman whose future in-laws lived out of town might never meet them until the day of her marriage for out-of-town trips were unthinkable.

It remained for the next generation—the children of the immigrants—to become builders and electricians, to acquire property and build their own homes, and to adopt American customs. Many an elderly immigrant refused to set foot inside the Overland automobile his son had acquired, maintaining that his feet had always served him well enough. Indeed they had![13]

13

CATALYSTS FOR CHANGE

Being
an Account of
Norwalk at a Time of Social Reform

HE TOWN'S never more than adequate school system was severely taxed by the steady stream of newcomers attracted to Norwalk's factories. Especially in South Norwalk teachers of primary grades felt hampered and frustrated facing classes made up of foreign-born youngsters who could neither speak nor understand the English language.[1] Teachers of upper grades felt equally perturbed that parents saw no need to keep their children in school but allowed them to drop out and go to work in factories. The greatest number left in grades five and six but no small number quit even earlier.

Yet when zealous truant officers forced unwilling scholars to attend school, classrooms became overcrowded. There might be as many as sixty pupils in a class so that as the conscientious Board of School Visitors reported, "The work must be done wholesale. [There is] no opportunity to give attention to the weak and wayward." At end-of-term ceremonies teachers awarded well-behaved students premiums, but throughout the year they punished dull, fractious, and insolent ones with sound whippings. In 1883 Norwalk's School Board banned whipping but reinstated it the very next year. These undesirable practices prompted many young people to avoid school whenever possible and to withdraw when they were legally able to do so.

In 1893, appalled at the educational deficiencies of youthful workers, the state required every large town to maintain an evening school, subsidizing it

[1] These small printed cards praising the pupil's work were distributed with apparent abandon in the late 1800s.

by paying three dollars for each person enrolled. Illiterate youths fourteen to sixteen years old could no longer work in shops or factories unless they attended night school at least twenty consecutive evenings a school year.

The Evening School aroused a great controversy in town. When the Board of School Visitors decided not to open the school because they could find only eighteen students to attend, the selectmen took a rare pro-education stance, claiming there were almost 850 applicants. In an about-face the Board of School Visitors capitulated only to find the selectmen had preempted the facilities by leasing the schools for one hundred nights. A rising Irish politician, Jeremiah Donovan, and his cohort, John Kane, intervened by securing an injunction and retrieved the facilities for the School Visitors.[2] The selectmen seemed vindicated when a record 691 students enrolled in the fall to take such courses as mechanical drawing, arithmetic, bookkeeping, and basic English skills. By midwinter, however, attendance had fallen off so drastically that two branches were closed and the following year a discouraging attendance led to closing two others. Only the South Norwalk branch remained open to serve "a large foreign element." The ambitious plan to eliminate illiteracy had been reduced to one token institution.

Appointing School Visitors, hiring truant officers, determining the course of study, and opening new schools all fell under the jurisdiction of the town Board of Education. This body supervised the separate school districts, each of which maintained a primary or grammar school. School Visitors monitored district schools, assessed their strengths and

weaknesses, and made recommendations to the Board. The Board acted on these recommendations cautiously, usually exercising great fiscal restraint, for although the town received state appropriations for education the bulk of school financing came from school taxes levied in each district.[2] School Visitors had to state forcefully that a building was "dilapidated, absolutely unfit for school purposes, and merit[ed] condemnation" before a district felt compelled to replace the structure.

There were, of course, many practices in the schools to which Norwalkers could point with pride. Science, geography, and civics fleshed out the traditional study of reading, writing, and arithmetic. Singing, "one of the chief agents in bringing the teacher and taught into harmonious concert of action," drawing, and weekly physical exercises provided lighter moments in the day's activities. Teachers tried to impart proper social values through instruction on the adverse effects of al-

2 The amount spent in each district varied greatly. The Over River District, for example, spent $8,016.10 in 1893-1894. In contrast the South Norwalk District spent $22,929.87 in 1896-1897. The total education budget for Norwalk for 1896 was $45,280.

cohol drawn from Dr. Richardson's *Elementary Treatise on Alcohol.* Although physiology and hygiene were part of the curriculum, the carefully edited textbook used for instruction was so "devoid of charts" that even in those Victorian days the Norwalk Board of Education found it lamentably defective.

Parents had to supply their children's textbooks which were stocked by local bookstores and poor youngsters whose parents couldn't afford this expense frequently stayed away from school. When the School Board realized that regular attendance would increase Norwalk's share of state aid the townspeople voted to provide free textbooks to encourage children from poor families to attend. Even so the economy-minded Board bought new textbooks only once a decade. However, each school district could purchase supplementary reading materials and this policy became the nucleus for a school library system. By the turn of the century there were libraries in all district schools except one and nearly five thousand volumes on the shelves.

Another matter for pride was the change occurring in the philosophy of education. The old ABC method that stressed four exercises a day[3] was replaced by a new technique that "teaches 'things' [sic] rather than letters and words; that leads a child to observe closely and quickly . . . that keeps his faculties awake and active." Repeated references to the goals of "proper cultivation of reasoning powers and the development of thought" interject a modern note and reveal the earnest thoughtfulness of Norwalk's nineteenth-century School Visitors.

Through efforts of private citizens like Alfred Austin and John H. Light, both strong supporters of education who served many years as School Visitors, the first kindergarten opened in the winter of 1893 in Knudsen's Hall with seventy-five to eighty six-year-olds. Three other districts soon followed suit and the kindergarten concept became firmly established in Norwalk.

Much of the educational ferment can be attributed to the increasing professionalism of the teaching staff. In most of the nineteenth century a little learning went a long way and it was not uncommon for a job applicant to offer as her best qualification that "she would teach for three dollars per month less than anyone else."[3] To its credit the Board usually hired teachers with upper-school education or prior experience in a country school. In 1887 the Board established a Teachers' Library to encourage professional development. A Town Teachers' Association also strove to upgrade teachers through an annual lecture series.[4] By 1899 the Board required either normal school training which could be based upon an approved high school course or successful classroom experience as a prerequisite to employment. They certainly did not overpay the staff; salaries increased slowly over the last half of the nineteenth century but were never remarkable. Wages of female teachers rose from $20 a month in 1867 to $42.74 by the end of the century, an increase that was overshadowed by the $97.33 then paid monthly to male teachers.

No educational issue caused more consternation than the proposal to build one townwide high school "worthy of its name." Prior to the Civil War South Norwalk had taken advantage of a state law to consolidate two school districts into a union school district and to establish an upper school (a union school) that included grade ten. Upon payment of twelve dollars yearly tuition, "payable quarterly in advance," children from other Norwalk districts could attend grade ten, along with South Norwalk pupils, in the two "fine" rooms set aside for this purpose in the Concord Street School. Gradually the other districts introduced higher grades to some extent and eventually four districts instituted high school departments. In 1891 School Visitor John Slater suggested that expenses incurred in maintaining four separate departments would in fact adequately support one superior townwide high school. The crucial issue was where to locate the unified high school. South Norwalk's gnawing suspicion that it would be in Norwalk proper precluded any enthusiastic support by the lower district. Jealousy overshadowed reason at a South Norwalk Union School District meeting in 1897:

"Would it be located in Norwalk?" someone asked. Mr. John H. Light–"Probably it would. Norwalk would act like it does when a South Norwalk member of the School Board dies–want to appoint one from the upper end of town . . . It may be two years and it may be four years before a town high school is built."
Mr. [Asa] Woodward–"It might be forever."[4]

It was, of course, not forever although fully ten years passed before the town high school opened. The School Board's strategy of prescribing a uniform course of study for all high school departments and granting Norwalk High School diplomas to all graduates smoothed the way.[5] Finally in 1908 eight teachers under Principal E. H. Gumbart began instructing students in the new townwide yellow brick high school on West Avenue at Courtland Place—in Norwalk proper![6]

Over five hundred young people received their education outside the public school system. Of these more than four hundred had transferred to St. Mary's Parochial School when it opened in 1882. About a hundred day students from the town attended the boarding schools that continued to flourish in Norwalk. Here local children could associate with those of America's new industrialists and even with the offspring of New York City's

---

[3] In schools with several grades in one room children taught by this method might find themselves with "long intervals of idleness and play time."

[4] The Association had existed since about 1890. One particularly successful series was given by Professor Charles Zueblin of Chicago University.

[5] The first class to graduate from the Norwalk High School was the Class of 1902. Thirty graduates of the several high school departments received their diplomas in a graduation exercise held at the Music Hall on May 14, 1902.

[6] This building was razed during construction of the Route 7 Interchange with the Connecticut Turnpike in the 1970s.

Four Hundred. One of the best-known private schools was the Young Ladies Seminary founded in the 1830s by Mrs. Louisa Smith and later known as the Hillside School for Girls. In its handsome building on Prospect Hill young ladies studied English, Latin, Modern Languages, Piano, Guitar, Drawing, and Painting and learned to speak faultless French under tutelage of Madame Fabegon, "a Parisian lady of education and refinement."[7] The Harstrom School, a nearby boys' school that prepared young men for college and business, offered the girls an occasional diversion from their protracted studies. Miss Cornelia Baird's Institute, an exclusive finishing school on West Avenue, had the most imposing campus of all, boasting four large houses, a gymnasium, and an infirmary on spacious grounds set out with fruit trees. The school's advertisements alluded to its large and select library and assured

The Roosevelt School on East Avenue.

parents that "Miss Baird is thorough in her manner of discipline and instruction."

The best-known counterpart to Norwalk's female seminaries was the Selleck School on East Avenue, founded by the Reverend Charles Selleck in 1855. Although Selleck accepted some day students the majority were boarders who came from as far south as Texas and Louisiana, as far west as Michigan and Wisconsin, and even from Puerto Rico and Cuba. Selleck and four young male instructors taught college-entrance courses to their charges. Additionally Selleck employed a cook and six domestic servants to attend a household of some fifty boys.[8]

7 This school was later called Mrs. Mead's School for Girls and operated until 1941. When Mrs. Melville Mead was principal there were both college preparatory and primary departments.

8 There were fifty-three resident students in 1870; by 1880 the number had dropped to thirty-five and Selleck's staff showed a corresponding decrease.

In 1889 this school was sold to Colonel Frank S. Roberts and its name changed to the Norwalk Military Institute. In the twentieth century the venerable facility became the Overlook-Selleck Military Academy.

The town as a whole had settled into a pattern that was to remain fairly stable. Its twin shopping and business centers experienced little change except expansion up to the First World War. Its ethnic enclaves had hardened into neighborhoods. The railroad tracks created a line of demarcation between the Hungarians and Italians who lived on the wrong side of the tracks in Whistleville and the

Rev. Charles M. Selleck.

native-born, middle-class residents of Golden Hill around Flax Hill and West Street. The Irish were scattered throughout the town by this time. Their original small settlement around Chapel Street had flourished and Irish families now occupied many of the old Federal houses between West Avenue and the river. Dr. William Tracey, a well-known and respected member of the Irish community, owned a handsome Italianate residence on a large lot at the corner of Chapel Street and elegant West Avenue.

In the prevailing pattern of the day the rich lived on main thoroughfares while smaller houses occupied side streets. East Avenue was still a fine address. The entire length of West Avenue was lined with homes of the city's social and business leaders.[9] By modern standards these upper-class residential neighborhoods were undesirably close to noisy, smoke-belching factories. Arthur C. Wheeler's straw hat factory on Butler Street was little more than a stone's throw from West Avenue. South Main Street in the lower district was also the site of large, comfortable houses each maintained by three or four servants. This neighborhood was especially popular with doctors who maintained their offices in their homes. The popular Dr. Charles Bohannan, three times mayor of South Norwalk, was one of the physicians who lived here.[5] Surrounded on all sides by factories South Main would be the first section of town to lose its residential character. The Volk Hat Company on Day and Raymond Streets and Lounsbury, Mathewson's shoe factory were merely two of the many plants close by. When Crofut and Knapp moved their entire operations to Tolles and Day Streets, South Main's deterioration as a residential neighborhood was foreordained.

Residents sorrowfully observed the loss of many of the town's ancient elms about this time. Infestation by European elm beetles denuded street after street of the giant trees whose leafy arches had provided shade and beauty for so many years. Readers of the *Gazette* mourned along with Charles O.C. Betts when they read that he had been forced to cut down the pair of elms, four feet in diameter at the base, which his grandfather had planted over a hundred years before. Lost also was the "King of Elms" planted by Governor Fitch himself on his family's home-lot. Town officials did their best to save their heritage. The South Norwalk Board of Street Commissioners was willing to employ a "quite expensive" method, costing $121.88 for a single year, to wash down 353 trees with a kerosene emulsion[6] but nothing could save the afflicted trees. Imperceptibly the loss of the stately elms hastened the transmutation of the older neighborhoods.

A number of farms still operated within the town's limits. The *Directory* for 1885-1886 listed 216 farmers with postal addresses in Norwalk, 52 in Rowayton, 26 in Silvermine, and 77 in South Norwalk.[10] Some families maintained small farms separate from the family residence, as did the Bohannans. Although they lived in South Norwalk they

owned five acres along Gregory Boulevard in East Norwalk where one of their Negro yardmen cared for their coach and saddle horses, and a few cows, pigs, and chickens. The Taylor farm, handed down from planter Matthew Marvin, now sprawled over most of the shore area east of the Norwalk River, including beautiful Calf Pasture beach. Occasionally in the summertime families would picnic or tent along this shore. Not all of East Norwalk was farmland. The old Fort Point area and Seaview Avenue, which skirted the east bank of the harbor, were both residential. A scattering of summer houses dotted the river bank below Cedar Point.

Rowayton long remained an oystering village with three shipyards specializing in oyster boats located on Five Mile River. However, as more and more summer people learned about this inexpensive little seaport, its inhabitants began to turn their homes into boarding houses for summer visitors. Taking summer boarders gave an oysterman's family that bit of extra cash that often made the difference between mere survival and having a few of life's comforts. Some of the boarding houses expanded into small hotels to accommodate the many visitors who came to enjoy the leisurely pace and fresh sea breezes. Many artists summered in the village, attracted by its pastoral beauty and picturesque water views.

Roton Point amusement park brought many day visitors to Rowayton. Sometimes three excursion boats docked in a single day at the long pier at the end of the Point. People relished spending the day in its picnic grove, a knoll almost at the water's edge filled with fine old shade trees through which cool breezes swept even on the hottest summer day. The Point gradually developed a full-fledged amusement park with bath houses, restaurants, a pavilion, shooting galleries, merry-go-rounds, and roller coasters. The trolley ran from South Norwalk to the Point every twenty minutes. The fare was only a nickel and on warm summer evenings Norwalkers found it a pleasant diversion to ride out and back in the open trolley. As they neared the Point they could hear music wafting from the pavilion in the grove.

The amusement park was an economic asset to Rowayton merchants who provisioned its restaurants and to local boys who found summer jobs

---

9 To cut down the noise from clanging horseshoes this street was paved with large wooden blocks instead of the customary stone Belgian blocks.

10 These figures may be somewhat misleading since business and professional men such as Dudley Ely, Alfred Austin, Dr. Moses Pardee, and Elbert Woodward listed themselves as farmers, apparently for property tax purposes.

there. It was a noisy nuisance to families living nearby, however, and its presence precluded the kind of people who were hiring McKim, Mead and White to design their summer homes in exclusive resorts like Newport and Southampton. Thus Rowayton remained more homogeneous than those socially-stratified towns.

The Dibble family provides a typical example of how the more prosperous Rowaytonites lived.[7] Alonzo Dibble operated a successful grocery store on Rowayton's main street. He and his wife also took in paying guests in the summertime.[11] Hannah Dibble's good cooking and the beautiful location of the Dibble house at the bend in the Five Mile River just where the harbor widened brought so many guests that they had no difficulty filling their rooms. The diary of the Dibbles' teen-age daughter,

[11] Today this is the Seeley-Dibble-Pinkney House, 177 Rowayton Avenue, a museum maintained by the Rowayton Historical Society and the Sixth District.

The Marvin-Taylor Farm at the turn of the century.

Residence of Lewis G. Wilson.

Emma, indicates that the family enjoyed those old-fashioned, wholesome activities that lure wistful urbanites to the suburbs. Sleighride parties enlivened the otherwise dreary winter months. Snuggled in the hay-filled sleigh, harness bells jangling as the horses trotted along the snow-packed roads, Emma and her friends often traveled as far as Stamford or New Canaan on their expeditions. In the summertime there were many picnics and always at least one circus. When life was dull one could stroll up to the depot of an evening to pick up the mail. There was much friendly socializing in church activities; Rowayton's Baptists attended the Methodists' strawberry festivals and the Methodists attended the Baptists' lecture series. Visiting back and forth and "staying for dinner" was so customary that one wonders if any family ever sat down to a meal, even in the wintertime, without setting an extra place at the table.

For years Rowayton had to depend upon a bucket brigade when a fire broke out. In 1902, however, after Charles Thomes' grocery store burned to the ground and the fire threatened other buildings as well, the Rowayton Hose Company was organized.

The story goes that this volunteer fire company's social gatherings became so exclusive that a few years later some outsiders who had been refused membership formed their own firefighting unit, the Reliance Hook & Ladder Company. Both companies turned out for fires but each kept its own equipment in its own firehouse. To obtain funds for the new fire company wives of Reliance members put out a cookbook. The Reliance Cook Book contains what appears to be the only oyster recipe to be found in early cookbooks published by Norwalk's women's organizations—Mrs. William Doland's hearty oyster pie. Apparently oysters were so commonplace that no one even thought of including an oyster recipe!

Green and hilly Bell Island was also popular with summer visitors[12] although it acquired an unsavory but brief reputation when a house of prostitution catering to the town's racy young blades was discovered operating there.[8] But this little scandal was soon forgotten and the island's less sensational attractions, in particular its excellent beaches, lured

[12] Originally Roaton Neck and renamed after Captain Henry Bell.

solid, reputable citizens to its shoreline. Dan-buryites and Norwalkers themselves almost monopolized Bell Island but it drew visitors from other Connecticut towns as well as from Manhattan and Brooklyn. The family of State Senator John H. Ferris, for example, closed their three-story formal brick house on West Street every summer and moved to Cobble Cottage, their pretty seven-room stone house on South Beach with a beautiful view of Sheffield Island.[9] Popularity of monthly or seasonal rentals in this community encouraged the building of cottages solely to rent and Bell Island became more crowded than other shorefront developments in Norwalk.

Wilson Point with its beautiful wooded ridges and long shoreline developed in quite a different fash-ion. Prior to the Civil War Lewis G. Wilson, a New York City financier, acquired Belden's Point by marrying Isaac Belden's daughter after Belden had refused to sell him the property. Little by little Wil-son picked up other pieces of land there, mostly through foreclosure of mortgage loans made to other members of the Belden family. There he created a gentleman's farm, living on a grand scale in a beautiful stone villa surrounded by gardens in which white peacocks strolled and fanned their snowy plumes. Wilson lost his fortune in 1883 and his property fell into other hands but the area re-mained sparsely settled. A strip of land on Wilson Cove was owned for years by the D&N Railroad and later the Standard Oil Company acquired property on the Cove. In the 1890s the Knob Outing Club and Norwalk Yacht Club built clubhouses and boat-ing and beach facilities on Wilson Point, further restricting land use. Wilson Point, therefore, never became as densely populated as either Rowayton or Bell Island.[10]

According to a well-known study New England towns followed a fairly uniform pattern in electing political leaders.[11] Early in the nineteenth century they tended to elect "patricians," educated men from old, prosperous, highly-respected families. Around 1840 self-made men of Yankee stock were chosen and finally the Irish and other ethnic groups were able to put their men into office. Norwalk had its own variations of this general pattern. Its Irish were slow to seize a share of local government. New Haven elected its first Irish alderman in 1857 but in Norwalk no Irish politician became a councilman

until the last decade of the century.[13] The *Gazette*, a Republican newspaper, reflected the Yankee fear of Irish support for the opposition party.[14]

The election of 1885 saw the first victories for the Irish when, in a list of forty, James Farrell, Edwin Kelly, John Murphy, and Edwin O'Reilly were elected justices of the peace.[15] In 1887 Michael Sheedy and William McMullen were elected poundkeepers, jobs hitherto reserved for descen-dants of the old Protestant families. The fire com-panies, convivial male social clubs as well as fire protection units, remained political domains of "old" Norwalkers of the middle class. One seldom finds a foreign name, except for an occasional German, in their pre-1900 rosters with the excep-tion of Hope Hose Company. After its reorganiza-tion in 1894 names like Slattery, Duffy, and Costello began to appear on its lists. South Norwalk was a somewhat different story. Before the end of the century Democrats Michael McNerney and John McMahon, whose nephew was to become a United States Senator a generation later, had served on the Council.[16]

The rising star among South Norwalk's Gaelic politicians was Jeremiah Donovan. He was not a typical Irishman, however. For one thing, although the Norwalk-born Democrat had to go to work at the age of sixteen, he had had a better education than most. For another, he made his money in a less orthodox fashion. After holding briefly one or two

13 James Finney, a constable elected between 1857 and 1880, may have been Irish, but he was an Episcopalian.

14 The Democrats purportedly received Irish votes only by plying the naive newcomers with strong drink. At a time when there were only about a hundred newly-naturalized Irishmen in all of Fairfield County the *Gazette's* editor used St. Mary's fund drive to moralize: "Let the money that is usually wasted in maddening the brain of poor Pat on election day be given to build him instead a church."

15 This sudden success may have been related to Cleveland's popularity or it may have come about because the votes were more carefully counted. For the first time a tally appears in the Town Proceedings.

16 Except for Grover Cleveland, who always won handily in Norwalk, Republican presidential candidates received the town's vote throughout the last half of the century. But the Democrats always drew a strong minority vote and some-times the town would send Democrats to Hartford while voting for a Republican president. Norwalk's most promi-nent Democrat was James W. Hyatt who became Treasurer of the United States under Cleveland. Born in Norwalk, Hyatt left school at thirteen, worked his way up to a position of responsibility in LeGrand Lockwood's office, and after Lockwood's death became president of the D&N Railroad. He was a Whig in the 1850s.

low-paying jobs in Rowayton and South Norwalk Donovan went to work as a clerk for a grocer named Casey. When Casey died not long afterward the twenty-two-year-old Donovan married Mrs. Casey.*17* After her death only a few months following their marriage in 1874 Donovan inherited the grocery store. He continued to operate it, adding a saloon and liquor business. Living frugally above the saloon on Washington Street, by 1898 Donovan had accumulated a "comfortable fortune," enough to move with his second wife to a substantial house on stylish Flax Hill, and go into politics. In the meantime he had won local respect by fighting for the South Norwalk electric plant and supporting the lower district in its frequent quarrels with Norwalk proper.

Machine politics reached its peak in the 1880s and 1890s. Norwalk, in particular the Borough, came in for its share of criticism. At this date Norwalk's most prominent Republican was Ebenezer J. Hill, cousin of Ebenezer Hill, Jr., the son of banker-lumberman-industrialist Ebenezer Hill.*18* Ebenezer J. Hill's appointment to the Republican National Convention in 1884 gave him effective political visibility, and two years later he was elected to the state senate. By the 1890s he was acknowledged to be a top "boss" of the Republican machine, which was supported by local businessmen and controlled both Borough and town.[12]

In 1889 Connecticut's legislature passed a reform bill providing for the secret ballot but boroughs were not required to use this new method of voting. Thus after 1889 South Norwalk, a city, employed the secret ballot but in the Borough of Norwalk it was not unusual for party functionaries to follow a voter right to the ballot box, trying to buy or influence his vote. Under the existing open balloting method factory workers were often forced by their employers to vote Republican or not to vote at all.

17 Donovan's obituary in the Norwalk *Hour,* Apr. 22, 1935, states that he was then seventy-seven years old. His birth date is given as 1858. If that is correct Donovan was only sixteen when he married Mrs. Casey. It is more likely that the 1853 date given in the *National Cyclopaedia of American Biography* is the actual one.

18 The similarity extended beyond names. Their life spans were almost identical, Ebenezer J. being born in 1847 and dying in 1917, and Ebenezer, Jr. living from 1849 to 1915. The latter lived in his father's home (old Ebenezer died in 1875) at 46 West Avenue, while Ebenezer J. lived at 40 West Avenue. Their business activities appear to have overlapped, as well, thoroughly confusing their contemporaries, including newspaper reporters.

The Borough's Republican leaders resisted all efforts to adopt the secret ballot and in 1892 the matter came to a head when reformers petitioned the Court of Burgesses to adopt this electoral reform.

When the petition came before the Court of Burgesses, Hill stood up and denounced the proposal as a fraud and a swindle. Under the embarrassing heading: "Ballot Reform Not Wanted—Conn. Republicans Prefer Disgraceful Elections," the *New York Times* reported that the burgesses permitted Hill to continue an uninterrupted tirade but refused the reformers any opportunity to answer his

Congressman Ebenezer J. Hill.

outburst. The *Times* prophesied that no more would be heard about the secret-ballot petition since the Court of Burgesses had referred it to an all-Republican committee for study. But there were immediate repercussions. Of 787 new voters, the largest number ever to register in a single year, about 500 were Democrats.[13]

By the 1890s city status was an idea whose time had come and towns besieged the state legislature for city charters. Most citizens of the Borough, even Ebenezer J. Hill, supported the change. A few opponents claimed that a city charter would impede future consolidation of the town, a proposal some people were advancing. By 1893 proponents of city status had the majority and the Borough was granted a charter to become a city. The new charter provided for a six-man common council which retained most of the powers of the old burgesses. The newly-elected mayor Edwin C. Keeler and those who followed him exercised little power except to carry out regulations laid down by the council.

Hill's obstructionism *vis à vis* the secret ballot was forgotten by the voters and in 1894 he was elected on a Republican upswing to Congress where he remained for more than twenty years, piling up

Elevation of the railroad tracks through South Norwalk in 1895 made a noticeable change in the downtown business district.

outstanding majorities in several elections. One reason for Hill's success was his cultivation of Connecticut's newest immigrant group, the Italians. He was always willing to appear as a speaker at their social gatherings and by his presence give prestige to their all-important Columbus Day.[19]

Another reason for Hill's success was the control businessmen exercised over the workmen in their

19 He had less need to cultivate the Germans who, although a sizable community worth catering to, generally voted Republican anyway.

employ. His cousin, Ebenezer, Jr., like many a nineteenth-century employer, intimidated workers politically by pressuring them to join Republican clubs and participate in parades and other political activities. On at least one occasion Hill discharged three Democratic machinists at the Norwalk Iron Works with the explanation that "hostile tariff legislation" forced the layoffs. The *New York Times* inquired why, out of fifty-four machinists of whom only four were Democrats, the three who lost their jobs were all from that party. The *Times* found it hard to believe that poor business conditions had caused the firings when only two days later Hill announced that his company was "running overtime and expected to run nights."[14]

Congressman Hill probably thought of himself as a liberal. Although a strong advocate of the controversial protective tariff he supported both Roosevelt and Taft, and he worked for such progressive measures as rural free delivery of mail. In Congress he was considered an expert in tariff and banking matters and sat on the prestigious Ways and Means Committee.[15] His influence and his tariff views were of considerable help to Connecticut hatters, clothing and lace manufacturers, and to the communities in which they operated; this too redounded to Hill's benefit at the polls.

Norwalk was little different from other communities at this time in its cleavages between Democrats and Republicans, political machines and reformers, factory owners and factory workers. In the last years of the century many American cities were marked by such divisions. What set Norwalk apart was its bailiwick mentality. Localism as such is not necessarily discreditable but Norwalk's brand was ridden with negative and petty jealousies.

The only undertaking that united the entire town was still another effort to make Norwalk the county seat. The selectmen agreed willingly to appropriate one hundred thousand dollars to construct a court house even if the town had to borrow the money. A committee representing all sections and both political parties was created to lobby in Hartford. However, Bridgeport, which stood to lose the title of county seat, lobbied even more strenuously and, as it turned out, more successfully.[16] As a wag expressed it later the court house should no longer be called the County Court House, but the Bridgeport Court House, since Bridgeport had paid a quarter-million dollars to built it.[17]

Getting the county seat could have given Norwalkers the impetus to cooperate, pull the town together, and move forward, but the town's parochialism continued. A writer who completed a study of lower Fairfield County in 1890 asked why the Norwalks, "welded together by mutual interests and mutual progress," could not incorporate under one charter. This must have been one of the more polite comments for the *Gazette,* imploring the town to unite, cried: "If we could hear the ridicule and contempt heaped upon us by outsiders, we should blush to have it known that we had ever even rode [sic] through Norwalk."

The political parties, politicians, and town officials—as such—contributed little to the town's betterment. Progress did come about, however, through private initiative. The newspapers—there were now three of them—frequently served as forces of change. Although A. Homer Byington had gradually turned the running of the *Gazette* over to associates the paper continued to represent his views: progressive but business-oriented politics, Republicanism, and an interest in temperance.*20* When South Norwalk became a city the daily *South Norwalk Sentinel21* appeared. Devoted to the interests of the lower district, it was published for many years by the Golden family.*22*

An argument between a commuter and the New Haven Railroad led to publication of the town's third paper in 1871. When Brainard W. Maples, a daily commuter between Westport and New York City, mislaid his commutation book and refused to pay a cash fare, he was thrown off the train. The irate Maples sued the railroad. Since the existing papers refused to carry his side of the story he started the Westport *Hour* which soon moved to Norwalk and was renamed accordingly. Although his case dragged on in the courts for more than three years Maples eventually won it. The man had a talent for getting into rows; he and the popular John Light engaged in a name-calling bout during

20 In 1898 Byington, then seventy-two years old, was appointed consul at Naples, Italy, where he spent more than a decade.

21 This newspaper at times appeared also as the *South Norwalk Evening Sentinel* and the *Evening Sentinel.* It is customarily referred to in these pages as the *South Norwalk Sentinel.* Similarly the name of the *Norwalk Hour* was changed from time to time.

22 The *Sentinel* was turned over to Leigh Danenberg and others in 1924.

the evening school controversy that did neither man any good. Maples was one of those intelligent but contentious men whose nonconformist views ruffle people's feathers but in the long run often turn out to be correct. Dubbed by his competitors "the Ruffian of the Connecticut press" and his paper a "two-cent yellow journal," the crusty Maples nonetheless turned the *Hour* into a viable publication. When it became a daily in 1895 it put the venerable *Gazette* out of business.

Of the many civic-minded men and women in Norwalk no one was more committed to community projects than John Light. This attorney of inexhaustible energy not only headed or aided innumerable local endeavors but gained national fame for his stand in the Danbury Hatters' Case. Retained as counsel by workers who started a

The South Norwalk Library on Washington Street.

boycott during the strike of 1902, Light eloquently argued the case for the hatters but failed to sway the pro-business District Court. Light carried the case to the Supreme Court where, in a landmark decision that severely restricted labor's use of the boycott as an economic weapon, the Court ruled it a conspiracy in restraint of trade and therefore illegal under the Sherman Antitrust Act. Light's advocacy of the hatters may have harmed him politically. Although he was a state legislator, judge of Common Pleas, and served as the state's attorney general, he never attained national political prominence.*23*

23 Born in Carmel, New York, Light studied law in Levi Warner's office in Norwalk. His reputation as a Shakespearean scholar drew crowds whenever he lectured about the English playwright.

Another man to whom Norwalk owes much was General Nelson Taylor. He was a native of South Norwalk, had been brought up in New York City, studied law at New York University and Harvard, fought in the Civil War, served as a U.S. Congressman from New York, and then had returned to his native town. He was active in the Democratic Party but he refused public office and devoted his energies to community improvement, lending his name to and working on many committees.

Through the persistent efforts of citizens like these, and the support of local newspapers, Norwalk obtained public libraries earlier than most towns—a dozen years ahead of affluent New Haven. The library movement was part of the new educational philosophy that stressed helping adults continue their education. With General Taylor as the guiding spirit library supporters donated money and books to set up shop in a small rented space in South Norwalk in 1878. Within a few years they had managed to collect enough money to build a business block which they ingeniously rented out, using the income to operate the adjoining library.24 With Congressman Hill, Dr. James Gregory, and Miss Dotha Stone Pinneo as its major sponsors a similar committee established a library on Wall Street.

Shortly after the turn of the century Andrew Carnegie spread his largesse among American communities, offering funds to construct library buildings if city governments would agree to maintain them. The library boards leaped at the opportunity—it took city officials somewhat longer to make up their minds—and in both Norwalk and South Norwalk attractive buildings of more than adequate size for the time were constructed. Both the Queen Anne-style red brick library on Belden Avenue and the gray limestone classical structure on West Washington Street still stand. Thus Norwalk found itself with not only one, but two libraries, each with a limited collection of books. Cooperating with each other at times but competing for funds, for donations of books, and for members the libraries symbolize how Norwalk's localism attenuated its capabilities. Its citizens worked willingly for the town's betterment but primarily within the framework of their own parochialism.

24 South Norwalk's library had such a skimpy collection of books at first that its early regulations permitted members to borrow only one book at a time and to keep a maximum of three on loan.

Dr. William J. Tracey was a benefactor to all of Norwalk. When he became the town's health officer in 1893 citizens got almost more than they had bargained for.[18] Tracey was everywhere—peering into wells and watertanks, cesspools and sewers, privies and piggeries, marking mosquito-breeding pools, examining conditions in the Jail House, and tracking down the origin of every single case of typhoid fever. The year this conscientious man took office Norwalk's death rate was one of the highest in Connecticut. Within a few years it was one of the lowest. His competence and honesty gave him unchallenged authority which he never hesitated to use. When he marched into the East Norwalk School to find an overcrowded classroom deficient in lighting and ventilation he arbitrarily ordered the room closed and the School Committee had no

The second Norwalk Hospital on Armory Hill.

alternative but to rent two rooms in another building. East Norwalk was Tracey's bugbear. Its farming residents begrudged filling in the stagnant pools in the area, as required by state law, and the selectmen were loath to enforce the statute. This section was also slow to obtain sewers and for years many an East Norwalk homestead maintained its privy or cesspool close to the well in its back yard. "East Norwalk becomes more unsanitary every year," Tracey complained after a decade in his post.

Thanks to the health officer's relentless harping the public water supply—so polluted that as Tracey declared, "At times [even] the horses refuse to drink it,"—was cleaned up. Contagious diseases declined. In each annual report to the selectmen Dr. Tracey could point to a substantial improvement. Once a problem had been solved he was off on another crusade. Invariably he concluded his reports with little lectures, spelling out his next campaign: townwide garbage collection, or an isolation hospital for contagious diseases, or cleaner dairy farms, or physical examinations for pupils in Norwalk schools.

Duty compels me [he wrote in 1902] to call the attention of the public to the indiscriminate sale and use of poisonous drugs . . . It is better to suffer pain than to become addicted to the use of drugs . . . We have in our midst arsenic eaters, opium, acetaceilid and phenacetine habituates, who purchase these drugs at many of our drug stores as often as they wish.[19]

It was not difficult for readers of this report to foresee that local pharmacists would shortly be curbing their sales of habit-forming drugs and that doctors would be dispensing prescriptions for anodynes somewhat less casually.

After consolidation of the town Tracey reluctantly gave up the post he had filled for twenty years, but his good services were not lost to the townspeople. He became chief of staff of the Norwalk Hospital.[25]

Since the early 1880s there had been talk of obtaining a hospital for Norwalk but it took an accident along the railroad tracks and a campaign by some women hat trimmers to get action. In 1892 John Light used his legal talents to obtain a hospital charter from the Assembly; he remained for some fifty years as the institution's counsel. Others, including State Senator John M. Ferris, the hospital board's first president, solicited funds and supervised alteration of a small building on Leonard Street with a capacity of six beds. The hospital opened in July, 1893, and cared for thirty-one patients during the remainder of the year, only a portion of whom were able to pay in full the weekly charge of seven dollars. Six doctors were on call as the hospital's medical staff and a dozen local women formed a visiting committee, the nucleus of the present Women's Board of the hospital. Within a few years the little Leonard Street house was no longer adequate and a three-story structure with a capacity of twenty-six beds was built on Armory Hill.

25 Tracey rounded out his career with a return to the post of health officer and years of service on the Board of Education.

The hospital's visiting committee was merely one example of the many women's organizations of that day. Women were prime movers in community betterment. Through old issues of the *Gazette* and *Hour* one can observe a changing pattern of life. It is clear that women began getting out of the house more—not surprising in view of the lightened burden of housework. The public water systems alone reduced a housewife's workweek by several hours. Standard household equipment continued to improve. E. K. Lockwood's store carried eight varieties of clothes wringers and new manual washing machines promised to relieve the drudgery of the

Mrs. James J. Gregory, President of Central Club, in 1900.

washboard. But who needed to purchase these new appliances when there was an inexhaustible supply of Irish and Hungarian women willing to toil from dawn to dark at day wages that even an average family could afford?

Middle-class women waded into a multitude of good works. Women temperance workers became more bold, even calling at saloons and singing hymns and praying for the men lined up at the bar. Brainard Maples, considerably less sympathetic than Byington to the temperance cause, inquired editorially: "We wonder if the dishes are all washed and the mending all done before the ladies start out on their philanthropic mission?" Although his sour remarks may have lost Maples some subscribers they did not deter members of the Ladies Temperance Union who bravely continued to invade establishments like Becker's and Lee's saloons, exhorting the Saturday-night drinkers to go home to their wives and children.

Other women, no longer content with church and temperance work or with literary societies, organized new social welfare and reform groups. These often led progressive action, as witness the Ladies Union which pushed for a library for the uptown district several years before an effective library committee functioned. The Norwalk Woman's Club, one of the oldest women's clubs in Connecticut,[20] was created in 1885 to stimulate intellectual activities for local housewives; it broadened its pursuits to social causes and town beautification. The Central Club formed for philanthropic purposes became interested in women's rights and made a comprehensive study of the effect of Connecticut's laws on women.

Norwalk women did not have to take a back seat at all as far as lasting influence goes. Two outstanding librarians, Dotha Stone Pinneo in the Borough and Angeline Scott in South Norwalk, brought a professionalism to their work that must have impressed even the Carnegie grant committee. Angeline Scott went to work at the South Norwalk library in 1890 and remained there fifteen years. She was an innovative and spirited young lady who—among other activities—set up superb exhibits of paintings at the library, arranged enrichment courses and organized a Chautauqua Union in Norwalk. She held responsible offices in the state library association and wrote articles for several publications. Although she resigned from her professional position after her marriage, Angeline Scott continued for many years in "faithful, unselfish service to the public" as a volunteer of the South Norwalk Library Association.

After helping to plan the Borough's library, Dotha Stone Pinneo became its first librarian. During her twenty-eight year tenure she was responsible for establishing the East Norwalk Library which began with one hundred books donated by her and sixty volumes loaned by the state. Miss Pinneo was ahead of her time in opening library shelves to the public at a period when most libraries would not allow people to browse among the stacks for fear of theft. To supplement her meager librarian's salary the hardworking Miss Pinneo gave literary recitals and even had to turn her hand to public stenography.

New people, new politics, modern education, labor's broadened outlook, women's social spirit, and the ideals of civic-minded progressives were all catalysts for change. Reluctantly or willingly, Norwalk would have to accept these obtrusive forces as it headed into the twentieth century.

he valley, which lies along the

Norwalk river, and in which the

PART FOUR

town is built, is beautiful. Few

richer prospects of the same extent can be found

MODERN CITY

than that, which is presented from the neighbouring

eminences of this ground; the town . . . the

1913 / 1961

river . . . the farms . . . together with an unlimited

view of the Sound and the Long Island shore."

Timothy Dwight / 1822

14

CONSOLIDATION AND COMPROMISE

*Being
an Account of
Norwalk in the Dawn of the Twentieth Century*

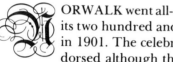ORWALK went all-out to commemorate its two hundred and fiftieth anniversary in 1901. The celebration was widely endorsed although the women's clubs deserved the credit for the hard work of organizing the festivities. Events ranged from spectacular pageants and visits to historic sites like the Reverend Hanford's dwelling place[1] to speeches by visiting dignitaries and an epic poem composed for the occasion.

There was an undercurrent of discontent, however, as evidenced by apologetic remarks in the volume commemorating the anniversary. "The popular opinion is that Norwalk has not lived up to her possibilities and, therefore, has little reason for boasting," admitted the author of the section on industry.[1] Although the writer went on to state that Norwalk was not unimportant in the world of business, the examples he gave—hatting, locks, oystering, corsets—were all less impressive than other Connecticut towns could boast. Danbury was the state's acknowledged hatting center. Chance and a technological breakthrough had put Yale & Towne above the Norwalk Lock Company. Both New Haven and Bridgeport surpassed Norwalk as corset-making centers. In Bridgeport the Warner Company alone had 80 percent more workers in its employ than R&G Corset. In oystering 11,797 acres were under cultivation in Norwalk whereas in New Haven a single firm cultivated 15,000 acres. At a

period in American life when expanding commerce and industry were measures of a city's success Norwalk had only passing marks.

Knowledge of the town's failure to live up to its potential was one reason why so many people of good will joined forces to make the townwide celebration memorable, hoping it would lead to further cooperation. The Reverend Paul Strayer, a featured speaker, seized his opportunity on the platform to plead for unity. Scolding uptown and downtown alike he accused Norwalkers of being petty, antagonistic, and jealous. It had come to the point, said the pastor of the Second Congregational Church, where if South Norwalk wanted something Norwalk vetoed it in town meeting. "Indeed," Strayer stated with a bluntness that must have offended more than a few listeners, "what cause[s] the disagreement between the two cities is not that they have so little in common but that they have so much in common selfishness."[2]

Whatever impetus may have been derived from the anniversary festivities it was not enough to bring the town together and in spite of several subsequent efforts to draft consolidation charters, unification eluded Norwalk. The governments remained overlapping and inefficient.

In 1905 a welfare scandal hit the town which gave reformers another argument for consolidation. Criticism of aid given to the so-called "outdoor poor," those people living at home and receiving monthly stipends from the town, had led to the appointment of an investigatory committee. The

---

1 All that remained was part of an old well.

170

Residence of George Holmes on Main Street, 1901.

Town Hall was packed to the doors when the committee made its report. The *New York Times* publicized the episode and Norwalk joined the list of notorious cities in the clutches of corrupt officials.2 The town's traditional practice of listing welfare recipients by name had ceased, a change that maintained privacy for those unfortunates but also threw a convenient cloak of secrecy over welfare expenditures. Investigation revealed that with a population of only 20,000 Norwalk was spending as much annually on welfare as New Haven and Hartford combined, although their total population was 150,000. A few cases appeared to be the result of laxity, as in the instance of the immigrant woman who—while working steadily for ten years—had collected benefits and with motherly devotion had sent them to her son in Poland. Other cases, those where well-to-do taxpayers had been continued on the "pauper" list for more than twenty years, involved downright dishonesty. The uproar arose, however, over cases where welfare funds were dispersed through grocery orders paid directly to grocers and rent orders paid directly to owners of tenements where welfare recipients lived in "unspeakable conditions of neglect."³ Much of the

money finally landed, the *Times* reported, "in the pockets of certain powerful politicians, who own the tenements," and in the bank account of a certain grocery company in which several prominent political figures had financial interests.

Norwalk found itself once more at cross purposes in 1909 when union hatters, seven hundred from Crofut and Knapp alone, walked out in support of a unionwide strike in major hatting centers along the eastern seaboard. This dispute gave Dr. Charles MacFarland, the new progressive pastor of the Second Congregational Church, ample opportunity to put into practice his teachings about a minister's responsibilities. A lecturer on pastoral functions at Yale Divinity School, MacFarland taught his students that a modern minister must foster a close and sympathetic working relationship with unions, encourage their higher ideals, and provide wise guidance.₃

MacFarland crusaded tirelessly to bring the two sides together as the strike, which started in January, stretched into the spring with no settlement in sight. He and his ally, Christian Swartz, influenced South Norwalk's mayor, Dr. Francis Burnell, to appoint a negotiating committee. MacFarland and Mortimer M. Lee, the most dedicated

---

2 Norwalk was by no means alone in Fairfield County in having to admit to kickbacks. Only a few years later muckraker Lincoln Steffens was chagrined to find corruption in his small village of Greenwich.

3 *The Defender*, May-June, 1909. MacFarland's lectures were collected in a book entitled *The Christian Ministry and the Social Order*, and published by Yale University Press.

members of the group, confidently shuttled back and forth between owners and workers. During the course of the strike members of the Association of Hat Manufacturers reverted to the open shop and refused all overtures toward reconciliation. Crofut and Knapp brusquely asserted, "The Company is entirely satisfied with the present condition inside its factory, and so far as the Company is concerned the strike is over."[4] Even MacFarland's provocative Labor Sunday sermon, "Morals in Modern Business," urging arbitration and conciliation in labor disputes, could not pry the owners from their position.

The strike never really ended; it simply ran out of steam. At the onset the striking finishers, makers, and trimmers received small weekly strike benefits from their unions. But as the strike dragged on the financially-strapped hatters reluctantly drifted back to work, even in the face of vicious verbal assaults from the holdouts. One by one the long-idle factories reopened in late spring. A new hatting firm started production in May; another in August. Crofut and Knapp retained the open shop. Animosity between union sympathizers and non-union men, working side by side in C&K's open shop, was never too well disguised and a chance remark could trigger assaults so violent that the perpetrators ended up in jail. Even this did not cool tempers for the supporters of the injured party were known to line up in front of the jail and shout vile names at the incarcerated men.

The end of the labor troubles did not signal any sudden surge in the local economy. The dual Boards of Trade in Norwalk and South Norwalk, each of which had been formed to seek ways of attracting industry to its section of town, continued to search for new businesses and, as a result of their efforts, two or three lacemaking firms moved into town. A Troy-based shirt company, Cluett, Peabody, opened a branch factory in South Norwalk in 1909 for manufacturing men's dress shirts. The expansion of Nash Engineering Company, maker of a new type of air pump, was one of the more heartening events. The inventor of this new device, Lewis H. Nash, was a native of Norwalk and descendant of an early tanner in town. After his company outgrew its quarters above a store on Water Street he constructed a large concrete building on a tract of land on Wilson Avenue and began operations there in 1911.

In 1912 the Boards of Trade belatedly realized that if the two Norwalks, each slightly less than 10,000 in population, had been united they would have been included in a U.S. Department of Labor Bulletin listing cities of over 10,000 that wanted to attract new industries. The same year, after the Thermos Bottle Company considered locating in Norwalk and turned it down in favor of upstate Norwich, the dismayed boards agreed to cooperate.[5] These two events coming so close together prompted another look at consolidation proposals and the town appointed a seven-man committee, representing all sections, to draft a unification charter.

New charters are always difficult to agree upon, generally because they eliminate political offices whose holders object to losing their prerogatives. In Norwalk's case more was involved. South Norwalk was the stumbling block. For years the lower district had surpassed the upper as South Norwalk's electric plant and its superior school system testified. Furthermore, the Borough's refusal to share its water system forty-five years earlier had never been forgotten, nor had the rancor over the location of the high school fully subsided. An embattled group, the South Norwalk Protective League, declared they would fight to the last ditch to retain the *status quo*. League members charged that when South Norwalk was little more than a marsh and Norwalk a flourishing center, "the citizens of the upper borough stuck up their noses at the Plebian oystermen." Now that South Norwalk was the dominant city the "old mossbacks in Norwalk [who] wouldn't give up a dollar to build anything themselves" wanted to move in on South Norwalk. "Our City, First, Last, and Forever!" cried the *Sentinel*.[6]

A unification charter was drafted nevertheless and sent to the General Assembly for approval, only to be rejected by Norwalk voters in February, 1913, while the Assembly was still considering it. Voters finally accepted a watered-down charter in June.[4] The following October the new system with Dr. Burnell as mayor was put into operation. The seven-man Common Council was composed of two councilmen from each of the two large districts and a single councilman from East Norwalk. Silvermine and Rowayton were granted one representative each on the Council. Norwalk was united at last!

[4] A majority of those voting in both South and East Norwalk opposed unification but the overwhelming vote in the First District overbalanced the negative ballots and the measure won by a vote of 2,256 to 1,606.

Or was it? First of all, the existing political framework remained essentially unchanged since the First and Second Districts corresponded to the old ones. The two water districts continued to operate as separate systems as they do to this day. The Second District kept its own generating plant to supply that area with electrical power. The Third District (East Norwalk and the former East Norwalk Fire District) also kept its own electrical system to distribute electrical power which it purchased from a public utility for its residents. People in the rest of the city obtained their electrical power from the same public utility but paid a different price for it. Because of these and other differences in city services, accepted in the compromise charter, the city

There She Is a Waitin' at the Church

Political cartoon from the "New York Journal," 1913.

now had to be divided into separate taxing districts. As the city grew these changed somewhat but, as the following excerpt from a study by a long-time resident and an authority on municipal administration indicates, they might confound a Philadelphia lawyer:

The taxing districts of Norwalk, eight in all at the present time [1959], may be roughly grouped in three categories. In the first place, there are four districts (fourth, fifth, seventh and eighth) which exist essentially for the purpose of computing differential tax rates for the conduct of city services, and the properties of which belong to the city government; secondly, there is the sixth district, which *provides limited local services and owns some non-utility property; and, thirdly, there are the three districts (first, second and third) which provide certain local services and own and operate essential city utilities along with some other properties.[7]*

Given the schisms of 1913 it is a wonder Norwalk achieved any consolidation at all; yet the new structure contained built-in devices that would delay unification, differential tax and utility rates being the greatest barriers. The average citizen might have only a foggy notion of the city's governmental structure but if he glimpsed any prospect of an increase in his taxes or utility rates he was ready to vote "No" to further consolidation. The boards and commissions controlling the several utilities also rejected proposals that would have endangered their power bases. A minor but graphic example of the unfinished nature of the 1913 charter was the South Norwalk City Hall rented to the new city government on a temporary basis. The rent, a nominal one dollar per year plus expenses, was still being paid to the Second District sixty-five years later.

Rowayton took advantage of this loose structure to obtain a separate status in 1921 that made it a kind of city-within-a-city.[5] Commissioners of the new district, with the obvious approval of its citizens, maintained vigilant guard over their unique properties, Bayley Beach in particular, which Rowayton later developed for the exclusive use of its residents. The Sixth District arrangement showed that parochialism was alive and well in Norwalk.

But such developments were in the future and in 1913, shelving unsolved problems and breathing sighs of relief that their city was at long last unified, the people of Norwalk turned complacently to their private pursuits. Preoccupation with their own interests obscured the war brewing on another continent an ocean away. While crisis upon crisis brought Europe's two opposing camps closer to war, Norwalkers remained immersed in the routine of everyday living.

Expansion of public utilities was making Norwalk a more attractive place in which to live. Completion of a much-publicized modern water purification plant worth a million dollars and touted as "the best in New England" encouraged real estate develop-

[5] In 1926 the court held the act under which the Sixth District was created to be valid although it was defective as originally created.

ment. When a New Jersey builder developed Marvin Beach Tract he was able to promise prospective purchasers street lights and a safe water supply in addition to the panoramic view. Summer visitors swelled the population too, and an unprecedented demand for cottages at Bell Island drove summer rentals upward of one thousand dollars a season. Other visitors—Catholic laymen on retreat at Manresa Institute on Keyser's Island, as well as impoverished, work-weary New York mothers vacationing at St. James' Summer Home on Strawberry Hill Avenue—enjoyed briefer sojourns away from the bustle of a big city.

In 1916 James Augustus Farrell added a second grand mansion to the town when he constructed Rock Ledge to replace a smaller house that burned down during the wedding reception of one of his daughters. The Irish millionaire, president of the United States Steel Corporation and Farrell's Steamship Line, built an even more imposing residence. Rock Ledge was set on fifteen acres above Hickory Bluff Road with a superb view of Wilson Cove. It was a reproduction of an Elizabethan great house replete with timbered ceilings, oak paneling, leaded windows, and even a fully-consecrated chapel. Although the house was considerably out of keeping with the casual summertime style of life

along this shore Rock Ledge became Rowayton's chief ornament.

Pleasure-seeking residents found many diversions within Norwalk. They enjoyed concerts by the Firemen's Mandolin Orchestra, a group of music-lovers from the South and East Norwalk Departments. On Saturday nights young people took the trolley to Dorlon's Pavilion to dance the tango, the latest step, to the beat of Fiedler's Orchestra, assured by the management that there would be no wallflowers. When Roton Point Amusement Park announced completion of a new roller coaster thousands of local people flocked to the park to try the thrilling ride at least once, while the most daring tested it ten times! At the Norwalk Country Club members converged on the new Roque courts and competed at this Americanized and "scientific" form of croquet.

Norwalkers could hop into their Pierce Arrow, Overland, or Moyer Model A, or rent a chauffeured car for a "spin through the country." To do so was to flirt with danger for horses and wagons still cluttered the roads. An impatient motorist who attempted to pass but failed to clear such an obstruction found the law courts more sympathetic to the wagoneer than to the driver. Highways which were merely old wagon roads not yet redesigned for safe

The Howard family at Roton Point in 1914.

motoring could also be treacherous. But no road was a greater challenge than that portion of Westport Avenue approaching the intersection with East Avenue where hardly a week passed without a death or serious accident. So many cars and drivers came to grief on the steep incline with its sharp S-curve that it earned the name Mortuary Hill.

Even in the summer of 1914 Norwalkers were more interested in a novel beautification project, the Children's Market, than in news about Europe. When townspeople and touring motorists could spend a pleasant Saturday morning picking from among the bunches of bachelor buttons and pinks and baskets of peas and beans grown by local children, it was difficult to worry about Austria-Hungary's declaration of war on Serbia. It is true that a Norwalk company of the Connecticut National Guard, the Sixth Company, Coast Guard Artillery, Captain Albert Mossman commanding, did drill regularly. Their shooting practice in South Wilton occasionally turned into outings crowned by "a meal fit for the gods" from the pots of company cooks. But the general complaint throughout Connecticut was that membership in the National Guard had declined.

Imperturbable Norwalkers occupied themselves with the 1914 Congressional elections. A bitter post-election dispute between Ebenezer J. Hill and Jeremiah Donovan also diverted attention from Europe. In 1912 Donovan had won Hill's long-held seat in Congress and when Hill regained it in 1914 Donovan charged him with spending in excess of what the law allowed for campaign expenditures. It was more than two years before the House of Representatives found in Hill's favor.

American complacency was shaken in 1915-1916 as headlines recounted bad news more often than not: heavy losses of British and French troops on the Western front, Germany's heinous use of poison gas, U-boat activity that jeopardized neutral shipping. The war was brought even closer when Norwalkers read about the military adventures of three former Dresden Lace Works employees who had joined the British Expeditionary Forces and were serving in far-off Mesopotamia. Readers shivered over an account of the near-drowning of a young Norwalk seaman, Daniel Novak, hurled from the liner *Silius* into the waters off Havre, France, when the ship exploded during a German torpedo attack. They experienced battle conditions vicariously when a visiting War Ambulance Corps driver or a wounded British officer shared harrowing adventures with church groups and showed lantern slides of battle scenes.[8]

Throughout America in 1916 people began to realize that the war might be a long one and that the United States might eventually become a participant. In an about-face Norwalkers, like Americans everywhere, became strong advocates of preparedness. The *Norwalk Hour* condemned "peace at any price" and urged its readers to get involved in patriotic causes. When Marjorie Sterrett, a sweet little girl with sausage-curls, appeared at the Regent Theater to solicit contributions for a U.S. battleship financed by public subscription, the *Hour* did its utmost for the project. Local businessmen demonstrated their commitment to national defense by paying regular salaries to those employees in the National Guard released for a two-week encampment at Fisher's Island. During the summer of 1916 a contingent of local men voluntarily spent a month at the officers' training camp at Plattsburgh, New York, and nearly one hundred women plunged into practical nursing and first aid courses at the Armory.

War preparations were stepped up early in 1917. In January Governor Marcus Holcomb ordered every Connecticut community to compile a military census and an inventory of local resources. Volunteers flocked to City Hall. Over a ten-day period Boy Scouts, high school students, and housewives unstintingly gathered information which city employees tabulated on typewriters commandeered from the high school. By late March they were able to send Hartford a list of 8,002 males aged sixteen and older together with an inventory of local vessels with military potential and a list of persons who understood telegraphy or could repair steam engines. Even those who could swim or had taken Red Cross courses were included on this list. A newly-formed Norwalk War Committee headed by General Russell Frost effortlessly recruited volunteers for a Home Guard of men aged seventeen to sixty to protect bridges, railroad property, and factories from enemy sabotage. Members of the Norwalk Rifle Club joined as a body. The response to a call for volunteers for auxiliary police and fire forces surpassed all expectations.

Contributing to the preparedness effort was infectious. When industrialist E.B. Gallaher purchased a Lewis machine gun to protect the city and sponsored the Gallaher Machine Gun Battery[6] other merchants and manufacturers, not to be out-done, matched his generosity by contributing funds for a machine gun "primarily for the defense of the first district." To help employees combat rising food prices C&K acquired the former Comstock Dahlia Farm in Silvermine and gave its workers small plots on which to raise vegetables. But no one could match Henry Rose's patriotism; the head of the Rose Oyster Company offered his entire oyster farm business to the federal government!

Shortly before war was declared President Woodrow Wilson ordered the National Guard mobilized for federal service. Connecticut National Guard units were brought up to full strength and, together with their counterparts in the other New England states, were organized as the Twenty-Sixth Division of the United States Army, with the 102nd Infantry Regiment distinctly a Connecticut unit.

Men in the Connecticut Coast Artillery, including Norwalk's Sixth Company, were mobilized in late July. The city gave the one hundred nineteen members of this unit a rousing farewell but those who lined the route to the railroad depot must have been moved when they saw the remaining aged, white-haired "Boys of '61" marching side-by-side with the "Boys of '17." Part of the Sixth was absorbed into the Third Long Island Sound Company and served guard duty at strategic points along the East Coast.[7] The remainder, assigned to batteries of the Twenty-Sixth Division, saw action in France.

The Twenty-Sixth, the Yankee Division, embarked for England in the fall of 1917 and from the staging points there was ferried to LeHavre where the men were greeted with a tumultuous welcome. They were then detailed to Lorraine or Brittany for a period of intensive training under conditions that replicated those of the battlefield.[9] Foul weather and a shortage of supplies notwithstanding, there were lighter moments. Antonio Carione, who signed his letters "Pride of the Italian Colonial Club," reported that he was "having a good time, outside of my drilling . . . the girls are very nice over here and I am learning to talk French."

---

6 This corps of civilians displayed their prowess to admiring spectators during Cranbury Drill Ground reviews.

7 As moral support for their comrades, Norwalkers in the Third L.I.S. Co. regularly purchased war bonds out of the paltry $30.00 a month these homefront "doughboys" earned. In a little over two months in 1917 they purchased $6,000 in war bonds.

The interlude of flirting with French girls ended when the Division was sent to the Chemin des Dames sector in February, 1918, and got its baptism of fire. Here for the first time they experienced German night raids and a twenty-four hour bombardment by mustard, phosgene, and hyperite gas shells that left many men badly burned, their lungs seared and their eyeballs scorched. This was only the onset; the men of the Twenty-Sixth fought in the Aisne-Marne, Champagne, Oise-Aisne, and Meuse-Argonne campaigns and before the guns were silenced in November, 1918, they had been in the thickest of battles: Seicheprey, Remieres Wood, Belleau Wood, Château-Thierry, Saint-Mihiel, and Verdun.[10] For months they were pounded with high explosives, suffered gas shell attacks, advanced on the enemy and learned to dive for the security of the trenches. Some, like Private Clayton Bell, 104th Ambulance Co., received the Croix de Guerre for extraordinary valor on the field. Others, like the light-hearted Antonio Carione and four comrades of Co. D, 102nd Regt., were captured, listed as missing in action, and eventually turned up in the German prison camps of Limbourg and Damstadt. Some were severely gassed, wounded, or like Robert O'Riley, limped home on crutches. A considerable number of men in the Twenty-Sixth lost their lives in battle.

Other Norwalk men served in the Regular Army. There were those like Frank Godfrey, who had been in the Regular Army in both the Spanish American War and the Mexican Border in 1916, who reenlisted when the Great War started. Others served in the U.S. Cavalry, the American Engineer Corps, and the Aviation Service, all branches of the Regular Army. Black men from long-established local families went off to Fort Devens to join a newly-formed "colored regiment." Age was no deterrent to a determined man: James Costello, Norwalk's oldest volunteer who admitted only to "thirty-nine," became a machinist in the U.S. Army Ordnance Corps.

As might be expected in a community where so many men made their livelihood from the water, the Naval Coast Defense Reserve, the Naval Militia, and the Merchant Marine attracted their share of volunteers. Duty with the Merchant Marine could be as perilous as that of an infantryman on the front line and more than one Norwalk seaman could match Leland Walsh's story of his experience on the transport *Mount Vernon,* when a German shell put a hole "as large as an Army truck" through its hull.

When national conscription came into effect in June, 1917, a total of 2,575 Norwalk men ages twenty-one to thirty-one, including married men and aliens, came forward to enroll "without a murmur." Because so many had already enlisted it was often difficult to meet assigned draft quotas and for this reason Local Draft Board No. 14 showed little sympathy toward Class 1-A men who requested deferment. In the early callups an appreciative community presented each draftee with a wrist watch at a farewell dinner at Dorlon's the evening before they began "the start of a trip to Berlin." But as callups became more frequent the city had to resort to cigarettes and writing paper and breakfast at the Mahackemo Hotel on the morning of departure.

Norwalkers did their utmost, however, to support the war effort by fulfilling and sometimes even surpassing the city's quota in every Liberty Bond drive. At massive bond rallies forceful orators inveighed against the Huns and the women's chorus of the Mayehoff factory added spirit to some of these occasions with its stirring renditions of the National Anthem and "Over There." Businesses occasionally closed for part of an afternoon so that employees could march en masse in bond-buying parades. The sight of Mayehoff's female employees, strikingly attired in white dresses and red liberty caps, stepping smartly along the parade route and waving patriotic banners and American flags helped to sell over a million dollars worth of bonds in one drive alone. Mr. Mordecai Mayehoff even gave employees a raise accompanied by the directive that they use the money to buy Liberty Bonds.

This was a period of great prosperity as "the spirited whir of industry's wheels [was] heard throughout the city." Manufacturers large and small reaped benefits of war contracts. Muller Mills operated twenty-four hours daily to satisfy a government order for several billion yards of gauze. Norwalk Lock received war contracts for small fittings used in marine construction and could boast that it had made every hinge, lock, and door pull installed on the battleship *North Dakota*. Lockwood Manufacturing Company produced components for the Lake submarine. A relative newcomer, Norwalk Tire and Rubber Company, trebled its business manufacturing tires and inner tubes for every conceivable kind of military vehicle from motorcycle to lorry. The Arnold Foundry, a smaller

firm, cast utilitarian pancake griddles for field mess kitchens. American military men wore hats made by Rosenwald Wimpfheimer and underwear made by Jacobs and Sons, the old Union mill, while R&G corsets were the mainstay of Red Cross nurses. At Wilson Point the United States Emergency Fleet Corporation commandeered Standard Oil's dock and D&N Railroad property for use as a huge storage facility and transshipment center for lumber.

The unprecedented demand for a work force to fulfill war contracts drove salaries upward. Norwalk Tire hired workers at $2.00 daily with the promise that after a few weeks on the payroll they would be earning $5.00 a day. In appreciation of jobs well done and to avoid strikes, management periodically raised wages 10 and 15 percent and handed out generous bonuses. All 196 employees of the American Hat Company enjoyed a "royal" Christmas in 1917 when they received an unexpected bonus of anywhere from $12 to $48. A raise did not necessarily guarantee a better standard of living; drastic increases in the cost of foods, housing, and fuel offset wage gains. To set a traditional Thanksgiving table in 1917 a housewife had to pay 42c a pound for turkey and 75c for a jar of Heinz' mincemeat. Potato prices had climbed to $2.20 a bushel and a dozen eggs cost nearly a dollar. Even at these prices certain foods were scarce. As shortages became acute Norwalkers pledged themselves to honor meatless Tuesdays followed by wheatless-bread Wednesdays and Thursdays. Giving up bread was actually no great sacrifice for oleomargarine, the government-mandated substitute for butter, was unpalatable.

Of all wartime crises the fuel shortage during the bitter winter of 1917-1918 hit the town hardest. Although coal prices had climbed to more than ten dollars a ton it became almost impossible to replenish dwindling local supplies. Many households were down to their last few bushels. The one remaining hope for relief was dashed when barges carrying twenty-five thousand tons earmarked for Norwalk were battered by ninety-mile-an-hour gales and sank off Tavern Island. To conserve fuel, street lights and hotel, theater, and bowling alley signs were turned off twice a week. When some uptown merchants insisted on keeping exterior lights burning for the convenience of Christmas shoppers their patriotism was called into question.

As temperatures dropped to -6° F, the Sound

froze over between Westport and Greenwich, preventing vessels from entering the harbor. By January only Raymond Brothers' yard had any coal left—a meager four hundred tons. Pipes froze throughout the city and Norwalk's Fuel Administrator, Judge John Light, was besieged by hardship cases pleading for even one or two scuttles full. A few householders fortunate enough to have stockpiled coal shared generously with those in need; Mrs. John Keogh turned over twelve tons of nut coal to Judge Light for distribution to the Day Nursery and the needy. Schools closed and saloons stayed open three fewer hours a day while churches made plans to band together to offer a single uptown and single downtown service. R&G Corset shortened its workday. Finally as the crisis worsened almost every local factory was shut down by federal order. Nearly ten thousand workers remained idle until the weather moderated and coal became available.

Norwalk residents of Germanic extraction not only had to cope with inflation and shortages like everyone else but bore the added onus of cruel anti-Teutonism. Even before America entered the war rumors of suspected German spy activity were

rife. Surely the German family who sold gasoline from the pump in front of their home on Westport Avenue used it as a front for the wireless station inside the house; after all, they were always out of gas. The curious, well-dressed man who asked so many penetrating questions about the U.S. government cutter docked at Captain Miller's shipyard was undeniably a German spy. So eminent a spokesman as Christian Swartz pledged the loyalty of the German community and Pastor Martin Steup of St. Peter's Evangelical Church assured Norwalk that German residents were "Americans first, last and all the time;" but they could not dispel the mounting antipathy. When local boys in the Naval Militia were called into active service as the result of reports that a German raider had been sighted off Nantucket their families found it hard not to show antagonism toward neighbors with German names. In truth Norwalkers were probably no better and no worse than people in dozens of other American communities who hounded their hapless neighbors, but even so Norwalk's German-Americans had to carry on under difficult conditions.

With the United States entry into the war all unnaturalized Germans and Hungarians were declared enemy aliens and every male fourteen years of age and older and all adult women had to register at the police station, be fingerprinted, and submit photographs of themselves. Each received a permit to live in the city and even to work in war plants but their movements were restricted. To violate the provisions of registration cards was a serious offense that could lead to arrest as three enemy alien lacemakers discovered to their sorrow. After a pleasant day at Roton Point Park, a permissible zone, they loitered in saloons, became inebriated, and were on the streets after eight o'clock at night, violations that led to their arrest.

Loose lips sometimes led to grievous slips, a lesson Ernest Boessmann, a workman at Norwalk Tire and Rubber Company, learned the hard way. Boessmann boasted that Liberty Bonds wouldn't be worth thirty cents after the Germans had licked the Allies and was waylaid by irate colleagues as he was leaving the shop after a day's work. Faced with the choice between kneeling and kissing the American flag or being heaved into the river, Boessmann quickly sank to his knees. A pro-German remark made by a Waterbury man at Montgomery's Lunch Wagon in South Norwalk sent Constable John Mills in hot pursuit of the perpetrator who had left town on the Bridgeport trolley. Mills caught up with the offender in Westport, made the arrest, and returned the man to Norwalk where he was promptly clapped into jail by Judge Nehemiah Candee.

Federal authorities intervened in cases involving the Espionage Act. The Department of Justice requested arrest of Arnold Hanson and Henry Briderbush, skilled machinists who operated complex imported machinery at a local plant. Money and incriminating papers found during a search of their hotel room were used as evidence to substantiate the charge that the two enemy aliens were "sending and receiving messages in German or code by means of carrier pigeons, which they were releasing from the windows of a downtown hotel." In a sadder and more complex case the U.S. Alien Property Custodian impounded R&G Corset Company stock on the grounds that Julian Goldschmidt, a founder of the company who still held one-third of the shares, was an enemy alien. Goldschmidt's son, a vice president of the firm, claimed that his father had taken out citizenship papers in 1887 but the elder Goldschmidt was unable to step forward and offer proof. Shortly before the war he had

taken Mrs. Goldschmidt to Hamburg, Germany, because of her poor health and there had been no word of the couple since.

One did not have to be an enemy alien or have a foreign surname to be chastized by the community. Author Robert Wason of Silvermine, "a quiet little colony of professional people . . . all true Americans," was asked to resign from the Silvermine Neighborhood Club because of his "socialistic views." Wason admitted that he had questioned the constitutionality of conscription and had expressed sympathy for the plight of German children. He also conceded, "I may have suggested that the Silvermine River was too shallow for U-boats," but denied that this in any way constituted aid and comfort to the enemy.

The chauvinistic atmosphere so overwhelmed Americans whose forebears had been latter-day immigrants that they felt compelled to demonstrate their loyalty. The Italian Societies of Norwalk donated receipts from their Columbus Day celebration to the Red Cross, an effort duly noted in the newspapers. Polish employees of Muller Gloria Mills were singled out for their generous purchases of Liberty Bonds as was also the Polish Republican Club. The excellent turnout of Slavonic and Bohemian people at a patriotic meeting at the Palace Theater offered visible proof of their loyalty.

For women too it was a time of challenge and trial. As more and more men departed for military duty women began to fill positions formerly in the male bailiwick. They were employed as messengers at the Postal Telegraph Company, clerks in local banks, machine operators in war plants, "conductorettes" on the trolleys, and even mail carriers. Nor were their contributions confined to the home front. At least two dozen local women served as Army and Navy nurses,[11] many of them in hospitals close to the front lines in France. A handful worked with the YMCA, particularly in units assigned to the south of France where they conducted tours, organized social events, and taught basic literacy courses for soldiers on rest leave. Under auspices of the Red Cross, Norwalk's Director of Kindergartens, Fanniebelle Curtis, and two colleagues, Margaret Holmes and Sophie Brady, traveled to the war-devastated areas of Belgium and France to organize kindergartens. Filled with pity for war-stricken and orphaned French children the middle-aged Miss Curtis remained in France after the war to set up Kindergartens, Inc. This agency established peaceful havens for more than thirty-five thousand youngsters. The grateful city of Lievin, France, built a community house as a memorial to her work and named the Rue de Fanniebelle Curtis in her honor. The French government awarded her its illustrious Legion of Honor.[12]

The next logical step for women was securing full citizenship at the ballot box. Elsie Hill and Helena Hill Weed, daughters of Congressman Ebenezer Hill, spent the war years actively campaigning for woman's suffrage. These spirited young women were the organizing force behind the Norwalk Equal Franchise League and were officers in the Connecticut Woman's Suffrage Association. They planned public meetings, sparked letter-writing campaigns, and worked to win legislators to their cause. The spunky sisters participated in suffrage marches and demonstrations in Washington, D.C., protesting both Congressional procrastination and President Wilson's outspoken opposition to giving women the vote. The indomitable sisters responded with clever ripostes to the abuses heaped upon them. When Elsie Hill was arrested for climbing up General Lafayette's statue during a demonstration, she told the press: "During my years of suffrage work I've been told and retold that women's place is on a pedestal; and the first time I get on one, I'm arrested." Both women were seized by police for picketing in front of the White House and were hauled off before a disapproving judge. Given the choice between a twenty-five dollar fine or a jail sentence the militants chose confinement in Washington's antiquated, dank District Jail. There they further dramatized their cause by staging a hunger strike. By 1920 embattled politicians could no longer resist the persistent, coercive tactics employed by suffragettes like the Hill sisters and the Nineteenth Amendment became the law of the land.

Every whistle, siren, and bell in the city rang out for four continuous hours when news of the Armistice flashed over the telegraph wires at three o'clock on the morning of November 11, 1918. From this moment on, a shouting crowd gathered at the intersection of Main and Wall Streets and incessantly thumped on every kind of makeshift noisemaker—boilers, pans, kettles, and pails. At daybreak the jubilant celebrants formed a ragged line of march and spontaneously paraded through the streets. Here and there marchers dragged dummies decorated with signs proclaiming "To Hell with the Kaiser." Schools and factories closed for the day so that everyone could "Come Out and Bury The Kaiser" at city-organized afternoon ceremonies but this formal celebration could not match the emotional pitch of that earlier spontaneous gathering.

Airing pent-up emotions offered only momentary relief for with the war's end a new set of problems emerged. The wounded began to arrive home.

World War I homecoming celebration at Baxter Camp Grounds in 1919.

Elsie M. Hill in 1916.

Gassed, maimed, and shell-shocked though they were, they were among the fortunate. In November and December the War Department released updated lists of casualties incurred in the last massive drive against the enemy. The inclusion of some Norwalk boy's name on almost every new death list confirmed the worst fears of anxious parents and friends. Rarely did a family enjoy so blessed a Christmas gift as the one received by the Coppola family. James Coppola, reported initially as severely wounded in battle and later as dead, actually walked into his father's house on Christmas Day. More often than not, however, the casualty lists were heartbreakingly accurate.

Whatever joy Norwalkers could take from the return of their sons was dampened by the dread Spanish influenza epidemic that swept through the city during the winter of 1918-1919. A few mild cases in the Muller Hill area in September gave no hint that by month's end the number of cases would double from day to day and affect all parts of the city. November's unseasonably warm weather did not help although flu victims in the Ely Avenue section could be seen pitifully clinging to fence posts and porch rails in the hope that the pale autumnal sun and fresh air would restore their vitality. Doctors worked day and night caring for the most extreme cases while Red Cross volunteers, who had learned first aid and nursing techniques during the war, assisted those less desperately ill. When all else failed families resorted to home remedies like frequent rubdowns with camphorated oil and liberal doses of hot wine. To care for the vast number of victims the new modern Norwalk Hospital, still under construction, opened ahead of schedule after Samuel Roodner sent a corps of his own workmen to complete it. All winter the epidemic persisted, sometimes claiming two members of the same family within a few hours of each other. Those same church bells that had so joyously pealed out the Armistice now tolled almost every day announcing in muffled tones the death of yet another influenza victim.

To many of the returned veterans it seemed that life in the old town had changed drastically and they sought companionship with wartime buddies in the newly-formed American Legion. Members named the local post in honor of Frank C. Godfrey.[8] The Legion helped to stage a Welcome Home party at Baxter Camp Grounds in September, 1919, and to plan the first celebration of Armistice Day in November, 1920. This occasion was meant to serve as a tribute to the heroic dead and an acclamation for the living. Norwalk's survivors of the Great War, some seven hundred strong, marched along the thoroughfares of the city in a nighttime parade that culminated in a genial block party and carnival. The celebration allowed them to forget for a while the hard problems that veterans, even more than other Americans, faced in a world returned to peace.

[8] A battalion sergeant major at the time of his reenlistment, Godfrey was commissiond a second lieutenant after graduation from Officer Candidate School in France, and was assigned to the 328th Infantry. This stouthearted company commander who led his men into the thick of the fighting in battle after battle was killed while on front-line duty at Château-Thierry in August, 1918. He lies buried in a military cemetery not far from this battlefield.

15

TURNING TO UNCLE SAM

*Being
an Account of
Norwalk in Affluence and Depression*

ITH THE end of the war Americans expected to settle into the comfortable routines of "normalcy." Instead they were confronted with a prodigious number of unsettling events: severe inflation coupled with mounting unemployment, labor unrest with a rash of strikes, and radical organizations that openly advocated drastic changes in the economic system.

A countervailing wave of nativism swept the nation and accusations were hurled at aliens, immigrants, Jews, and Catholics, all looked upon as different from "100 percent Americans." The threatening doctrines emanating from the new Bolshevik regime in Russia influenced patriotic organizations to urge deportation of "agents of Lenin," "tools of foreign agitators," and those who defamed "the American way of life."[1] As the mood of the nation turned increasingly punitive United States Attorney General A. Mitchell Palmer began a brief but massive drive to arrest dangerous radicals, mostly aliens suspected of Communistic and anarchistic activities.

Norwalkers escaped Palmer's dragnet in the November, 1919, raid but because of its large foreign population the city was visited by agents who quietly investigated suspects. They had slim pickings here for in the January, 1920, roundup only one resident was seized—Fred Baer, a long-time Norwalker of German descent. Agents found "pamphlets in four different languages and cards in red color" in Baer's home, enough evidence, one federal agent bragged, "to hang him."[2] The charges proved to be unsubstantiated. The harassed Nor-

walker was released the very night he was arrested and was back at work at the Loth Silk Company the next morning.

In politics Americans sought a return to normalcy by rejecting the party of Woodrow Wilson. Although the Twenties belonged to the Republicans in Norwalk the Democrats made a strong showing in the 1920 presidential campaign. Two days before the election the young Assistant Secretary of the Navy and candidate for vice-president, Franklin Roosevelt, came to town to pick up undecided votes but in spite of excitement generated by the visit of such a prominent personage Norwalk voted Republican.

The mayoralty election the following year put Jeremiah Donovan out of significant political office for good. Donovan had gained national commendation for his generosity in turning over his entire mayor's salary to the Norwalk Hospital. Quite possibly the popular Democrat might have won had it not been for his penny-pinching tactics.[1] Donovan also lost the women's vote because, despite his courtly manner, he had opposed suffrage.[3]

Women from all walks of life had registered and the 1920 record vote was attributed to their addition to the voting rolls. Militant Elsie Hill looked upon the suffrage amendment as only the beginning of the battle to achieve woman's full rights. Miss Hill, who flouted convention by retaining her maiden name after marriage, was now directing her

---

1 He had antagonized both parents and teachers by opposing a Board of Education appropriation for teachers' salaries although he had offered to advance their salaries from his own pocket.

energies to a Woman's Bill of Rights. As chairman of the Executive Committee of the National Woman's Party she lobbied in nine states to interest legislators in her cause. Briefly promoted as a candidate for Congress on the Farmer-Labor ticket in 1922, she scotched these efforts when she told the press she would not run for Congress "on any ticket." Most women, however, were quite content with their gains and satisfied to organize Republican or Democratic Women's Clubs.

Less than a month after Republican Mayor Calvin Barton took office in 1921 members of the Frank C. Godfrey Post demanded a public works program to employ veterans. Fortunately the mayor and council were in a position to do so for a decade earlier the state legislature had authorized one hundred thousand dollars for alterations to the Washington Street Bridge. City officials had never completed this project₂ and some money was still available. Barton was able to tell the veterans to sign up at the Highway Department office.[4]

Although the Great Red Scare subsided nativist sentiment remained strong and expressed itself through other channels. The Ku Klux Klan enjoyed a spectacular revival nationwide. In Stamford, Darien, and New Haven, local dens or Klaverns were formed. By 1923 Norwalk had a Klavern of its own,[5] whose native-born, white Protestants singled out Jews, Catholics, and the foreign-born as their whipping boys. That summer, cloaked in anonymity and protected by the cover of darkness, members of the Invisible Empire set fire to a mighty cross thirty feet high with twenty-foot crossarms at Calf Pasture Beach. A *Stamford Advocate* reporter was tipped off in advance and watched the men erect the cross but could not identify them. Several persons who said they had seen a truckload of men driving to the beach remained mum. Nor did anyone know who painted a large KKK on the stone wall surrounding industrialist James Farrell's Rock Ledge. When a man standing in the vicinity of a cross blazing on West Rocks Road was questioned he claimed that he was directing people to a picnic. Perhaps silence was the best shield for a downtown insurance man and a professional man who spoke out against the hooded band received threatening letters.[6]

Even in 1926, when the Klan had ceased to be a

2 The delays stemmed partly from the war but largely because of a political battle over location of the entrances to the bridge.

dynamic force in Connecticut, local Knights continued to set fire to wooden crosses wrapped in tar-soaked burlap on the heights of Garner Street and on West Rocks Road. Norwalk's Knights made it quite clear that Negroes were not the object of their dislike for in 1926 when the AME Church was raising funds to repair its weatherworn building on Knight Street the KKK contributed a hundred-dollar bill to the Deacon Taylor Fund. The pastor of this poor little church received several telephone calls from persons opposed to the church's keeping this money but who, apparently still fearful of Klan

Removal of central span of 1867 Washington Street bridge in 1913.

intimidation, did not wish to be identified.

As the decade progressed Norwalk began to hit its stride. The city's reputation for being up-and-coming was such that twenty families left depressed Leominster, Massachusetts, and settled in Norwalk. In 1923 157 manufacturers, representing more than a hundred different kinds of enterprises, did business in town and employed 7,900 workers. Many businesses specialized in products complementary to other manufacturers. J&J Cash manufactured labels, frillings, and tapes, and found local customers in R&G Corset, the shirt companies, and dress manufacturers like Mayehoff's and Rosenblatt and Hollub, as well as the hatters.

Norwalk hatting enjoyed the prosperous Twenties which brought enough business to keep eighteen hat companies humming. Crofut & Knapp continued to lead the field. John Cavanagh, C&K's president, was well-versed in the operational end of the business, having started out as a young man stoking stoves for brim curlers. While working his way to the top he invented a process known as the Cavanagh Edge which increased a hat's durability. He is also credited with establishing year-round

Prestigious hat boxes conveyed the quality of the product within.

operation of the factory, eliminating the customary slow season. In 1926 C&K moved to a large new fireproof plant on Van Zant Street which incorporated improvements in structure and operations, including one of tremendous significance to the workers—storage of mercury mixes in an airtight room to eliminate the danger of haphazard mercury poisoning. With 1,800 employees the new plant had the capacity to produce a million and a half hats per year.

C&K partially eliminated the middleman by joining with Dobbs & Co., fashionable retail hatters whose shops on Fifth Avenue, in Palm Beach, and other exclusive locales catered to an upper-class clientele. Crofut & Knapp's management had a

knack for merchandising, best illustrated by their snappy-looking hat boxes. These were copied after old bandboxes and conveyed an impression of old-fashioned quality and up-to-date style in hats for both men and women.[3] Next C&K launched a national advertising campaign, becoming the first hatting firm to take full-page color ads in the popular *Saturday Evening Post.* Those days every man invariably wore a hat on the street, a derby in winter, and a straw hat in summer. C&K's ambition was to persuade every man that he needed more than two hats. As a result of its advertising, soft felt hats, sporty caps, and pearl-gray or black fedoras, still worn occasionally by diplomats and lawyers, all became popular between the two world wars. For the man who could afford it C&K still produced a stylish beaver hat which retailed for forty dollars.

An airport on West Rocks Road where Central Catholic High School stands today gave additional evidence of the strength of Norwalk's economy. Although Norwalk harbor had declined in significance a few coasters still unloaded their cargoes at the aging docks. One of the most picturesque sights was a sailing ship of the St. George Paper Company, manufacturers of newsprint for several New York City dailies. Well into the twentieth century these three-masted schooners sailed upriver at high tide, carrying wood pulp from Nova Scotia to the company's processing plant on Smith Street.[4]

Restructuring the Boston Post Road during the First World War and again the following decade shortened the distance between the City and Norwalk although the latter was far from being a satellite of New York. Widening, straightening, leveling, and paving the winding Old King's Highway drastically altered neighborhoods and encouraged construction of a host of gas stations, garages, and small stores along the thoroughfare. Out-of-town automobiles sped along the Post Road causing concerned residents to write letters to newspaper editors and providing challenges that local policemen on their new motorcycles were only too happy to meet.

The close of the First World War swept Norwalk into the automobile age. City directory pages were

---

3 In 1928 Cavanaugh-Dobbs, Inc., a holding company, was formed. It controlled the stock of Crofut & Knapp and Dobbs & Company.

4 The company was taken over by the International Paper Company.

The Crofut & Knapp plant on Van Zant Street.

Pulp schooners at the St. George Paper Company dock off Smith Street.

covered with automotive advertisements: Webb Brothers, who advertised: "Rubber Tires, Welding, Rim Cuts, Blow Outs"; Hyman Jaffee, whose ad read: "Junk Dealer and Second Hand Tires"; and the Royal James Garage whose specialty was repairing Fords. Carriagemaker Luther Wright was now an agent for Mitchell and Grant motor cars, repaired autos, sold auto supplies, rented an automobile bus to "Pleasure Parties," did long-distance trucking, and still shod a few horses. By 1926 even the editors of the *Hour,* who had a tendency to nostalgia, agreed that the old hitching posts and stepping stones would have to go. There was no longer any need for them.

One inventor, Charles Barker, who came to Norwalk to manufacture a two-cylinder gasoline marine

their age with dignity. Still the erosion had begun. In 1923 Gulf Refining Company purchased the eighteenth-century Van Buren house near the Armory and erected a gas station in its place. In vain the *Hour* tried a few years later to collect funds to have the historic Belden house at the north end of West Avenue moved to another site. This pre-Revolutionary structure, used as a way station by General Garth's men during the burning, was demolished to make way for a Standard Oil station.

Faced with such threats to residential property Norwalk was ready to accept zoning after the Supreme Court upheld its validity in 1926. Even the business-oriented Board of Trade threw its weight behind zoning regulations. Russell Frost, Jr., who built the first segment of a commercial block on

The Frost Building on West Avenue.

engine for oyster boats to replace the naphtha engine, found new customers in the automobile age. The C.L. Barker Works on Crescent Street turned out four-cylinder engines which were used in Barker heavy-duty, five-ton trucks and in fire engines that could chase off to fires at speeds of thirty-five miles per hour.

The key now to the character of a street was the amount of traffic flowing through it. It would not be accurate to say that West Avenue or Main Street changed overnight. Victorian houses, some occupied by the widows or children of the men who had built them, still lined these through-highways. A few had become rooming houses but they were well cared for and carried

West Avenue prior to zoning, had to appeal to the new zoning board for a variance when he wished to erect two more sections on this residential street. Yale-graduate Frost put up three connected two-story structures with facades of tan seam-faced granite cut from the same quarries as the buildings on the Yale campus,[8] making the block an attractive shopping area. The handsomely designed Frost Building was another step toward commercialization of West Avenue. The same inevitable changeover from residential to commercial was occurring on other thoroughfares; the rate would accelerate after the Second World War.

At the end of the Twenties the city lost a famous landmark—the William Kellogg James mansion which the younger generation knew as the Royal James Inn. Set back slightly from the street behind an iron fence and shaded by some of Wall Street's remaining elms the Royal James retained the architectural grandeur of the original house. When a modern concrete commercial building rose in its place Norwalkers realized that an age had ended.

A few inhabitants mourned the loss of these old houses but most welcomed signs that the city was moving ahead. The Grand List had showed a solid, steady growth and stood at $44 million in 1925, double the 1910 figure; the First and Fourth Wards each asked for an extra councilman because of added population. In 1927 there were 465 new houses built and the population reached nearly 36,000.

The growth was gratifying but it forced the city to face up to new problems. The most troublesome was waste disposal. Although sewers had been laid in all heavily-settled sections of Norwalk the city had not built a sewage treatment plant. For years everyone had tossed trash and garbage into a marshy area in the river just below the Washington Street Bridge. This unsightly and unsanitary mound, a breeding place for flies and rats, was crudely enclosed with chicken wire in a slipshod effort to prevent its contents from floating away.

The city's casual attitude toward sewage and garbage disposal was devastating to an already-faltering oyster industry.[5] Between 1927 and 1929 while the Grand List was rising the value of local oyster grounds fell by two-thirds. Oystermen had learned to control such natural enemies as starfish and drills by sweeping the bottom of the Sound with huge string mops, using water suction dredges and chemical treatments, but they were helpless in the face of man-made pollution. Everyone deplored the situation and for at least three decades there had been demands for a clean-up of the Seaview Avenue dump but, as was the case so often, city officials dragged their feet.

Then the state banned shellfishing in Norwalk waters altogether and in 1929 Captain Frederick Lovejoy, a prominent East Norwalk oysterman, sued the city, charging that his business had been ruined through its negligence. Other oystermen

instituted similar suits. The matter ended in a kind of compromise when the city agreed to build a sewage disposal plant.[6] By the time the state lifted the ban in 1933 most local oystermen had already adopted the practice of moving the crop from inshore areas to deep offshore waters for purification before marketing but before the hard-pressed industry could recover completely the hurricane of 1938 struck a crippling blow. Many small firms closed their doors forever or consolidated with larger companies that began to specialize in growing seed oysters.

An achievement of the Twenties was acquisition of Calf Pasture Beach, completing a process begun in 1917 when the legislature authorized Norwalk to

The Royal James Inn on Wall Street.

create a public park along this beautiful stretch of shoreline. Condemnation proceedings began in 1919 and moved slowly but amicably. In 1922, much to everyone's delight, the Marvin, Taylor, and Betts families who had inherited the property gave the land outright to the city.[9] The Council promptly accepted the generous gift and expressed the city's gratitude, praising "the public spirit which prompted the proposal of this valuable benefaction." The city fathers responded appropriately by authorizing construction of a broad divided park-

---

5 The public's growing preference for shrimp and its distrust of oysters following several epidemics attributed to unsanitary packaging, as well as changes in the natural environment, had already harmed the industry.

6 The Seaview Avenue dump was not done away with completely for years and then it was replaced by another one upriver.

Miss Katherine Bee, first public health nurse in Norwalk, makes a house call.

way to the beach. Salt meadow was filled in to make about thirty-five acres of usable land on which bath houses, a pavilion, walks, landscaping, and a jetty were constructed eventually. In May, 1924, Calf Pasture Beach was opened ceremoniously although all the work had not been completed.

The town made strides in public health and social work too. These were years for benefactions. In 1922 several civic-minded citizens gave a Chevrolet coupe and a year of "free mechanical repairs" to the city for use by the school nurse. Two public health nurses were hired through the Norwalk Dispensary Association. Energetic fund-raising and a generous outpouring of contributions by the entire community over several years were rewarded when the large, modern YMCA on West Avenue opened its doors in 1928.

Even during this period of expansion and prosperity, the city continued to be niggardly in expenditures for education despite pressure from businessmen who perceived a good educational system as a requisite for continued growth. Although the school budget crept upward to half a million dollars by the end of the decade,[7] the old wooden elementary school buildings became more dilapidated than ever and more than one thousand high school students were crammed into the overburdened quarters on West Avenue designed for three hundred and fifty students. Norwalk developed a reputation for paying its teachers poorly, a condition publicized in a front-page story about a well-regarded high school teacher who left to take a position in New York City at an increase of one thousand dollars over her Norwalk salary. Such

[7] Center Junior High School, Roger Ludlow Junior High School and Broad River School were built during this time.

attrition coupled with a general inflationary trend brought modest increases in salaries.

Norwalk was assailed by land and by sea during the prohibition era. Bootleggers boldly sashayed in cars or trucks up the Post Road and rum-runners deposited illicit cargoes in secret lairs on the Norwalk Islands. Although many arrests occurred earlier in the Norwalk area 1926 was a top year for apprehension of violators. As a rule investigations and arrests were left to federal agents and State Police; rarely did Norwalk's own law enforcement officers participate.

Whatever imbibing Norwalk's officials may have done in private, publicly they were prepared to uphold the law with considerable vigor as one unhappy councilman discovered. This man had approached a local police officer for help in obtaining liquor. When other council members learned of their colleague's overt flouting of the law they held a "trial" in Corporation Counsel William F. Tammany's office at which the errant councilman was present along with his lawyer, old Judge Light. To the councilman's discomfiture both the police officer and the bootlegger's wife were on hand to testify. Declared by his peers to be guilty, the councilman was dismissed on the spot.[10]

Bootleggers attempted their runs through Norwalk winter and summer. Bottles and gallon jugs frequently nestled under innocent-looking bushels of cucumbers or crates of chickens. Once they had managed to slip past "Lone Wolf" Anderson, the Darien motorcycle policeman who seemed capable of literally sniffing out even a single ounce of alcohol, bootleggers generally thought they were home free. Occasionally, however, a sharp-eyed officer on the Norwalk stretch of the highway would glimpse something amiss, as the time a State Policeman cruising on his motorcycle along Westport Avenue noticed that every time a certain car hit a bump the springs sagged noticeably. He halted the vehicle and found 162 quarts of champagne and wine.

One of the largest hauls ever made in Connecticut occurred at the Wilson Point dock of the New York, New Haven, and Hartford, where 1,480 cases of "alum" had been transferred from a lighter to the railroad cars. An observant freight agent noticed alcohol dripping from one car and called revenue officers who promptly confiscated more than one hundred thousand dollars worth of French liquors.

Did Norwalk's ethnic inhabitants take the prohibition against manufacturing alcoholic beverages more lightly than Anglo-Saxons did? Were their operations easier to apprehend? Or was the *Norwalk Hour* simply more inclined to publicize a violation if the alleged moonshiner had a foreign-sounding name? Certainly the great majority of the *Hour's* reports of liquor raids involved minority residents. One Jewish second-hand clothier defended himself against the charge of selling moonshine on the grounds that he had been turned in by a disgruntled customer for refusing to take back a suit. Unimpressed by this explanation the judge fined him a hundred dollars. A raid on the White Eagle Hall netted the president of the American Polish Society who was allegedly serving homebrew and wine to members. Hungarians in all parts of the city had their small stills and "two gallons of hootch" or "fifty gallons of mash" confiscated. Italians were found purveying wine and liquor quite openly from little grocery stores or at their social clubs. Forty customers of a "colored" club on Water Street who were enjoying bootleg beverages during dice and card games were hauled in during one raid.

These forays were all petty ones to revenue agents who were more interested in the high-powered boats that cut their engines and glided into silent coves where they stashed valuable cargoes of Scotch, Canadian whiskey, and French wines and champagnes. Rum-running was big business and although the Long Island side of the Sound saw larger operations the Norwalk Islands drew their

8 Moonshiners had used the islands as far back as Civil War times and perhaps earlier. A shallow channel in those days between Cockenoe Island and the mainland allowed molasses to be hauled over by oxcart.

share of illegal commerce.8 Coast Guard cutters could not be everywhere and like the Tory whaleboat raiders of olden days rum-runners slipped in and out among the islands abetted by accomplices on the shore. Oystermen quickly discovered that their knowledge of the waters paid off more handsomely hauling forbidden liquor than dredging for bivalves in polluted waters and more than one joined the ranks of the rum-runners. A man might tell himself as some did, "When I make fifteen thousand dollars I'm going to knock off and get myself a nice fishing boat." Sometimes he would quit; more often he did not.

Mysterious sloops quietly rode at anchor off Calf Pasture and Gregory's Point while their cargo was transferred to waiting automobiles. A clandestine cove on one side of Sheffield Island was also purported to be a favorite with rum-runners who would leave liquor under a tarpaulin in the leafy underbrush until it could be safely unloaded at the dock of the Norwalk Country Club. One cold March night in 1926, following a ten-day stake-out at the nearly deserted Country Club dock, State Police captured the 42 foot sloop *Notus* as its crew attempted to unload 150 cases of liquor. The *Hour* was careful to point out that the suspected consignee was not a member of the Country Club and that Club officials stood ready to assist authorities. It is doubtful that the man identified as captain was actually in command of the *Notus*. Men who knew their way along the shoreline at night were too valuable to lose. Professional rum-runners usually took óne man along who was provided with papers identifying him as captain. If the boat was captured this expendable individual was left with the tedious details of arraignment, trial, and possible imprisonment.

Although the Norwalk Islands gained notoriety from these unauthorized expeditions most visitors to the tiny spits of land came to enjoy their natural beauty and the feeling of remoteness from the workaday world. The beauty of sun-dashed dappled waters and the silence broken only by the cries of sea birds were balm to land-bound humans. For years day-long outings to the islands had been popular; hardy souls even camped there overnight. Some families like the Eben Hills on Tavern Island had such comfortable cottages that they rarely left them during the season.

Out-of-town vacationers stayed at "Sheffield-on-the-Sound," a small resort on Chimmons Island. Owners Warren and Millard Smith, grandsons of Gershom Burr Smith who had purchased the islands one by one in the nineteenth century, leased acreage on Chimmons to a developer, the Sheffield-on-the-Sound Corporation. Guests stayed in small cottages and congregated at the main building, the Casino, for entertainment and meals including the house specialty, a superb lobster dinner. The corporation suffered a setback in 1926 when Warren Smith brought suit charging that the developers had never fulfilled the contract. Robert Corby opened The Island Club on nearby Sheffield Island in 1923. It was a posh resort that offered pleasure-seekers a dazzling array of facilities: a golf course, tennis courts, a landing strip for small planes, and even stables for racing horses and polo ponies. Corby invested unstintingly—the main house and "bungalow" alone cost over one hundred thousand dollars—but he overestimated the bounties of nature. The ambitious undertaking failed in 1937, victim of an inadequate fresh water supply.[12]

On Betts Island a tall, forbidding watchtower cast long shadows over oyster beds in the surrounding waters. In the heyday of oystering poachers plundered the staked-out grounds so regularly that oystermen had purchased the island and erected the tower from which to patrol the beds. As oystering fell to its low ebb in the late Twenties oystermen abandoned their watches and in 1929 sold the island to Clarence Merritt and Captain Frederick Lovejoy. Hoyts Island, purchased by a Wilson Point resident solely to protect his view, remained unoccupied. The islets (some less than an acre in size) were havens for waterfowl and migratory birds.

The majority of Norwalkers lived routine and conservative lives during the Roaring Twenties. They avidly followed news of America's Sweetheart, Mary Pickford, and her dashing husband, Douglas Fairbanks. They viewed John Barrymore in "The Sea Beast" at the Palace in South Norwalk where matinees cost thirty cents and evening performances forty cents, vaudeville included. The Palace, known in the theatrical world as "the theater you play before you play the Palace in New York," brought topflight entertainment to the city. Comics Weber and Fields; the buxom Mae West; the first hero of the "Westerns," William S. Hart;

and the great Harry Houdini were only a few of dozens who played the Palace. The entire population seemed to crowd onto the Washington Street Bridge one day to watch as Houdini was bound, placed in a trunk, and lowered into the Norwalk River. He emerged in minutes and the crowd breathed a loud sigh of relief.

Old-time Norwalkers deplored the goings-on around Ely Avenue where, as reported almost daily in the newspapers, Italian men used guns, knives, homemade stilettos, and even teeth in their no-holds-barred fracases. Boating mishaps added excitement and provided conversational tidbits. Rowaytonites watched in fascination one summer day as the crew of the departing excursion steamer *Crescent* rammed her on a reef off Roton Point at the start of her return trip to New York City. En route to the Park captain and crew had sampled confiscated booze stashed in the pilot house by a police officer. It was only with difficulty that the crew managed to dock the steamer and they were in worse shape when the *Crescent* left the wharf. Rowaytonites talked for weeks about the dramatic rescue of the terrified passengers.

New styles sometimes caused more consternation than pleasure. A local woman charged in a divorce complaint that her husband had bound her hand and foot and snipped off all her hair after she had disobeyed him by having her long locks bobbed in the popular shingle style. Parents of Norwalk High School students fretted about plans to hold school dances in the evening instead of the afternoon as in the past. Dr. Tracey spoke for many fathers and mothers when he damned the innovation declaring: "There will be a lot less opportunity for the hip flask and the cigarette in the afternoon than the evening," adding, "The children have enough distractions now with radios, flivvers, and movies." The redoubtable doctor notwithstanding, the afternoon tea dance went the way of the hitching post.

Norwalk's introduction to the Great Depression came when Cluett, Peabody & Co. closed down its shirt factory in 1930 with a loss of four hundred jobs. This first depression year, a time of discouragement and dismay, was most of all a time of bewilderment. The complete disintegration of the American economy was not yet apparent; the crumbling of the faulty financial structures of the Twenties not yet visible. Men and women who lost their jobs during these first few months often felt themselves somehow to blame for their predicament.

By 1932 at least 150,000 men and women were unemployed in Connecticut and it was estimated that 45 percent fewer workers were engaged in manufacturing than in 1929.[13] The legislature gave $3 million to the towns to pave dirt roads but this sum was soon spent. Governor Wilbur Cross was sympathetic to the financial distress of the people and the towns but even in the fall of 1932 he refused to call the Assembly into special session to consider local relief problems although clergymen throughout the state added their pleas to those of the mayors.

Norwalk city officials floundered in 1930 and 1931, baffled by the flood of out-of-work citizens, and Mayor Anson Keeler was criticized for not responding more promptly to the crisis. The administration did appoint an Unemployment Committee whose chairman, Edward M. Gans, reported that immediate help was needed. The Council responded by appropriating twenty-five thousand dollars to ease the situation and started a work program. By June, 1931, the Unemployment Committee had given work to 821 citizens during the previous ten weeks.

In the fall of 1931 voters agreed to a one-mill tax increase to be turned over to the Unemployment Committee, but voting a tax and collecting it were two different matters. Tax receipts had begun to fall off, partly because firms were going bankrupt; in fact the city had already borrowed one hundred and fifty thousand dollars on a short-term loan and early the following year borrowed an additional four hundred thousand dollars in anticipation of taxes. Meanwhile pleas for tax abatement poured in:

This is to ask for leniency in regard to taxes on our house on Ingleside Avenue ... Mr. —— was out of work all last Winter and this Winter has only worked part time.
We have four little children and it is hard to "make ends meet." We are trying at present to meet the interest which comes due on the mortgage at the bank, but will pay a little on the taxes just as soon as we have paid the interest.
I suppose no leniency of the interest on the Taxes on account of unemployment?
Thanking you for any help you can give us.
Mrs. ————[14]

What could the Councilmen reply to such letters? They felt forced to continue their policy of providing tax relief only to "needy" cases—widows left with three or four small children, severely-crippled men, aged and destitute maiden ladies.[9] When tax collections fell off by 20 percent during the autumn of 1932 the tax collector's office announced it was imposing the prescribed penalty for late payment. Hapless property owners who could not pay their taxes on time because they were out of work forfeited the additional sum.

Fiscal restraint was the watchword; elected officials may have heard of the new economic theory of deficit spending but they were not about to apply it to Norwalk. To help balance the budget, the Council reduced salaries of city employees. In 1933 an experienced elementary teacher who had earned $900 the year before found her salary cut to $800, but for a woman who might be the sole support of an aging mother and an unemployed brother, the pittance was preferable to the dole. Other employees suffered even larger cuts. Officials endeavored, however, to continue necessary public works—laying sewers, repairing streets, and similar projects, all of which provided employment. The Department of Charities[10] also doled out free food from time to time from its office behind City Hall. It was a pathetic sight to see dozens of illclad people sitting on City Hall steps patiently awaiting distribution of potatoes, onions, or flour.[11]

Between December, 1932, and March, 1933, the nation's industrial production fell to an all-time low. Norwalk's economy continued to deteriorate.[12] At

9 The city was quite generous in such abatements. When Mrs. Delia Sanford reached the age of 100 the Council voted to remit her taxes, apparently more on the basis of age than need, and continued to do so faithfully although she lived beyond the age of 107.

10 This was renamed the Department of Welfare.

11 Prior to 1933 people still hoped that America's traditional voluntary approach to community needs could offset a large measure of unemployment. Hence Norwalk's Relief Committee asked townspeople to help less fortunate neighbors with clothing, food, and jobs. Under Fairfield County's Share-the-Work Program, with Douglas E. Nash as Norwalk's chairman, householders hired unemployed men to put up storm windows or do yard work, tasks a homeowner might ordinarily have done himself. Share-the-Work brought out the generosity of Norwalkers but was ineffectual.

12 The birthrate, that reliable barometer of economic conditions, dropped from 51 in 1933 to 38 in 1934, a 25 percent decrease.

this point the federal government came to the rescue of American communities with the first of a multitude of New Deal programs. Under the Federal Emergency Relief Act (FERA) towns contributed funds for materials and the federal government paid salaries of those hired. Paul James, city engineer, recalls: "I remember that at one-thirty one evening I got a call from Mayor Charles Swartz. He had a telegram from Washington and wondered if we could get six hundred men employed, and I think they gave us about ten days. We did. We met the quota."[15]

In the first rush many jobs were of a make-work nature but the city soon organized worthwhile, lasting projects. Under FERA Seaview Avenue was repaired, Calf Pasture Beach improved, sidewalks were widened, sewers and storm drains installed, and a number of similar public works projects undertaken.[13] FERA workers ranging in age from eighteen to seventy were given a free evening course in surveying and substantially expanded the capacity of the city's tiny engineering staff. For a man who had held an office job using a pickax was sheer torture for a week or two, but there was little grumbling for most men were desperate for work.[14] Eventually many more than six hundred worked under FERA and the later programs. In April, 1935, with over nine hundred families on relief, the government increased the city's share of FERA funds and many work programs were able to continue.

Norwalk's depression years were not as rigorous as those in other towns for the city's industrial character militated in its favor. Its many small manufacturing companies benefited the local economy in ways that larger corporations failed to do. Owners and executives often lived in Norwalk, felt a sense of responsibility and local loyalty, and did not simply regard the community as an area to be drained to make profits for shareholders. At least in part because of the diversified nature of local business all the Norwalk banks were able to reopen after

the bank holiday in March, 1933. In fact only one, the Central Fairfield Trust Company, ever closed and this only briefly.[15] What had been an economic embarrassment in 1901—Norwalk's failure to attract growth industries—had turned out to be a blessing in disguise. Factories did close, it is true, among them the respected old firms of R&G Corset and Lounsbury and Bissell, but none was so large as to throw the town into complete economic disarray. Moreover the city's many skilled workers, men and women, were adaptable. Finally Norwalk's proximity to New York City as well as its cheaper rents and lower taxes encouraged a number of firms to leave the metropolis and settle in this smaller, less expensive industrial city.[16]

The Chamber of Commerce worked diligently to bring new businesses to town through all those years. Several small factories and three or four retail establishments came to Norwalk in 1935 and a larger firm, the Manhattan Shirt Company, bought the old R&G Corset factory to manufacture soft-collar shirts. The first three months of 1935 showed a payroll gain of 49 percent over the same period in 1934.

The building trades continued at low ebb, however. Few families were prosperous enough to commission architect-designed houses and builders could not afford to build "on spec." When they did they had to offer good value as shown by a builder's ad for a two-bedroom house with breakfast nook, heated garage, and hardwood floors at an asking price of $4,400, "$500 down and the balance like rent." The newspapers were not exaggerating when they described the moderate-sized Christian Science Church begun that year on West Avenue as "one of the most important building enterprises undertaken in Norwalk for several years." This gold-domed brick edifice of classical Georgian style was handsomely appointed and its construction gave employment to a wide range of artisans. Con-

---

13 Some work was also done under the Civil Works Program.

14 As time went on the Highway Department sometimes found it hard to assemble a complete work crew. "The majority of men now working are the older men," complained the *Norwalk Hour* in a front page article, "while the younger, stronger men are the ones who refuse." In other towns men on relief who refused city jobs were thrown into jail; the editor implied this might not be a bad idea in Norwalk.

15 Central Fairfield, reopened under the name Merchants Bank and Trust Company, was actually closed only two months. The People's Trust Company in South Norwalk was rescued in 1931 when the South Norwalk Trust Company bought it.

16 That a few of these might have been sweatshops during the first year or so is likely since Connecticut's labor regulations were less stringent than those of New York. The *Norwalk Hour*, Oct. 11, 1932, pointedly deplored sweatshops in an editorial which, although couched in general terms, might have referred to a local situation. By the end of 1933 the Assembly had prohibited sweatshops and passed a minimum wage law and the evil subsided.

sidering the straits of Norwalk's building trades the *Hour* exercised considerable courage when it led the opposition to the Bank of Norwalk's petition for a zoning change to allow a gas station at the Green. Bowing to strong public disapproval the bank quickly withdrew its petition.

Construction of a new high school was an exceptional boon to the building trades. With a grant from the Works Progress Administration and a city bond issue of $500,000 the city acquired property on East Avenue and construction began in 1936.

Entrance to Norwalk High School on East Avenue.

The modern facility replete with auditorium, gymnasium, and athletic field opened in January, 1938. At the start of the new school year in September 1,388 students marched through the doors. The magnificent, wood-paneled library would have done justice to a small private college. Students must have gazed spellbound at the striking murals that decorated the walls of the foyer. John Steuart Curry whose work hung in the Whitney Museum and in university art galleries rendered the murals under a WPA artists' project. He selected Norwalk's

early industry as the theme for one panel, portrayed aspects of the hatting industry in another, and devoted three panels to oystering. The latter were so skillfully rendered that they were featured in the art columns of *The New York Times*.

The city then turned its attention to elementary schools, refurbishing several of the old wooden structures through FERA and WPA funds. Winnipauk School built in Civil War days completely of stone was demolished to make way for the Merritt Parkway and with a $45,000 federal grant a new school was built on upper Main Avenue.[17] The *Hour* turned public attention to the grossly neglected Springwood section and, labeling its school buildings a "disgrace," admonished readers: "We must not be selfish for our own section and thereby defeat the progress of the city." A new generation of

The Columbus School on Concord Street.

Springwood parents, no longer mute and compliant as their own parents had been, took up the fight. On Labor Day, 1938, in a colorful ceremony that brought out both the St. Ann and Giuseppe Verdi bands, the cornerstone—purchased through contributions from every Italian-American organization in Norwalk—was laid for the Columbus School.

Depression-weary townspeople found several things to be happy about in 1936. Only 17 persons per 1,000 were unemployed in Norwalk contrasted with 52 in Stamford and 58 in Bridgeport; Norwalk's retail sales were 23 percent higher than those

17 The *Hour* assured taxpayers that the city's own $35,000 investment would soon pay for itself since the modern school would attract housing and business to that part of the city.

NORWALK
*an historical
account*

194

in Connecticut as a whole and 41 percent higher that the nation's.[16] A large U.S. post office was completed in Norwalk and another begun in South Norwalk. The harbor was dredged and the silt used to fill in the old dump and create Seaview Avenue Park. Crofut and Knapp, now the Hat Corporation of America, announced a profit of nearly a million dollars and distributed more than seventy-five thousand dollars in Christmas bonuses to its employees. Culminating the year's good news was an announcement by the Edwards Company, a New York City electrical manufacturer, that it would move to Norwalk and employ 250 persons.

People were also excited about the Merritt Parkway, a state highway connected to Westchester County's Hutchinson River Parkway. In 1935 the state started purchasing land along the Norwalk stretch of the route and work commenced the following year.[18] A local contractor, the Daniel Deering Company, received large contracts for grade approaches, bridges, paving and drain work, giving a real boost to the town's construction business. The new highway provided accesses at New Canaan and Main Avenues, made Norwalk more accessible to

New York City, and set the stage for development of Winnipauk and Cranbury. The highway was finished on schedule and in June, 1938, Governor Cross dedicated the eighteen-mile stretch between Greenwich and Norwalk.

Without federal funds the city would have found it impossible to undertake large capital improvements and officials soon learned to take advantage of federal help. As Mayor Frank Stack pointed out in his 1937 report: "Norwalk, I am told, has received a larger percentage of PWA allotments than any other city in the state of Connecticut."[17] WPA and PWA funds were used extensively to blacktop miles of city streets. The existing gravel roads, although routinely oiled to keep down dust and pro-

18 Shortly before the first leg was completed, allegations of improprieties in the state's land purchases led to a grand jury investigation of both the winding route and the prices paid for acreage, including land in Silvermine. Several Fairfield County real estate brokers and the state purchasing agent were charged with criminal conspiracy. Although one Norwalker was indicted and the bank accounts of a former mayor examined, the bulk of the charges pertained to people and firms in Greenwich and Westport, and Norwalk escaped the stigma of involvement in the messy deals.

vide a hard surface, were often left with dangerous ditches and pot holes after heavy rains and paved roads were now an absolute necessity. Using federal funds a Housing Authority supervised slum clearance and the construction of Washington Village, the city's first low-rent project for a hundred and thirty-five families.

Another substantial accomplishment was the city incinerator. After a three-year delay while residents fought over its location, a site on Crescent Street was acquired in 1939. An ironic and unexpected side-effect developed when the incinerator was put into operation and people stopped taking their garbage to the old dump at the river. Thousands of rats living at the dump suddenly found their food supply cut off and swept over the Water Street area like an invading army, devouring unprotected foodstuffs, infesting restaurants, offices, and private homes, and occasionally attacking human beings. It was months before they were controlled.

Of all city undertakings officials were most proud of acquiring the magnificent Mathews estate. Obtaining LeGrand Lockwood's old "Elm Park" for city use had long been the dream of scores of Norwalkers but Miss Florence Mathews, the sole remaining daughter of the man who had purchased the property in 1876, refused to sell it. After she died in 1938 at the age of ninety the Common Council leased the property from her heirs with an option to purchase it for $160,000[19] which was done two years later. After the meeting at which acquisition of Elm Park was approved, delighted councilmen stood around the Council chamber congratulating each other like proud fathers. Only a few townsfolk other than the Mathews' family servants had ever been beyond the gatehouse, much less seen the inside of the mysterious mansion, for the family had not mingled with local people. When Norwalkers read in the *Sentinel:* "On August 1, at noon, one may walk boldly into the grounds and satisfy all his curiosities," hundreds of them did just that.

Voters of the 1930s did not lack issues on which to express their opinions at the polls. Besides the state of the economy there were the matter of repeal of the Eighteenth Amendment,[20] fears of centralized

government, and the growing debate over American involvement in the European war.[21] Local politics was ridden with "bossism" of a rather unusual variety since Richard H. Ireland, Republican boss, and Paul Connery, Democratic boss, shared the same law office. When a local scandal which erupted in 1932 over construction of the new city sewer plant forced a Republican councilman to resign, Ireland, backed by the powerful state Republican organization, was able to retain control of the local party organization. However, the affair, along with the nationwide swing to the Democratic Party, put Charles Swartz in the mayor's office in 1933 and started a trend that would keep Democrats in City Hall until 1943. Paul Connery drew strength from improved party organization and extended his power upward to the national level, becoming a close friend of James Farley and as a national committeeman exercising marked influence in Washington. Both Ireland and Connery ruled their domains with an iron hand. One Norwalk lawyer recalls entering the mayor's office to find him occupying a chair at the side and Connery sitting at the mayor's desk. The tableau was, unfortunately, only too accurate—especially with Norwalk's weak-mayor system of governance.

When President Franklin D. Roosevelt decided to tour the state that had given Hoover a plurality four years earlier local Democrats became ecstatic upon learning that the city was to be a stop on the president's swing through New England. This was the first time in anyone's recollection that a president of the United States had paid a visit to Norwalk and the city made elaborate preparations for FDR's visit. Schoolchildren were released from classes, factories shut down early, and the Norwalk local of the Journeymen Barbers International Union closed all barbershops in town that day. A crowd of 20,000 so clogged East Avenue that State Police had to cut a path for the president's car. Mayor Stack had the honor of introducing Roosevelt to the wildly cheering mob at the Green. "Women fainted," reported the *Hour,* "children separated temporarily from their parents cried out lustily as the cheering stampede converged on the President's machine." Among the eminent Democrats who rode in official

19 The arrangement involved a rebate of taxes for the remaining Mathews heirs during the extent of the lease.

20 Norwalkers voted "wet" five to one in 1932.

21 With record-breaking numbers at the polls and thousands of new registrants added to voting lists, about 3,000 in 1932 alone, most elections were tossups between the two major parties. Republicans lost ground in 1932, lost the mayoralty in 1933, but gained ground in the state elections in 1934. In 1936 FDR won by 9,216 to 7,191.

NORWALK
*modern
city*

195

limousines behind the president's automobile was Judge Brien McMahon, a rising politician from the Second Ward. He had been rewarded for his hard work on behalf of the party by being appointed Attorney General Homer Cummings' special assistant in 1935. Roosevelt's visit to Connecticut paid off on November 2. He carried the state ticket to victory and for the first time in many years Norwalk voted for Democrats for Congress.

Perhaps the clearest indication that the city rode through the Great Depression with less trauma than other manufacturing cities is found in the singular lack of success of the local Socialist Party. Other cities had gone in this direction and at times there were enough Socialists in the Assembly to influence legislation. The guiding lights of the Norwalk Socialists were the two Freese brothers, Arnold and Irving. Members of this industrious little group gathered for frequent study and strategy meetings at Socialist Hall on West Avenue. They bombarded the Common Council with "good government" proposals such as demands for a local civil service system, few of which stood much chance of success but which brought the party, and Arnold and Irving Freese in particular, into the public eye.

The inside columns of Norwalk newspapers abound with such an array of articles about social and cultural gatherings that a reader might never suspect how much depressing economic news covered the front pages. Lack of money may have discouraged some Norwalkers from social activities but others bravely continued as best they could in impoverished circumstances. Ladies with mended gloves collected clothing for the poor; men whose shoes had been resoled for the third time sang in choral societies or devoted an evening a week to the Boy Scouts; girls in hand-me-down dresses took part in Norwalk High School plays or debating contests.

The Springwood Neighborhood Center in South Norwalk was a sociable gathering place for all ages. It offered a program of children's activities and was the focus for more than twenty clubs catering to interests that ranged from gardening to stamp collecting. No activity was more breathlessly awaited than its annual Christmas party. During these years, Christmas parties took on added significance and almost every group in Springwood tried to soften the austerity that had to be practiced at home by

providing inexpensive gifts and holiday sweets at Christmastime. At the Saint Maria Della Murgia Society party children received toys and candy distributed from beneath the fragrant, decorated Christmas tree.

People learned to take advantage of free events like the WPA concerts. Shortly after acquisition of the Mathews property nearly a thousand people, possibly motivated as much by a desire to get a glimpse of the old house as to hear the music, crowded into the mansion to hear one of these "high class concerts," as Mayor Stack pridefully called them. Dancing at Roton Point was inexpensive and young couples danced away the summer evenings there to big-name bands: Glenn Miller, the Dorsey brothers, Glen Gray, Cab Calloway, and Guy Lombardo, all of whom played the Pavilion. For a while Norwalk had a Civic Opera Company which performed light operas such as *Naughty Marietta*.

The Norwalk Symphony Orchestra offered still another opportunity for individuals to continue the pattern of enriching community life. It was put together in 1939 when Edward Kreiner, a violist with the NBC Symphony; Lad and Stanley Kaplan who owned a violin string shop; and Dr. Louis G. Simon collected a group of local musicians. Simon, a competent violinist as well as physician, played in a string quartette with another talented amateur, Dorothy Langlie, whom he drew into the group. Her husband, Dr. Theos Langlie, became president of the first board of governors. Except for a hiatus during the Second World War the orchestra grew and thrived. Quinto Maganini, its first permanent conductor, remained for more than twenty-five years, refining and improving its performance to the point where internationally-known artists were proud to appear with the group.

Householders with flooded cellars were not surprised to read in the papers on Monday, September 19, 1938, that 4.1 inches of rain had fallen over the week end. The rain washed debris down Norwalk's hills blocking catch basins and making streets impassable. As the downpour continued—nine inches by Wednesday—the foaming Silvermine, Norwalk, and Five Mile rivers poured over their banks.

On Wednesday morning school authorities ordered the schools to close at midday and, therefore, children were safely home that afternoon when a hurricane struck. The storm tore down giant trees, disabled power lines, and dashed boats to pieces. Sidewalks were thrust completely aside by the roots of toppling trees. The high water level—an hour before high tide and six feet higher than anyone had ever seen—threatened the sewage plant but the quick work of City Engineer Paul James and his crew, who threw up makeshift "sandbags," saved it. It was the only area plant in operation the next day.

By about nine o'clock in the evening the wind began to die down and the water level dropped. The following morning people could start to appraise the damage although the rivers were still beyond control. Pounding waves had demolished dock and pier at Roton Point, washed away buildings and sidewalks at Calf Pasture Beach, and had torn two hundred bath houses at the Shore and Country Club from their foundations, dragging them down the shore. Hundreds of houses were left with broken windows, crumpled roofs, and flooded basements, and several hundred boats were destroyed or swamped. Tons of lumber which had lain on the dock at Hatch & Bailey's lumberyard in South Norwalk were strewn around like a pile of jackstraws or washed into the harbor.

The hurricane had struck inland as well as along the coast and losses in Connecticut came to more than $58 million. Norwalk's $1 million loss was less than that of towns farther up the coast. Within a few days normal railroad service in the area was restored and with the work of a hundred WPA men the harbor was soon cleared. Even in November oystermen were still trying to estimate their losses—or gains. The furious storm had plucked complete oyster-beds from the floor of Long Island Sound and moved them to other locations, shifting innumerable bivalves to new owners with no way for the losers to regain title to oysters they themselves had planted![18]

16

FIGHTING
FOR UNCLE SAM

*Being
an Account of
Norwalk in the Forties*

HEN POST NO. 141, Jewish War Veterans of Norwalk urged a boycott of German-made goods in the mid-1930s few Norwalkers regarded German politics as their concern. This isolationist mood prevailed even after the German Blitzkrieg in Poland, the occupation of Norway and Belgium, the conquest of France, and the Battle for Britain. Like other Americans Norwalkers were unrealistic. Almost everyone wanted to see the Axis defeated but they worried that the United States would be drawn into the conflict.

By the autumn of 1940, however, Norwalk people were made aware of the grim effects of this war. Some eighty European refugees had already settled in the town. A group of Polish residents had organized a Polish Relief Committee to aid their captive relatives. The newly-formed Norwalk chapter of the Committee to Defend America by Aiding the Allies, a nationwide organization particularly active along the eastern seaboard, began to crusade for massive aid to Britain. From their pulpits Norwalk's ministers condemned the selfish nationalism of Americans who tolerated "the long dark night" that had fallen on Europe. The *Norwalk Hour* struck a martial pose in an editorial that warned: "Those outside the country should remember that these are the UNITED States and that they will always find that we are a united people when anything is done to interfere with our democratic way of life."

Aid to Great Britain along with Roosevelt's will-

ingness to seek a third term in defiance of tradition were issues in the 1940 presidential election in spite of FDR's efforts to downplay the likelihood of American involvement in Europe's war. The third-term possibility made some Americans almost distraught and more than a few lifelong Democrats decided to vote for Wendell Willkie, the Republican candidate. In Norwalk over a hundred Republicans, Independents, and Democrats handed out bumper stickers, pamphlets and buttons on "National No Third Term Day" in October and all kinds of peripheral groups were organized, including a Grandparents-for-Willkie Club headed by General Russell Frost, then ninety years old. The excitement may have been engendered by the personable Willkie who made an appearance in Norwalk in early October and drew a crowd of ten thousand to a giant rally in Mathews Park.

Ethnic politics intensified during this campaign. Second-generation Italians and Hungarians who had achieved stature in the community by joining together in political and social organizations were now a force to be reckoned with.[1] The Hungarian Democratic Club, for example, could attract five hundred persons to a fund-raising benefit. There was much crossing of party lines during this election, particularly among Italians. One rally of the

[1] City officials and politicians paid attention to officers of the Italian-American Senior Civic League like Dr. Ralph Padula who articulated "important matters pertaining to the Italians of Norwalk."

Independent Willkie Club led by Daniel Caruso, a former Fifth Ward Democratic leader, drew eight hundred persons to St. Ann's Hall. Many traditionally Republican Italians, on the other hand, had been lured into the Democratic fold by New Deal programs like FERA and the WPA. Norwalk's Polish-American Club, appreciative of Roosevelt's outspoken opposition to the Axis, remained true to the Democrats.

As election day drew near, with both parties predicting victory by at least fifteen hundred votes, excitement became almost unbearable. When ballots were counted Willkie had squeaked through by a margin of two hundred votes. FDR's drawing power throughout the state, however, was sufficient to give the governorship and all five U.S. Congressional seats to the Democrats. Of the 22,151 eligible voters in Norwalk, 20,345 cast ballots—an incredible 92 percent![2]

America's preparations to defend itself began in earnest with passage of the compulsory military-training act in September, 1940. Two local draft boards were established.[3] With good-humor and a spirit of camaraderie reminiscent of World War I, more than seven thousand men of ages twenty-one to thirty-five, many of them on release time from factories, registered at local schools in a massive one-day effort.[1] Draft Board members worked long into the night to order the lists in time for the national lottery and on October 29, 1940, the distinction of being assigned Number 158, the first number chosen in the lottery, fell to Edgar Hobbs of Bell Island, a chemical engineer, and Patrick McDonough, a hatter living on Lakeview Drive. Volunteers were given an opportunity to fill the first conscription quota in November. A man might enlist in the Navy, which set up a recruiting station in town, or he could join Battery "C," the local unit of the 192nd Field Artillery, National Guard, which had a few vacancies, including one for a bugler. To be certain it filled the assigned quota each Draft

Board sent the draft questionnaire to the first fifty men on its list.[4]

The nation's effort to arm brought prosperity to the city and the Depression was forgotten when jobs became plentiful as local factories turned to war production. Norwalk Lock, now a subsidiary of Segal Lock and Hardware Company, operated on a three-shift, seven-day-week schedule to complete a large Navy Department contract for anti-aircraft parts. By late 1941 its business had so expanded that it had to build an addition, completed just in time to provide work space needed to expedite a quarter-million dollar military contract for forgings. Engineers at Sparks-Douglas Company were designing machines to manufacture shells and guns, and Nash Engineering had been awarded a government contract for pumps. A French firm whose officials sought anonymity for fear of reprisals opened a plant in Norwalk to make parts for bomber engines. Norwalk Tire and Rubber was producing such quantities of tires that the Office of Production Management, the government agency that monitored resources, ordered the firm to cut back on the use of already scarce rubber. The shortage of skilled workers rapidly became so acute that those in non-defense jobs were encouraged to switch to defense work or take parttime jobs in defense industries. By October, 1941, OPM designated Norwalk a defense area; of its over 11,000 factory workers more than 2,000 were engaged in defense production.[5]

An influx of workers to Norwalk created a housing shortage. Although construction was brisk, with as many as eighty-one building permits issued in one three-week period in the autumn of 1940, housing was at a premium. The designation of Norwalk as a defense area gave private contractors priority-rating to construct defense housing units. This temporarily alleviated the problem but did not solve it and the housing shortage became so grave by 1943 that a New Canaan group who owned Roton

---

4 To encourage volunteers, Edwards Company adopted the policy of giving a month's salary and granting full seniority rights to employees who entered military service, and social organizations like the South Norwalk Council of the Knights of Columbus paid dues for one year for members in the military forces.

5 Although not a defense industry per se, the Microstat Company, a small firm on the Post Road specializing in precision microfilming, which guaranteed preservation of industrial records, developed a nationwide market among defense plants.

---

2 Norwalkers sent Democrats to the state legislature but gave Governor Raymond Baldwin a 240-vote margin. Baldwin had promised the city a trade school if Republicans gained control of both houses.

3 Draft Board 26A included the second, third and fifth wards of Norwalk and the town of Darien, and Draft Board 26B covered the first and fourth wards of Norwalk, as well as Wilton and New Canaan.

Point Park considered opening its old hotel to war workers.

During 1941 Norwalk became a city on a wartime footing in a country not yet formally at war. More than four hundred area men, a few at a time, received their draft notices, took their physicals in Hartford, and were inducted into the U.S. Army. In March Battery "C" and Headquarters Battery, Second Battalion, 192nd Field Artillery of the National Guard was called to active duty. Now part of the 43rd Division, U.S. Army, members underwent intensive training at Camp Blanding, Florida. Other Norwalkers had voluntarily enlisted in various branches of the armed services or like Harry Herbert, the director of the Norwalk Jewish Center who was operating a mobile USO center, had entered military-related service. Twelve young licensed pilots had joined the U.S. Civil Air Patrol. The number of marriages skyrocketed as young women rushed to tie the knot before their beaux departed for military service.

Norwalk's Civilian Defense Committee was planning the defense of the city "if the worst comes" and, with a trifling five thousand dollars allocation from city funds,[6] had developed a master plan for orchestrating the activities of twenty groups. Volunteers were compiling an accurate registry of the citizenry to aid in the event of an air bombardment and Chief Air Warden Eric Malmquist was conducting training sessions for volunteer wardens. More than six hundred residents attended the first session of the air raid precautions school. From watchtowers on the Merritt Parkway and on West Rocks Road air raid spotters identified airplanes flying overhead and with the help of Norwalk Amateur Radio League members forwarded the sightings to Mitchel Field on Long Island. Auxiliary police were sworn in and regularly drilled at the Armory. Local yachtsmen marshaled by Commodore E.B. Gallaher became watchdogs for sabotage along the coast. Women joined the Red Cross Motor Corps and the Norwalk USO sent off 665 Christmas presents—a two dollar check to each Norwalk man in the armed forces.

East Coast residents preoccupied with European events did not seriously consider the prospect of war with Japan even though newspapers began to mention growing tension between the United States and the Japanese. A stunned populace was hardly able to digest the news broadcasts announcing Japanese attacks on Pearl Harbor and the Philippines on that wintery afternoon of December 7, 1941.[7] Before nightfall defense plants had doubled the number of guards on duty and maintained this complement until the Norwalk unit of the Connecticut State Guard was mobilized for guard duty. That evening city officials closed The Owl and the M and J restaurants, Japanese-owned establishments on West Avenue, and stationed police guards around the buildings to prevent ugly acts of vengeance.

The following day about sixty Japanese living on Merwin and Orchard Streets, the majority of whom worked in the two restaurants, were brought to Police Headquarters for fingerprinting. Their alien registration cards were placed on file but they were not detained. For the remainder of the war these Japanese nationals were confined to their homes. Haohiro Sasaki, who had opened The Owl in 1937, later said, "We were closely watched,"[2] but unlike West Coast Japanese they were not subjected to the indignities of internment camps. Within a few weeks the restaurants reopened under the supervision of American managers and townspeople once more began to enjoy the triple-decker sandwiches that had been Mr. Sasaki's specialty.

All aliens of Germany and Italy, estimated at about a thousand in South Norwalk alone, had to register. A federal order requiring them to turn in all cameras, handguns, and short-wave radios created a crush at Police Headquarters.

The "day of infamy" was of immediate, personal concern to a dozen or more local families whose sons or husbands were stationed at Wheeler Field, quartered in Scofield Barracks in Hawaii, or attached to the Pacific Fleet. As weeks passed without substantial news of individual men, rumor was rife and gloom settled on the city. Finally on December 22 the Charpentier family received a heavily-censored letter from their son indicating that he and, as far as he knew, other Norwalk boys in Hawaii had come through the attack "without a scratch." Throughout the holiday season cable-

---

[6] The Civilian Defense Committee of Greenwich, a residential community with little industry, had $50,000 as an initial allocation.

[7] The Stamford-Greenwich-Norwalk Chapter of the isolation-minded America First Committee, which lost its *raison d'etre* with the attack, canceled its Sunday night meeting and suspended all activities for the duration.

grams were delivered to other families wishing them a Merry Christmas and cryptically noting, "Everything okay." But the War Department telegram to Arthur Werner's family notified them he had been seriously wounded in action in the Philippines.[8]

In February Mr. and Mrs. John Radley of Norwalk received a first-hand account of those terrifying hours from their daughter-in-law who was living in Hawaii with her husband Lee, a Navy man.

Lee and I were asleep on Sunday morning when we were awakened by the bombing. Of course, we said, "Oh, it's just another drill." So we just forgot it.

. . . the lady next door turned on her radio, full blast, and we heard the announcer ordering "all Navy, Army, Marine and defense workers to report to their stations immediately, because the island of Oahu is under enemy attack."

We . . . rushed to the roof, and, in the direction of Pearl Harbor, we could see planes in dogfights. They were easily identified as Jap planes. We could see the red marks and the planes themselves were the funniest things—odd in shape. And we could see fire and smoke from all over out there and hear our own anti-aircraft artillery in action.

Although U.S. defense authorities considered Norwalk relatively safe from the danger of air raids, city officials raced to mobilize manpower and acquire equipment needed in event of an attack. For once penny-pinching took a back seat. This uncharacteristic loosening of the purse strings can be attributed in small part to retirement of the Washington Street Bridge improvement bond and, in the main, to genuine concern that as a war production center Norwalk might be bombed.

Acting upon recommendations from the Civilian Defense Committee, which set up a control center "somewhere in Norwalk" (its location known only to a few key workers), the Council appropriated funds for an emergency disaster hospital, containers for blood plasma, a search light for the harbor, a two-way ship-to-shore radio for the harbor patrol boat, and finger-printing equipment. It increased the Fire Department budget, hired ten new firefighters, and built two sump wells to enable

8 The selection of a limited number of individuals cited in this chapter is in no way intended to overlook the hundreds of other Norwalk servicemen and women whose wartime contributions and experiences are of equal interest; those mentioned here were chosen as representative examples.

firemen to draw water if hydrants were destroyed in an air raid.[3]

A Salvage Committee that operated on the principle that "everything that can be taken will be taken" investigated reclamation of tin and iron scrap from garbage and the city incinerator. The old trolley tracks which yielded one thousand tons of exceptionally high grade steel were ripped up for salvage. A proposal to remove the iron fence at Mathews Park generated a lengthy debate that ended in the decision to take this step only as a last resort, scrapping the iron pipe from its greenhouses instead. Scrap collection drives in the early years of the war were extraordinarily successful and in one drive Norwalk's average of fifty-nine pounds per person was the largest for any city of its size in the state.

Individuals through their jobs and social organizations gave unstinting support to the war effort and with uncommon good grace endured inconveniences and adapted to shortages. Over three thousand volunteered for civilian defense activities: air raid wardens, first aid and rescue teams, transportation or messenger duty, or demolition and rescue work. School teachers worked as clerks, typists, and line-attendants at the Selective Service and fuel oil registrations. Residents contributed thousands of volumes during a drive for books to servicemen and somewhat more reluctantly parted with their typewriters for the same cause. The Norwalk USO raised thousands of dollars through such events as a "Keep 'em Smoking" dance at Shorehaven Country Club, the proceeds of which were used to give each inductee four packs of cigarettes. The Federation of Hungarian Societies contributed $1,539 for purchase of an ambulance[4] and the Norwalk Post of Jewish War Veterans organized an ambitious fund-raising effort to purchase six pursuit planes, one of which would be named *City of Norwalk*. Every ethnic, fraternal, and social organization regularly contributed to the Red Cross whose services to men in battle areas one young Norwalk soldier summed up by the popular colloquial expression of the time, "Gee, it's the nuts."

Frequent air raid drills in the schools and simulated evacuations of large residences like the Children's Home on Westport Avenue kept everyone on the alert. Dimout regulations sent householders rushing to the Fitzgerald Awning Company on Liberty Square to buy blackout shades made to government specifications since violators could be fined five hundred dollars or sentenced up to six months in jail. Motorists cautiously threaded their way through darkened streets guided only by the dim light cast by the lower half of their automobile headlamps.

Tires were the first commodity to be rationed. The area Tire Rationing Board was uncompromising and meted out its limited allotment only to such vital agencies as the State Police, electric service company and medical personnel. Milk dealers cut home deliveries and local grocers informed housewives that, once tires wore out, no further home deliveries would be made. When Norwalk Tire and Rubber Company announced that it had developed a retreading process known as the "Victory Camelback" civilians speculated that the supply would be more plentiful but their optimism was dashed when the federal government added retreads to the list of rationed items. Drivers coddled their "baldies" and some even put their cars up on blocks for the duration. On occasion a war worker coming off the night shift hopped into his automobile, started the motor and, as he tried to pull away was greeted with horrendous noises that sounded like a broken axle. Quick inspection showed that a sneak thief had stolen a tire, thoughtfully leaving the jack in place of the missing wheel. The problem of deteriorating tires became moot when gas rationing was instituted and, still later, pleasure driving banned.

Long lines often formed at the two rationing boards headed by Thomas Collins and manned mostly by volunteers who doled out ration books. Sugar, butter, coffee, meat, and processed foods were on the rationed list, as were shoes and fuel oil. Even if a petitioner succeeded in acquiring extra ration stamps he faced the hurdles of genuine shortages and inflated prices (food prices doubled between 1940 and 1943). The black market flourished, especially in meat, despite the government's efforts to track down slaughter houses that violated price ceilings and exceeded their quotas.

The public learned to substitute and improvise. Faced with a fuel oil shortage residents converted to coal and city officials closed school auditoriums. Following the example set by the White House, people planted Victory Gardens in their backyards or in plots on the old Rowayton School property. Several dozen children emulated their elders by planting vegetable gardens at Mathews Park. So many participants enrolled in the Home Canning Project in the old high school that the project paid

for itself.

The city simply outdid itself in purchasing war bonds. In the second bond drive alone Norwalkers subscribed to $4,750,000 worth of bonds, the largest amount ever raised in any drive in this city. WOWS, the Woman's Organization on War Savings in Norwalk, hit upon an appropriate reward for patriotism; they provided a ride in an Army jeep to anyone buying a bond. The Norwalk Branch of the American Association of University Women plowed the money customarily used for student loans into war bonds. School children bought defense stamps weekly but none matched those at St. Mary's School where 465 pupils purchased $3,178 worth of bonds and stamps on one day alone. St. Mary's, one of only seven schools in the state to be so

Miss Fanniebelle Curtis and nurses inspecting greenhouses in Mathews Park as victory garden sites in June, 1942.

honored, was awarded a special war bond flag because 95 percent of its students regularly purchased stamps and bonds.

Defense industries ran at full tilt. More and more women filled the boots of men who left for military service. In fact local firms preferred to hire women since they were not draftable. To meet the shortage of skilled workers the Board of Education expanded the industrial arts program in the high school placing emphasis on welding and airplane engine assembly. The Norwalk Chamber of Commerce was so successful in one campaign to get women to take war jobs that more than five hundred women joined the ranks of war workers as a result. Retail merchants sold quantities of denim overalls and coveralls since in this war women on the assembly line donned male garb.

Local defense firms maintained remarkably high levels of production against such odds as delayed shipments and chronic shortages of workers and vital metals. Impressive ceremonies in which the government acknowledged importance of their contributions to the war compensated for these frustrations and setbacks. When the Norwalk Com-

Senator Brien McMahon.

pany was awarded a gold production star to add to the Army/Navy E Flag already earned, and told that its compressors went "Wherever the Navy goes, Midway, Wake, Guadalcanal or other far-flung lands," each employee could take satisfaction in his share of this honor. When the Edwards Company was awarded the Maritime "M" pennant and a Victory Fleet Flag, Congresswoman Clare Booth Luce publicly announced that equipment made by its six

hundred employees was saving the lives of Merchant Marine crews all over the world. Automatic Signal, 70 percent of whose employees were women, concentrated almost all its production on items vital to the military. Some Norwalk products were so sophisticated that workers had no understanding of their application. Machlett Laboratories with plants in Norwalk and Springdale received three Army/Navy commendations for consistently high production. Only after the atomic bomb was dropped on Hiroshima did employees learn that the high voltage electronic tubes on which they had worked were vital to the success of the Manhattan District Project.

Norwalk's wartime senator, Brien McMahon, gripped by the terrible implications of this unprecedented type of warfare, set himself to studying its technological and political facets. Holding his first elective office at the age of forty-four[9] this rather cynical New Dealer became so expert on the subject that he was chosen to head the Joint Congressional Committee on Atomic Energy, an unusual honor for a freshman senator, and he led the successful effort to have the Atomic Energy Commission placed under civilian control.

Additions to the list of names on the Honor Roll Board set up in Mathews Park and the service flags proudly displayed by neighborhood and social organizations were constant reminders of the growing number of Norwalk men and women in the armed services.[10] By war's end over seven thousand Norwalkers had served in every branch of the armed forces and in every theater of operations around the world. Some families had as many as five children in the service at one time. For Ralph Ferrandino, owner of the Hi-Ho Grill on West Avenue, and Charles Mace of the Norwalk Fire Department, this was their second war for as young men both had served in World War I. In the 1942 draft registration forty-two-year-old Hugh Marron, a World War I veteran, registered alongside his twenty-

9 Brien McMahon was born in Norwalk in 1903, graduated from Norwalk High School, Fordham University, and the Yale Law School. He received a post with the Department of Justice where he made a name for himself by prosecuting some of the gangsters of the Thirties and in 1935 he became the youngest assistant attorney general to hold this position. In 1950 Senator McMahon was briefly considered as a candidate for the presidency but his ill-health precluded his entering this race.

10 Male bastions like the Eagles Athletic Club had to close their club rooms for the duration.

NORWALK

modern city

203

year-old son Edward. Most servicemen were little more than youths thrust into an alien milieu and their letters mirror the pain of adjusting to new circumstances: "Army life is swell once you get used to being pretty far away from home," and (during the invasion of North Africa) "just no such things as chewing gum, candy or ice cream." One young recruit pleaded:

> *Just sit right down and write to me*
> *Tho' its [sic] just a long Hello,*
> *For a letter to a soldier*
> *Is the greatest lift I know.*

Capt. Edward B. Giorchino.

Norwalk men were assigned to every conceivable duty; they were Navy deep sea divers, Army paratroopers, Army Air Corps dentists, Rough Riders in the Motorcycle Corps of Armored Divisions, Army Amphibian Engineers, construction workers with the Seabees, Marine Corps shock troops, crewmen on Merchant Marine vessels and, by far the greatest number, infantrymen who fought inch by inch to gain precious toeholds in enemy-held territory. Norwalk's daring flyboys provided air cover for the Allied landings at North Africa and Sicily, dropped their payloads on enemy oil refineries and aircraft

installations in Occupied France and Germany, and maneuvered speedy little P-51 Mustang fighter planes in combat against German Messerschmitts. Like Lieutenant Lloyd Aronson, marooned for fourteen days in a mountain village on the Tibet-China border when his transport plane was forced down, they lived with danger and acquitted themselves bravely. Sergeant Robert Rockwell, for example, who had enlisted at eighteen and was a top turret gunner and first engineer on a B-17, had been awarded the Air Medal, four Oak Leaf Clusters, the Distinguished Flying Cross and two Bronze Stars by the time he was twenty years old! Many, far too many, airmen never had the opportunity to recount their exploits to home town friends. Captain Ed Girochino, for example, who left Dartmouth and joined the RAF after he flunked the Air Force physical, later transferred to the U.S. Army Air Corps and had earned the DFC and four Oak Leaf Clusters before he lost his life.

When local churches held services commemorating residents in military service they offered prayers for men and women alike for Norwalk women were represented in the woman's corps of every branch of service. Local women in the WAAC served in the unglamorous but vital positions of surgical corps technician and baker/cook. Norwalk WAVEs trained for positions as pharmacist's mates or communications workers. RNs enlisted in the Army Nursing Corps and on occasion, as in the King family, two sisters served at the same time. Many of these professionals worked in base hospitals in North Africa and Europe where they sometimes ran into other Norwalk women who were staffing Red Cross centers just behind the forward lines.

The American effort to defeat the Axis powers can be readily traced through letters of Norwalk servicemen which were often printed in the *Hour*. During the late summer and early autumn of 1942 large numbers of infantrymen were shipped to England, the staging area for invasion of North Africa. In those lazy late-summer days Norwalkers observed the peculiarities of British life and some of them even acquired a taste for fish and chips. It was here that Lieutenant Colonel Edson Raff of Wilson Point trained the U.S. parachute troops who acquitted themselves so nobly during the Tunisian campaign.

Among those in command of U.S. troopships headed for North Africa was Lieutenant Commander Duncan Cook who survived the sinking of his ship off Algeria during the first landing on that coast. John Daniels, a turret gunner who was part of a contingent of U.S. Navy torpedo bombers that provided air cover for the landings, recalled they flew so low that the enemy shot at them with rifles from rooftops. Lieutenant Colonel Raff celebrated his thirty-fifth birthday landing on and capturing a Tunisian airdrome. Fighting on rugged terrain at temperatures well over 100° without a tree in sight left infantrymen feeling they had "climbed nearly every mountain in North Africa." Dentist "Doc"

Salerno and fought their way north to Rome. It was at Serre d'Aino in the last great assault of the Italian campaign that Private John D. Magrath of the 85th Mountain Division met his death, the only enlisted man in his regiment to be recommended for the Congressional Medal of Honor. The heroic young soldier destroyed three machine gun nests and killed, wounded, or put to rout more than fifty Germans during the deadly Battle on Hill 909.[5]

Other veterans of North Africa were given a well-deserved rest period and next saw action in the D-Day invasion of Normandy. PFC Earle Smith,

Lt. Comdr. Duncan Cook, familiarly known as Captain.

Pvt. John D. Magrath.

Goldman reported that his patients were nervous but not from his drill and that he often had to stop drilling to dive into a foxhole. Those fortunate enough to get a pass to Casablanca were crestfallen to find that prices had doubled with the arrival of American servicemen but thanks to a farmer's gift of a big hog, one lucky contingent enjoyed a Christmas dinner that featured roast pork.

After the Americans had mopped up North Africa the Allies turned to Sicily where some Norwalk men participated in the landings there and at

attached to one of the first outfits to land, found Normandy Beach "infested with mines, boobytraps and snipers" and he soon learned "the true value of a foxhole: it cannot be dug too deep." Jack Sniffen, s/1 U.S. Coast Guard, was a member of an assault transport barge at Normandy, the fourth invasion in which he had participated. Sergeant Stephen Kish, part of a small group chosen to reconnoiter the best route after hitting the beach, had to leave the landing barge while it was still in such deep water that the jeeps they were unloading sank to the bottom. It was each man for himself as the landing party walked, waded, and swam ashore, rifles held high over their heads. Facing into German artillery fire that included "everything but the kitchen sink," Kish and his comrades "took off across the beach like striped baboons."

Norwalk men, too, were part of the great war machine that island by island smashed Japanese control in the Pacific. At Guadalcanal was Marine Private Eugene Palmer who was wounded at his machine gun post. Marine Alvin Heerdt was in the thick of the fighting there for four long months until laid low by malaria. During the Battle of Tulagi, Navyman Thomas Connell was on the destroyer *Duncan.* During combat marked by blank range firing at close quarters the *Duncan* was hit by Japanese shell fire and went up in flames and Connell spent eleven hours in shark-infested waters before he was rescued. His experience was no more grim than that of Navyman George Simon who was blown off the flight deck of the carrier *Franklin* during a kamikaze attack and spent five hours in the water before being picked up. For Private Renwick Lewis, who was part of a "main stage production and the seats from this vantage point are of the boxseat variety," New Guinea was "quite comparable to the Inferno of Dante." Seventeen-year-old Bobby Burt might have echoed Lewis' sentiments for he spent two years in Japanese prison camps in Taiwan and Tokyo.

"New U.S. Atomic Bomb Blasts Japan," the headline emblazoned across the August 6, 1945, issue of *The Norwalk Hour,* kindled hope that the end of hostilities was near. At that time the city was putting final touches on its plans for "Christmas In Connecticut," a lavish party for 107 Norwalk servicemen home on leave while en route to the Pacific. The celebration expanded into a gigantic victory party; some fifty thousand citizens, a crowd unrivaled since Armistice Day, 1918, lined Norwalk streets to view the Christmas parade. Later in the evening twenty thousand turned out for the party at Mathews Park where Santa Claus distributed gifts to the honorees as a hundred-member choir sang carols. When the Japanese surrendered a week later there was pandemonium. Myriad bits of torn paper eddied around marchers as tens of thousands jostled each other along the parade route. All businesses were closed for two days and the entire police department roster stayed on duty lest impromptu street parties turn into brawls.

The hangovers had hardly dissipated when the boom descended. The war was over and so were government contracts. Five hundred employees of Norwalk Lock Company were the first affected; when night shift workers reported they were told to go home and pick up their final pay the following morning. General Aircraft Equipment Company laid off six hundred workers at its three plants, and Leroy Downs, Fairfield County War Manpower Commissioner, predicted that 20 to 25 percent of Norwalk's war workers would lose their jobs in the next few weeks. There were, however, a few bright spots. Edwards Company announced that it would not reduce staff; indeed it planned to rehire the one hundred and fifty employees still in uniform. E.H. Hotchkiss Company, manufacturers of stapling machines and drills, planned to convert to peacetime production and Norwalk Tire actually hired workers. Nash Engineering reassured its employees that it did not plan layoffs and Rabhor Robes ran half-page ads for experienced sewing machine operators.

Between December, 1941, and August, 1945, day-to-day affairs of the City had to be dealt with, wartime disruptions notwithstanding. Voters switched from the Democrats to the Republicans in the local election of 1943 bringing Robert B. Oliver, an executive with General Electric, to City Hall as mayor.[11] His administration plunged into a battle over revision of the City Charter. Ever since 1913 one charter revision committee after another had been trying to undo some of the inequities of the consolidation charter or, to put it another way, had been trying to complete the unification of Norwalk. A few changes had been effected but nothing substantial was achieved.

Frank P. Dunn, chairman of the new Charter Revision Committee, candidly informed the Common Council that his committee could either make genuine revisions or they could "tinker;" he hoped he would get enough cooperation to make worthwhile changes. The Council promised him full support and the Committee came forward with a major change: extension of the Fourth Taxing District to incorporate all areas where sewer lines had been installed. Sewers had aleady been laid beyond the

_____

11 This was a great upset for Oliver beat incumbent Frank Stack by 8,379 to 5,344.

Fourth District and would inevitably be extended still farther as the city's population grew. At a public hearing in February, 1944, Dunn spelled out the problem:

I told you that in the beginning this city was consolidated, but the consolidation was not effective, and so the Fourth District was created in the hope that this would become the central city and we could have in time two districts–an inner and an outer district. These services which are laid on the Fourth District are garbage collection, sewage disposal, police and fire protection. These people [in the outlying areas] have been receiving those services. Somebody has been paying for those services. The persons who have been paying for those services live within the Fourth District. It seems so fair and equitable that here are those people on the fringe of the serviced area, who have been receiving the services; and now we are asking them to pay for them.[6]

Residents of the Fifth District who were most affected by this charter change packed the Council chambers and proceeded to muddy the waters with conflicting demands. Some insisted that if they were going to have to pay Fourth District taxes they should have every city service, including street lights. Others opposed street lights because "they shine in bedroom windows." A Cranbury man spurned police protection for his safe neighborhood while others claimed this was their uppermost need. Thanks to support by citizens like Irving Freese, who spoke in favor of the Fourth District extension even though his own taxes would rise, the Charter change was adopted in a referendum. Henceforth as sewer lines were extended new areas were incorporated into the Fourth Taxing District and a fairer tax structure emerged.

Growing pains had accompanied the wartime prosperity. Between 1943 and 1944 the Grand List increased by $1 million, almost all due to new war plants and business buildings. Traffic and parking problems, especially in the Wall Street area, seemed to increase daily but when the Common Council talked of installing parking meters such cries of protest arose that the Council speedily dropped the idea. Another trouble spot was the little mountain of garbage and industrial trash slowly rising south of the new incinerator on Crescent Street. However, Councilmen assured complaining citizens there was no need to worry; as soon as the city could obtain a bulldozer—hard to come by in wartime—

the dump would be leveled and covered over and that would be the end of it.

With obvious need for planned growth, one of Oliver's first acts as mayor was to appoint a Planning Committee. Since policy decisions were always made by the Council the output of planners usually fell far short of their dreams. An earlier Commission appointed by Charles Swartz in 1933 had drawn up ambitious blueprints for a beautiful Norwalk, only to see them gather dust when Mayor Stack and subsequent Common Councils gave priority to other matters. The Planning Committee achieved stricter rules for new real estate developments such as proper drainage and better layout of streets but, like its predecessor, found its more progressive plans pigeonholed by an indifferent Council.[12]

It was during Oliver's administration that for the first time some attention was paid to housing for Norwalk's blacks. Credit goes to a group of white residents who, given a glimpse of Norwalk's "colored" neighborhoods on a tour with Miss Margaret Pantzer, director of the Family Service Bureau, were dismayed that in 1943 black people in Norwalk were living in tenements where a single outdoor privy served as bathroom to several families. After a fire destroyed a decrepit four-family house near the D&N tracks these altruists together with leaders from the black community persuaded the Council to authorize condemnation of substandard structures in the area. Led by Dr. Edward Sterling they garnered funds for the Carver Apartments which were laid out on expansive grounds on Butler Street.

The Democrats were back in City Hall in 1945. Mayor Oliver's efficient administration had left the city in good shape for them.[13] The new mayor, Edward J. Kelley, a well-known local politician and long-time Council member, was devoted to the town[14] but was not the businesslike type of chief

---

12 In 1947 a Special Act of the legislature gave planning bodies more power by requiring that the Planning Commission review all city projects involving more than $10,000 and allowing the Council to overturn the Commission's ruling only by a two-thirds vote.

13 In addition to the charter change, methods of bidding for city contracts had been improved and purchasing procedures tightened.

14 Kelley's contribution of fifty Norway maples for planting along Ludlow Parkway beautified the approach to Calf Pasture Beach.

executive Norwalk needed for he was too apt to accept existing practices, to "go along" with local politicos, and to allow control to pass into other hands. Almost his first act as mayor was to appoint Paul Connery as Corporation Counsel. Immersed in time-consuming routine decision-making, Kelley and the Common Council failed to take a long-range view of Norwalk's needs and undertook few capital projects unless they could get federal funding.

With 2,900 veterans back home by February, 1946, a woeful shortage of housing developed. Hoping to provide dwellings cheaply and quickly a Mayor's Committee investigated feasibility of pre-fabricated houses but when the Norwalk Building Trades Council pointed out that such housing did not conform to existing building codes the committee dropped the scheme. Only fifty-two veterans and their families were lucky enough to be allotted units in the old barracks buildings which had been obtained through the Federal Housing Agency from an army camp in Pennsylvania and moved to a site near Norwalk Hospital.

The Mathews Mansion, utilized during the war by the Rationing Board and for storage of snowplows and voting machines, appeared to some to be a white elephant and the Council busied itself in prolonged discussions of its future. The city's building inspector suggested that the elaborately-carved mantels and woodwork could be dismantled and sold, but a few councilmen vetoed this idea. Lester Gilman implored: "Let's save this priceless treasure." Lacking consensus on every proposal, the Council took no action.

Troubles struck Mayor Kelley in rapid succession during his second year in office. The Police Department was ridden with discontent over working hours, hiring practices, and the mysteriously-administered Police Benevolent Fund. The Welfare Department continually operated beyond its budget and came under investigation when it was bruited about that Norwalk's welfare costs were higher than either Bridgeport's or Stamford's. Angry Board of Estimate members insisted that the mayor appoint a nonpartisan committee to look into practices of the Welfare Department. This committee's report disclosed an unbelievable state of affairs brought about by laxity of the Welfare Board which had delegated all responsibility for operation of that department to the Welfare Supervisor, Miss Dorothea Murray. According to their

report Miss Murray ran her domain in a highly arbitrary and inconsistent fashion, neglecting to check the financial status of recipients, failing to keep case records, and keeping her browbeaten underlings in the dark about certain welfare cases.[7]

During its investigations the committee visited Naramake Home, the city's poor farm, a depressing set of filthy, run-down buildings set on ten acres on Strawberry Hill. An overworked superintendent and his wife operated the farm and cared for a handful of inmates. The institution was such a picture of squalor that shocked committee members could scarcely find words to convey their indignation. "The Naramake Home is probably the blackest page in Norwalk's album . . . Civic pride changes to civic shame after visiting the premises," their report stated.

The administration also had to engage in an unexpected tug of war when Norwalk's ordinarily submissive teachers united to demand better pay. Struggling along on salaries that had not kept pace with inflation they found postwar living costs unbearable. Female faculty members hired on a salary schedule pegged five hundred dollars below that of males found it especially hard to make ends meet, even when they were single women living with their parents. One study showed that the thirty-four Norwalk teachers in this category had an average living cost of $2,317 on an average salary of $2,218.[8]

In January, 1946, the Norwalk Teachers Association presented the Board of Education with a set of proposals that called for equalization of men's and women's salaries and a salary schedule with a $2,000 minimum and a $4,500 maximum. Their earnestness was underscored by their request for contracts with a definite wage by early June so that they could seek jobs in other school systems if salaries here had not improved sufficiently. The Board of Education acquiesced to the NTA proposals and forwarded them to the Board of Estimate and Taxation together with a budget request of $1,020,112 for teachers' salaries. The latter board, already sensitive to taxpayer complaints about high tax rates, slashed the allocation to $813,000.[9]

Lengthy negotiations over the summer months brought the parties no closer to a settlement. In mid-August negotiations broke down completely when the Board of Education withdrew its recognition of the Teachers Professional Committee, the authorized bargaining agent of the Norwalk Teachers Association. Despite a city ordinance that prohibited city employees from striking or "in any way adversely affecting the efficiency . . . or operation of the City of Norwalk," the NTA voted 220-1 to return their contracts unsigned and to delay returning to work until a proper contract was signed and the Association given full recognition. The Board of Education reacted with an ultimatum: the deadline for returning contracts was noon, August 22. On that date members of the TPC with Miss Alice Cole, chairman, appeared at the office of Superintendent of Schools Philip Jakob and delivered 225 contracts—all unsigned.

Since the teachers had not signed their contracts, were they still city employees? Opinion in the city was split. Some Board of Education members advocated hiring replacements immediately but were blocked by a suit seeking a temporary injunction to restrain the Board. Others rejected drastic steps for as Councilman William Barnett accurately pointed out the teachers "have been our friends and neighbors, even our relatives, for too long to be treated in such a manner." It might in fact have been difficult to get experienced replacements for the executive secretary of the State Teachers Association had posted letters to all members cautioning anyone contemplating employment in Norwalk to do so only after careful consideration. The Connecticut State Commissioner of Education, Dr. Alonzo Grace, was far less subtle. He notified the Norwalk Board of Education that if there was no reasonable compromise on teachers' salaries and schools did not open on September 4 he would recommend a full investigation of the local school system.

At Grace's behest the Board of Education once again recognized the NTA and the two parties resumed consultations with the teachers submitting a "rock bottom figure" of $90,112 over the $813,000 already allotted and the Board of Education making a "final offer" of $31,000 above it, leaving the parties $59,112 apart.[10] Prodded by the PTA council Mayor Kelley made a last-ditch effort to break the deadlock by calling a joint meeting but "rock bottom" and "final offer" remained as far apart as ever.

"Probably not since the British burned the town in 1779 has Norwalk had such a day of excitement," was *The New York Times* description of the opening day of school. Almost the entire instructional staff of 225 teachers, including both the mayor's daughter and the wife of one School Board member,

failed to report to duty. Turned away from school house doors, children cheered the extended vacation and scooted off to play, dipping into their lunch bags as they raced away. The day held yet another surprise for distressed parents and glum officials: Dr. Alonzo Grace ordered the city to close its public schools until Monday and announced an immediate investigation of the school system. Charging that the Board of Education had "passed the buck" to the Board of Estimate and Taxation he termed the teachers' request as "perfectly equitable, since, as a whole, teachers have been substantially underpaid for a long time."[11]

Governor Raymond Baldwin now intervened in this first teachers' strike in Connecticut, ordering disputants to meet in his chambers in Hartford. After a four-hour session that made little headway Baldwin ordered the parties to continue negotiations in Norwalk, threatening that if they did not come to an agreement the State would sign contracts with the teachers and assess the city for the costs.

In the next round of meetings the city offered teachers two proposals, both of which would require voter approval through referendum. Teachers rejected both offers and the scenario shifted back to the governor's chambers. At the close of yet another four-hour conference between town officials, representatives of the NTA, and the governor's aides Baldwin announced that a settlement had been reached: a $65,000 increase in the teachers' salary budget, recognition of the NTA as the official bargaining unit, and establishment of a committee of educational experts to make recommendations on Norwalk's salary question. Children were not too happy to learn that the ten school days lost would be made up in June. Schools opened on September 16 and, when the contract was signed three days later, Dr. Grace canceled the investigation of Norwalk's school finances, satisfied that "the community can settle its own problems now."

At almost every Council meeting there was Irving Freese sitting just outside the railing that separated citizens from councilmen and ready to bring up matters that would embarrass the Democrats. Many of Freese's criticisms centered on Corporation Counsel Paul Connery whom he charged with dereliction of duty and conflict of interest for failing to try to collect $21,000 in back taxes owed since 1943 by General Aircraft Equipment Corporation. Connery was the lawyer for this company,[15] which had received large government contracts during the war but had been unable to make a successful transition to peacetime production. Connery had lost a son in the war and his sympathizers accused Freese of picking on Connery "now that he is in a little jam." However, even the Democratic Town Committee became openly disenchanted with Connery for his high-handed way of dispensing city jobs without consulting them and Freese used this to attack the Democrats, since he had long been a strong proponent of civil service for city employees.

Kelley had run for mayor reluctantly in 1945 and refused to be a candidate in 1947 so the Democrats nominated Councilman Robert Howard. The Republicans put up former Mayor Oliver. Irving Freese, the Socialist candidate, picked up votes from both parties and easily outdistanced his competitors. In a sweeping victory he carried eleven Socialists to the Council, leaving only one incumbent, the conscientious Lester Gilman—a Republican—on that body.

Minutes after they took their oaths of office Freese and his councilmen passed a resolution stating that "the spirit of civil service shall prevail henceforth in the hiring, replacement and advancement of all city employees."[16] The new mayor called upon the police commissioners to eliminate "certain irregularities" in that department and, disappointed in the response, replaced them.[12] He had somewhat more difficulty with Paul Connery and Dorothea Murray, both of whom at first refused to resign, but by the end of the year Freese had taken control of the city's major departments.[13]

All was not clear sailing for Freese. He disillusioned some supporters when, after having stated that responsible city employees "need not fear the broom," he removed Stephen Dokus as comptroller and replaced him with his own man. In most instances, though, his appointments were praised as being the first time "this kind of job was placed on merit and not a political plum." He overruled the Council when they gave a contract to a local firm over the lowest bidder, an out-of-town company. He was also successful in having real and personal property reevaluated to more realistic figures; the Grand List jumped by over $10 million as a result. Like all administrations the new mayor and Council spent many hours listening to a never-ending series of citizen complaints and petitions. There were new faces now outside the railing in the Council Chamber; some of them were black. A few resolute Negroes stood up before the Council and made public the discrimination this isolated and unheard group had so long endured. Their work resulted in an ordinance empowering the mayor to create the Citizen Inter-Group Commission as a clearing house for charges of discrimination or denial of civil rights.

Their conscientious mayor satisfied the citizens of Norwalk. Freese was easily reelected in 1949. In 1951 he broke with the Socialists and organized the Independent Party, which he led to victory that fall, inaugurating the multi-party system Norwalk has retained ever since. Even while he wore the Socialist label, however, Freese was a combination of the two other parties—Republican in his concern for fiscal caution and efficiency in government, and Democratic in his understanding of what the average voter wanted. He won again in 1951, although by a smaller margin—the only Norwalk mayor in the twentieth century, other than Frank Stack in the 1930s, to be elected for four successive terms.

15 Letters sent to Connery in his capacity as corporation counsel were sometimes addressed to him at General Aircraft Equipment Corporation.

16 This was a symbolic gesture from a strictly legal point of view since a civil service system required a change in the charter. To date Norwalk has not seen fit to adopt a city-wide civil service system although certain departments maintain their own personnel requirements.

17

THE
TERCENTENARY DECADE

Being
an Account of
the Beginning of Norwalk's Fourth Century

O OLD-TIMERS the Norwalk of 1950 with a population of 49,460, an increase of 10,000 since 1940, was beginning to look unfamiliar. The town still retained many of its village characteristics, however, especially in West Norwalk and Silvermine where country roads meandered through meadows and woodland and over little bridges that spanned the many tiny streams feeding into the Five Mile and Silvermine Rivers.*1* The following decade put an end to this bucolic scene for no sooner had the GIs of World War II finished their interrupted schooling, found jobs, and married than they and their families looked for houses in the suburbs. The government's generous mortgage policy for veterans encouraged the trend. Weary Planning Commission members spent much personal time reviewing plot plans for new developments with enticing names like Elite Homes or Holiday Estates. In 1960 alone the Commission approved 156 subdivisions.[1]

The census tally of 1960 showed that Norwalk's population had jumped to 67,775, a 35 percent increase. Not all the newcomers were middle-class native Americans occupying "colonial ranch" houses in new developments. By 1960 three to four thousand Hispanics lived here,*2* most of them from Puerto Rico, Costa Rica, and Colombia. The need for workers in war plants brought a surge of Puerto Ricans to the United States in the early 1940s but most of those who came to Fairfield County went to Bridgeport. The few who came to Norwalk generally had to go to Bridgeport for their social life. The great immigration of Puerto Ricans to Norwalk began in 1950*3* when the Zell Corporation opened a factory on Main Street for manufacture of leather and metal specialty products. This company paid for the transportation of people from Puerto Rico to Norwalk. Following the pattern of earlier immigrants these newcomers encouraged relatives and friends to join them so that today most of Norwalk's Puerto Ricans are either from the agricultural village of San Lorenzo or from the commercial city of Mayaguez. The differing customs and educational backgrounds of the two groups have not made for a congenial relationship even though they speak the same language. Many Puerto Ricans who came originally to Norwalk have moved on to New Haven, Bridgeport, or other upstate communities.*3*

---

1 The long-term effects of the severance of Canaan and Wilton Parishes from the town in 1805 show up most clearly at this time. Norwalk had never developed an exclusive back-country "estate" area, as Greenwich and Stamford had done; its zoning regulations were less restrictive; and, more important, its tax structure was quite different from that of Greenwich, which could retain a low mill-rate because of its high-priced back-country section.

2 This figure is based upon studies by Norwalk's Spanish-speaking residents. The 1960 U.S. Census figures contain no separate category for Hispanics, a classification that was not begun until 1970. According to local sources the 1970 Census figure of 3,240 living in the city is far from accurate, a more likely number being 10,000.

3 The first Puerto Rican to settle in Norwalk was Carlos Morales, who came with his New York company when it moved to Norwalk in 1929. The second one, a woman, Mrs. Maria Aguayo, arrived in 1944 with her small son Jaime.

Costa Ricans also came under contract to Norwalk, migrating in such numbers that they eventually outnumbered Puerto Ricans in the city. Costa Ricans tended to be better educated than other Latin American immigrants. Quite often they were young men who had finished high school but—because of poor economic prospects in their native land—came to America for a better life. So many congregated in Norwalk that to help them with their problems, Fernando Carranza, an early immigrant, was appointed consul, the first Costa Rican consul in the United States.[4]

Blacks who constituted somewhat less than 8 percent of the city's population found their circumstances improved in the 1950s. Previously they could be sure of a welcome only at the two or three black cafes in town; now other restaurants were more willing to serve them. A small group of middle-class blacks, most of them members of Grace and Calvary Baptist Churches and Bethel AME Church, continued to work for advancement of civil rights. The NAACP with the persevering Andrew Wise as president was their most effective vehicle.[5]

One of the NAACP's goals was to convince corporations that blacks could be successful in management positions. Executives from fifty area companies were invited to an industrial luncheon where Charles Ukkerd, a top salesman for Pitney-Bowes and an NAACP member, was a featured speaker. Another long-term undertaking, persuading black girls and boys to complete their education, was furthered by publicizing the careers of successful black men and women as role models for the younger generation. One was Marguerite Fuller, the first black student chosen for the National Honor Society at Norwalk High School, and later the first black teacher in the school system.[3] Dr. George I. Johnson, a dentist who became Norwalk's first Negro councilman, was another example, as was Dr. W.H.N. Johnson, who was accepted on the Norwalk Hospital staff in 1943 and was a member of the Rationing Board during the war.[6]

Village Creek, a deliberately integrated residential development on a 66-acre tract between Manresa Island and Wilson Point, produced more than a flurry of controversy. The modernistic architecture of Village Creek was probably as disturbing to tradition-minded Norwalkers as the reputed left-wing political philosophy of the artists and other professional people who moved there in the fifties. As the years passed Village Creek's architecture no longer seemed avant-garde and a new political climate modified anxieties about its residents.

As plans for one subdivision after another were removed from drawing boards and rendered into three-bedroom, split-level houses, a battalion of school-age children overwhelmed the existing schools. Construction of new buildings and erection of "prefabs" on the grounds of older ones provided the elementary school classrooms so urgently needed. Even as this phase was being completed the high school on East Avenue was engulfed by a horde of teenagers. Although several hundred young Norwalkers attended Central Catholic High School, a coeducational school on West Rocks Road that opened in 1959, or the Thomas School, a private school in Rowayton,[7] the surge of public school secondary students compelled the city to build another high school. Brien McMahon High School, a sleek building wrapped around gardens and pools and large enough for fifteen hundred students, opened in 1960.

The education specialist who guided the school system through this period of extraordinary growth was Dr. Harry A. Becker, appointed superintendent of schools in 1953. More often than not involved in projecting needs and planning new facilities, Becker also introduced innovative instructional techniques like team teaching, known as the Norwalk Plan in educational circles.[8] In the Sputnik era, when critics were lashing out against the inadequacy of science and mathematics instruction in American schools, Becker encouraged adoption of

---

4 The Costa Rican community in Norwalk today is said to be the largest anywhere outside Costa Rica itself.

5 The Norwalk branch of the NAACP was founded about 1940 by Nathaniel Hopkins and several others.

6 Young blacks began to aspire to a broader range of positions. For example, Larry Bentley, a Norwalk High School graduate and a Navy veteran, applied for and was given a job as messenger at the Merchants Bank and Trust Company. This was the beginning of his career in banking.

7 Miss Mabel Thomas founded The Thomas School in 1922 using the living room of Graycote, a small summer cottage on her father's property, as the classroom for the eleven children who enrolled in the first class. She remained head of the institution until 1953 when the school was incorporated as a non-profit institution. A decade later the board of trustees moved the school across the street to the former Farrell estate and constructed a classroom building on that property.

revamped programs of study in those disciplines and of advanced placement courses.

Becker's name is identified with yet another noteworthy educational innovation for he laid the groundwork for establishment of Norwalk Community College, the first city-supported community college in Connecticut. Shortly after he assumed the school superintendency Becker, formerly dean of the Junior College of Connecticut,[9] broached the idea of a city-run, two-year college that would make higher education available at a modest cost to residents of the then seventh-largest city in the state. The proposal won support of Norwalk's state legislators Abner Sibal and Louis Padula; of civic leaders Marvin Gruss, Max Lepofsky, and Mrs. Charlotte Chen; and of presidents of educationally-minded organizations like Mrs. Lynn Savitsky of the Central Council PTA and Mrs. Madeline Bernard of the American Association of University Women. Each worked unstintingly toward establishing the school; State Senator Sibal and House Majority Leader Padula were responsible for enabling legislation that allowed the Norwalk Board of Education to establish and maintain a two-year college contingent upon voter approval in a referendum.[10] Civic leaders[11] testified at hearings in Hartford, enlisted support of club memberships, and spoke at citizen gatherings, all so effectively that in the November, 1960, referendum voters sanctioned the college by a vote of 10,324 to 2,192.[4] Norwalk Community College opened in September, 1961, using the new $4 million Brien McMahon High School as the campus for 140 students who attended liberal arts or secretarial studies classes in the afternoon or evening.[12] Its motto affirmed its function: "In a democracy, educational opportunity for all."[5]

8 Under this plan teams of three cooperating teachers instructed as many as ninety students at a time. Drawing upon their competency in a special area, the teams provided the kind of expertise ordinarily unattainable in self-contained classrooms.

9 The Junior College of Connecticut became the University of Bridgeport in 1947.

10 A 1955 bill introduced by Senator Louis Lemaire had been defeated and Sibal's first attempt in 1957 was unsuccessful when the bill was tabled.

11 The League of Women Voters, the Chamber of Commerce, and a newly-organized Citizens Committee for the Community College were among those working most diligently toward establishment of the institution.

12 In January, 1966, Norwalk Community College became a unit of the State System of Regional Community Colleges and receives financial support as a state agency.

The community's enthusiasm for the new college which *The Hour* termed "indubitably the most significant civic enterprise in the history of our city" somewhat overshadowed the fact that a second post-secondary school also opened its doors in September, 1961. Norwalk State Technical Institute,[13] the handwork of a Citizens Committee of representatives from area industries and of Louis Padula, who introduced the enabling act in the legislature, offered programs of study designed to train technicians for industry. Sixteen laboratories equipped for study of chemical, electrical, metallurgical and tool engineering technology were a prominent feature of the Institute's three inter-connecting buildings located on a seventeen-acre tract on Richards Avenue. The school reached its maximum full-time enrollment of seven hundred within five years and drew hundreds of part-time students after it adopted a five-year associate degree evening program designed to upgrade workers in local industries.[6]

The city struggled mightily to keep up with the stream of newcomers and to improve the quality of life. One step in this direction was building Samuel Roodner Court, a gigantic project costing $2.3 million that provided 220 families with housing. These well-appointed apartments, located on a ridge above Ely Avenue and surrounded by manicured lawns and carefully tended shrubbery, were a source of pride to both the administration and citizenry. Acquisition of Shady Beach with its delightful wooded area for picnic tables adjoining Calf Pasture almost doubled the public beach area. On sunny Sundays as many as 14,000 persons enjoyed the beaches, keeping seventy lifeguards on watch.

Although the city could have done considerably more to put the harbor in better shape for the hundreds of pleasure boats that swarmed in Norwalk waters during the summer months, it did inaugurate a Police Marine Division. A young policeman and former Navy coxswain, Sergeant Thomas Brigante, was placed in charge of the new unit and given a 23-foot Seaskiff to patrol the islands and twenty-one miles of coastline.

Citizens, distressed that the city had failed to obtain magnificent Roton Point when it came on the market some years earlier, were now determined that Norwalk should acquire Manresa Island, a

13 In June, 1967, the State Board of Education changed the Institute's name to Norwalk State Technical College.

large point jutting out in the direction of Chimmons Island.[14] They proposed making this into a public recreational area with a marina. A highly political fight developed which was carried from the Council Chambers to the Assembly in Hartford and finally to the people in a referendum. Proponents of the park might have won had it not been that Connecticut Light & Power Company, its facilities strained by lower Fairfield County's rapid growth, wanted the site for a power station. When the $1.6 million cost of purchasing and developing Manresa was balanced against the taxes CL&P's power station would pay the outcome was inevitable.

Dr. Bern Dibner with an electrical machine made by Nicholas T. de Saussure of Geneva, which is now in the Burndy Library.

One man who labored to obtain Manresa for the city was Henry Davis Nadig, editor and publisher of the crusading little magazine, *Mark*, whose first issue appeared in 1954. *Mark* became the voice of those good citizens who were not content to see

14 Roton Point was snapped up by private clubs and by the Sixth Taxing District, which named its new private area Bayley Beach, after the owner of Roton Point who for many years operated the amusement park. Bayley had to close the Point during World War II because of the gas shortage. Like Norwalk, the Town of New Canaan ignored this opportunity to pick up a portion of the beach for its use.

their city drift into decline through official procrastination or astigmatic financial policies. More booster than critic, Harry Nadig preferred carrot to stick but whenever the city fathers failed to reach the high standards he demanded—which was fairly often—Nadig would let them know it. In every issue he promoted Norwalk's potential as a top residential community and asked provocative questions: "When has the Zoning Commission last talked with the Planning Commission? . . . If the water at the Country Club beach tests 'so badly' as it reportedly does how about the water at nearby Calf Pasture Beach? . . . Whatever became of the almost-created Heritage Commission?"[7] The editor sensed that Norwalk's future lay not in the declining textile or hatting industries but in research and development facilities of corporations, and he gave such firms excellent publicity.

Perkin-Elmer and the Burndy Corporation had arrived early in the decade and typified the kind of company Nadig had in mind. The former, originally an optical company, now manufactured precision electronic instruments. Burndy's sensational growth derived from success of the unique electrical connector it manufactured. Along with his corporation, Bern Dibner, the company's founder and a cultivated and imaginative man, brought to Norwalk an extensive scientific and technological library that contained not only modern volumes but rare treatises by Europe's earliest physicists and chemists.[15]

Another newcomer was the Automatic Signal Division of Eastern Industries, Inc., which owed its continued growth to America's neverending need for modernization of traffic control equipment. The Norwalk Police Department's up-to-date semaphores and traffic direction signals were largely attributable to the local Automatic Signal firm.[16] The Norden Company, made famous during World War II by the Norden bombsight and now a division of United Technologies, arrived in 1960.[17] With their emphasis upon research and development these companies hired employees of

15 In the 1960s Dr. Dibner had a spacious, classically modern library built to house these volumes, along with his extensive collection of early scientific instruments. He later donated a large portion of his collection of books, including incunabula, books printed prior to 1500, to the Smithsonian Institution.

16 The Nov. 23, 1957, issue of *Mark* contains an advertisement (page 6) showing the first radar traffic signal in the United States, installed on East Avenue and St. John Street.

higher than average education and skill (in 1956 650 of Burndy's 2,150 employees were engineers),[8] whose commensurably higher income made them welcome additions to the community.

It seemed that oysters would never reign again as king for in the postwar period the industry was plagued by set failures and oystermen abandoned the waterfront for other means of livelihood. Old-timers attributed the decline to pollution of the waters by untreated chemical wastes dumped into the river and to silting of the harbor from commercial dredging operations.[18] At the end of the 1950s

vanced aquaculture techniques facilitated the revival and helped astute businessmen like the Bloom Brothers, owners of Talmadge Bros. Company, to become one of the largest oyster businesses along the Connecticut shoreline.[19] Sharp-eyed readers of the local newspaper could find occasional advertisements that began: "Wanted Oyster Boat Deckhands."

During the cold war, the superpowers—the United States and the Soviet Union—played out their struggle through brinksmanship confronta-

*In 1953, efforts of the Grace Baptist Building Fund Committee resulted
in the purchase of the Jewish Center property on West Avenue for a new church.*

the industry came alive again. Availability of seed oysters from shellfish hatcheries in years of set failure, more efficiently designed equipment, and ad-

tions and many Americans became fearful that the nation's strength was being sapped by crypto-Communists in their midst. Norwalk made front-page news for two months during the wave of accusations exposing disloyal citizens,[9] when the Mulvoy-Tarlov-Aquino Post of the VFW divulged that it was turning over to the FBI names and ad-

17 The Grand List shows an increase of $15 million between 1955 and 1957 of which only $7.5 million represents dwellings indicating that the flood did not slow down Norwalk's industrial growth.

18 When Connecticut Light and Power Company contributed to silting of the harbor by dredging to lay cables to Long Island in the mid-1960s the company donated $30,000 to the State Shell Fish Commission which distributed the money to local oystermen as compensation for their losses.

19 In the late 1960s the revenue from Norwalk oyster beds was estimated at $5 million, about half the industry's annual income, according to Arthur Layton, "Shellfish Industry Going Down for Third Time," *Fairfield County Courier,* Sept. 18, 1969.

dresses of residents whose records or activities were deemed to be Communistic.[20]

The disclosure was intended to attract new members to the Post but it set in motion a nationwide controversy that pitted hardliners against civil libertarians. Chairman of the House Un-American Activities Committee Harold Velde suggested that the VFW turn over names of suspected Communists to it, as well as to the FBI. "An excellent idea," Senator Joseph McCarthy asserted. On the other hand the state branch of Americans for Democratic Action condemned the VFW for not allowing those charged to answer the accusations, and the chairman of the American Veterans' Committee, Bill Mauldin, censured the action as "vigilante tactics which violate the spirit of Americanism." Even President Dwight Eisenhower was drawn into the polemic. Asked at a news conference to comment on the Norwalk VFW's stand, he replied that no one could be prevented from reporting suspects to the FBI and that since the VFW was not making the names public there was no basis for libel or slander.

Attempts to clarify the imbroglio added to the confusion. The original story had placed the onus for sifting data and forwarding names to the FBI on a special committee allegedly formed from among Post membership of men "from all walks of life." When the national VFW commander appeared before the House Veterans Committee he unequivocally stated there had been no committee, no investigation, no evaluation, and no discussion of suspects among the Norwalk Post membership. On NBC television the local commander stated the Post "never screened, never evaluated material, and never publicized it." In a radio broadcast, Mrs. Suzanne Silvercruys Stevenson, founder of the Minute Women of America and a member of the Norwalk VFW Auxiliary, labeled the committee story a myth. She explained that a timid person had shared his suspicions about an individual with Communist leanings with the Post commander and that when the informant was reluctant to turn in the name the Post commander had done so in his behalf.[21]

The spotlight on Norwalk was particularly embarrassing because the community was playing host to a group of newspaper men from NATO countries, here under sponsorship of the State and Defense Departments to visit "a typical American town." What they saw was a community not only rent by the VFW incident but one in the midst of a prolonged strike involving the city's major industry.

Fifteen hundred members of the five Norwalk locals of United Hatters, Cap and Millinery Workers had voted almost unanimously to strike the Hat Corporation of America on July 9, 1953, after protracted contract negotiations reached an impasse on the union's demand for a job stability clause. The Hat Corporation had already moved its lower-priced straw hat operations to Winchester, Tennessee, and intended to move its higher-priced straw hat and finishing operations there also—a switch that would leave two hundred employees jobless. The union regarded the company's decision as the onset of "the slow process of dying" and demanded a contract guaranteeing that the company cancel its plans. The Hat Corporation for its part disclaimed any responsibility to remain "fixed like a cabbage to a spot." After persistent efforts by state and federal mediators failed to break the stalemate the employees began the first general strike at the plant in forty-four years.

The phrase "slow process of dying" could accurately have been applied to the hatting industry as a whole. For whatever reason, perhaps because returning servicemen wanted nothing resembling a uniform, younger men stopped wearing hats after the war.[22] Women were slower to abandon hats but eventually they too became willing to appear hatless on the street, especially in summertime. In 1947 the Hat Corporation's sales hit a peak of almost $21 million; by 1950 they had dropped to less than $18 million[10] and the decline continued. Following the example of dozens of other New England manufacturers the corporation turned to the South's non-union labor to cut production costs.

For a month, in two-hour shifts, orderly strikers uneventfully manned the picket lines thrown up around the corporation's production plants and storage buildings. On August 18 an unmarked truck crashed through the picket line and sped off to the Railway Express office with a load of hats. In his haste to unload the driver inadvertently ran

---

20 The Post's action was consistent with a resolution adopted at the organization's 1926 national encampment that made it a duty of the membership to report any person believed to be engaged in subversive activity.

21 Interest in Communism subsided so rapidly that when the Norwalk Junior Chamber of Commerce arranged a three-lecture series entitled "Freedom Answers Communism" in May, 1958, they had to cancel the third lecture.

22 In Norwalk wearing a hat on the street was still demanded, especially if a man hoped to do business with a local firm.

down a member of the union's Executive Board who was on picket duty at the railroad station, triggering a rough-and-tumble melee. The police quelled the milling crowd and arrested the driver for improper registration but he was released a short time later with bail money provided by the Hat Corporation.

Relying on a twenty-five to thirty-dollar weekly strike benefit and tapping their savings to meet expenses, all except sixteen strikers held out all winter and into the spring.[23] Although there were a few cases of arson, assault, and illegal entry into the lodgings of scabs,[24] there was little violence. Occasional rumors of a settlement enlivened the humdrum but negotiations always ended in the usual deadlock. The break finally came in May. Using an injunction hearing on the Hat Corporation's charge of union obstruction and the union's counterclaim and suit for ten million dollars as the means to bring about a settlement, Judge Elmer Ryan of the Superior Court brought the opponents to his chambers and smoothed the way for a three-year "peace pact." With only ten opposing votes the union membership ratified a contract that preserved the union shop and provided a company-financed pension plan, an improved grievance procedure, and a severance pay plan.[25] Since the corporation had all but completed moving the remaining straw hat operations to the South, some workers found the severance pay of immediate use. On May 24 workers, "tickled pink" to return to work after the ten-and-a-half month hiatus, began normal full production. Relieved local merchants hailed the settlement as they looked forward to a burst of buying.[11] But the heart of Norwalk's hat production was gone and with it the great days of hatting.

In mid-October, 1955, a flood of such overwhelming scope swept over Norwalk that when it receded it left behind a city not only devastated but permanently changed. On Friday, October 14, a

23 In addition to the sixteen rank-and-file workers, fifty foremen returned to work late in August.

24 Someone set fire to the car of a scab living at Green Pastures Inn, Darien. Car and contents were destroyed.

25 The most complex part of the new contract was a "red circling plan" which guaranteed an employee the wage of a higher-paying job for a sixty-day period if he returned to work, found his original job occupied, and had to accept a lower-paying job. After that period his seniority would advance him to the higher paying job. If the job no longer existed he would get severance pay under the new contract.

gale swept the eastern seaboard from Cape Hatteras to Maine. That afternoon Paul James, Commissioner of Public Works, was with local Civil Defense Director Seth Wiard studying the latest weather reports which forecast a "heavy drizzle." The two men glanced out to West Avenue and saw rain pouring so heavily that water already reached the top of the curb, looking like "an overgrown trout stream."[26]

The city had weathered many heavy storms and, although officials kept cautious watch, not until 10:00 P.M. Saturday did the Police Department, on Mayor Freese's authorization, put its Emergency Mobilization Plan into operation, notifying city agencies and Civil Defense units, and asking neighboring police and fire departments to stand by for help.[12] By this time the Silvermine River had inundated the Broad Street bridge. Drivers everywhere in town were abandoning autos and trying to reach home as fast as they could on foot. The worst was yet to come for rain and wind would continue until by Monday 12.89 inches of rain had fallen and upriver dams had crumbled, pouring out thousands of tons of water.

The police had scarcely activated their emergency plan when they learned that the Cross Street bridge, which handled most of the in-town through traffic, had collapsed and the Wall Street bridge was obstructed by debris. Traffic was hurriedly rerouted all the way to the Washington Street bridge. Although blocked temporarily the Wall Street bridge's sturdy stone arch anchored in solid rock at either end held fast, attesting to the competence of the stone masons who had rebuilt it in 1898.

Next the New Canaan Avenue bridge over the Merritt Parkway became impassable while the Silvermine Avenue bridge collapsed completely. Travelers either attempted to fight their way through snarled traffic to the Washington Street bridge or gave up and sought shelter near the parkway. Winnipauk School was hastily turned into a refuge for stranded travelers and Silvermine residents who had fled from their endangered houses.

The heavy rain and swollen rivers were not alone responsible for the damage; it was the debris—tree trunks, boxes, lumber, cars, trucks, even entire houses—that washed up against bridges and

26 James tried to put up stakes in the rivers to measure the rate at which the water was rising but he soon realized that this was a waste of time because of the rapid rise.

created temporary dams. Water could not rush harmlessly over the top but instead collected behind the mounting debris and finally tore bridges away from their moorings.[27] In a replication of the 1854 flood the rising water surged through the Danbury line's tunnel just west of the river and then tore through Mechanic Street wreaking havoc on everything in its path.

The Red Cross, Salvation Army, and other volunteer organizations had swung into action immediately and by Saturday volunteers were pouring in to help, seven hundred from the Red Cross alone.[28] That organization's ability to respond quickly with food, clothing, shelter, and money was a godsend to frightened families and distraught travelers. The Red Cross turned the Jewish Center

Mayor Freese set up headquarters in a taxi office on Wall Street from which, assisted by Council President Raymond Rayner, he directed operations during the entire emergency. Early Sunday at the mayor's request Governor Abraham Ribicoff called out the National Guard. These soldiers began rescue work promptly and as the waters subsided they were assigned to keeping people out of dangerous zones and preventing looting.

The reluctance of people to abandon their homes hampered rescue operations and cost police and firemen many wasted hours. Fortunately only four persons lost their lives, three from a Clark Street house that was swept into the river. Many newspapers carried the pathetic story of seventy-one-year-old Mrs. Susan Kelly whose bobbing head came into

Cross Street Bridge was engulfed at floodtide on October 16, 1955.

Mayor Freese, U.S. Civil Defense Director Peterson, and Governor Ribicoff confer.

in South Norwalk into a shelter where it housed between ten and twenty people for a week. The Red Cross also operated a twenty-four-hour switchboard, a most helpful supplement to police emergency radio and telephone communications.

27 Commissioner James who only two months earlier had observed a flooded upstate area was at first confident of avoiding similar devastation. "I had told them they should have placed equipment at the bridge to keep it cleared out and they wouldn't have lost it," he says, "but when it happened to us . . . the debris comes so fast you can't get slow-moving equipment moving fast enough."

28 The quick thinking of a local committee chairman alarmed at the flooding put the Norwalk-Wilton Chapter into emergency operation according to Seymour S. Weisman, *Case Study of a Flood-Stricken City* (New York, 1959), 22, from which many of the details given here are derived.

the rays of Mayor Freese's flashlight as she clung to a piece of wood after being washed from the wreckage of this house. She, her husband, and two women boarders had huddled in the dark in an upstairs bedroom while she tried to persuade them to accept a makeshift lifeline proffered by firemen. Her husband had refused to leave, responding testily: "Let me alone, you make me nervous." "You couldn't tell that man anything," commented his surviving spouse.[13]

Clean-up operations were hindered by mobs of sightseers who descended upon the city to gawk at the battered houses and boats, crushed trailer trucks, autos teetering on washed-out river banks, and in downtown Norwalk the weird sight of hundreds of yards of fabric swept along for blocks and wound around trees and poles by the violent force of the water.

On Monday afternoon when it became possible to take stock of the damage the governor flew in from Hartford and landed by helicopter on the high school athletic field. His main concern was the traffic, backed up for eight miles in both directions along the Merritt Parkway because it had to be rerouted through Norwalk's almost impassable streets.[29] Eastbound railroad operations had also come to a halt with the wreck of a freight train at Noroton Heights and service was not restored for almost a week.

Nearly every firm in the Norwalk River valley lost machinery and equipment damaged by mud and

picked up part of the tab for repair and replacement of streets, water mains, and bridges.

Most observers were struck not so much by the magnitude of the business losses, as heavy as they were, but by the piteous sight of families trying to reclaim odds and ends from flood-ravaged houses. Forty were lost completely and hundreds damaged. The fact that some of these, in the Cross Street section in particular, were small and dilapidated added to the pathos. Six brand new houses built on the bank of the Silvermine River were swamped.[31]

Homeowners and businessmen were unable to collect insurance for flood losses to their real estate since under the terms of most insurance policies water damage was not recoverable, but the Small Business Administration opened an office in Nor-

Post-flood ruins of the Commercial Building on Wall Street.

Temporary Bailey bridge at Cross Street . . . a reminder for years to come.

silt. Thousands of dollars worth of inventories were water-soaked and ruined. Total losses including public property and dwellings were at first estimated at over $8 million but this figure was later pared down to something over $4.5 million.[30] Since the city's borrowing power was tied to its Grand List the abrupt loss of so much property was a hardship. However, both state and federal governments

walk a week after the flood and made $800,000 in low-interest, long-term loans to businessmen. The Red Cross provided close to $50,000 in loans to homeowners and small businessmen. The emotional and psychological toll paid by those who had

29 The New Canaan Avenue bridge was cleared by Monday and a Bailey bridge erected over the Silvermine a few days later, opening the Merritt to through traffic. The traffic problem remained with Norwalk for many months, since a permanent bridge over the Silvermine was not completed until December, 1957. Construction of the Cross Street bridge did not commence until the end of 1957.

30 Of this, according to the Flood Survey Commission, business losses amounted to $3,110,000, loss of city property came to $920,000, and residential losses were $450,000. It is believed, however, that the last figure is not accurate since it was based on tax abatement requests which not all property owners filed even though entitled to do so.

31 A real estate developer built these dwellings on this spot after the Common Council overruled the Planning Commission, which had rejected the proposed development as being dangerously close to the river. The developer later replaced these houses.

The Lockwood-Mathews Mansion.
"... the magnificent interior of the building has the best
frescoed walls I have ever seen in this country, and the lavish-
ness of the marble and wood inlay work almost defies description in the museum quality of its workmanship." Dr. William
Murtagh, Keeper, National Register, Washington, D.C.

been in the water's destructive path was impossible to calculate.

During his visit Governor Ribicoff expressed the optimistic view that the flood had provided an extraordinary opportunity to rebuild a better Norwalk under the new Urban Renewal Program. Many local observers shared his optimism, especially when they noticed the speed at which clean-up operations proceeded and normal conditions were reestablished. From this point on, however, plans and programs became choked in a tangle of conflicting aims and methods and snarled duplication of bureaucratic agencies each with its own variety of red tape.

The city's Redevelopment Agency through which federal funds for restoration were channeled had the greatest power but it had to take the new Parking Authority into account. The Planning Commission and the Redevelopment Agency sometimes went their separate ways. Norwalk's Flood and Erosion Control Board had to subordinate its work to that of the State Water Resources Commission. Location of Route 7, a key connecting link to Danbury, depended upon decisions of the State Highway Commission. The looming shadow of a superhighway then in the planning, the New England Turnpike, fell over the entire center of the city and to complicate matters further a new mayor took office in the very midst of the first clean-up work.

No decisions affect the manner in which a city develops as much as those pertaining to land use. Hence the Redevelopment Agency's plans excited everyone's interest, especially that of uptown and downtown merchants. Despite suggestions of Planning Boards from time to time the city had never adopted a master plan on which restoration might be patterned.[32] What the Redevelopment Agency decided to do in effect was to complete what the flood had started. It acquired for renewal twenty-six acres on the north side of Wall and Main streets as far west as Belden[14] Avenue, an area heavily damaged by flood waters. Many buildings and streets in this section were shabby specimens of urban blight. The redevelopment plan involved widening the in-

tersection of Wall and Main streets to improve the flow of traffic, and clearance of surrounding land[33] to allow for open space as well as a modern shopping area with adequate parking. While redevelopment languished awaiting federal government approval, which was not forthcoming until July, 1959, the center of Norwalk resembled a bombed-out city. Work did not get under way until the 1960s.[34]

The Agency did not even apply for federal funds for South Norwalk renewal until 1958, bringing a flare-up of the old resentment, especially since that part of town was growing shabby and its property values were slipping. In the long run, however, more money was poured into South Norwalk's renewal than into Norwalk's.[35]

The two separate renewal projects left Norwalk and South Norwalk with their separate shopping areas, but it is difficult to envision a central project that would have been acceptable to both sections which were already facing changed shopping patterns. Intracity bus service was becoming a thing of the past while construction of scattered shopping plazas pulled shoppers away from the old central areas that their parents had patronized. After the New England Turnpike opened in 1958 the centrifugal pull accelerated for now shoppers could spin down to Stamford almost as easily as they could drive to Wall Street.[36]

In the last years of the fifties keen interest arose over proposals for charter revision to create a more

[32] Although citywide plans for parks, schools, etc., existed by the 1960s Norwalk did not adopt a master plan until 1973 nor had the Norwalk Redevelopment Agency, in existence since 1950, completed any Urban Renewal projects. Prior to 1955 most of its attention was devoted to the obsolescent area around Commerce and Isaac streets. The Agency was beginning to consider the Wall and Main section as a prospect for renewal when the flood struck.

[33] Much clearance was done by the Army Engineers who removed many buildings left in dangerous condition.

[34] By 1967 Irving C. Freese Park at the corner of Wall and Main streets had been built, River Street relocated, many modern buildings erected, and utility lines put underground in this area. Over two thousand feet of flood walls were erected along the river in the redevelopment area. Flood-control measures in other parts of town included enlarged storm drains and debris-free bridges. However, some vital flood-control work had to await decisions on relocation of Route 7.

[35] The first phase of South Norwalk Urban Renewal encompassed the area between Spring Street and the New Haven tracks below North Main. Through early land acquisition this got under way by 1961. To house families left homeless when dwellings and tenements were razed, the plan provided for both low and moderate cost housing as well as a modern shopping area and appropriate parking space.

[36] The Turnpike also played a part in keeping the two Norwalk districts apart, since it cut between them. However, it made Norwalk better for industries of the type that could be accommodated to the city's industrially-zoned land.

efficient government through some form of the city manager system. In practice, however, politics continued to be as much a matter of personalities as issues.[37] Losing in 1955 to George Brunjes, a well-liked retired school principal and Democrat, Irving Freese bounded back in 1957 but was overwhelmingly defeated by Republican John Shostak in 1959. Shostak declined to run in 1961 and another Republican, Frank J. Cooke, was elected.

The Common Council's plan to tear down the stately Mathews mansion and erect a large modern city hall in its place brought Norwalk's tercentenary decade to a cacophonous close but the fight to save the grand old building was a heartening display of public spirit. The controversy pitted people against politicians because the City Hall Building Committee, the Planning Commission, and Council President Cooke, who became mayor in the midst of the battle, were all bent on demolishing the mansion. As soon as the city's plans became known Miriam Lynch, a Wilson Point resident, and Elsie Hill, as formidable at seventy-seven as in her suffragette days, spearheaded the move to save it.

A city hall in Mathews Park[38] was not a completely ill-advised idea for this was a central location midway between Norwalk and South Norwalk. The mansion was too small for a city hall and could not be enlarged adequately. Doubtless officials looked forward also to the prosperity a new piece of construction would generate in local building trades. To Cooke and his associates a fine new city hall seemed definitely preferable to a dismal old Victorian mansion. At the time, the interior of LeGrand Lockwood's beautiful house resembled a junkyard. A few of its rooms housed city agencies but the rest were filled with miscellaneous equipment and trash. Its frescoed walls were smudged by stacks of

dusty city record books and power mowers stood in the entrance hall, propped against the caryatids that adorned the hall's massive walnut fireplace, and dripped oil on the floor of Italian marble.

The energy with which save-the-mansion forces launched a campaign to prevent its demolition astonished city officials.[15] Mansion supporters formally organized the Common Interest Group whose members asserted that bulldozer and wrecker's ball did not necessarily ensure progress. The CIG cleverly began to refer to the house as the Norwalk Mansion, emphasizing its age, elegance and uniqueness. Other organizations such as the Norwalk Historical Society joined the fight. More than four thousand visitors toured the building under auspices of save-the-mansion groups and the *Hour,* which favored razing the structure, was swamped by expressions of support for the mansion. Astounded but stubborn city officials persisted in plans for the city hall but were pushed eventually to the point of submitting the matter to a referendum. To their immense chagrin the proposition won by a handsome margin of 2,500 votes with voters in every ward favoring preservation of the fine old structure.[39] When the mansion was declared a national historic landmark the good service rendered by the CIG was abundantly demonstrated. Citizens, too, could take satisfaction in the knowledge that their votes had helped save Norwalk's "priceless treasure."

Three times during the tercentenary decade citizens had turned out in massive numbers to give direction to their elected officials through a referendum. Public-minded men and women from all sections of town had pulled together in causes that, to their way of thinking, would benefit the city. Through their efforts a priceless landmark has been saved and a new institution, a community college, had been created.

37 One issue in 1955 was Freese's refusal to compromise in the matter of the school budget. His rather rigid nature, which made him such an effective opponent while out of office, was not an asset when he held office. He also ran into trouble during the flood crisis when he arbitrarily ordered some men arrested for entering a restricted area without a pass. They were found not guilty when it was learned that they were contractors looking at prospective work. The newspapers and Democrats made much of the mayor's hasty act.

38 A memorial for veterans was projected for the site and in the 1950s this was called Veterans' Memorial Park. Almost as soon as the property was acquired the city had begun to nibble at the Mathews property, constructing a garage for the Department of Public Works where the greenhouses had stood and in 1959 taking over the gardens directly behind the mansion for a Police Court and jail.

39 City officials refused to accept defeat and proceeded with plans for a city hall. In 1963 they dredged up a state fire ordinance and on its basis the state fire marshal closed the building to the public. The CIG began a taxpayers' suit based on the city's original purchase of the Mathews property "for park purposes." The taxpayers won, the city appealed but lost again in 1965 and was permanently enjoined from turning the property into a city hall and parking lot. This case, *Baker et al. vs. City of Norwalk,* one of the first in which taxpayers defeated a municipality on an issue of this type, became a landmark case. The Junior League of Stamford-Norwalk restored and maintained the mansion temporarily. Today it is operated as a non-profit museum by the Lockwood-Mathews Mansion Corporation.

EPILOGUE

To travelers speeding along the New England Turnpike Norwalk is just another industrial city on the urbanized east coast. To the U.S. Census Bureau it is a metropolitan statistic. But megalopolis can never swallow up a city completely, and to its inhabitants Norwalk is their "town," their home, and the locus of their hopes for the future.

Fashioned by the responses of the early settlers to its physical characteristics — the River and the Sound, rich farmland, and a protected harbor — the tiny Congregational outpost became a placid little agricultural community. During the age of sail, as a stouthearted vanguard of merchants, shipmasters, and sailors turned to the sea for their livelihood, Norwalk prospered as a seaport. However, just as its small harbor relegated Norwalk to secondary importance as a maritime center, so too the capriciousness of its river constricted its industrial development. Not until the use of coal did factories loom over the landscape, rail lines intersect at its hub, and steamships take on tons of industrial freight at its docks. Today, in the third quarter of the twentieth century, the modern city is shaped by myriad external influences over which it can exercise little control: state social policies, federal tax regulations, overseas markets, even international monetary fluctuations.

Nevertheless, the city has been able to exert some authority over its development. One lesson from the past is that Norwalk's shortcomings were partly of its own making. As the Wall Street area and Old Well developed in tandem to become separate cities within the town, their unremitting economic rivalry was a detriment to both. Since each maintained a separate political identity as well, they were unwilling to join together in common cause, and the terms "uptown" and "downtown" came to conjure up deep-rooted suspicion and contentious rivalry. Even after consolidation in 1913, Norwalk retained a network of separate taxing districts that allowed narrow-minded localism to prevail. Its persistence is evident today in the neatly-printed white signs that proclaim a park, a beach, or even a wooden bench, the property of a specific taxing district.

Norwalk's tendency to pursue an independent political course also adversely affected its fortune. Often out of step with both state and national trends, isolated from the center of power, and shy of political figures able to establish wide political bases, the community as a consequence frequently failed to garner a substantial share of political patronage. Norwalk never succeeded in its bids to be a shire town, a county seat, or a customs port, and was even unable to block the loss of its outlying parishes. Today the community is sometimes bypassed in favor of cities with more conspicuous urban problems or better political connections.

The influence of public-spirited men and women on the community's development is another theme that pervades Norwalk's annals. The persistent efforts of a handful of humanitarians provided many of the services and amenities that made Norwalk a more attractive place in which to live. From LeGrand Lockwood's generous subscription that enabled the city to meet its quota of soldiers during the Civil War to present-day efforts in historical reconstruction and preservation, inhabitants have

223

worked unselfishly to found libraries, a hospital, a symphony orchestra, and even a municipal college. When town officers procrastinated or settled for makeshift solutions in the name of fiscal restraint, these same public minded residents were sure to be found in the ranks of those who pushed officials into taking appropriate action. Many of the institutions and programs that serve Norwalkers today rest upon the work of these devoted individuals.

Norwalk's history has been further characterized by its remarkable ability to absorb generations of newcomers in vastly larger numbers than surrounding communities. Inhabited for two centuries by typically New England Yankees, its homogeneity gave way to diversity in mid-nineteenth century as a profusion of immigrants from Northern Europe made Norwalk their home. These and later newcomers from Central and Eastern Europe contributed to the city's cultural diversity. Norwalk continues to attract in-migrants; today Latin Americans, West Indians, and a sizable number of Greeks account for a significant percentage of the new arrivals. In the past the bulk of each group of newcomers entered the labor market at the level of unskilled labor. Each in turn moved up the economic ladder and was absorbed into the middle class. Whether this pattern will continue remains to be seen. What is apparent, however, is that the city's heterogeneous population has lived together in remarkable harmony for over one hunderd years.

Careful scrutiny of those who have made Norwalk their home reveals one other link connecting the past with the present. Picture first the Amerind aborigine who lay aside his chopper and knife to reflect upon his good fortune in finding a secluded workplace sheltered from danger and accessible to the tidal flats that provided an ample food supply. Centuries later a middle-aged proprietor rhythmically swinging his scythe through knee-high salt hay praised God for guiding him to these virgin farmlands. A hearty sea captain hastened to his comfortable Pudding Lane home after completing a profitable West Indies voyage, grateful to the Providence that brought him to this snug port. A burly oysterman skillfully wielded rake and tongs, cheered by the thought that this year's plenteous harvest would provide the wherewithal for his family in their "neat white cottage." A penny-wise Whistleville housewife counted out the coins from the family's pay envelopes and secreted them in a sugar bowl toward that satisfying day when they

would add up to the price of a piece of land. From the verandah of an elegant mansion set high on Prospect Hill a prosperous manufacturer looked out over town and Sound, content in the knowledge that all was well in his world. Surveying the wooded half acre plot from the patio of his house, a proud new home owner was assured that his children would thrive in this pleasant suburb. To each person in this kaleidoscopic array Norwalk provided a refuge, a livelihood, and the hope of economic security.

Norwalk still fulfills these dreams. One young newcomer, André L. Pardo, has spoken for today's seekers in his poem "Norwalk, South Norwalk":

*Fly freely little bird,
here you are loved.
This is your home,
the town of all
the kids who want to play with you.
    Now I know!
We're always saying,
"Eagle, come home,"
and you think we've forgotten you.
    No, little bird,
    Come home also.
Come join
the blacks, the whites
and the Puertoricans,
and pick up your pieces of bread.
    If you get hurt,
don't be afraid to come down
to a Haitian, a Chinese,
a Greek, or an Italian.
Anyone will take care of you.
    As I tell you this,
from the window of my house
    I am observing a beautiful town
    Called Norwalk, South Norwalk!*

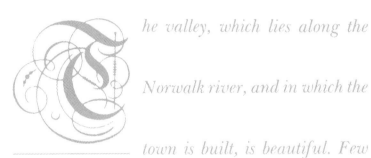

The valley, which lies along the Norwalk river, and in which the town is built, is beautiful. Few richer prospects of the same extent can be found

APPENDICES

than that, which is presented from the neighbouring eminences of this ground; the town . . . the river . . . the farms . . . together with an unlimited view of the Sound and the Long Island shore."

Timothy Dwight / 1822

FOOTNOTES

CHAPTER 1

1. Edwin Hall, ed., *The Ancient Historical Records of Norwalk, Connecticut* (Norwalk, 1847), 31.
2. John M. Taylor, *Roger Ludlow: the Colonial Lawmaker* (New York, 1900), 112.
3. Hall, *Ancient Historical Records*, 30.
4. Charles M. Selleck, *Norwalk* (Norwalk, 1896), 12.
5. Hall, *Ancient Historical Records*, 35-36.
6. *Public Records of the Colony of Connecticut, Prior to the Union with New Haven Colony*, Vol. I, 1636-1665 (Hartford, 1850), 20-21.
7. Public Records Office, London, England. A copy of this map was made in 1867 and reproduced in *United States Coast and Geodetic Survey Report for 1850* (Washington, D.C., 1850), Plate 71.
8. Joseph Sabin, *Dictionary of Books Relating to America* (29 vols., London, 1917), XIX, 248.
9. Leslie Stephen and Sidney Lee, eds., *The Dictionary of National Biography* (22 vols., London, 1917), XVII, 1165-1166.
10. A copy of this map, a tracing on linen made in 1872, is at the Connecticut State Library.
11. Extracts of the Prince Letters, *Connecticut Historical Collections* (31 vols., Hartford 1860-1967), III, 313-315.
12. Timothy Dwight, *Travels; in New-England and New-York* (3 vols., New Haven, 1822), III, 503.
13. Mark Tangard, "Man and Movement in the 'Reluctant Suburb'." Unpublished paper submitted for the B.A. Degree, Middlebury College, Spring, 1974, 30.
14. Martin Goldstein, *Waterfront, A Study of the Norwalk Waterfront, Off- shore Islands, Port, and Recreation Facilities* (Norwalk, 1967), 3-4.
15. Charles Townshend, "The Early History of Long Island Sound and its Approaches," *Papers of the New Haven Colony Historical Society* (10 vols., New Haven, 1865-1951), V, 279.
16. City Planning Commission (Norwalk), *The Norwalk Islands* (Norwalk, July, 1970).
17. "History of the Norwalk Chain of Islands," typewritten manuscript in the Rowayton Historical Society Archives.
18. Major H. H. Adams, Army Corps of Engineers, *Report of Survey of Norwalk Harbor*, October, 1895. Federal Archives and Records Center, Waltham, Mass.
19. Albert VanDusen, *Connecticut* (New York, 1961), 26.
20. Bernard Powell, "First Site Synthesis and Proposed Chronology for the Aborigines of Southwestern Connecticut," *Pennsylvania Ar- chaeologist* (April, 1965), 30-37.
21. Bernard Powell, "Spruce Swamp: A Partially Drowned Coastal Midden in Connecticut," *American Antiquity* (April, 1965) 30:4, 400- 469; "A Curious Scratched Design on a Connecticut Paintstone," *Ibid.,* (July, 1964), 30:1, 98-100; and "Aboriginal Trephination: Case for Southern New England?" *Science* (November 13, 1970), 170:3959, 732-734.
22. Powell, "A Chronology for Aborigines of Southwestern Connect- icut," 36.
23. John Swanton, *The Indian Tribes of North America* (Washington, D.C., 1952), 45-46.
24. Samuel Weed, *Norwalk After Two Hundred and Fifty Years*, (Norwalk, 1902), 102.
25. Norwalk Town Records I, 147. Connecticut State Library, Hartford, Connecticut and Selleck, *Norwalk,* 68-69.
26. Norwalk Town Proceedings (NTP), Book I, December 25, 1669, 90 and June 4, 1674, 112. Archives, City Hall, Norwalk, Conn.
27. Daniel Gookin, *Historical Collections of the Indians in New England* (Towntaid, 1970), 14.
28. *Public Record of Connecticut (PRC)* (5 vols., Hartford, 1850-1890), I, 529-530.
29. NTP I, February 21, 1658/59, 44; December 14, 1659, 48; and De- cember 18, 1666, 78.
30. U.S. Department of Commerce and Labor, *A Century of Population Growth* (Washington, D.C., 1909), Table 86, 164 and Table 87, 166- 167.
31. John DeForest, *History of the Indians of Connecticut* (Hartford, 1851), 359.

CHAPTER 2

1. NTP I, April 18, 1655, 3.
2. *PRC* I, 49.
3. Jacob R. Marcus, *Early American Jewry* (Philadelphia, 1951), 172- 173.
4. Hall, *Ancient Historical Records*, 46.
5. J. Hammond Trumbull, ed., *The True-Blue Laws of Connecticut and New Haven and the False Blue Laws Invented by the Rev. Samuel Peters* (Hartford, 1876), 116-117.
6. *PRC* II, 27-28.
7. D. Hamilton Hurd, *History of Fairfield County, Connecticut* (Philadel- phia, 1881), 519.
8. Robert Albion, *The Rise of New York Port* (New York, 1939), 89.
9. Richard L. Bushman, *From Puritan to Yankee: Character and the Social Order in Connecticut, 1690-1765* (Cambridge, Mass., 1967), 41.
10. Erna Green, "The Public Land System of Norwalk, Connecticut, 1654-1704: A Structural Analysis of Economic and Political Rela- tionships." Unpublished Thesis, Department of History, University of Bridgeport, 1972, 55.

CHAPTER 3

1. *Collections of the Massachusetts Historical Society, Fourth Series* (10 vols., Boston, 1878), VII, 623; Hall, *Ancient Historical Records;* 85; Selleck, *Norwalk,* 135; Augustus C. Golding, comp., *Descendants of Rev. Thomas Hanford*, Vol. I: *Six Generations* (New York, 1936), x-xii.
2. Alice Morse Earle, *The Sabbath in Puritan New England* (New York, 1891), 58.
3. Hall, *Ancient Historical Records*, 76-77.
4. Bushman, *From Puritan to Yankee*, 132.
5. *PRC* I, 242; II, 112; Hall, *Ancient Historical Records*, 48.
6. Ecclesiastical Affairs (Conn.), Vol. I, Documents 1-130, 51. Ar- chives, Connecticut State Library, Hartford.
7. Purcell, Richard J., *Connecticut in Transition: 1775-1818* (Middletown, 1963 ed.), 63.
8. Samuel Whiting, *The Connecticut Town-Officer* (Danbury, 1814), 268- 69.
9. Isabel Mitchell, *Roads and Roadmaking in Colonial Connecticut* (New Haven, 1934), 17, 25.
10. Malcolm Hunt, "Norwalk Town Proceedings," 26-28, 34, Archives Lockwood House Museum, Norwalk, hereafter cited as LHM Ar- chives; NTP I, Mar. 1, 1658/59, 44.
11. *PRC* II, 202.
12. Roland Hooker, *Boundaries of Connecticut* (New Haven, 1933), 29.
13. Affidavit, May 5, 1679, signed and attested to by Nathaniel Grayes, Thomas_____ and Thomas Barnum. Ecclesiastical Affairs I, I, 55.
14. *PRC* III, 59.
15. Ltr, Hanford to Mather, July 15, 1682. *Collections of the Massachusetts Historical Society*, VII, 623-24.
16. Henry M. Benedict and Elwyn E. Benedict, *Genealogy of the Benedicts in America* (Albany, New York, 1870, 1969), 1969 ed., 19-20.

CHAPTER 4

1. NTP I, Mar. 25, 1687, 137.
2. *Ibid.*, Feb. 21, 1698, 170.
3. NTP II, Aug. 12, 1726, 93.
4. Ecclesiastical Affairs III, 207a and b.
5. Liz Wilson, "Port of Norwalk," *Mark*, Mar. 26, 1960, 7:7, 6.
6. Fairfield County Court Files, 1757-1759, Vault 11, Box 187, RG3. Archives, Connecticut State Library, Hartford.
7. Roland Mather Hooker, *The Colonial Trade of Connecticut* (New Haven, 1936), 25.
8. Benno Forman, "The Crown and York Chairs of Coastal Connecticut and the Work of the Durands of Milford," *The Magazine Antiques*, (May, 1974), 1147-1154.
9. Frederic Boyer and Herbert Poole, "The Quintard Family in America," reprinted from July and October 1955 issues of *The New England Historical and Genealogical Register*.
10. See George Dow, *The Arts and Crafts in New England, 1704-1775* (Topsfield, Mass., 1927), 48, for a reproduction of the *Gazette* advertisement of April 18, 1763.
11. Benjamin Trumbull, *A Complete History of Connecticut: Civil and Ecclesiastical* (2 vols., New London, 1898), I, 159.
12. John Josselyn, *New Englands rarities discovered* (London, 1672), 46-47.
13. Benjamin Trumbull, *A Century Sermon* (New Haven, 1801), fn., 31.
14. Ltr., Leaming to Sec. for Society for the Propagation of the Gospel, Apr. 7, 1761. Francis L. Hawks and William Steven Perry, eds., *Documentary History of the Episcopal Church in Connecticut, 1704-1789* (Hartford, 1959), 11.
15. Ltr., Jonathan Hoit to Jonathan Law, Stamford, July 5, 1744. *Connecticut Historical Society Collections, II, Jonathan Law Papers*, 205-06.
16. The Connecticut Archives, Crimes and Misdemeanors, 1662-1789, Index, has sprinkled throughout its pages countless cases against counterfeiters.
17. Herbert Thoms, *Yale Men and Landmarks in Old Connecticut (1701-1815)* (New Haven, 1967), 247.
18. Parker Bradley Nutting, "Thomas Fitch: Charter Governor." Unpublished Master's Thesis, University of North Carolina, 1968, 11-12.
19. Ltr., Fitch to Moore, Feb. 24, 1766. *Fitch Papers II, 1759-1766, Collections of the Connecticut Historical Society*, XVII, 386.
20. *Rolls of Connecticut Men in the French and Indian War, 1755-1762, Collections of the Connecticut Historical Society*, IX, 88.
21. *Fitch Papers*, I, 356.

CHAPTER 5

1. Ltr., Fitch to Lord Halifax, Nov. 12, 1764, from Norwalk. *Fitch Papers*, II, 295.
2. Hall, *Ancient Historical Records*, 126.
3. Thomas C. Barrow, *Trade and Empire: The British Customs Service in Colonial America, 1660-1776* (Cambridge, Mass., 1967), 241.
4. Report to Treasury, "Ports, Districts & Towns..." PS 53582, SC No. 51459. Add Mss. 15484. Archives, The British Library, London.
5. George Spencer to William Pitt, Dec. 14, 1760. C.O., 5/60, Pol. 161-164. Archives, Public Records Office, London. Cited in Barrow, *Trade and Empire*, 146.
6. Ltr., spring of 1775. Cited in North Callahan, *Royal Raiders: The Tories of the American Revolution* (Indianapolis, 1963), 67.
7. Norwalk Revolutionary War Series 1, Vol. 5, Part 2, 416. Archives, Connecticut State Library, Hartford.
8. Frank Moore, *Songs and Ballads of the American Revolution* (Port Washington, L.I. 1964 reprint) 11.
9. *Ibid.*, 350-361.
10. Size Roll, Eighth Company, Capt. Rogers, Third Connecticut Regiment. *Connecticut Historical Society Collections*, VIII, 102.
11. Extracts from Norwalk Revolutionary Records, 1774-1784, 5. Archives, Connecticut State Library, Hartford.

12. Louis F. Middlebrook, *History of Maritime Connecticut during the American Revolution, 1775-1783* (2 vols., Salem, Mass., 1925), II, 10.
13. Gordon Casagrande, "Tory or Rebel," *Fairfield County Magazine*, Dec. 1975, 141.
14. Robert A. East, *Connecticut's Loyalists* (Chester, Conn., 1974), 24; Lois Bayles, comp., "Norwalk Loyalists," unpublished list of Loyalists collected 1975. LHM Archives.
15. Huntington, Long Island, Town Records, 3, fn., 5 and fn., 18. Town Hall, Huntington, N.Y.
16. Eliphalet Lockwood Accounts. LHM Archives.
17. *Huntington Papers, Connecticut Historical Society Collections*, XX, 41, 313.
18. Joseph Plum Martin, *Private Yankee Doodle* (Boston, 1962), 56.
19. Ltr., Thaddeus Betts, Stephen St. John, Eliphalet Lockwood, Hosmer St. John, John Hanford, Ozias Marvin, Abijah Betts, to Gov. Jonathan Trumbull, Jan. 19, 1781. Trumbull Papers XIV, Part I, 48ab. Archives, Connecticut State Library, Hartford. This may be exaggerated, for Norwalk was under heavy attack at this time.
20. Oscar Zeichner, *Connecticut's Years of Controversy, 1750-1776* (Richmond, Va., 1949), fn., 355.
21. Callahan, *Royal Raiders*, 67.
22 Robert McDevitt, *Connecticut Attacked: A British Viewpoint, Tryon's Raid on Danbury* (Chester, Conn., 1974), 29. All the shore towns were similarly fortified, and Tryon had a hard time finding a safe place to land.

CHAPTER 6

1. William B. Willcox, ed., *The American Rebellion, Sir Henry Clinton's Narrative of his Campaigns, 1775-1782* (New Haven, 1954), 130. For the view that Tryon's expedition was sent as a relief to Connecticut Loyalists, see Rev. Samuel Peters, *General History of Connecticut* (New York, 1877), 260.
2. Charles S. Hall, ed., *Life and Letters of Samuel Holden Parsons* (Binghamton, N.Y., 1905), 255-56.
3. Pay Role [sic] for Horse Travel, *Connecticut Historical Society Collections*, VIII, 202.
4. Marcus, *Early American Jewry*, 172.
5. Henry Carrington, *Battles of the American Revolution, 1778-1781* (New York, 1877), 471.
6. Hall, *Life and Letters*, 254.
7. Ltr., Leaming to unknown recipient, July 28, 1779, cited in Mary E. Drake, comp., "The Life of the Rev. Jeremiah Leaming," unpublished compilation of articles and excerpts from secondary works. Archives, St. Paul's-on-the-Green, Norwalk, Conn.
8. Samuel Rezneck, *Unrecognized Patriots, The Jews in the American Revolution* (Westport, Conn., 1975), 64.
9. Gen. G. Selleck Silliman to Gov. Trumbull, Jan. 3, 1781; St. John to Trumbull, Jan. 8, 1781. Trumbull Papers XIV, Part I, 1781, 20a, 22ab. Archives, Connecticut State Library, Hartford.
10. *RSC* VII, 453-57.
11. George Matthew Dutcher, *George Washington and Connecticut in War and Peace* (New Haven, 1933), 11.
12. Arlene St. John, *St. John Genealogy*, cited in the *New Canaan Historical Society Annual* (June, 1946), 54.
13. Revolutionary War Series I, XXVI, 247a-248.
14. Ltr., Charles Grandison Street to Mrs. M.A. Street, May 26, 1892. Street's cabinet shop stood for many years near Union Park. Ltr. in possession of Mrs. Polly Apperson, Street's great-granddaughter.

footnotes

CHAPTER 7

1. "Norwalk, Connecticut, Shipbuilding in," Catalog No. 1806, New-York Historical Society Records. The catalog covers Vincent's activities, 1810-1820.
2. *Sun of Liberty*, Vol. 1, No. 52, July 18, 1801, Houghton Library, Boston.
3. *Independent Republican*, Vol. 1, No. 15, Sept. 21, 1802. Houghton Library, Boston.
4. *New London Bee*, Apr. 4, 1798, cited in Eugene P. Link, *Democratic Republican Societies, 1790-1800,* (New York, 1942), 113.
5. Elizabeth Wilson, "Republicans vs. Federalists," unpublished paper. LHM Archives.
6. LHM Archives.
7. Entry of Aug. 15, 1800. Thomas Robbins, D.D., *Diary* (2 vols., Boston, 1887), I (1796-1825), 120-124.
8. *Independent Republican*, Dec. 29, 1802.
9. NTP II, Sept. 21, 1812.
10. O.S. Mills, "History of Rowayton," typewritten manuscript. Archives, Rowayton Historical Society, Rowayton.
11. Letter, William Lockwood to Buckingham Lockwood, Oct. 17, 1808. LHM Archives.
12. Letter, William Lockwood to Buckingham Lockwood, Oct. 17, 1808. LHM Archives.
13. Letter, William Lockwood to Buckingham Lockwood, Sept. 16, 1796. LHM Archives.
14. See the Registry of Ships belonging to the Lockwoods, compiled by John Kochiss, Mystic Seaport, for the Lockwood House Museum, Norwalk.
15. James Swank, *History of the Manufacture of Iron in All Ages and Particularly in the United States from Colonial Times to 1891,* (Philadelphia, 1892), points out that wrought nails were not replaced by wire nails until about 1852.
16. License to Tan Leather, February, 1802. LHM Archives.
17. Ralph Bloom, " 'Rockcliffe,' Historic Beard House, Majestically Overlooks South Norwalk," *Mark* Vol. 9, No. 5, March 10, 1962, 9.
18. Algernon Beard Account Book, 1830. LHM Archives.
19. The account of Norwalk potteries draws heavily from Andrew Winton and Kate Barber, "Norwalk Potteries," *Old-Time New England,* XXIV, No. 3 (Jan. 1934), 75-92, and XXIV, No. 4, (April, 1934), 111-128, and from Lura W. Watkins, *Early New England Potters and Their Wares,* 1968 reprint, Archon Press, 198-206.

CHAPTER 8

1. "Diary of a Journey through the United States, 1821-1824," (anonymous), 3 vols., Archives, New-York Historical Society, Manuscript Collection.
2. Extrapolated from John C. Pease and John M. Niles, *A Gazetteer of the States of Connecticut and Rhode-Island* (Hartford, 1819).
3. Henry P. Sage, "Ye Milestones of Connecticut," *Papers of the New Haven Colony Historical Society,* X, 1951, 65-68; and John D. McDowell, *Connecticut's Vanishing Milestones* (Litchfield, 1970), 1. See also NTP II, Dec. 9, 1765, 147.
4. Selleck, *Norwalk*, 422.
5. Clark Map of Norwalk, 1851; Vol. IX, No. 1, unpaginated; *Norwalk Hour* Tercentenary Edition, 186.

6. M.D.C. Terry, ed., *Old Inns of Connecticut* (Hartford, 1937), 189.
7. *RSC* XI, Appendix, 367.
8. John Hayward, *The New England Gazetteer* (Boston, 1849), ninth edition, unpaginated.
9. *Ballou's Pictorial* (Nov. 24, 1855), Vol. IX, No. 21, 328.
10. Elijah Middlebrook, *Middlebrook's Almanack* (Bridgeport, 1830), 17-24.
11. Attachment, Norwalk and New York Steamboat Association, 1827. LHM Archives.
12. "History of the Norwalk Chain of Islands," a typewritten manuscript from the Millard Smith family files. Archives, Rowayton Historical Society, Rowayton.
13. *Norwalk Hour* Anniversary Edition, Sept. 10, 1901.
14. "Expenses from the Commencement of Housekeeping, April 1, 1853, (through 1863) of Julia Ann (Seeley) Tristram." The young wife recorded every single household expense, making this small book a superb catalog of daily life in Norwalk. Archives, Rowayton Historical Society, Rowayton.
15. Rudy Favretti, *New England Colonial Gardens* (Stonington, Conn., 1964), 4-5.
16. *The Kitchen Directory and American Housewife, Containing the Most Valuable and Original Receipts in all the Various Branches of Cookery.* (Author anonymous.) (New York, 1841), 32-33. This probably belonged to one of the ladies in the Dibble family. Archives, Rowayton Historical Society, Rowayton.
17. Letter, Gaylord to Treadwell, Aug. 5, 1842. LHM Archives.
18. *Norwalk Gazette*, Oct. 2, 1844. According to Julia Tristram's housekeeping accounts, in 1858 a dentist charged $.25 for pulling a tooth.
19. David H. VanHoosear, comp., *A Complete Copy of the Inscriptions Found on the Monuments, Headstones, &c in the Oldest Cemetery Norwalk, Conn.* (Bridgeport, 1895), xxxii.
20. Harold Martin, comp., *Historical Papers Concerning the First Congregational Church on the Green, Norwalk, Connecticut* (Norwalk, 1955), 75.
21. Thomas Duggan, *The Catholic Church in Connecticut* (New York, 1930), 71-72.
22. Black Book of Rising Star Division, No. 94, of the Sons of Temperance of South Norwalk, Connecticut (New York, 1870). Archives, Rowayton Historical Society, Rowayton.
23. *Ballou's Pictorial* (Nov. 24, 1855).

CHAPTER 9

1. Extracted from the Population Schedules of the Census of the United States, 1850. National Archives, Washington, D.C.
2. Connecticut Archives, Series 2, Towns and Lands, I, 143, 147. Connecticut State Library.
3. Population Schedules of the Third Census of the United States, 1810, Roll I, Conn. National Archives, Washington, D.C. Also *Niles National Register*, Sept. 1840-Oct. 1841 (Baltimore, 1841), 275.
4. Mrs. H. Crosswell Tuttle, "Reminiscenses of Rowayton," a typewritten manuscript in possession of the Rowayton Historical Society, Rowayton.
5. Prices at Niagara Post Exchange, cited in J. R. Dolan, *Yankee Peddlers of Early America* (New York, 1964), 76.
6. N. G. Osborn, ed., *History of Connecticut in Monograph Form* (5 vols., New York, 1925), IV, 279; undated newspaper article, LHM Archives.
7. *The C & K Book,* Prepared by the Publicity Department of Crofut and Knapp (New York, 1924), 7 ff. LHM Archives.
8. The material for this and succeeding paragraphs pertaining to the Norwalk Lock Company is taken from a lengthy article printed in the *Gazette* of Nov. 16, 1858. The writer had been given a thorough tour of the plant and an explanation of its processes and business methods.
9. Alvin F. Harlow, *Steelways of New England* (New York, 1946), 177.

footnotes

228

10. Mel Cooke, "The New Haven Railroad — A History, Part I," *Mark*, Jan. 14, 1956 (Vol. 3, No. 2), 4.
11. Sidney Withington, *The First Twenty Years of Railroads in Connecticut* (New Haven, 1935), 12.
12. Stowell Rounds, "A Railroad for the Valley," *Wilton Heritage*, Fall, 1964, 2-9.
13. Charles Dunn, "The Danbury and Norwalk Railroad," a typewritten manuscript, 9. Archives, Rowayton Historical Society, Rowayton. *Norwalk Gazette*, Aug. 8, 1882.
14. Amos G. Hewitt, "The Long Island and Eastern States Express," *Journal of the New Haven Colony Historical Society*, (Sept., 1964) Vol. XIII, No. 3, 32-44.
15. Charter and By-Laws, Borough of Norwalk, Proceedings of Burgesses, I. Vault, First District Water Department, Norwalk.
16. Proceedings of Burgesses, II, July 3, 1859, 32.

CHAPTER 10

1. Deed of Sale, Mar. 9, 1748/49. LHM Archives.
2. Bruce Stark, "Slavery in Connecticut: A Re-examination," *Connecticut Review*, Vol. 9, No. 1, Nov. 1975, 77. Stark points out that merchants were more likely than farmers to accumulate money enough to purchase slaves.
3. John Adams Comstock, *A History and Genealogy of the Comstock Family in America* (Los Angeles, 1969), 20-21.
4. Norwalk Land Records, Vol. XIV, 421.
5. Population Schedules of the First Census of the United States, 1790. National Archives, Washington, D.C.
6. Population Schedules of the Third Census of the United States, 1810. National Archives, Washington, D.C.
7. List compiled by Malcolm Hunt, taken from Norwalk Land Records. LHM Archives.
8. *Independent Republican*, Oct. 6, 1802.
9. See Lester Card, Norwalk Records (Marriages), Supplementing Hall's Annals of Norwalk bringing the Records to 1875. Typewritten manuscript. LHM Archives.
10. *Fifth Annual Report of the Executive Committee of the American Anti-Slavery Society* (New York, 1839), 138.
11. James Knox, *A Token of Affectionate Remembrance, Being a Farewell Discourse Delivered in the Second Congregational Church in Norwalk (Conn.) Sunday, March 31, 1839* (Philadelphia, 1839), 36. File Box, South Norwalk Congregational Church Records. LHM Archives.
12. Horatio T. Strother, *The Underground Railroad in Connecticut* (Middletown, Conn., 1962), 118-119, 120.
13. John Niven, *Connecticut for the Union* (New Haven, 1965), 31-32.
14. W. A. Croffut and John M. Morris, *The Military and Civil History of Connecticut: the War of 1861-65* (New York, 1868), 53.
15. *Norwalk Gazette*, Dec. 2, 1862, May 12, 1863; Francis Trevelyan Miller and H. S. Commager, eds., *A Photographic History of the Civil War* (10 vols., New York, 1957 ed.), 40, 42; Philip B. Kunhardt, Jr., "Images of which history was made bore the Mathew Brady label," and "Hold Still — don't move a muscle; you're on Brady's Camera," *Smithsonian*, Vol. 8, No. 5 (July, 1977), 20-21, 27, 33; and No. 6 (Aug., 1977), 66. The story of the guard's ignorance was taken from a "home letter" of Whitney's, dated Mar. 18, 1862.
16. Ltr., William O. Godfrey to his friend "Gyp," (probably Jessup St. John), Feb. 26, 1863. St. John Family Papers, LHM Archives.
17. *Norwalk Gazette*, May 26, 1863.
18. "Comrades, I am Dying," Dedicated to the Memory of Lieutenant Douglass (sic) Fowler of Norwalk, Conn. Words by Thomas Manahan, Music by Edgar C. Spinning (Chicago, 1865). Archives, Burndy Library, Norwalk, Conn. The GAR of South Norwalk later named a post in Fowler's honor.
19. St. John Family Papers. LHM Archies.
20. NTP IV, Aug. 5, 25, 1862, 87; Aug. 1, 1863, 113; Sept. 14, 1864, 134.

CHAPTER 11

1. *Norwalk Gazette*, Apr. 21, 1863.
2. George Haven Putnam, *A Memoir of George Palmer Putnam* (2 vols., New York, 1903), II, 102-03.
3. Alexander R. Callow, *The Tweed Ring* (New York, 1966), 203.
4. *Norwalk Gazette*, Apr. 28, 1868.
5. Records, City of South Norwalk, Vol. 1, 1870-1875, 1, 14, 32.
6. Report of South Norwalk Electric Works, years ending 1903, 1907; Report of Chief Engineer, Fire Department, South Norwalk, 1911. LHM Archives. The plant began operations in 1892.
7. Archibald Ashley Welch, *A History of Insurance in Connecticut* (New Haven, 1935), 8; William T. Davis, ed., *New England States* (4 vols., Boston, 1899), II, 983; D. Hamilton Hurd, *History of Fairfield County*, 546.
8. Letters, U.S. Treasury Department to Central National Bank, Norwalk, Feb. 2, 9, 1877. Archives, Town House. Weed, *Norwalk After Two Hundred and Fifty Years*, 260-61. New names appear among this bank's organizers. They include Ambrose S. Hurlbutt, John P. Beatty, H. P. Guthrie, C. M. Holmes, P. L. Cunningham, William Smith, Charles Smith, and Sherman Morehouse.
9. Letter, Oliver Seeley to Hannah Dibble, Feb. 5, 1891. Archives, Rowayton Historical Society, Rowayton. Rowaytonite Seeley had made several trips west in the Gold Rush era and finally settled in Iowa where he raised cattle.
10. Martin Goldstein, "Waterfront, a Study of the Norwalk Waterfront, Offshore Islands, Port and Recreation Facilities," E-3, 4. Typewritten manuscript, 1967. LHM Archives.
11. James L. Kellogg, *Shell-Fish Industries* (New York, 1910), 195; Kochiss John, *Oystering from New York to Boston* (Middletown, 1974), 24. Rampant dissatisfaction with the policy was allayed when the law was modified to allow a ten-year leasing plan with option to renew.
12. Harry Leroy Crockett, "Rowayton, Conn." Typewritten manuscript. Archives, Rowayton Historical Society, Rowayton.
13. "Rowayton Natural Growth Oyster Sloops, ca. 1895, taken from a list of vessels licensed to work upon Connecticut Natural oyster beds, from Connecticut Shellfish Commissioners' records." Typewritten manuscript. Oscar Mills, "History of Rowayton," Typewritten manuscript. Archives, Rowayton Historical Society.
14. A speech made at a National Labor Union Conference, reported in Thomas Brooke, *Toil and Trouble, A History of American Labor* (New York, 1964), 46.
15. Philip S. Foner, *History of the Labor Movement in the United States* (4 vols., New York, 1955), II, 15, 20.
16. Nelson Burr, *The Early Labor Movement in Connecticut* (West Hartford, Conn., 1972), 21-22.
17. Knights of Labor, Record of the Proceedings of the General Assembly, 1st-26th regular session. This figure was given in the Record of the Proceedings of the Seventh General Assembly.
18. Knights of Labor, Record of the Proceedings of the Tenth Regular Session of the General Assembly, October 4-20, 1886, 106.
19. John R. Commons and Associates, *History of Labour in the United States* (2 vols., New York, 1966 ed.), II, 463.

footnotes

CHAPTER 12

1. Unless otherwise noted, information regarding the German settlement has been culled from the Population Schedules of Norwalk, United States Census for 1860, 1870, and 1880, and the Norwalk *City Directory* for 1892, 1895, and 1900. The Tax Assessment lists for 1896 were also helpful.
2. *Fifty Years in South Norwalk, 1874-1924,* a small pamphlet published by the Davis Clothing Store to commemorate fifty years of business. LHM Archives.
3. Stephen Thernstrom, "Immigrants and Wasps: Ethnic Differences in Occupational Mobility in Boston, 1890-1940," in Stephen Thernstrom and Richard Sennett, eds., *Nineteenth-Century Cities* (New Haven, 1969), 157-158.
4. John Lindeberg, "Groceries from Barrels," *Mark,* Aug. 4, 1956, 5.
5. Mrs. George Weddle to Gloria P. Stewart, March 28, 1978. Mrs. Weddle is Samuel Roodner's daughter. She graciously shared the reminiscences included in this section with the interviewer.
6. Robert A. Slavitt, to Deborah W. Ray, March 27, 1978. For early presidents and gaboyim of the Beth Israel Synagogue, see "Generation to Generation," a pamphlet distributed at the dedication of the new Beth Israel Synagogue on King Street, December 2, 1973.
7. John Lindeberg, "Scandinavian-Americans Contribute Much to Norwalk," *Mark,* Vol. 3, No. 7, Feb. 18, 1956, 4. Ericson spelled his surname Erich in the 1870 Census.
8. Extrapolated from the Birth, Marriage, and Death Registers of Hungarian Reformed Church of South Norwalk, 1895-1907.
9. Much of the information in this section was provided by Mr. and Mrs. William Sontra, Andrew Kurimai, Mrs. Stephen Soltesz, Sr., Miss Elizabeth Szecs, Joseph Magyar, and Thomas Yocsik, all descendants of early Hungarian families who settled in Norwalk.
10. Dr. John Butosi, comp., *Diamond Anniversary Album, The Hungarian Reformed Church, United Church of Christ, South Norwalk* (Denville, N.J., 1968), 5-9.
11. H. Lee Conner, *et al.,* "The Magyars of Norwalk," 35, 37. Federal Writers' Project Reprint from University of Connecticut's People of Connecticut Project, Storrs, Conn.
12. *South Norwalk Sentinel,* Oct. 6, 7, 12, 1909.
13. Many of the experiences related in this section have been culled from the reminiscences of Mrs. Richard Kotulsky, Mrs. Nicholas Granata, Mrs. Joseph Sulla, and Ralph Tucciarone.

CHAPTER 13

1. Information in these pages is derived from School Visitors' Reports between 1883 and 1897, Reports of Superintendent of Schools, and Board of Education Reports 1883-1914. LHM Archives.
2. *New York Times,* Dec. 10, 1893.
3. Broad River School District Records, Apr. 3, 1867. LHM Archives.
4. "Schools," *South Norwalk Sentinel,* June 25, 1897.
5. Miss E.L.D. Bohannan to Deborah W. Ray, Jan. 12, 1978. Miss Bohannan is Dr. Bohannan's niece.
6. Report of Board of Street Commissioners, South Norwalk, 1903. 72-73. LHM Archives.
7. For information about the Dibbles, see *Norwalk Gazette,* Apr. 7, 1868; Population Schedules, Census of the United States, 1870, Schedule 1, Inhabitants of Norwalk, Conn. National Archives, Waltham, Mass.; Rowayton Library Records, 1867; Letter, Emma Dibble to Gertie Dibble, Mar. 9, 1880, and Diary of Emma Dibble. Archives, Rowayton Historical Society, Rowayton.
8. Letter from "A Citizen" to the *South Norwalk Sentinel,* Aug. 25, 1880.
9. John H. Ferris, grandson of Senator Ferris, to Deborah W. Ray, Feb. 7, 1976, Norwalk, Conn.

10. Nelson Hayes, *The Destiny of an Indian Village* (South Norwalk, 1933), 58 ff; Angeline Scott, "Norwalk, Connecticut," *New England Magazine,* XII, No. 5 (July, 1902), 588-606.
11. Robert A. Dahl, *Who Governs?* (New Haven, 1961).
12. *New York Times,* Aug. 5, 1892.
13. *New York Times,* Nov. 3, 1892.
14. *New York Times,* Dec. 10, 1893, and Dec. 12, 1893.
15. *Memorial Addresses on the Life and Character of Ebenezer J. Hill* (Washington, D.C., 1919), 13, 15 and 40.
16. *Bridgeport and Norwalk: A few facts and figures to show that the Court House should remain in Bridgeport* is an example of pamphlets prepared by Bridgeporters. File 974.61 F1 5 br. "Pamphlets on Retaining the County Seat at Bridgeport rather than Norwalk." Archives, Connecticut State Library, Hartford.
17. *Stamford Advocate,* May 21, 1886.
18. Information about Tracey is derived primarily from his reports as Health Officer. Norwalk Annual Reports, 1903 through 1913. LHM Archives.
19. Report of Health Officer to Selectmen, 1902. LHM Archives.
20. Dotha Stone Pinneo, ed., *Conn. State Federation of Women's Clubs Official Directory* (New Haven, 1900), 123-124.

CHAPTER 14

1. Weed, *Norwalk After Two Hundred and Fifty Years,* 357.
2. *Ibid.,* 169
3. *New York Times,* May 28, 1905.
4. *South Norwalk Sentinel,* May 6, 1909.
5. *74 Years of Continuous Service, 1889-1963, The Chamber of Commerce of Norwalk, Conn., Inc.* (Norwalk, 1963), 9, 11.
6. *South Norwalk Evening Sentinel,* Apr. 19, 1912.
7. A. E. Buck, "The Norwalk Taxing Districts, Part I — The General District Picture," *Mark,* Vol. 6, No. 12 (June 6, 1959), 16 ff., the first part of an excellent three-part series on Norwalk's government.
8. Except where otherwise noted, all material relating to the First World War was taken from the *Norwalk Hour,* between March, 1916, and November, 1918.
9. Emerson G. Taylor, *New England in France, 1917-1919* (Boston, 1920), 40-46.
10. Irene Mix, *Connecticut's Activities In the Wars of This Country* (Washington; U.S. Government Printing Office, 1932), 61.
11. "Women on Connecticut Town Rolls of Honor," a photocopied list of names collected by the State of Connecticut Department of War Records. Connecticut State Library, Hartford.
12. *Norwalk Hour,* November 28, 1942.

CHAPTER 15

1. Robert K. Murray, *Red Scare, A Study of National Hysteria* (New York, 1955), 87-92.
2. *Norwalk Hour,* Jan. 6, 1920.
3. Donovan's obituary in the *Norwalk Hour,* Apr. 22, 1955; *New York Times,* Oct. 4, 1921.
4. City of Norwalk Record Book (NRB) Vol. 2, Nov. 1, 11, 1921, 151, 158.
5. David Chalmers, *Hooded Americanism* (Garden City, N.Y., 1965), 268.
6. *Norwalk Hour,* June 30, 1923.
7. Osborn, ed., *History of Connecticut,* IV, 446.
8. Russell Frost, Jr., to Deborah W. Ray, Feb. 25, 1978, Norwalk, Conn.
9. NRB 2, June 10, July 8, Aug. 12, 1919, 12, 16, 24; Jan. 20, 1921, 90; June 22, 1921, 115.
10. NRB 2, Special Council Meeting, Aug. 11, 1922, 226.
11. See *Norwalk Hour,* Jan. 9, 25; Feb. 6, 22; March 1, 6, 9, 17, 20, 22, 1926.
12. Jeff Bolster, "A History of The Norwalk Islands," 8. Typewritten Manuscript. Archives, Rowayton Historical Society.

footnotes

13. Herbert Janick, *A Diverse People: Connecticut 1914 to the Present,* (Chester, Ct., 1975), 29.

14. Ltr., Feb. 6, 1932, in NRB 3, 596.

15. Paul James to Deborah W. Ray, Apr. 28, 1978, Silvermine, Norwalk, Conn.

16. *74 Years of Continuous Service,* 33, 35.

17. Mayor's Report, NRB 5, Sept. 28, 1937, 243.

18. *New York Times,* Nov. 1, 1938.

CHAPTER 16

1. Except where otherwise noted, all material pertaining to World War II is drawn from issues of *The Norwalk Hour,* October 1, 1940, through August 29, 1945.

2. The *Hour,* Dec. 1, 1977.

3. NRB 6, 365, 368, 375, 383.

4. Rev. Zoltan Szabo to Gloria P. Stewart, Feb. 2, 1978, Norwalk, Conn.

5. *Mark,* Vol. 7, No. 24 (Nov. 19, 1960) 6.

6. NRB 7, 101.

7. NRB 8, 323 ff, 429 ff.

8. *New York Times,* Feb. 27, 1947.

9. *New York Times,* Aug. 22, 1946.

10. *New York Times,* Aug. 29, 1946.

11. *New York Times,* Sept. 5, 1946.

12. *New York Times,* Oct. 10, Nov. 12, 1947.

13. *New York Times,* Oct. 10, Nov. 12, 15, Dec. 19, 1947.

CHAPTER 17

1. Report of Mayor John Shostak, *Norwalk Hour,* Aug. 11, 1961.

2. Telephone interviews: Ephraim Cotto, Norwalk, Conn., Aug. 5, 1978; Jaime Aguayo, Maria (Aguayo) Blevens, Aug. 7, 10, 1978.

3. *Black People Making History in Norwalk,* published by the Norwalk Public Schools (undated, probably 1971); telephone interviews with the Reverend John P. Ball, and Andrew Wise, Norwalk, Conn., Aug. 7, 1978.

4. *The Norwalk Hour,* Aug. 25, 1961.

5. Information pertaining to the history of Norwalk Community College was taken from materials in the Archives, Norwalk Community College and from Kenneth B. Barclay, "The Origins of the Community College Movement in Connecticut 1946-1961," an unpublished dissertation for the Ph.D., Kent State University, 1976.

6. Material relating to the history of Norwalk State Technical Institute was drawn from the Archives, Library, Norwalk State Technical College.

7. *Mark* Vol. 5, No. 20, (Nov. 22, 1958), 7.

8. *Mark* Vol. 3, No. 17, (May 12, 1956), 13.

9. *New York Times,* Jan. 27, 28, 29, 30, 31; Feb. 1, 4, 5, 7, 8, 12, 16, 17; Mar. 1, 1954.

10. The *Hour* Tercentenary Edition, 203.

11. *Norwalk Hour,* issues from Jan. 17, 1953 through May 28, 1954.

12. Seymour S. Weisman, *Case Study of a Flood-Stricken City* (New York, 1958), 18.

13. *New York Times,* Oct. 17, 1955.

14. *Norwalk Rebuilds, A Progress Report on Urban Renewal,* published by the Norwalk Redevelopment Agency, 1966.

15. Information derived from Charter and By-Laws of Common Interest Group, Minutes of Common Interest Group, miscellaneous newspaper clippings between 1961 and 1965. LHM Archives. Mary Mason Brewer, "Alumna Battles City Hall," Miss Hall's School Alumnae *Bulletin* (Pittsfield, Mass., Spring, 1965), 8-10.

footnotes

BIBLIOGRAPHY

PUBLIC DOCUMENTS AND RECORDS

Local

Norwalk, Borough of. Charter and By-laws; Proceedings of Burgesses, Vols. I, II, III. Vault, First District Water Department, Norwalk.

Norwalk, City of. Record Book (NRB). Vols 1-9. City Hall, Norwalk.

Norwalk, Planning Commission. "The Norwalk Islands." City Hall, Norwalk.

Norwalk Town Proceedings, (NTP). Vols. I-IV. City Hall, Norwalk. Tax Assessment Lists, 1860-1896. City Hall, Norwalk. Land Records, Vol. XIV. Vault, City Hall, Norwalk. Board of Education and Superintendent of Schools Reports, 1883-1926. Lockwood House Museum (LHM) Archives, Norwalk. Book of First School Society in Norwalk, Jan. 1799-Mar. 1847. LHM Archives. Broad River School District Records, Apr. 3, 1867. LHM Archives, Norwalk. School Visitors' Reports, 1883-1897. LHM Archives, Norwalk. Annual Reports, Selectmen. City Hall, Norwalk.

Norwalk Redevelopment Agency. *Norwalk Rebuilds, A Progress Report on Urban Renewal* (Norwalk, 1966).

South Norwalk, City of. Report of Board of Street Commissioners, 1903. LHM Archives, Norwalk. Electric Works, Reports, 1903, 1907. LHM Archives. Fire Department, Report of Chief Engineer, 1911. LHM Archives.

State and Federal

Public Records of the Colony of Connecticut, Prior to the Union with New Haven Colony, Vol. I, 1636-1665 (Hartford, 1850).

Public Records of Connecticut (PRC), Vols. I-XV. (Hartford, 1850-1890).

Records of the State of Connecticut (RSC), I-VII, XI (Hartford, 1895-).

Connecticut Archives. Connecticut State Library, Hartford: Crimes and Misdemeanors, 1662-1789, Index. Ecclesiastical Affairs (Conn.) Vols. I, II, III. Industry, 1747-1820, Series 2, Manufactures, Mines and Mining. Norwalk Revolutionary Records, 1774-1784. Norwalk Revolutionary War Series, I, Vol. 5, Part. 2. Towns and Lands, Series 2, Vols. I, IV, IX. Trumbull, Governor Jonathan, Papers of.

Fairfield County Court Files, 1757-1759. Vault 11, Box 187, RG3. Archives, Connecticut State Library, Hartford.

Huntington, Long Island. Town Records. Vol. 3. Archives, Town Hall, Huntington, Long Island, N.Y.

U.S. Coast and Geodetic Survey Report for 1850 (Washington, D.C., 1850).

U.S. Department of the Army, Adjutants-General Office. *Record of Service* (Hartford, 1869); *The Record of Service of Connecticut Men in the Army and Navy of the United States During the War of the Rebellion* (Hartford, 1889).

U.S. Department of the Census, Population Schedules for 1790, 1800, 1810, 1820, 1830, 1840, 1850, 1860, 1870, 1880. National Archives, Washington, D.C.

PRIMARY WORKS

Autobiographies, Reminiscences, Memoirs, Collections, And Published Correspondence

Alexander, Orline. *The St. John Genealogy* (New York, 1907).

American Anti-Slavery Society. *Fifth Annual Report* (New York, 1839).

Applications and Recommendations for Appointment. Records of Jefferson Administration, M418, RG 10-19-3, Roll 1, M418, RG 10-19-3, Roll 5. National Archives, Washington, D.C.

Beard, Algernon. Account Book, 1829-1835. LHM Archives.

Beard Family Papers. LHM Archives. Beard, August F. Personal Account Book. LHM Archives. Beard, Eliza to Edward Beard, Ltr., Nov. 14, 1862. File Box, Beard Family Papers. LHM Archives.

Benedict, Stephen. Day Book and Ledger, 1772-1776. Collection of Lawrence Hochheimer.

Anonymous. "Bridgeport and Norwalk: A few facts and figures to show that the Court House should remain in Bridgeport." Archives, Connecticut State Library.

Butosi, Dr. John, comp. *Diamond Anniversary Album, The Hungarian Reformed Church, United Church of Christ, South Norwalk* (Denville, N.J., 1968).

Common Interest Group (Norwalk, Conn.), Charter, By-laws, Minutes. LHM Archives, Norwalk.

Connecticut Historical Society. *Collections of the Connecticut Historical Society.* (31 vols., Hartford, 1860-1967), I, II, III, VIII, XVII, (Vols. I and II).

"Diary of a Journey through the United States, 1821-1824," (anonymous), 3 vols., Archives, New-York Historical Society, New York, N.Y.

Dibble, Emma. "Diary." Archives, Rowayton Historical Society, Rowayton.

Dibble, Emma. Letter to Gertie Dibble, Mar. 9, 1880. Archives, Rowayton Historical Society, Rowayton.

Dwight, Timothy. *Travels; in New-England and New-York* (3 vols., New Haven, 1822), III.

Fifty Years in South Norwalk, 1874-1924. LHM Archives, Norwalk.

Gaylord, Charles Seely to Treadwell, John P. Ltr, Aug. 5, 1842. LHM Archives.

Godfrey, William O. to "Gyp.", Ltr, Feb. 26, 1863. St. John Family Papers, LHM Archives.

Gregory's Point Horse Railway 1873. Assorted Documents, LHM Archives.

Hall, Edwin, ed. *The Ancient Historical Records of Norwalk, Connecticut* (Norwalk, 1847).

Hawks, Francis L. and Perry, William Stevens, eds. *Documentary History of the Episcopal Church in Connecticut, 1704-1789* (Hartford, 1959).

Hungarian Reformed Church of South Norwalk. Birth, Marriage, and Death Records, 1895-1907. Vaults, Hungarian Reformed Church, South Norwalk.

James, Maria Philips Selleck. Last Will and Testament, 1911. LHM Archives, Norwalk.

The Kitchen Directory and American Housewife, Containing the Most Valuable and Original Receipts in all the Various Branches of Cookery (New York, 1841).

Knight, Sarah. *The Journey of Madam Knight* (New York, 1935).

Knights of Labor. Record of the Proceedings, Seventh General Assembly. Record of the Proceedings, Tenth General Assembly.

Knox, James. *A Token of Affectinate Remembrance, Being a Farewell Discourse Delivered in the Second Congregational Church in Norwalk (Conn.) Sunday, March 11, 1839* (Philadelphia, 1839). LHM Archives.

Lockwood, Eliphalet. Accounts. LHM Archives.

Lockwood, E. & Sons. Account Book, May, 1796-1814. LHM Archives.

Lockwood, William to Buckingham Lockwood. Ltr, Sept. 16, 1796, Oct. 17, 1808. LHM Archives.

Lockwood, W. & B. Day Book, Slitting Mill, 1818-1835. LHM Archives.

Manahan, Thomas and Spinning, Edgar C. "Comrades, I am Dying." Archives, Burndy Library, Norwalk.

Martin, Joseph Plum. *Private Yankee Doodle* (Boston, 1962).

Massachusetts Historical Society. *Collections of the Massachusetts Historical Society, Fourth Series* (10 vols., Boston, 1878).

Memorial Addresses on the Life and Character of Ebenezer J. Hill (Washington, D.C., 1919).

Miscellaneous Correspondence Regarding Impressed Seamen, Records of Jefferson Administration, Boxes, 1, 2, 7, RG 59. National Archives, Washington, D.C.

Norwalk Chamber of Commerce. *74 Years of Continuous Service, 1889-1963* (Norwalk, 1963).

Norwalk City Directory, 1886, 1890, 1892, 1895, 1900, 1919, 1920.

Norwalk Quartette Club. *Program, Centennial Anniversary Concert.* (Norwalk, 1975).

Opie, Catharine T. *A Light That Shone* (Ayer, Mass., 1969).

Papers of the New Haven Colony Historical Society (10 vols., New Haven, 1865).

Pinneo, Dotha Stone, ed. *Conn. State Federation of Women's Clubs. Official Directory* (New Haven, 1900).

Republican Society of Flax Hill. Minutes. LHM Archives.

Robbins, Thomas, D.D. *Diary* (2 vols., Boston, 1887), I.

St. John Family Papers. LHM Archives.

St. John's Lodge No. 6 F. & A.M., 1765-1965 (Norwalk, 1965).

School Society Book, 1840, Norwalk. LHM Archives.

Second Congregational Church, South Norwalk. Records. File Box, LHM Archives, Norwalk.

Seeley, Alfred. Journal, Document No. 19, Sloops, Trade. Pinkney Collection, Archives Rowayton Historical Society.

Seeley, Oliver to Hannah Dibble, Ltr., Feb. 5, 1891. Archives, Rowayton Historical Society. Rowayton.

Sons of Temperance of South Norwalk, Rising Star Division, No. 94. Black Book. Archives, Rowayton Historical Society, Rowayton.

Street, Charles Grandison to Mrs. M.A. Street, Ltr., May 26, 1892. Collection of Mrs. Polly Apperson, Street's great-granddaughter.

Tristram, Julia Ann (Seeley). "Expenses from the Commencement of Housekeeping (April 1, 1853 through 1862)." Archives, Rowayton Historical Society, Rowayton.

Tryon, General William. Reports to Sir Henry Clinton, July 12, 20, 1779. The Clinton Papers, The William Clements Library, University of Michigan. Ann Arbor, Mich.

Tuttle, Mrs. H. Crosswell. "Reminiscences of Rowayton." Archives Rowayton Historical Society.

U.S. Treasury Department to Central National Bank, Norwalk, Ltrs., Feb. 2, 9, 1877. Archives, Norwalk Town House.

SECONDARY WORKS

Albion, Robert. *The Rise of New York Port* (New York, 1939).

Barber, John Warner *Connecticut Historical Collections* (New Haven, 1838).

Barrow, Thomas C. *Trade and Empire: The British Customs Service in Colonial America 1660-1775* (Cambridge, Mass., 1967).

Baughman, James P. *The Mallorys of Mystic: Six Generations in American Maritime Enterprise* (Middletown, 1972).

Benedict, Henry M. and Elwyn E. *Genealogy of the Benedicts in America* (Albany, N.Y., 1870, 1969).

Blaikie, Alexander. *A History of Presbyterianism in New England* (Boston, 1881).

Bouton, Nathaniel. *An Historical Discourse in Commemoration of the Two-Hundredth Anniversary* (New York, 1851).

Boyer, Frederic and Poole, Herbert, "The Quintard Family in America," reprinted from July and October 1955 issues of *The New England Historical and Genealogical Register*.

Brooke, Thomas. *Toil and Trouble, a History of American Labor* (New York, 1964).

Burr, Nelson R. *The Early Labor Movement in Connecticut* (West Hartford, 1972).

Bushman, Richard L. *From Puritan to Yankee; Character and the Social Order in Connecticut, 1690-1765* (Cambridge, Mass., 1967).

Butterfield, H.L., Friedlander, Marc, Kline, Mary-Jo, eds., *The Book of Abigail and John* (Boston, 1975).

Callahan, North. *Royal Raiders: The Tories of the American Revolution* (Indianapolis, 1963).

Callow, Alexander R. *The Tweed Ring* (New York, 1966).

Carrington, Henry. *Battles of the American Revolution, 1778-1781* (New York, 1877).

Chalmers, David. *Hooded Americanism* (Garden City, 1965).

Commons, John R. and Associates. *History of Labour in the United States* (2 vols., New York, 1966 ed.).

The C & K Book (New York, 1924). LHM Archives.

Comstock, John Adams. *A History and Genealogy of the Comstock Family in America* (Los Angeles, 1949).

Croffut, W.A. and Morris, John M. *The Military and Civil History of Connecticut: The War of 1861-1865* (New York, 1869).

Dahl, Robert. *Who Governs?* (New Haven, 1961).

Danenberg, Elsie N. *The Romance of Norwalk* (New York, 1929).

Davis, William T. *The New England States* (4 vols., Boston, 1899).

DeForest, John. *History of the Indians of Connecticut* (Hartford, 1851).

Destler, Chester *Connecticut: The Provision State* (Chester, Conn. 1972).

Dolan, J.R. *Yankee Peddlers of Early America* (New York, 1964).

Dow, George *The Arts and Crafts in New England, 1704-1775* (Topsfield, Mass., 1927).

Duggan, Thomas *The Catholic Church in Connecticut* (New York, 1930).

Dutcher, George Matthew. *George Washington and Connecticut in War and Peace* (New Haven, 1933).

Earle, Alice Morse. *The Sabbath in Puritan New England* (New York, 1891).

East, Robert A. *Connecticut's Loyalists* (Chester, Conn., 1974).

Favretti, Rudy. *New England Colonial Gardens* (Stonington, Conn., 1964).

Foner, Philip A. *History of the Labor Movements in the United States* (4 vols., New York, 1955).

Four Cities and Towns of Connecticut (New York, 1890).

Golding, Augustus C., comp. *Descendants of Rev. Thomas Hanford, Vol. I, Six Generations* (Norwalk, 1936).

Gookin, Daniel *Historical Collections of the Indians in New England* (Towntaid, 1970).

Hall, Charles S., ed. *Life and Letters of Samuel Holden Parsons* (Binghamton, N.Y., 1905).

Harlow, Alvin F. *Steelways of New England* (New York, 1946).

Hayes, Nelson. *The Destiny of an Indian Village* (South Norwalk, 1933).

Hayward, John. *The New England Gazetteer* (Boston, 1849).

Hooker, Roland. *Boundaries of Connecticut* (New Haven, 1933). *The Colonial Trade of Connecticut* (New Haven, 1936).

Hurd, D. Hamilton. *History of Fairfield County, Connecticut* (Philadelphia, 1881).

Ingersall, Ernest. *A Report on the Oyster Industry of the United States* (Washington, D.C., 1881).

Janick, Herbert. *A Diverse People: Connecticut 1914 to the Present* (Chester, Conn. 1975).

Jenkins, Stephen. *The Old Boston Post Road* (New York, 1913).

Jones, Mary J. *Congregational Commonwealth* (Middletown, Conn., 1968).

Josselyn, John. *New Englands rarities discovered* (London, 1672).

Kellogg, James L. *Shell-Fish Industries* (New York, 1910).

Kochiss, John *Oystering from New York to Boston* (Middletown, 1974).

Lathrop, Elise. *Early American Inns and Taverns* (New York, 1926).

Lecky, William. *The American Revolution, 1763-1783* (New York, 1898).

Link, Eugene P. *Democratic Republican Societies, 1790-1800* (New York, 1942).

Marcus, Jacob R. *Early American Jewry* (Philadelphia, 1951).

Martin, Harold, comp. *Historical Papers Concerning the First Congregational Church on the Green, Norwalk, Connecticut* (Norwalk, 1955).

McDevitt, Robert. *Connecticut Attacked: A British Viewpoint, Tryon's Raid on Danbury* (Chester, Conn., 1974).

McDowell, John D. *Connecticut's Vanishing Milestones* (Litchfield, 1970).

Middlebrook, Elijah. *Middlebrook's Almanack* (Bridgeport, 1830).

Middlebrook, Louis F. *History of Maritime Connecticut during the American Revolution, 1775-1783* (2 vols., Salem, Mass., 1925).

Miller, Francis Trevelyan and Commager, H.S., eds., *A Photographic History of the Civil War* (10 vols., New York, 1957 ed.).

Michell, Isabel. *Roads and Roadmaking in Colonial Connecticut* (New Haven, 1934).

Mix, Irene. *Connecticut's Activities in the Wars of This Country* (Washington, D.C., 1932).

Moore, Frank. *Songs and Ballads of the American Revolution* (Port Washington, L.I., 1964). *The Diary of the American Revolution, 1775-1781* (New York, 1967).

Murray, Robert K. *Red Scare, A Study of National Hysteria* (New York, 1955).

Morse, Jarvis M. *Connecticut Newspapers in the Eighteenth Century* (New Haven, 1935).

National Cyclopaedia of American Biography (56 vols., New York, 1898), II, X, XXVII.

Niven, John. *Connecticut for the Union* (New Haven, 1965).

Osborn, Norris Galpin, ed., *History of Connecticut in Monograph Form* (5 vols., New York, 1925), II, IV.

Norwalk Public Schools. *Black People Making History in Norwalk* (Norwalk, Conn., undated).

Pease, John G. and Niles, John M. *A Gazetteer of the States of Connecticut and Rhode-Island* (Hartford, 1819).

Peters, Rev. Samuel. *General History of Connecticut* (New York, 1879 ed.).

Pratt, Fletcher. *The Navy, A History* (Garden City, N.Y., 1941).

Purcell, Richard J. *Connecticut in Transition, 1775-1818* (Middletown, Conn., 1963 ed.).

Putnam, George Haven. *A Memoir of George Palmer Putnam* (2 vols., New York, 1903), II.

Quarles, Benjamin. *The Negro in the American Revolution* (Chapel Hill, 1961).

Rezneck, Samuel. *Unrecognized Patriots, the Jews in the American Revolution* (Westport, 1975).

Rosenbaum, Jeanette. *Myer Myers, Goldsmith, 1723-1795* (Philadelphia, 1954).

Sabin, Joseph. *Dictionary of Books Relating to America* (29 vols., London, 1917), XIX.

Selleck, Charles. *Norwalk* (Norwalk, 1896).

Spargo, John. *The Potters and Potteries of Bennington* (Southampton, N.Y., 1926).

Spiess, Matthew. *The Indians of Connecticut* (New Haven, 1957).

Steiner, Bernard. *History of Slavery in Connecticut* (Baltimore, 1893).

Stephen, Leslie and Lee, Sidney, eds., *The Dictionary of National Biography* (22 vols., London, 1917), XVII.

Stiles, Ezra. *Extracts from the Itineraries* (New Haven, 1916 ed.).

Strother, Horatio. *The Underground Railroad in Connecticut* (Middletown, Conn., 1962).

Swank, James. *History of the Manufacture of Iron in All Ages and Particularly in the United States from Colonial Times to 1891* (Philadelphia, 1892).

Swanton, John. *The Indian Tribes of North America* (Washington, D.C., 1952).

Taylor, Emerson G. *New England in France, 1917-1919* (Boston, 1920).

Taylor, John M. *Roger Ludlow: the Colonial Lawmaker* (New York, 1900).

Terry, M.D.C. *Old Inns of Connecticut* (Hartford, 1937).

Thernstrom, Stephen and Sennett, Richard, eds., *Nineteenth-Century Cities* (New Haven, 1969).

Thoms, Herbert. *Yale Men and Landmarks in Old Connecticut (1701-1815)* (New Haven, 1967).

Thompson, Edmund. *Maps of Connecticut Before the Year 1800* (Windham, Conn., 1940).

Trumbull, Benjamin. *A Complete History of Connecticut: Civil and Ecclesiastical* (2 vols., New London, 1898), I. *A Century Sermon* (New Haven, 1801).

Trumbull, J. Hammond, ed. *The True-Blue Laws of Connecticut and New Haven and the False Blue-Laws Invented by the Rev. Samuel Peters* (Hartford, 1876). *Indian Names of Places* (Hartford, 1881).

Van Dusen, Albert. *Connecticut* (New York, 1961).

U.S. Department of Commerce and Labor. *A Century of Population Growth* (Washington, 1909).

Van Hoosear, David H., comp. *A Complete Copy of the Inscriptions Found on the Monuments, Headstones, &c in the Oldest Cemetery in Norwalk, Conn.* (Bridgeport, 1895).

Watkins, Lura W. *Early New England Potters and Their Wares* (Hamden, 1968 reprint).

Weed, Samuel, ed., *Norwalk After Two Hundred and Fifty Years* (Norwalk, 1902).

Weisman, Seymour S. *Case Study of a Flood-Stricken City* (New York, 1958).

Welch, Archibald Ashley. *A History of Insurance in Connecticut* (New Haven, 1935).

Weld, Ralph F. *Slavery in Connecticut* (New Haven, 1935).

Whiting, Samuel *The Connecticut Town-Officer* (Danbury, 1814).

Willcox, William B., ed. *The American Rebellion, Sir Henry Clinton's Narrative of his Campaigns, 1775-1782* (New Haven, 1954).

Wilson, Lynn. *History of Fairfield County, 1639-1928* (3 vols., Hartford, 1929).

Withington, Sidney. *The First Twenty Years of Railroads in Connecticut* (New Haven, 1935).

Woods, Frederic J. *The Turnpikes of New England* (Boston, 1917).

Zeichner, Oscar. *Connecticut's Years of Controversy, 1750-1776* (Richmond, Va., 1949).

UNPUBLISHED MATERIAL

Adams, Maj. H.H. "Report of Survey of Norwalk Harbor, October, 1895." Federal Archives and Records Center, Waltham, Mass.

Adams, Virginia. "History of Sheffield Island, Norwalk, Connecticut." Archives, Rowayton Historical Society.

Barclay, Kenneth B. "The Origins of the Community College Movement in Connecticut, 1946-1961." Unpublished doctoral dissertation, Kent State (Ohio) University, 1976.

Bayles, Lois, comp. "Norwalk's Loyalists." LHM Archives.

Bolster, Jeff. "A History of the Norwalk Islands." Archives, Rowayton Historical Society, Rowayton.

Anonymous. "Diary of a Journey through the United States, 1821-1824." (3 vols.) Archives, New York Historical Society, Manuscript Collection.

Card, Lester. "Early Norwalk School District Records, 1800-1867." LHM Archives. "Norwalk Records (Marriages), Supplementing Hall's Annals of Norwalk, bringing the Records to 1875." LHM Archives.

Conner, H. Lee, et al. "The Magyars of Norwalk," Project Reprint, University of Connecticut's People of Connecticut Project, Storrs, Conn.

Crockett, Harry Leroy. "Rowayton, Conn." Archives, Rowayton Historical Society, Rowayton, Conn.

Drake, Mary E., comp. "The Life of the Rev. Jeremiah Leaming," unpublished compilation of articles and excerpts from secondary works. Archives, St. Paul's on-the-Green, Norwalk, Conn.

Dunn, Charles. "The Danbury and Norwalk Railroad." Archives, Rowayton Historical Society.

Goldstein, Martin. "Waterfront, A Study of the Norwalk Waterfront, Offshore Islands, Port, and Recreation Facilities." (Norwalk, 1967) LHM Archives.

Green, Erna. "The Public Land System of Norwalk, Connecticut, 1654-1704: A Structural Analysis of Economic and Political Relationships." Unpublished Thesis, Department of History, University of Bridgeport, 1972.

Anonymous "History of the Norwalk Chain of Islands." Mss., Archives, Rowayton Historical Society.

Hunt, Malcolm, comp. "Norwalk Town Proceedings." LHM Archives. "Norwalk Land Records." LHM Archives.

Kochiss, John. "Registry of Ships belonging to the Lockwoods." LHM Archives.

Mills, O.S. "History of Rowayton," typewritten Mss. Archives, Rowayton Historical Society, Rowayton.

"Norwalk, Connecticut, Shipbuilding in," Catalog No. 1806. New-York Historical Society, New York, N.Y.

Norwalk Redevelopment Agency. *Norwalk Rebuilds, A Progress Report on Urban Renewal* (Norwalk, 1966).

Nutting, Parker Bradley. "Thomas Fitch: Charter Governor." Unpublished Master's Thesis, University of North Carolina, Chapel Hill, N.C. (1968).

"Report to Treasury, Forts, Districts & Towns." PS 53582, SC No. 51459, Add Mss. 15484. Archives, The British Library, London, England.

Tangard, Mark. "Man and Movement in the 'Reluctant Suburb.'" Unpublished paper submitted for the B.A. Degree, Middlebury College, 1974.

Wilson, Elizabeth. "Norwalk Federalism — Republicanism, 1793-1803." Unpublished paper, LHM Archives.

"Women on Connecticut Town Rolls of Honor." Archives, Connecticut State Library, Hartford.

Wolfinger, John J. "A Test of Faith: Jane Elizabeth James and the Origins of the Utah Black Community." Archives, Church of Christ of Latter-Day Saints, Salt Lake City.

"Journal History of 1845." Archives, Chuch of Jesus Christ of Latter-Day Saints, Salt Lake City.

PERIODICALS

American Antiquity (April, 1965), 400-469; (July, 1964), 98-100.

Bulletin of the Massachusetts Archaeological Society (April-July, 1965), 53-63.

Ballou's Pictorial (Nov. 24, 1855); (July 7, 1859).

Connecticut Quarterly (January, 1895), 271-273; (December, 1895), 281-287.

Connecticut Review (Oct., 1971), 53-59; (Nov., 1975), 75-81.

Connecticut Historical Society Bulletin (January, 1975), 8-18.

County (December, 1967), 24-27; (December, 1968), 18-19.

Fairfield County Magazine (February, 1974), 28-29; (December, 1975), 64-67, 134-141.

Journal of the New Haven Colony Historical Society (September, 1964), 32-44.

Mark January 14, 4; 21, 3; February 4, 4-5; 18, 4; May 12, 13; August 4, 5; November 10, 1956, 6-7; August 17, 7; 31, 10-11; November 23, 1957, 6; November 22, 1958, 7; June 6, 1959, 16; March 26, 6; April 9, 8-10; November 19, 1960, 6; March 10, 1962, 9, March 6, 1965, 11-12.

Miss Hall's School *Alumnae Bulletin*, Spring, 1965, 8-10.

New Canaan Historical Society *Annual*, June, 1946, 90-100.

New England Magazine (July, 1902), 588-606.

New England Historical and Genealogical Register (July, 1955).

Old-Time New England, January, 1934, 75-92; April, 1934, 111-128.

Pennsylvania Archaeologist (April, 1965), 25-33.

Science (November 13, 1970), 732-734.

Smithsonian (July, 1977), 21-33; (August, 1977), 58-67.

The Magazine Antiques (May, 1974), 1147-1154.

Wilton Heritage (Fall, 1964), 2-9.

NEWSPAPERS

Charter Oak, May, 1839.

Connecticut Courant and Weekly Intelligencer, February 22, 1780.

Fairfield County Courier, September 18, 1969.

Independent Republican, September 21, October 6, December 29, 1802.

Norwalk Gazette and *The Norwalk Hour*

These newspapers were researched as follows: *Norwalk Gazette:* 1818-1900; *The Norwalk Hour:* 1913-1961, in addition to the Anniversary Edition, 1901, and the Tercentenary Edition, 1951.

The New York Times, August 5, November 3, 1892; December 10, 12, 1893; May 28, 1905; October 4, 1921; November 1, 1938; August 22, 29, September 5, 1946; February 27, October 10, November 12, 16, December 19, 1947; February 1, 4, 5, 7, 8, 10, 16, 17, March 1, 1954; April 22, October 17, 1955; August 11, 25, 1961; July 3, 1976.

South Norwalk Sentinel (The Sentinel, South Norwalk Evening Sentinel), August 25, 1880; December 25, 1884; June 25, 1897; May 6, October 6, 7, 12, 1909; April 19, 1912.

Stamford Advocate, May 21, 1886.

Stamford Sentinel, February 15, March 23, 1835.

Sun of Liberty, July 18, 1801.

MISCELLANEOUS

Clark Map of Norwalk, 1851.

Deed of Sale, "Dick" to Moses St. John, March 9, 1748/49. LHM Archives.

License to Tan Leather, February, 1802. LHM Archives.

Norwalk and New York Steamboat Association, Attachment, 1827. LHM Archives.

The Thomas School, 1970. Descriptive Viewbook. LHM Archives.

INTERVIEWS

Aguayo, Jaime, Aug. 7, 10, 1978, Redding, Conn. (Telephone interview). Maria, Aug. 10, 1978, Redding, Conn. (Telephone interview).

Ball, Reverend John, Aug. 7, 1978, Norwalk, Conn.

Bohannan, Miss E.L.D., Mar. 12, 1978, Norwalk, Conn.

Cotto, Ephraim, Aug. 5, 1978, Norwalk, Conn. (Telephone interview).

Ferris, John H., Feb. 7, 1976, Norwalk, Conn.

Frost, Russell, Jr., Feb. 25, 1978, Norwalk, Conn.

Granata, Mrs. Nicholas, September 9, 1977, Norwalk, Conn.

Kurimai, Andrew; Magyar, Joseph; Soltesz, Mrs. Stephen, Sr.; Szecs, Elizabeth; Yocsik, Thomas, August 30, 1977, Norwalk, Conn.

Sontra, Mr. and Mrs. William, July 23, 1977, Norwalk, Conn.

James, Paul, Apr. 28, 1978, Norwalk, Conn.

Kotulsky, Mrs. Richard, September 14, 1977, Norwalk, Conn.

Slavitt, Robert A., March 27, 1978, Norwalk, Conn. (Telephone interview).

Sulla, Mrs. Joseph, September 20, 1977, Norwalk, Conn.

Szabo, Reverend Zoltan, Feb. 2, 1978, Norwalk, Conn.

Tucciarome, Ralph, September 6, 1977, Norwalk, Conn.

Weddle, Mrs. George, March 28, 1978, Norwalk, Conn.

Wise, Andrew, July 23, 1978 Norwalk, Conn.

bibliography

ILLUSTRATIONS AND CREDITS

The illustrations in Norwalk, being an historical account of that Connecticut town *came from many sources. Photographs and source material from public archives were augmented by similar material from local residents and the authors are deeply grateful to all who provided illustration specifically for this volume. We are indebted to the late Mgrdich H. Manugian and the late Charles d'Emery of Manugian's Studio, South Norwalk, for having copied and restored many of the photographs which were selected for inclusion.*

All illustrations are listed chronologically as they appear in the book. The abbreviated title of each, where such information was available, is followed by the photographer's or delineator's name, the source, and the page number on which the illustration appears. In this listing, the archives of the Lockwood House Museum are abbreviated LHM, and the Norwalk Historical Society NHS.

236

illustrations

237

INDEX

index

index

241